Citizen Quigg

A MAYOR'S LIFE OF CIVIC SERVICE

Mark S. Foster

Fulcrum Publishing
Golden, Colorado

For Virginia Shafroth Newton

Quigg's indespensable partner

Text © 2006 Mark S. Foster
Photos © 2006 Newton family collection

Library of Congress Cataloging-in-Publication Data
Foster, Mark S.
  Citizen Quigg: a mayor's life of civic service / Mark S. Foster.
     p. cm.
  Includes bibliographical references.
  ISBN-13: 978-1-55591-548-3 (pbk. : alk. paper)
  ISBN-10: 1-55591-548-5
  1. Newton, James Quigg, 1911-2003.   2. Mayors—Colorado—Denver—Biography.   3. Denver (Colo.)—Biography.   4. Denver (Colo.)—Politics and government—20th century. 5. Commonwealth Fund—Biography. 6. College presidents—Colorado—Boulder—Biography.   7.   University   of   Colorado, Boulder—Biography. I. Title.
  F784.D453N484 2006
  978.8'83033092—dc22
  [B]

                                          2006021451

Printed in the United States of America by Color House Graphics, Inc.
0 9 8 7 6 5 4 3 2 1

Design: Patty Maher
Editorial: Sue Collier, Faith Marcovecchio
Cover photo: Newton family collection

Fulcrum Publishing
4690 Table Mountain Drive, Suite 100
Golden, CO 80403
800-992-2908 • 303-277-1623
www.fulcrumbooks.com

CONTENTS

PREFACE

In the late spring of 1929, Quigg Newton was a seventeen-year-old, finishing his final year at Andover, a highly respected eastern prep school. He was, by almost any measure, a promising young man. He was from a well-to-do and highly respected Denver family. Although Quigg had not yet demonstrated sustained academic excellence, he had done well enough to gain acceptance into Yale University's next freshman class. At Andover, he was a varsity letterman in football, and he had participated in other sports. Quigg's extracurricular activities, however, set him apart from many of his peers.

He was chosen as business manager for the school's yearbook, the Phillipian. It proved to be a wise decision. By tradition, the business manager was allowed to keep any profits the yearbook earned. Previous managers had been content to break even, or earn a very modest profit. Quigg, however, sold so much advertising that the yearbook earned a net profit of $1,000, a significant sum back then. Many young entrepreneurs would have kept the money, or perhaps thrown a big party for themselves and their friends. But when Quigg informed his father, Jim Newton, about the windfall, the elder Newton suggested that he return the money to the school. Ever the dutiful son, Quigg tried to do so without fanfare. The headmaster was so impressed by this gesture that he used the money to set up a small scholarship in Quigg's name. Today, thanks to continuing support from the Newton family, and occasionally from other sources, the scholarship fund is still assisting deserving young scholars. To be sure, Jim Newton applied relentless pressure on his son always to "do the right thing," but looking after others' needs came naturally to Quigg from his earliest years.

The incident portended the life of service to others that Quigg Newton would lead. With his family's contacts, its comfortable financial situation, and its secure social standing in Denver, Quigg might easily have settled for an easy life of light work and nearly full-time leisure and self-indulgence. Instead, he led an exemplary and consistently challenging life of service to his city, his state, and the nation. He developed both an interest in civic affairs and a deep social conscience at a very youthful age. Although in most respects a very "conventional" prep school student and collegian, Quigg worked hard to broaden his understanding of complicated public policy issues from his early twenties forward. By his late twenties, he had already become a noted community leader in Denver, and he was attracting highly favorable national attention. His election as the city's youngest mayor, at age thirty-five in the spring of 1947, was simply the first of many public achievements in his extremely full life.

Newton's two terms as mayor of Denver were filled with significant innovations, as he helped streamline and modernize city government. He also helped set the stage for intergovernmental regional cooperation. After a brief stint as a vice president of the Ford Foundation, he returned to Colorado to serve as president of the University of Colorado from 1956 until 1963. Although these years were marked by profound unrest and controversy, they were also packed with achievements. Under his stewardship, the university grew quickly in both size and prestige; scholarly research, particularly in science and technology, assumed a far more significant role than ever before. When Newton left the university in 1963, he moved to New York City, where he served as president of the Commonwealth Fund. He stayed there for twelve years, his longest stint in any capacity. The Fund promoted many of the most significant initiatives in medical education. Perhaps most important, thanks in part to Newton's initiatives, the Fund helped "democratize" medical education: thousands of young Americans previously excluded from realistic opportunities in the medical field could pursue exciting and rewarding careers in a wide variety of areas. Quigg's efforts with the Fund also helped greatly expand the availability of affordable community health services. During his years with the Fund, dozens of new medical clinics appeared in many of the nation's poorest and most underserved urban areas.

A few words concerning how I came to write a biography of Quigg Newton appear to be in order. In the summer of 2002, I was considering conducting research on the impact of the post–World War II "red scare" and McCarthyism in Colorado, devoting special attention to the Front Range. Since Newton had served as mayor of Denver and later as president at the University of Colorado during many of those years, I considered him one of the key people with whom I should test my ideas. I had long been aware of his distinguished service as mayor and university president. I also had a slight acquaintance with him, thanks to a few brief conversations we shared as we both exercised at a local gym. I called him in mid-August, and he was willing to meet with me at his home. Within minutes of starting our initial conversation, I sensed that examining the life of this modest, unassuming leader would be more interesting than my original project. At the initial meeting, I asked him if he would be willing to be the subject of a biography. He appeared surprised, but he stated that he would think it over and render a decision after talking with his extended family.

Fortunately, after some initial hesitation, his family voiced enthusiasm and encouraged him to go ahead with the project. Their cooperation has been complete, as well as inspirational. Quigg and his wife, Ginny, allowed me unrestricted access to approximately a dozen boxes of family and other personal correspondence never before revealed to other scholars. Before his sudden death in April 2003, we had conducted approximately forty hours of verbal interviews. Ginny Newton sat in on all of our conversations, and she provided frequent, telling insights. Gathering these recollections, along with the opportunity to listen to a series of earlier interviews conducted by noted Colorado historian Stephen Leonard, permitted me to gain deeper understanding of Newton's life, character, and achievements.

With Quigg's death three years ago, an account of his life appears timely. He was one of Colorado's finest public servants, and recognition of his multifaceted contributions already seems overdue.

—Mark S. Foster
Denver, Colorado
June 2006

ACKNOWLEDGMENTS

In the course of their work, authors invariably depend on numerous individuals who are willing to share their expertise and time. Quigg Newton, the subject of this book, graciously allowed me numerous interviews over almost a year. We spent roughly forty hours together, usually two hours at each meeting. He was remarkably open to all of my questions, and he permitted me to examine correspondence never before revealed to people outside of the family. Virginia Newton also sat in on all of our conversations, and her shrewd, insightful comments added depth to my understanding of her remarkable husband. Virginia allowed full access to family photos, and she read numerous drafts of the manuscript. She contributed so much of herself to this project that she could be listed as a coauthor. For these and many more reasons, the book is dedicated to her. I also benefited from conversations with two of the couple's daughters, Abby and Nan, who also read and commented on all or parts of the manuscript.

I conducted research in the Quigg Newton Papers in the Western History Collection at the Denver Public Library, and I am very grateful for the kind assistance of James X. Kroll and several staff members. The staff at the Rockefeller Center archives at Pocantico Hills provided highly efficient and friendly assistance. Linda Tietjen, a member of the Auraria Library staff, provided me additional research leads and helped me obtain relevant secondary sources. Bruce Rockwell, Gilbert Kerlin, and Dr. Robert J. Glaser (M.D.) also provided insightful interviews.

Several colleagues at the University of Colorado at Denver provided crucial help. James Whiteside, the noted historian of sports in Colorado, helped me fully unravel the football scandal at the Boulder campus. Dr. Thomas J. Noel, nicknamed "Dr. Colorado" on account of numerous books on the state's history, read the entire manuscript. Finally, Dr. Pamela Walker Laird also read the manuscript and offered particularly illuminating comments on Newton's remarkable networking abilities. Sue Sethney, the department's unflappable staff assistant, fielded dozens of phone calls and helped me retain a sense of proportion when I was feeling undue stress.

I am also indebted to my publisher, Bob Baron, president of Fulcrum Publishing. He voiced enthusiasm for the project at the outset, and his own book on leaders in American enterprise inspired me. Sam Scinta provided valuable guidance, as did Patty Maher in design and Shannon Hassan in marketing. My editor, Faith Marcovecchio, patiently helped me overcome nettlesome computer problems and saved me from countless errors and inconsistencies in the finished product. It goes without saying that any errors still extant are my responsibility alone.

Finally, family members helped in important, if intangible ways. My wife, Laurie, listened to many Newton family stories and raised thoughtful questions of her own. My stepchildren, Sarah and Scott Maxwell, helped me maintain a sense of balance when I veered on becoming overly immersed in my topic. I am grateful for all of this support.

CHAPTER 1

∞

FAMILY ROOTS

When asked to trace their roots, prominent people routinely glorify their forebears, ascribing heroic virtues to certain revered relatives that were presumably passed down through generations—legacies that supposedly help explain their own achievements. To be sure, many accomplished individuals built upon and enhanced desirable traits that had been demonstrated by parents or grandparents. Robert E. Lee, J. Pierpont Morgan, John Quincy Adams, and others come to mind.[1] Other famous people seem to emerge as if by sheer chance from generations of mediocre ancestors, including Abraham Lincoln, Ulysses S. Grant, Henry J. Kaiser, John D. Rockefeller, and Thomas Edison.[2] One suspects, however, that the vast majority of distinguished people come from very "average" extended families containing a handful of accomplished members, plus far larger numbers of people who experienced very ordinary lives. On very rare occasions, inspired human beings seemingly rise out of the muck, surviving squalid upbringings, poor health, and unimaginable adversity.

However, the majority of influential people emerge within environments where they are *positioned* to succeed. They might be raised by one or two parents who, whether consciously or otherwise, endow them with a deep passion to pursue specific avocations, such as music or painting; in such cases, financial resources might be less critical to their success than attitudes encouraged. But in larger numbers of cases, money does matter; most "successful" people come from financially secure families.[3] They usually receive excellent educations. Parents and

1

extended family members provide business, professional, and social contacts. In short, they learn vital "networking" skills at an early age.[4] That was certainly the case with Quigg Newton.

Newton's Colorado Connection

Ancestors on his father's side of the family can be traced back to early seventeenth-century England.[5] After several generations of Newtons achieved varying degrees of success in Massachusetts and Pennsylvania, Quigg's great-grandfather, Ezra Artemus Newton, became the driving force in guiding the Newton clan farther west, and eventually to Colorado. As a young man, Ezra taught school in Carbondale, about thirty miles west of the family homestead in Buckingham, Pennsylvania. He had a burning desire to achieve a college education, and he studied during evenings and weekends to prepare for entry into Carlisle College. Although admitted with "fair prospects," poor health forced him to interrupt his studies.

While living in Carbondale, he met and married seventeen-year-old Ruth Ann Wilbur in October 1841. Although frail in health, Ezra possessed driving ambition; ever alert to new opportunities, he entered the world of commerce. Just before the Civil War, Ezra moved west to Wisconsin, where he started up lumber operations in Oshkosh and Fond du Lac. Family records reveal that at various points in time he made land investments and began merchandising operations in several other midwestern towns. During the 1860s, the family also spent brief periods in Ripon, Spring Grove, and Monroe, Wisconsin, and later in Freeport, Illinois. Evidently, this generation of Newton men was more interested in business than patriotism and combat, since there is no mention of any Newton family members serving in the armies on either side during the Civil War.[6]

The peripatetic merchant and lumber entrepreneur had heard a great deal about new opportunities in Denver, a booming frontier town in the recently "settled" Colorado Territory. In 1868, he decided to come take a look. Ezra was impressed by the energy local boosters were generating in successfully attracting railroad investors, and he eventually decided to locate his family there. They arrived in Denver in 1871, the same year railroad service was inaugurated. Another reason for the move west may have been an attempt to expose their son Wilbur to the salubrious clean air of the West.[7] If so, the move failed to create magic, as Wilbur, just twenty-five years old, succumbed to what may have been tuberculosis, in 1872. Ezra quickly moved into leadership positions in the emerging frontier city, becoming a director of the City National Bank. He also engaged in cattle operations in El Paso County. While on a business trip back East, Ezra died suddenly in Waukesha, Wisconsin, in the summer of 1878, at the age of sixty-one.[8]

Ezra's son George, twenty years old when his family moved to Colorado, demonstrated sufficient ambition and energy to gain his father's trust. Family records indicate that, following his attendance at Racine College, George may have been the first family member to receive a college degree. Ezra helped him follow family tradition in establishing a lumber business in Pueblo in the early 1870s. George succeeded in building the state's largest lumber manufacturing enterprise during the 1880s, adding yards in Colorado Springs, Cañon City, Colorado City, Rocky Ford, Florence, and northern New Mexico. Unfortunately, George Newton failed to enjoy robust health, and he died in 1891 at age forty. After his death, his younger brother, Whitney, took over the business. Whitney was Quigg Newton's grandfather.[9]

Although Whitney had been born in Monroe, Wisconsin, in 1858, in many respects, he was a true son of Colorado. Arriving in Denver as he entered his teenage years, young Whitney entered the first public schools, and he was in the first graduating class at Denver High School in 1875. By then, his father was well established in business in Denver, and Whitney was sent to Cornell University in Ithaca, New York. While a student at Cornell, Whitney courted Mary Rose Quigg, who was four years his senior and a daughter in one of Ithaca's leading families. Whitney returned to Colorado, where he became a founder, cashier, and co-owner of the Bank of Breckenridge. His romance with Mary Rose Quigg flourished despite their lengthy physical separation, and the couple was married in 1881. Shortly thereafter, his older brother George persuaded him to help run the flourishing lumber business in Pueblo.[10]

The early 1880s were a propitious time to be in the lumber business on the Front Range, and Pueblo was an ideal center for business operations. Railroad operators replaced wooden railroad ties every five years or so. Mining operations in nearby Leadville, and elsewhere in the region, required massive amounts of timber for building and supporting underground mine shafts. Roads into remote mountain towns were surfaced with wood in some places, and bridges required wooden supports. As long as cities and towns continued to grow and expand, builders required millions of board feet to construct businesses and homes. Ambitious businessmen and their wives often envisioned magnificent domestic monuments to themselves built out of granite, or at least brick, but many eventually settled for more modest wooden structures. Some homeowners relied on wood-burning stoves. In an era preceding scientific resource management, only a few lonely voices noted that the mountainsides as well as the few stands of trees along the banks of streams had already been largely denuded.[11]

Whitney solidified the Newton family's emerging reputation as leaders in business in the Rocky Mountain region, and he expanded his activities into the political arena as well. In partnership with Charles Boettcher, Mahlon Thatcher, and Harry C. James, Whitney helped organize what evolved into the Ideal Cement Company. In many respects, this endeavor made sense, as it had obvious links to his lumber interests. He also became involved in state politics. After Colorado gained statehood in 1876, Whitney became an early statewide chairman of the Republican Party. Between 1903 and 1905, he served as Colorado's treasurer, helping modernize administration of the state's finances.

During his term as a public official, Whitney moved his family to a home at 1165 Grant Street. The Denver neighborhood was already known as Capitol Hill, and many of the leading citizens of Colorado lived there. Some of Whitney's friends and business associates urged him to run for governor, or perhaps the U.S. Senate or House, but he resisted these entreaties. He was content to run his various enterprises and enjoy his fraternal associations with fellow members of the Masons, where he rose to the thirty-second degree of the Order. Whitney also enjoyed other social organizations. He was a member of the prestigious Denver Club, and he was among the founders of the Denver Country Club.

Whitney and Mary Rose Newton raised five children, all boys. The oldest was Quigg Newton's Uncle Wilbur, born in Pueblo on February 2, 1883. By the time the family had moved to Denver, Wilbur was off to college. Like his father, Wilbur attended Cornell University, graduating in 1905. Wilbur concentrated on business courses in preparation for his lifelong commitment to the corporate world. Returning to Colorado after graduation, Wilbur helped run the family's lumber business in Pueblo. Later, he moved to Denver and became a key "inside man" with the Boettcher Newton Investment Company, cofounded by his younger brother James Quigg, known as Jim. Wilbur was fascinated by challenges of bringing greater efficiency to every enterprise he studied.

Years later, his nephew Quigg Newton quickly gained a reputation as a modernizer who brought a new sense of order to all of his endeavors. Quigg may have inherited some of these qualities from his uncle Wilbur. Wilbur also helped establish family traditions in contributing his expertise to various civic causes. He served as treasurer at the University of Denver; later, Quigg would serve as president of the board of trustees at that school. Uncle Wilbur also became a trustee of Clayton College, an orphanage for boys. Toward the end of his life, Wilbur was honored by the regents of the University of Colorado in 1944 for helping that institution bring order to its investment policies. His nephew Quigg would step into an even more important capacity with the University of Colorado when he became president in 1956. Quigg generally admired and looked up to his uncle.

Quigg's Father, Jim Newton

Of all of Quigg Newton's forebears, his father, Jim, may have been the most complicated and interesting. Without question, Jim had by far the most profound influence on Quigg Newton's life. The second son of Whitney and Mary Rose Newton, Jim was born in Pueblo on December 31, 1885. The family may not yet have been wealthy, but their lifestyle was certainly comfortable. By then, Jim's father had become one of the most prominent men in town, and the family lived in a huge, rambling Queen Anne–style brick home in the best part of town. Nevertheless, Jim's parents may have attempted to imbue him with the qualities of Horatio Alger's heroes, or at least convince him that the poorhouse was just around the corner. Jim recalled, "When I left something on my plate, I'd be told to eat it up, that some poor boys would be glad to get it. I was afraid of poverty. I started out to make enough money to put me beyond its clutch."[12]

Some of his attempts to avoid poverty may have escaped the notice of adults; they almost certainly would not have received their approval. Jim claimed that as a youth in Pueblo, he was always trying to figure out how to get others to do his work for him. He recalled that he hated working in the family's lumberyard during summers, so he organized a poker game, "which was profitable, and much more entertaining." By his own account, at least, Jim was something of a hellraiser as a youngster. Late in life, he described himself as a combination of Tom Sawyer and Huck Finn: "I was probably the orneriest brat that was ever brought up in Colorado. … I think that I wasn't expelled from school simply because they'd sooner have me where they could keep an eye on me." According

Quigg Newton's father, James Newton.

to Quigg, when he started school in Denver more than two decades later, one of his veteran teachers, who had transferred from Pueblo, asked him if he was related to the notorious Jim Newton of Pueblo, whom she had taught years earlier. When informed that he was indeed Jim's son, the teacher allegedly said that she hoped he "did not take after his father."[13]

One suspects that Jim was playfully attempting to "sell" an exaggerated bad-boy image late in life for his own, or for a 1941 reporter's amusement. Other evidence strongly suggests that, although he may have had a devilish streak, he was in all important respects a dutiful and conventional turn-of-the-century youth. The Pueblo High School annual, published in the year of his graduation in 1903, conveys an image of a sober, industrious seventeen-year-old. Among forty-five members of the "cadet corps," as a senior, James was the third ranking officer, listed as a first lieutenant. Above him were a captain and a major. He was the business manager for the yearbook, as well as being a member of the board of editors of that publication. The senior class of 1903 at Pueblo High numbered thirty-four graduates, twenty-four of them girls. Jim was the only boy (along with six girls) who took the so-called "classical" course of study. One hundred years ago, this academic track was usually the one taken by youths intending to go to college. There is little indication of his being an accomplished athlete. In schools with such small enrollments, almost any boy with even moderate interest and skill in any sport was welcomed on various teams. Jim played in a handful of *indoor* baseball games (unfortunately, the yearbook provided no description of the facilities used), but he apparently did not play for the team in baseball games outdoors.[14]

Jim Newton was not mentioned among the school's academic standouts, but he was evidently sufficiently prepared to carry on a family tradition and be admitted into his father's alma mater, Cornell University. He went straight from high school to Cornell, where he revealed an immense intellectual curiosity and an appetite for always seeking new challenges. These may have been the most important qualities he eventually passed down to his son, Quigg. James participated in crew, headed the junior prom committee, and even joined a religious society. He devoted sufficient attention to his academic courses to graduate with his classmates in the spring of 1907, with a concentration in law.

Jim briefly returned to Pueblo to help out in the family lumber business, but it was soon evident that he sought a larger stage on which to prove his mettle. He found time to court and eventually marry Nelle Singleton in Chicago in October 1908. Quigg's mother's family can be traced back as far as the Newtons'. Christopher Springer, of German birth, became a wealthy businessman in Sweden in the mid-seventeenth century. He sired three sons. Charles, his second son, was serving in the Swedish Embassy in London when he was captured by bandits, shipped to Virginia, and sold for a five-year term as an indentured servant. Charles quickly escaped, found his niche in a Swedish enclave in Delaware, and achieved wealth. Two generations later, his grandson John joined Daniel Boone's initial foray into Kentucky, then returned east and fought as a private in a Maryland militia company during the American Revolution. John and his wife enjoyed uncommonly good health, as did their eleven children, all of whom survived into adulthood. Two generations later, John's grandson John T. Springer was born in Jacksonville, Illinois, and lived most of his life there. He attended Illinois College, and as a teenager, he participated in the California gold rush. Evidently, he did not uncover a fortune, and he returned to Jacksonville, where he practiced law. He and his wife had three children, the youngest being Lulu Springer, Quigg's grandmother. Lulu married John Singleton, and in 1891 the couple welcomed a daughter, Nelle, Quigg's mother.[15]

Quigg's Mother, Nelle Singleton Newton

Unfortunately, Nelle Singleton's upbringing was, in many respects, the direct opposite of Jim Newton's. Whereas Jim had been raised in a solid, upper-middle-class nuclear family with strong extended family connections, Nelle, an only child, was virtually an orphan. Her father, John Singleton, a traveling salesman, was almost constantly on the road. Two years after Nelle was born, in 1891, her mother died after falling down the stairs in what was termed an accident. John Singleton apparently had neither the interest nor the ability to be a real parent to the suddenly motherless youngster, so Nelle was sent to live with her grandparents on a farm outside of Jacksonville. John Singleton was an unsuccessful drifter for the remainder of his life. He eventually remarried and moved to the Pacific Northwest. On several occasions, he asked his daughter for financial help, and although she provided modest support, they had little, if any meaningful contact.[16]

Little is known of the circumstances under which Jim and Nelle met or their courtship, but it appears that Jim kept these experiences secret from his family for many months. His mother, Mary Quigg Newton, had five sons and no daughters, and she apparently had no inkling of how to relate to other women, particularly young and attractive competitors for the attention and affection of her sons. Jim's brother Whitney had been so leery of informing his mother he was married that he kept it a secret from both of his parents for some years. Fortunately for Wilbur, he married a strong woman who managed to establish reasonable boundaries with her mother-in-law.

Jim was somewhat less reticent about his own courtship and marriage than Whitney was, but not by much. Shortly after his wedding, Jim allegedly sent a telegram to his mother reading something like, "You are married, and I am too!" Unfortunately, Nelle was no match for her mother-in-law, who virtually ignored her and consistently shunted her aside. Mary's treatment of all her sons' wives bordered on cruelty. According to Quigg, at Thanksgiving, she invited all five sons to dinner but refused to include their wives! Nelle had moved west to be with her husband, and she had no family in Colorado. Given these circumstances, Nelle was clearly at an enormous emotional and psychological disadvantage. Having been brought up in a home with four brothers but no sisters, Jim had little understanding of women's needs. Even if he were so inclined, he had little sense of how best to nurture his young, insecure wife. By most accounts, they were an odd couple. Jim was confident and gregarious, while Nelle, not surprisingly, lacked self-confidence and was somewhat withdrawn.

Jim was concerned, first and foremost, with achieving a place in the business community in Denver. His father was well established, and Jim would expand the family's influence in the Mile High City. He first established the Newton Investment Company in 1908, the same year he was married. He and Nelle also began to establish a family. In 1909, their first child, Ruth, was born. Two years later, on August 3, 1911, their only son, James Quigg Jr., was welcomed into the world. Back then, virtually all children were born at home, and the infant took his first breaths at a temporary family home at First Avenue and High Street. Two years later, a second daughter, Nancy, arrived, and Jim and Nelle Newton's family was complete.

Quigg's older sister, Ruth, his mother, Nelle, and infant Quigg in 1911.

CHAPTER 2

YOUTH

In later years, when questioned by reporters, Jim Newton often described the years immediately following his son's birth as uncertain, a period during which hard times were never far from the door. In Denver, he had formed Newton Investment Company, a brokerage business. Jim Newton was gregarious and well liked. Other family members were settling into the local community, and he made friends with many of the region's most influential people. In all likelihood, he could have enjoyed a comfortable and essentially unchallenging life handling investments for family members and his well-heeled friends.

As he approached thirty, however, he was feeling adventuresome, wanting to test his business skills in a larger arena. In about 1915, Jim moved his family back to the New York City area and went to work in the financial district. By his account, he approached Wall Street with a little money, and "the wolves stripped [me] clean in a little more than thirty days." As Jim recalled, "There I was with a wife and three kids, a home in Short Hills, N.J., two cars and servants and broke—broke!"[1] James claimed that the only work he could get was as a "messenger" for Guarantee Trust Company at a salary of $100 a month. He stated that he also sold briefcases and suitcases on the side to help make ends meet. But if he experienced any economic deprivation, it was very brief. Senior management at Guarantee Trust quickly identified him as an up-and-comer, and within three years he was head of its new business department.

Quigg's Earliest Memories

Young Quigg, then about four years old, remembered going back East, very likely by train. He didn't recall Short Hills or any hard times. His father soon moved the family into Manhattan: the Apthorp Apartments on West Ninetieth Street. The family's initial sojourn in New York City lasted about three years. When Quigg was five or six, his parents enrolled him in kindergarten at the well-known Collegiate School for Boys, located on the Upper West Side.[2] In 1918, partly through family connections, Jim landed a job in Washington, D.C. Two brothers were in military service, and another brother, Whitney, was an aide to one of President Woodrow Wilson's closest advisors, "Colonel" Edward M. House.

Whitney may have brought Jim's name to the attention of influential men in the Wilson administration. After the United States declared war on the Central Powers and war preparations geared up in earnest, the Guarantee Trust Company "loaned" Jim to the administration, where he became assistant executive secretary of the Capital Issues

Quigg and his sisters in 1915. Ruth is on the left. His younger sister, Nancy, is on the right. Quigg is four years old.

Committee in the Treasury Department.[3] This fledgling entity was the embryonic forerunner of the Securities and Exchange Commission.

The family move to Washington, D.C., occurred as Quigg approached his seventh birthday. The family lived in a row house, and there were lots of other kids around. Quigg played outdoor games popular at the time, such as kick the can and run sheep run. As for indoor hobbies, baseball cards were, for a time, one of Quigg's consuming interests. The great flu pandemic struck in the fall of 1918, taking approximately 600,000 lives in the United States, and perhaps as many as 40 million worldwide.[4] Many children's parents confined them indoors until the worst of the epidemic faded the following year, but young Quigg didn't recall any such limitations on his social activities.

One indelible memory involved his younger sister, Nancy, who somehow got hold of a bottle of strychnine poison and swallowed some. Quigg ran to a nearby doctor for help, and the doctor used a stomach pump to save Nancy's life. Another incident involving a doctor in which Quigg's behavior was less heroic may have occurred during the flu pandemic of 1918–1919, when doctors were constantly on the run making house calls. Young Quigg remembered being led astray by an older boy who "snitched" a doctor's bag of implements, then talked him into going home with the bag. When Jim found out about the incident, he turned it into an opportunity to impart a lesson to the impressionable youngster. After Jim returned the bag to the doctor, rather than paddle Quigg, he verbally reprimanded him and gave him a lecture about not being led down the wrong path by misguided older youths.[5]

Following the armistice in November 1918, Jim moved the family back to New York, but they didn't stay long. In 1919 or 1920, the family moved back to Denver and took up temporary quarters in Jim's mother's home at 1165 Grant Street. Today, that stretch of Grant Street is a busy one-way thoroughfare, with some stately, well-preserved older homes surrounded by apartment houses and an occasional hotel, restaurant, or other business. Eighty-five years ago, Capitol Hill was home to many of Denver's elite. It was still surprisingly rural in atmosphere. Mary Rose Quigg's substantial property contained a barn, and although she did not tend them herself, she kept a cow and some chickens. Quigg's grand-mother also owned an electric car, which her recently deceased husband had bought.

Early Boyhood in Denver

Living with his family in his mother's house must have seemed stifling for an up-and-coming young entrepreneur, since she was an opinion-ated, powerful, and controlling woman. For Nelle, who felt very intimidated by her imperious mother-in-law, the living arrangement must have been insufferable. The young family didn't stay at the Grant Street home very long. Jim was very good at buying and selling Denver properties, including family residences, for profit. He soon moved the family to a house on Pearl Street, and then bought a large home at 801 York Street. The York Street home remained the family's headquarters for many years. Today, the area is built up with very expensive homes, but in the early 1920s, the neighborhood was interspersed with numer-ous vacant lots. Then, Eighth Avenue and York Street were still unpaved.

For a young boy who had lived in apartments and cramped row houses for much of his life, it was paradise. Young Quigg may have finally felt settled, sensing that the family would remain rooted for a time. For the first time in his life, he was able to establish some lasting friendships. He and his chums played for hours on end in vacant lots, built caves, and hid out among the gravestones in the cemetery located in what is now Cheesman Park. As an adolescent, he also joined the Boy Scouts, and he enjoyed the outdoor challenges that scouting offered. One of his closest boyhood friends was Henry Van Schaack Jr., the son of Henry C. Van Schaack, founder of an important real estate company.

Quigg and Henry often went fly-fishing and small game hunting. Jim Grant, a close family friend, had a large rural retreat in the moun-tains near North Park, and Quigg and young Van Schaack spent many glorious days and nights at Grant's spread, engaging in campouts and boyhood game hunts. In a safer and more innocent age, their parents may have occasionally allowed them to hitchhike to Grant's retreat, but more than likely, they were accompanied by adults on most of their trips into the mountains. During one summer, Quigg spent some time with an uncle "roughing it" on a ranch in Pagosa Springs. He learned horseback riding and how to handle pack mules. In the middle of the summer, he wrote home: "When I have nothing else to do I read the Bible and those little books. I am keeping clean, about every three or four days I take a bath in the river and change my clothes. We have to wash our own clothes because there is nobody else to do them."[6]

Just before his twelfth birthday, in the summer of 1923, the youngster had his first significant experience far from home: several weeks at the famous Culver Military Academy in northern Indiana. According to Quigg, his father considered the exposure to a very mild form of military discipline to be "the sort of experience every boy should have."[7] Their correspondence reveals that Quigg was highly enthusiastic about the trip, and several of his Denver friends, including Henry Van Schaack, were set to accompany him on the adventure. Jim considered the trip "payment for meritorious [academic?] work done during the winter." In a letter to the director of the academy, Jim noted that Quigg had broken a small bone in his ankle, and he had been leaning toward delaying his son's trip back East. But Quigg had his heart set on accompanying his friends. Jim asked the authorities to keep an eye on his enthusiastic offspring, because he would undoubtedly test his body to the limit. Yet Jim wanted Quigg to try any sport he desired, and he particularly encouraged him to continue boxing.[8]

By his own account, Quigg thoroughly enjoyed his weeks at Culver. Although the campers wore a type of military uniform, did some marching and drill, and heard the playing of taps and reveille, the entire experience was mostly a summer vacation. Quigg enjoyed the regimentation and occasional "inspections," but far more of his time was spent swimming, playing individual and team sports, and working on various Boy Scout merit badges. He had to spend some time in the infirmary because he suffered a deep gash in his foot during a swim, but that did not lessen his enthusiasm for the place. Toward the end of his stay at Culver, Quigg wrote an ebullient letter home describing his efforts to win top scores, or "notches," in numerous areas where the boys' efforts were evaluated and rewarded.[9] Even as a preadolescent, he was already demonstrating sensitivity to how his performances were perceived by others. This proclivity for self-evaluation was a characteristic that would be prominent in letters written deep into adulthood.

Quigg was large for his age, a definite advantage for young boys growing up, and he quickly became a leader among his peers. He enjoyed football in particular, and as a preadolescent, he played for the Sagamores, a neighborhood sandlot team managed by a woman. Memorabilia from his boyhood years includes a picture of a proud eleven-year-old sporting his first real football uniform. He also learned to swim, wrestle, and box at the Denver Athletic Club. His friend Henry Van Schaack was a golf enthusiast and persuaded Quigg to take it up. Although Quigg enjoyed the sport on a social basis, he never claimed to be very good at it. He may have broken 100 on a few occasions.[10]

Quigg was the son of increasingly affluent parents who joined the Denver Country Club and lived close to that symbol of the local "establishment." That did not, however, grant him immunity from typical boyhood trials as he grew into adolescence. Because he achieved physical maturity quickly, he occasionally became a target for other boys hoping to test their fighting skills. One epic battle was with Henry Stark, which evolved over a disagreement about ownership of a kite. "It was a real nose-punching boyhood scrap. … We must have been eleven or twelve years old. I think we fought for an hour, at least, resting only when we were so weak we couldn't fight any longer. I think it must have been a tie. Anyway, we had a lot more respect for each other afterwards."[11]

One afternoon, another friend, but also a rival, Putnam "Putty" Humphreys, challenged Quigg to a fistfight. They made arrangements to fight the following morning. Young Quigg worried overnight about the outcome and lined up a couple of other chums as seconds. They gathered at Quigg's home at Eighth and York and walked to Humphreys' home near Eighth and Logan Streets. To Quigg's great relief, when they showed up at his adversary's house at the appointed time and called him outside, Putty's mother poked her head out of the window and told them that her son was sick and that they should go home. Quigg recalled that although he did partake in a few other bare-knuckle brawls, on that occasion he was secretly relieved at being spared another such ordeal.[12]

Since Quigg was large for his age, as well as being handsome and well mannered (except for occasional fisticuffs), he was quite popular with the girls. Having two attractive sisters probably helped him receive coveted introductions as well. Quigg recalled being interested in the opposite sex as early as seven. At one point, he was smitten with Henry Van Schaack's sister, Clara, and he later formed a serious attachment to Nancy Toll, a daughter in another prominent Denver family. Nevertheless, in his adolescent years, almost all of his interactions with girls were of an entirely innocent nature at closely chaperoned social gatherings at the homes of parents, the Denver Country Club, or one of Denver's many private parties.[13]

Quigg's parents, particularly his father, were quite generous in rewarding their son for good behavior, and birthday and Christmas cel-ebrations brought him impressive harvests of material goods. Yet, like most other adolescents, Quigg was very interested in acquiring and con-trolling his own pocket money, and he devised some ingenious ways to get it. On hot summer days, he managed a pop stand on Eighth Avenue, near his family's home. In the early 1920s, black-and-white silent motion pictures were still something of a novelty, and he sold booklets of tickets for attractions at Harry Huffman's local theater for a percent-age of the proceeds. He soon acquired his own movie projector, and after borrowing movies from a local Episcopal church, he offered them to younger kids in the neighborhood for a few cents per showing. Another business venture was selling Christmas wreaths door to door.

The Newton family lived in a comfortable home, and by all out-ward appearances, they were enjoying the American dream. Jim and Nelle were socially active, partnered in bridge amongst their friends, and presented a united front in public. Relations between the couple were strained, however, and they frequently argued at home. Jim thoroughly dominated the household, and he believed that only men should deal with serious issues. These views strongly affected Quigg. Early in his life, he realized that his father basically patronized both his wife and his daughters and discussed important affairs only with him. For example, although Quigg was two years younger than his sister Ruth, Jim often shared with Quigg his concerns about what he should "do with" her.[14] From his earliest years until Quigg was a grown man, Jim constantly lectured his son. When Quigg was fourteen, his father wrote him a long letter full of moral lessons, urging him to live a clean and virtuous life and to look after his sisters. He cautioned his son, "Don't let the world run your actions. Always try to do right."[15]

Early Schooling

As for his schooling, it seems evident that in his earliest years, Quigg considered it a necessary evil. He was a dutiful and not particularly gifted student. He attended Corona (now Dora Moore) Elementary, followed by Morey Junior High (now Middle) School. He could only remember one of his teachers in his early grades, more for her beauty than the intellectual stimulation she provided. On one occasion, Jesse Hamilton, the principal at Morey Junior High School, advised Quigg's parents: "[He] and I have had a little talk and for certain reasons I am not giving him his report cards this time. I am sure you will feel the marks achieved next time are worth waiting for."[16] Although his parents did not make too much of Quigg's mediocre grades, they made it clear from the beginning that he would attend college. Jim was a graduate of Cornell University, an Ivy League school, and Quigg understood that he was expected to perform academically. At Morey, there was a "classical" educational track for students whose parents expected them to go to college, and Quigg took that course.

Like most men of his era, Jim Newton believed that only men counted in the realm of the serious affairs of life. Although he had two daughters, there is no surviving evidence that he thought seriously about their futures. He evidently believed that if they completed finishing school, attracted good husbands, and raised conventional families, he really didn't need to worry much more about them.[17] In contrast, he had big plans for Quigg. As a graduate of Cornell, he was determined that his son would be admitted into an excellent school. But Jim doubted that Quigg would receive adequate preparation for college in Denver's public schools. When Quigg was about nine years old, his father started scouting out New England prep schools, sending inquiries to several institutions.[18] He eventually settled on the Phillips Academy at Andover, Massachusetts. Jim's younger brother Bob had been sent there and had enjoyed a very good experience. Bob may have talked Jim into sending Quigg to Andover. Quigg recalled that his father made the decision unilaterally; he was simply told that he would be leaving Denver to spend his high school years on the East Coast. Even then, prospective students had to take entrance examinations to assess their academic skills. Quigg remembered performing miserably on these tests, but eighty years ago the determination of prominent parents and promises that the boy would "buckle down" to his studies were sufficient to convince the authorities at Andover to admit Quigg.[19]

Self-Discovery at Andover

Young Quigg was a compliant boy; if he felt he would be homesick and miss his family and friends in Denver, he hid his concerns. When the school year started at Andover in the fall of 1926, he had just turned fifteen. Several of his father's friends and business associates had sent their sons to the school. They may have given him advice in advance, and they provided "introductions" to some of the social clubs (quasi-fraternities) on campus. Just before Quigg left for Andover, his Uncle Bob, wrote him a letter urging him to join his old club, AUV, but he also

Quigg looking very mature at age sixteen. He was a student at Andover.

urged him to "go into the one where the biggest majority of your friends might be." His uncle also pressured Quigg to perform well: "Your record in college will be a repetition of what you do at Andover. The boys that you go to school with there will follow you to college and your mark must be made there."[20] One of his father's business partners imparted his own conventional words of wisdom: "It is a great privilege to be able to go to a school like Andover ... and you must remember that it is a very small percentage of young men that have the opportunity you possess ... I know from my own experience what it means to a young man, I, myself, not having had the privilege which you are now enjoying."[21] Shortly after Quigg arrived at the school, his father wrote him to remind him to be sure to "take the letters [of introduction] ... and present them at once. ... I am sending this letter air mail because I want to be sure you present your letters. It is very important for you."[22]

Thus, Quigg departed for Andover with the full weight of his extended family's and their friends' expectations squarely on his shoulders. Happily, it seemed that he needed little help, as he fit into the school almost immediately, at least socially. As Uncle Bob predicted, he roomed with two boys who would become lifelong friends. C. Davis Weyerhaeuser, from Tacoma, Washington, was a direct descendent of the founder of the huge lumber empire bearing that name. Richard M. Davis became one of his closest friends; he would eventually become Quigg's law partner in Denver and marry his younger sister, Nancy. Although Quigg liked his roommates, school food left something to be desired. "I was sure glad to get Mary's fudge and so were the boys in the house. ... I miss home cooking very much because we have such rotten food here."[23]

His Denver connections may have helped Quigg become noticed by members of two of the most prominent "fraternities" at Andover. But some of the "fast" social behavior of his peers bothered him. After he went out for football, one of his older teammates invited him to attend his social club's evening function, and Quigg went. "[W]e went to a frat house with lots of other boys (all smoking, I didn't), though much offered. I was asked to come to that frat again. ... That was the first time

I was rushed. *It was not AUV*" (emphasis his). The pressure of "rush" took its toll, as he confided to his parents, "I think I would almost rather join a club that I didn't have to have pull to get into."[24] Eventually, he received bids from both PAE and AUV. He quickly accepted a bid from AUV, but later had second thoughts. After pledging to AUV, he began spending more time with boys from PAE: "I went around with them so much that I liked them terribly well. When the day came along for the cards to come out, I was a little sorry that I had made my choice. ... " He rhetorically asked his parents, "Do you exactly blame me for not daring to say no to boys three years older than I am."[25]

Quigg's letters home were amazingly insightful and remarkably intimate for a teenager. He readily shared many of his feelings with his parents. There were times that he admitted extreme homesickness. A few weeks after his term began, he wrote, "I hold continually in mind the things that you both have told me all through my life. Sometimes I think that I am getting along very well and sometimes I am almost ready to give up and go away and cry."[26]

Although Quigg quickly adjusted to the school's social life, he took on a big academic load and signed on to play football. From the very start, he urged his parents not to expect too much from him academically, since he was trying to make up for his deficiencies by taking on extra course work.[27] According to Quigg, the typical student at Andover took seventeen hours of course work, and he was taking twenty-one.[28] A few weeks into his first semester, he wrote home, "The studies are very hard and the teachers very strict."[29] At times he voiced utter discouragement: "In my English here I will hand in a paper that in Denver I would get an A, while here I get a D. ... In my algebra it seems that I haven't got a very quick mind because I can't work any of the problems without help. I failed a test the other day but I hope that I can make it up."[30] Two weeks later, he wrote, "You will very soon receive a letter telling you that I have failed in two subjects, French 2 and Algebra. ... I am very ashamed although I have tried very hard. ... I am sure you will feel very bad and will think that I am not doing what you expected of me and that makes me feel worse than anything could."[31]

After his first semester at Andover, Quigg conveyed utter depression over his academic performance: "I flunked three rating exams in succession. I don't know why, but I am not doing so well here. I don't know whether or not my teachers think I am working (I don't think they do) but I think I am. I don't know how to study, I am beginning to realize that I come home to study an awful lot but I waste most of my time. … I am low in everything this month."[32] During Quigg's three years at Andover, worries over inconsistent academic performance along with promises to apply himself and do better in the future were staples in his correspondence with his parents.

Quigg had enjoyed athletic success in Denver, particularly in football, and he dreamed of making his mark at Andover. When he went out for football, he quickly discovered that his prep school coaches taught a different brand of ball, and he would have a hard time competing against upperclassmen. During his first year, he played halfback on the "first club" (intramural) team, but he considered himself basically a "scrub." "From a lack of playing before I don't do very well so the coach bawls me out about '50' times each practice." Still, he expressed hope he might be "chosen for the all club team that plays Exeter though if I were I would be very frightened."[33] A few weeks later, Quigg reported that he "bent his collar bone" and had been put out of a game "on account of my shoulder." In addition, he had not made the all-club team, which meant that he would not be playing against the school's biggest rival, Exeter. Despite these setbacks, he seemed to enjoy the physical challenge and team camaraderie. At the end of the football season, Quigg did not get to play in Andover's first win over Exeter in six years. He did win his numerals, however, and he was enormously pleased with the outcome of the Exeter game.[34] Although he informed one relative that he was "not so good an athlete as most other boys," he was determined to go out for track during his first winter at Andover.[35]

Quigg undoubtedly considered life at Andover serious business, and he was, by all accounts, a dutiful, conscientious teenager. But, like any youngster, he looked forward with great anticipation to breaks from the pressure to perform. Within two months of his arrival at Andover,

Quigg had managed to get off campus at least twice, and he definitely enjoyed himself in Boston. As described in letters home, the trips were wholly innocent in nature: day trips with other boys, during which they might eat lunch at a restaurant, then see a show. He reassured his father that he had *not* spent $25 on a single trip to Boston, but rather a total of $18 in two separate trips there. He also claimed, "We never see any girls of any kind here and I am just as glad."[36] His father evidently trusted him always to do the right thing, even going so far as to write the headmaster a letter stating that Quigg had requested permission to leave school and spend nine days in Boston over Thanksgiving break, and that he wanted to "go on record as saying that any request made by my son has my approval, and I have absolute confidence in his judgment and ability to take care of himself."[37]

Although his father gave Quigg free rein as long as he acted "responsibly," his mother's dealings with him often bordered on suffocation. Quigg loved his mother, who provided sweet and gentle support, but her influence on his life basically involved "fringe" issues. Nelle's letters and actions reflected her own deep insecurities. Several months after Quigg left for Andover, she wrote him, complaining that his letters were "few and far between," at least compared to those from his older sister, Ruth, who was already living on her own in New York City and allegedly writing home about twice a week. Nelle even interjected herself directly into Quigg's social life. As Valentine's Day approached in 1927, she urged Quigg to write a note to one of his female friends in Denver: "She had a bet ... whether you would write her or Betty, and she lost. She is crazy to get a letter from you, even if it is only a few lines." A few days after Valentine's Day, she informed her son that she had almost sent a card in his name, but then decided not to in case he had already done so.[38] One can only imagine Quigg's consternation regarding his mother's intrusion into his most personal affairs.

By the spring of 1927, Quigg was beginning to sense that if he was to make a major mark at Andover, it would be in extracurricular activities other than football. In the depths of the winter of 1927, he wrote to his parents of working out daily at track and wrestling:

"Perhaps someday I will be able to do something. I have been working out a lot also with the weights. I hope that when I see you, you will see a noted improvement in my muscles *as you have always told me that I am soft*" (emphasis added).[39] He also talked of trying out for the debate team, and he expressed early interest in joining the staff of the school's yearbook, the *Phillipian*.[40] If he couldn't make certain varsity teams, being elected team manager would be a major coup, because managers' knowledge and opinions apparently carried weight with their peers. On one hand, Quigg frequently worried about fitting in with his peers. On the other hand, he was appalled at some of the social behavior of Andover boys when they went in to Boston. One of his older "fraternity" friends indicated a willingness to include him in a junior and senior dominated class social function. While flattered, he demurred: "I am going to wait a little while before I go there because I don't fit with '18' year old girls. It seems that to get along real well with the boys you have to do the things they do and that is go in to BOSTON every weekend and take a girl to a show, smoke, and drink. ... They all believe that before the end of the year they will all have me smoking, drinking, and playing around like the rest, but I am going to fool them, I hope without getting the reputation of a 'goody goody.'"[41]

Quigg's first year at Andover was a major challenge for a Denver lad somewhat lacking in the sophistication and polish that some of his eastern classmates possessed, but in many ways it was a positive learning experience. By the end of the year, he was still struggling with academics. For the spring term in 1927, his marks were sixty-nine in Latin, eighty-seven in French 1, sixty-four in French 2, sixty-two in English, and just forty-six in algebra.[42] Although some of his grades were low, he was content at least in the notion that he had tried hard and done the best he could.

Unfortunately, in academics, his fall term in 1927 started on much the same terms his first spring term ended. Once again, Quigg quickly felt swamped by the coursework. Within days, he wrote to his parents that his Latin teacher was "the most terrible and dreaded of all teachers." The fates seemed to be conspiring against him: "I also have for

Geometry Mr. Dake the fellow I failed last year and Geometry I know will be hard for me. ... Now I am sure I will fail something."[43]

Quigg had gone out for football again, but he was still having trouble competing; he weighed about 145 pounds, and he estimated that some of his rivals weighed twenty-five pounds more. Within weeks, however, his athletic fortunes seemingly turned around. Coaches let him play in several varsity football games, and he even won his coveted school letter. Quigg wrote a long letter home, analyzing his performance and how it changed his schoolmates' perception of him. He discounted his performances in general terms: "I really don't see why they gave me my letter because I can't kick, catch or pass, but I suppose they will expect me to be able to do this next year." Yet he recounted in considerable detail warming up on the sidelines and then getting into one game. "I was congratulated by almost everybody in the school, but I realized beforehand that a football letter really means nothing." In his next sentences he seemed to contradict himself: "It also earns a good many enemies unless it is handled in the right way. I must act even more quiet than I did before because every false move I make a person will say, 'Well, no wonder. He is a letter man.'" Later in the same letter, Quigg spilled forth further needs and daydreams. Because he had won his major letter, he was disqualified from being a team manager in other major sports. "Now that I can't make that I must accomplish something else. I want to make the senior council for next year. These [class offices] are not elected until the spring, but I can be working toward it now." Perhaps more than anything, his letter reflected the natural and almost inevitable self-absorption of a typical sixteen-year-old.[44]

Tales of Quigg's gridiron efforts evidently made the rounds in Denver. Perhaps his proud father could not refrain from talking about his son. Jim informed Quigg that *The New York Times* had carried accounts of one game, and that his name had been "on the list." Within days, Quigg received congratulations from family friends back in Denver. One acquaintance of his father, who may have heard an embellished account of the game, gushed, "I just heard last night that after being shifted from the line to the backfield you played the whole Exeter

game through. ... At the present rate you are going I will not be surprised in the least to hear of you being one of Yale's star halfbacks."[45] Jim
Grant, another close family friend, also congratulated Quigg: "I would
have written you sooner to congratulate you on the splendid record you
have made this fall—in fact ever since you have been at Andover." Grant
added, "Incidentally, I have had some very good reports of you from
some of the officers at the school."[46]

Still, success at school entailed even more pressures. His father
suggested that Quigg's elevated status at Andover enhanced his ability to
take younger boys from Denver under his wing. Jim stated bluntly that
kindnesses extended to such young men would pay off handsomely
down the road. After mentioning by name the sons of two prominent
friends, Jim continued: "They are new there in the school and you have
made a place for yourself, so I believe you can help them in both morale
and in standing. The boys that come from Denver are the boys you are
going to live with the rest of your life and I want them to be sure to
understand that their interests are your interests."[47] In fact, the father of
one of the boys Jim Newton mentioned had written Quigg several
months earlier, specifically asking him to help his son adjust to Andover
life once he entered the school. "If you can get him in to the Adams or
any other good place, preferably with yourself, I will appreciate it. He
will be fortunate in having an old friend like you to give him pointers
when he enters next fall."[48] Well meaning as such letters were, they
undoubtedly added to the Quigg's sense of being hemmed in, to perform as expected and become a model prep school student in every way.
His father's letter also suggested that he had a clearly defined plan for the
directions Quigg's future life would follow. These letters provide striking
evidence of how the so-called old-boy network operated. Yet such expectations also exacted a toll from young members of the tribe.

During his first year at Andover, Jim Newton had asked the
school's headmaster to allow Quigg free access to Boston during various
holidays, indicating that he totally trusted his son's judgment. A year
later, he seemed to have second thoughts. Jim had never had a father-
son talk to Quigg about sex, but his suspicions may have been aroused

when he received word that Quigg had spent quite a bit of money during one visit to the city. Although Quigg evidently had done nothing in the past to heighten his father's concerns, he was achieving physical maturity, and Jim may have worried that if Quigg did visit the city with the wrong type of boys, he might succumb to carnal desires: "Keep away from the girls as you might ruin your whole life. Your cousin George ruined his life at Andover and died in Boulder crazy for [sic] a disease he got while at Andover. Remember this always."[49] If Quigg replied to his father's admonition, no evidence exists. At the time, he was probably only beginning to sense Jim's elaborate blueprint for how he was expected to live out his life. In later years, he would realize that his father's constant admonitions and instructions were, in some respects, even more oppressive than those of his mother.

At this stage in his life, however, Quigg was not yet ready to rebel against either of his parents. In letters home, it appears evident that although he was proud of his heightened standing among his peers at Andover, he still, even unconsciously, regularly sought reassurance and advice. Quigg's correspondence repeatedly mentioned his hope to be nominated and elected to one or more class offices, and he ruminated about how he should conduct himself around other students in order to improve his chances. He wondered whether becoming too friendly with the boys in his class would work to his disadvantage the following year if he hoped to be picked for several leadership posts. "A few boys have gotten up a junior society or secret club, not sponsored by the school, to rival a secret senior club. I was asked to join but don't know whether it could be a good idea. I must depend on the present seniors if I wish to make senior council for next year. I mustn't be considered too high hat if I wish to be elected to any upper middle office."[50] In remarkable respects, he was already thinking like the politician he would become when he ran for mayor of Denver two decades later.

This was a recurring theme in Quigg's correspondence. The sixteen-year-old was, in fact, amazingly sensitive to how he came across to his classmates, and his letters home were strikingly analytical of the "political" environment at Andover. In a long letter to his parents, he described in detail various political "types" at Andover. There were a number of nineteen-year-olds who "know just what's right from previous experience." If one wasn't careful around his peers, it was extremely easy to "form a reputation." Being either too quiet or too vocal was death to one's political ambitions; one had to "strike a happy medium." He described one class officer who was about the biggest boy in school but who "had a rotten reputation. He goes around slapping everybody on the back and talking to everybody for merely selfish reasons. This is the reputation I am liable to get if I don't watch out. People hate politicians because they aren't sincere." Yet he fully intended to play politics himself. In the same letter, Quigg mentioned, "I really ought to go out to Ohio (over Spring break). For various reasons I must see this fellow. One is that if I don't he will think I don't want to see him. He is going to be a big fellow here next year and I mustn't high hat him."[51] Achieving the self-knowledge to become a confident leader would take more time.

Quigg evidently felt on more solid ground in describing his efforts for the yearbook and literary magazines, the key being that he simply informed his parents about what he was doing and did not ask for advice. Early in the spring of 1928, he described in great detail the effort he was heading up to get out a large magazine for the school's sesquicentennial celebration in May that would contain articles from many leading alumni. It would run 125 pages. Quigg was on the editorial board. He was not responsible for any of the writing; rather he solicited the alumni for both literary contributions and purchases of advertising. In addition to his work for the yearbook, he spent many hours preparing for his school's debating contest.

Quigg found satisfaction, even amusement, in describing his work on both of these activities, but he was still anxious about his future in football. He shared his fear that if he failed to perform up to the standard expected of him, he would disgrace himself and, apparently, all of Denver. In Quigg's mind, football was now connected to politics: "If I make the team next year and play a good game all year I will probably be able to get almost anything I want, but if I don't I am lost. I shall tell you the straight truth. In my mind I didn't deserve a letter this year and as a result I am having a terrible time." He pleaded with his father to find him a football coach with whom he could work out over the following summer, "because it means my whole future here. Next year I won't be the fellow who received a letter and is to be congratulated. I will be a returning letter man and will have to show my stuff."[52]

However, his life at Andover wasn't totally focused on worries over football, politics, grades, and his precarious self-image. During the spring and early summer of 1928, young Quigg was involved in a couple of typical teenage capers involving automobiles. During his spring break from Andover, he visited his friend Jim Bannon in Ohio. Apparently young Bannon had access to a car, and the two drove through the night from Andover to Ohio. About 6:30 A.M., they realized that they were low on gas, so they stopped at a store that sold gasoline. The store was closed, so they tried to jimmy the available pump to drain enough gas so they could continue until daybreak. Their effort failed, but they continued on. Quigg recalled that he was driving, and he had nearly nodded off to sleep when he was awakened by a police siren. Almost eighty years later, he recalled, "If I believed in a sovereign God, I'd believe He was looking after me."[53] The officer stopped the boys, and then arrested them for attempted robbery. He took them back to the town they had left, and then hauled them before a judge. The boys lamely explained the situation to the judge, who was apparently satisfied concerning their basic innocence. It turned out that the store had been robbed a few days earlier, and the owner was naturally sensitive to the situation.[54]

Quigg may not have told his father about the incident, or else Jim laughed it off as a typical boyhood experience. After school let out for the year, Jim trusted Quigg to travel to Detroit, pick up a new car he had ordered for Nelle, and then drive it to Denver. Quigg even convinced his father that he should be allowed to stop off along the way at one or two house parties hosted by classmates at Andover who lived in the upper Midwest. Quigg arrived in Detroit by train early one morning and had some time to kill before the agency holding the vehicle opened. He went to a coffee shop, ordered breakfast, and engaged in casual conversation with a couple of men. Unfortunately, they were a

couple of con artists who, once they discovered that Quigg had some
money, offered to share a "sure thing" investment opportunity. They
insisted on *seeing* and counting his stash. Once the gullible youngster
showed them his modest bankroll, they deftly distracted him, then
pocketed a large portion before returning it with numerous bogus bills.
They quickly disappeared, and Quigg discovered he'd been the victim
of one of the oldest scams in the book. He sheepishly wired his father
for more money in order to get back to Denver: "Being a boob was
robbed by two thieves of money saved for trip."[55] Jim wasn't upset; he
promptly wired back money, saying that he was glad Quigg had learned
an important lesson in life. Quigg continued to St. Paul, where he visited
his Andover roommate C. Davis Weyerhaeuser before he returned
home to Denver.[56]

    As his senior year approached, letters home revealed that Quigg
was developing more maturity in sorting out his personal values. In one
letter, he commented at length about the sort of friends he most treasured. In his first year or two at Andover, he had been attracted to the
flashy and outgoing "politicians" and had expressed a longing to join
their ranks. Now he had second thoughts. "I know that to be with the
big fellows all the time hurts lots more than it helps. I have been staying
away from them just as much as I can. In fact, a lot of the ambition I
had I am beginning to lose because some of the examples of the fellows
who are now holding offices in school."[57] He claimed that he preferred
forming lasting friendships with the less gregarious, more modest,
thoughtful young men. At least in his own mind, he was also developing an uncommon seriousness of purpose. He described living in a
dormitory containing mostly younger students: "Some of them I like
very much, but I never am with them because I either haven't time or I
don't feel like fooling around ... most of the fellows are terrible 'foolers,'
in other words they are always wasting time, playing cards, and just
doing nothing."[58] In some respects, Quigg was feeling the stress of
hiding his growing frustration with what he considered a very superficial teenage culture on the campus: "This school, for gossip and talk,
is much worse than a small town. Everybody talks about each other. If

they do anything at all, someone does their best to make up something about them to lower them a little."[59]

Yet Quigg's apparent "maturation" process also revealed some rough edges. In typically teenage fashion, he immediately turned right around and engaged in gossip himself, dishing out decidedly unflattering opinions about certain classmates. Quigg professed disinterest in running for elected office: "I have lost some of my desire to make good in a political way. ... The present fellows who hold some of the offices are unpopular politicians. ... At present the president of our class is a very nice fellow but an awful drunk. ... The secretary is a perfect clod. He is terribly dumb, has been here for about four years already and is in a terrible fog, but he is captain of football."[60] In describing and assessing the campus culture, Quigg resembled a sociologist, even as he reassured his parents that he would never express such opinions publicly.

Quigg's final year at Andover was crowned with major success, particularly in his extracurricular activities. His tenure as manager of the *Phillipian* concluded with his significant gift to the school.[61] With hindsight of more than seven decades, Newton recalled thoroughly enjoying his Andover experience, yet he strongly believed that his social development exceeded the academic preparation he received. In fact, shortly after he entered college, he wrote a remarkably self-serving letter to Andover officials critiquing his experience there. Quigg acknowledged that school leaders were probably less than charmed to receive analytical, critical letters from alumni, especially recent graduates. Despite his own struggles with his studies, he claimed that he had not been sufficiently challenged academically. He believed that too much emphasis was placed on athletics and simply learning how to "get along." More importantly, "Prep school minds ... for the most part lack the stability accruing from a contact with reality." He continued, "Mental discipline is a difficult and decidedly unpleasant thing to learn. ... An intellectual atmosphere must permeate the life of the school. ... The intellectual side should not ... be relegated to those individuals who have acquired those tendencies from their home environment, or to those who are social outcasts and have nothing else to do with their time."

Continuing his astonishing lecture to Andover authorities, he stated, "[E]very other feature of life in prep school should be considered of negligible importance in comparison to it." Quigg recalled that intellectuals were openly ridiculed, considered oddballs or worse. "I myself can not remember coming into contact with any individual, with students *or* faculty, who stimulated me to a desire to learn or think more clearly" (emphasis added). He dismissed the faculty as "largely of old men who have lost their enthusiasm for developing young minds." As for the younger faculty, they were "of distinctly inferior caliber, usually athletic, and almost never capable of inspiring young minds to great thoughts." He claimed that in many respects the school was not doing as well as it should be, and that part of the trouble revolved around the social fraternities and the clandestine drinking occurring within their hallowed walls. Quigg allowed that "Andover men are better versed in the ways of the world than graduates of any other school." He concluded by writing that he "would never have felt the urge to write this letter … had I not heard so many of my friends … say that they will not send their sons to the school."[62] The recent graduate's letter combined a deep concern over his school and what could only be taken as breathtaking arrogance. If Quigg received a reply to this extraordinary screed, it has not survived.

In other ways, his Andover experience had matured him, and he was obviously ready to expand his horizons. In his last year at Andover, he at long last began to find himself academically. In his senior year, his grades improved significantly. When he took his college boards, he scored quite well: ninety-two in Latin, seventy in third-year French, and eighty-seven in geometry.[63] In the late 1920s, boys from affluent families who had performed reasonably well academically and who had superior extracurricular records in the nation's best prep schools gained virtually automatic admission to Ivy League Schools. Acceptance into Yale's freshman class in the fall of 1929 was a foregone conclusion.

After Quigg's graduation from Andover in 1929, Jim Newton took the family to Europe. It was Quigg's first trip abroad, and the experience helped expose him to important issues and a much larger world.

During the trip, the senior Newton, an investment broker, talked to a number of European bankers, some of whom were very critical of the feverish speculation in securities engaged in by American investors. On the ship back to New York, Jim wired his company to sell all of his stocks, as well as those of his brother George, thus saving the family from the financial disaster so many Americans suffered when the stock market collapsed just weeks later.[64]

Quigg turned eighteen a month before he reported to Yale for his freshman year in college. Although he may have felt that his academic preparation was less thorough than it could have been, he had lived away from home for three years, and he was anxious to partake fully of everything New Haven had to offer. Many of his Andover friends joined him at Yale. In some respects, New Haven was still a very cloistered world. Although the worst of the Great Depression played out during his four years there, Quigg was only vaguely aware of it, and then largely in abstract, intellectual terms. Perhaps more than anything else, the youngster eagerly anticipated distancing himself somewhat from the family nest.

CHAPTER 3

BRANCHING OUT

The eighteen-year-old Yale freshman riding a train from Denver back to New Haven in the fall of 1929 had changed markedly from the curious yet insecure boy who had ventured east to Andover under his father's wing three years earlier. In all likelihood, Quigg took a day coach, sitting up all the way from Denver to New Haven, eating dry sandwiches and stale cookies purchased from vendors, and grabbing catnaps on the hard upright seats when he could. He may have been accompanied by other fortunate youths from Denver headed for Yale or other nearby colleges. At the very least, Quigg looked forward to being reunited with many good friends from Andover. His prep school roommates, Dick Davis and C. Davis Weyerhaeuser, would also room with him at Yale. Despite his caveats about the lack of a stimulating intellectual climate at Andover, he had built a solid foundation of knowledge, and his grades had gradually improved. The prospect of confronting college-level academics did not intimidate Quigg. He would find that the pattern he set at Andover repeated itself. At Yale, he was far more engaged in extracurricular activities than solid academic subjects. Seventy years later, he recalled that, at the time, extracurricular activities were more meaningful to him and tested him more thoroughly than did his classes.[1]

Finding His Niche at Yale

If significant national and international events concerned Quigg, he seldom, if ever, mentioned them in letters to his family. With the exception of his father and a few other savvy investors, the collapse of the

35

stock market and subsequent Great Depression caught most by surprise. In the United States, at least, in the early fall of 1929 there seemed little cause for worry. To be sure, farmers had been experiencing hard times for a decade; as his train from Denver to New Haven passed through the Midwest, Quigg may have noticed more rundown properties and rural poverty than usual. He may also have seen large numbers of working men standing idly on street corners in larger towns along the railroad tracks, since some big plants were already laying off men because of steep declines in orders for durable goods. But the Big Bull Market was still going strong. Some of the nation's most respected economic fortune-tellers were claiming that the prosperity should continue into the foreseeable future and that everybody could be, and should be, rich.[2] When Quigg's train pulled into the railroad station at New Haven in September of 1929, the Wall Street crash was still a month off. For a time, at least, the Yale students could enjoy the serenity of seemingly untroubled times.

When the stock market collapsed in late October, Quigg was happily ensconced in his Yale dormitory, and he had thrown himself wholeheartedly into campus life. Jim Newton's investment firm suffered some losses, but thanks to his foresight in dumping most of the family's more risky securities before the break and quick action to protect customers once the crisis arrived, both the family's fortunes and the firm's assets experienced little negative effect.[3] Jim Newton had been in the habit of discussing business affairs and even sharing his worries with his son, but apparently he resisted any temptation to do so during harrowing times on Wall Street. Apparently, Quigg was largely shielded from personal worries. Some of his classmates were not so fortunate. The parents of numerous students who had already entered Yale could not afford the second semester tuition, and their sons were forced to drop out. Other young men took part-time jobs in laundries and waiting tables to help out with expenses. One good friend at Yale, Marshall Dodge, began selling insurance, and Quigg bought his first life insurance policy from him. As the financial crisis deepened and the Depression beat down relentlessly upon the nation's economy and social fabric, Quigg became more aware of it. He undoubtedly saw bread lines and encountered panhandlers on the street corners in New Haven and elsewhere.[4]

Young Quigg hit the ground running as soon as he stepped off the train in New Haven and immediately stamped himself as a leader among his peers. He became active in campus politics, being elected to the freshman student council then being chosen as its president by that body's members. Quigg claimed that his freshman class was the first in the history of Yale ever to create a governing body of its own. In the spring of 1930, he wrote his parents that his class had succeeded in overthrowing the rule that all freshmen had to wear hats, or "beanies." He and his fellow freshman council compatriots challenged other hoary Yale traditions as well. Evidently, Quigg played a leading rule in the struggle: "I am willing and will have to take the consequences. I thought the whole thing over, and have considered both sides of the thing, and I realize that I am hazarding my neck; this was told to me by the chairman at the [*Yale Daily*] *News*. I will tell you my reasons again even though you are probably against fool freshmen entering college and immediately trying to break to [*sic*] age old traditions."

In the same letter, Quigg then launched into an elaborate explanation of his perspectives on long-lasting and universally loathed customs on college campuses and why they were relatively easy to overthrow. "It would be a different proposition if college [students] now-adays were tradition loving and naïve. The whole class was discontented, and every class before it has been, but none of them have been willing to take any steps. Rightly or wrongly, our class has done the job, and whether or not I have been at the root of it, no matter, I must take all of the blame or at least part of it." By Newton's account, his class at Yale was uncommonly rowdy, and he described some of his classmates' actions with almost clinical detachment. "There was a riot last night which lasted until about two o'clock, and which resulted in about fifteen men in jail, and several in the hospital. ... The freshmen took everything possible and heaved it out the window ... this morning the whole place was littered about two feet thick with debris." If his parents may have feared that they had sent their son to a lunatic asylum, Quigg tried to reassure them that he hadn't personally taken part in the festivities: "I get out about the eighth of June and am coming home as fast as I can."[5]

As for the academic side of campus life, the serious-minded young man found himself drawn toward the study of American history and political institutions. He majored in history and attracted the attention of at least one of his professors, who taught historiography.[6] The instructor invited Quigg to take his specialized upper-level courses. Quigg was somewhat surprised when at one point the professor described him as an intellectual. He had never thought of himself in that way. Although Jim Newton regularly discussed ideas with him, this may have been the first time that anyone outside of his family had ever taken him seriously—or at least had let him know about it.[7] Quigg was, however, branching out intellectually. At Yale, he continued to develop his interest in debate, and he was generally good at it. But debate led directly to one of the most embarrassing moments of his college career. In his usually thorough and conscientious manner, Quigg had prepared long and hard for one contest, even memorizing his speech, which was ironically about self-control. When the time came to perform, he spoke confidently for several minutes, then completely forgot his next lines. For several excruciating minutes, he stumbled and rambled as he wound up his talk. When he concluded, there was awkward silence for a few moments, followed by a polite smattering of applause. As Newton ruefully recalled years later, "At Yale, at least in debate, peers never wanted to embarrass each other."[8]

Although Quigg was a serious student at Yale, he probably devoted more time to extracurricular activities than to academic subjects. In addition to debate and holding several class offices, he was publicity manager for the Liberal Club and cofounder of the Oyster Club. However, his primary love was journalism. At Andover, he had been business manager for the school yearbook. At Yale, he poured enormous amounts of time and energy into the *Yale Daily News*, rising quickly through the ranks of budding scribes. At the end of his junior year, he was elected to the position of managing editor, one of the prime jobs on the paper and one of the most prestigious undergraduate positions on campus. The paper was wholly independent of university financial sponsorship and faculty supervision and control. The students who ran the paper gained invaluable experience in managing finances, and perhaps even more important, in learning how to present news accurately and develop editorial policies designed to treat all sides of issues fairly.

Quigg reveled in the day-to-day operations of the paper. Young men who would make their marks in journalism worked on the paper, including John Hersey, who was two years behind Newton at Yale. Davis Weyerhaeuser, his roommate from both Andover and Yale, was also an editor. Newton was in fact so fascinated by journalism that for several years after he received his undergraduate degree, he seriously considered a career in that field.

Quigg may have been a serious student, but he was obviously well liked and respected. Early in his Yale years, he joined the Alpha Delta Phi social fraternity. At the end of his junior year, he was "tapped" to join the most prestigious club on campus, the highly exclusive and secretive Skull and Bones Society. Many Yale men dreamed of being tapped, but very few were so honored. Approximately fifteen members of each class received this high honor, which was reserved for captains of major sports teams or particularly outstanding athletes, the most brilliant students, and leaders in the most important extracurricular activities. Although Jim Newton was thrilled that Quigg had reached an inner circle of leadership among his peers, he warned his son against succumbing to hubris: "Your election to your society was a reward for what you have done to date. These rewards are not carried on and that is why they seem so empty, because one expects them to be a lasting reward and doesn't realize that each period in life is simply a heat in the race of life."[9] Still, Jim could not hide his pride in his son's achievements at Yale, and he rewarded the twenty-year-old with money to take a trip to Europe in the summer of 1932 to knock around with a few of his pals. Jim repeated his earlier warning about women: "Be careful of monkeying around with the women in Europe, because they have plenty of disease. Remember that if you should get hooked to get to a doctor as quickly as you can."[10]

Although Quigg came across as a sober-minded, serious young man, he was no stick-in-the-mud. He was involved in his share of collegiate high jinks typical of the period. Somehow Quigg had acquired a raccoon skin coat. Although the garment was basically a symbol of the more wide-open 1920s, he sported it proudly around campus. More to the point, it was wonderfully warm, a real attraction during New Haven's sometimes brutal winter days. Unbeknownst to Quigg, a friend received an invitation to fly an open cockpit airplane over New Haven on a very cold day and "borrowed" the coat. Unfortunately, the plane crashed in New Haven Harbor, and Quigg's friend barely escaped with his life. The coat evidently went down with the plane. In reporting the incident to his family, Quigg fudged a little. He informed Jim that the coat had been "stolen," and he hoped that insurance would cover it.[11]

As had been the case when Quigg was at Andover, other family members applied tremendous pressure on him to perform constantly and never fail to meet high expectations. His formidable grandmother Mary Rose ("Bamie") Newton informed him that his father was proud of him, that he had given him great pleasure. At the same time, Quigg should keep it up. "So happy it must make you to feel you have carried out his hopes and realized his ideals and not proven a disappointment." "Bamie" had not softened her attitude toward women in the family. Referring perhaps to Quigg's mother and sisters, she added cryptically, "He [Jim] has had too many [disappointments] and is getting no more from you than he deserves. ... As the years go by ... do not hesitate to send him a grateful message in appreciation for the opportunities he has made possible for you ... you are ... blessed with an unbroken family circle and that is really all that counts in this now crazy world that seems to have lost all sense of the real values of life."[12]

Jim Newton was doing all that he could to keep Quigg on the straight and narrow without help from his own mother. A cynic might argue that Jim bribed the young man to walk along an almost unnaturally righteous path during his undergraduate college years. He promised Quigg $1,000 if he avoided drinking until his twenty-first birthday. Quigg had, to be sure, taken occasional sips of his parents' drinks during cocktail hour at home, but his father did not consider that real drinking. Fulfilling the pledge was almost impossible at Yale, even during Prohibition in the early 1930s, but Quigg resisted the temptation to imbibe until just before his senior year. Seventy years later, he remembered his first serious encounter with alcohol, shortly before the birthday deadline; it was just after he was tapped by Skull and Bones, and his binge was a spectacular fiasco. Evidently, Jim Newton figured the young man had gotten close enough to legal drinking age, since he still offered Quigg the money.

Although Quigg was a class leader and popular at Yale, his delayed indulgence in alcohol suggested that he was somewhat behind many of his classmates in learning certain ways of the world. Evidently, Quigg had also dutifully followed his father's advice in avoiding "wayward women" during his trip to Europe after his junior year. During the spring of his senior year, however, an informal Yale rugby club traveled to Bermuda and engaged in several matches. Quigg and his good friend "Mac" Parsons joined the group. The young men had plenty of free time between matches, and they had other pleasures on their minds. Quigg evidently parted with his virginity in Bermuda, much to the approval of his peers. A class scribe recounting the adventure and assorted shenanigans concluded that the trip ended "with Newton experienced in life, everybody fairly happy, and a reunion in mind for next year."[13]

In the decades after his graduation from Yale in 1933, Quigg became a proud and extremely active alumnus, serving the university in a variety of capacities. As his sixty-fifth class reunion approached, he wrote to two classmates: "My affection for and feeling for my indebtedness to Yale has grown by leaps and bounds over the years. My degrees from Yale … have opened many doors and helped me immeasurably in my varied career. … I received many lasting friendships. Secondly, I got an insatiable life long thirst for knowledge and understanding of myself and of the world around me. … But there is something else of equal importance about Yale that I find difficult to describe, and that is its ethos which has served as an invisible guide post for me, and I am sure for other classmates, throughout my career."[14]

Post-Graduate Uncertainties

If in retrospect Quigg felt well prepared to define his life's goals and take steps toward achieving them, such feelings were not so apparent when he graduated in June 1933. Although a new, vibrant, and determinedly optimistic president—Franklin D. Roosevelt—had introduced an avalanche of legislation during his first "hundred days" in office, designed to combat hard times, the nation remained in the throes of the Great Depression. Even though Jim Newton could easily have placed Quigg in some sort of managerial position, either in his own investment firm or in some enterprise operated by one of his Denver friends, Quigg was undecided about his future, even in the short-term. Years later, he recalled that Jim did not really want him to join his investment firm: "[Father] was good at it [the investment business] but he might have preferred to do something else." Consciously or otherwise, Jim Newton steered his son away from the world of managing other people's money. Quigg recalled that his father thought law school would be "good" for him.[15]

    Although Quigg was beginning to chafe under his father's sometimes heavy-handed "guidance," he was not yet ready to strike out on his

own. He followed his father's advice, applied for Yale Law School, and was accepted. Yet even as he prepared to start classes, he fantasized about more-attractive short-term options. In an occasionally wistful letter to his father, Quigg mentioned that a well-heeled, doting father of a prep school boy in Connecticut wished to send his son around the world and that he wanted a responsible Yale man to accompany the youth, all expenses paid. "What an opportunity this would be for some fellow, just graduated, who does not want to settle down for a year."[16]

Quigg Newton at age twenty-five. He had finished his studies at Yale Law School.

Law School and Family Pressure

Nothing came of it, and young Newton enrolled in law school in the fall of 1933. He dutifully stuck it out during his first year. Yet from his letters home, Quigg appeared at first to be largely going through the motions. One almost gets the sense that he was trying to shock his parents or set the stage for possible failure. His letters bore a remarkable similarity to some he had written six or seven years earlier from Andover. As final exams approached in his initial year of law school, he voiced depression: "People in my class are all irritable and on edge. Exams start Monday and most everyone except me has studied into all hours of the night. I don't know how to cram, never did, and it is too late to begin learning. Either I know the stuff or I don't. It won't be too long until I find out. ... I waste tremendous time puttering. So my method is to hope I have learned enough to get by. Next weekend will be the worst ever staged in any school. Minute plans have already been thoroughly set forth. Just the right amount of beer to lay a proper foundation. ... Nothing will be remaining to do but draw the curtains."[17]

Was this a "confession" of sloppy study habits and the presence of beer, a mild form of rebellion, or the beginning of his quest for independence? Quigg's dark mood may have been a subconscious response to missives written by his father just a few weeks earlier. Although Jim Newton obviously loved Quigg, in hindsight it is equally evident that he persistently lectured and sometimes even hectored his still-dependent son. The Depression was still very real, and he didn't want Quigg to forget it. "If I were in your place, I would be preparing for a very stiff test of survival of the fittest." Law school would provide the foundation he needed: "Rules will be changed and the unfit will be governed by the fit—just as they have for the last many thousand years. ... Truthfully speaking, there are some things going on in the world outside of your college walls that you should know." He even tossed in what may have been an intentionally edgy, even cruel barb: "Life will be tougher than ever—even for sissies like yourself. ... Don't fail to read this letter more than once—I am suspicious that you don't read them at all."[18]

The senior Newton seldom addressed his son in this manner, and he may have intended for his tone to appear jocular. Quigg may have been hurt, or just irritated, but he hid his feelings well. And he did, indeed, perform. Lack of confidence over his exams and his ability to compete with his peers was almost certainly momentary. As Quigg immersed himself more thoroughly in his law studies, his interest gradually deepened. He was fortunate to be exposed to some brilliant minds, including those of law professors Thurman Arnold and William O. Douglas, both of whom served as his mentors.

Arnold was an unpretentious yet brilliant legal scholar. Born and raised in Laramie, Wyoming, he punctuated his classroom lectures with blunt, sometimes earthy human vignettes, which provided texture and color to sometimes dry legal concepts.[19] Quigg was very drawn to Arnold, and vice-versa. Arnold was evidently impressed with Newton's deep intelligence and dogged attention to detail. Among his other duties, Arnold supervised debate in moot court. If young Newton had a breakthrough or an epiphany in law school, it was his starring role in a debate competition toward the end of his first year. Evidently, Arnold extolled Quigg's acumen at higher levels of the school. Seemingly out of the blue, Quigg received a fancy invitation from the dean of the school to attend a formal Saturday night dinner then debate a brilliant fellow law student who happened to chair the law review. Distinguished jurists invited to judge the debate included a sitting member of the U.S. Supreme Court and the chief justice of the Connecticut Supreme Court. Predictably, Quigg was apprehensive. Would he freeze up and forget his lines as he had a few years earlier in one undergraduate debate? At about that time, he began to suffer from periodic stress headaches that would recur at unpredictable times throughout his life. Fortunately, Quigg rose to the occasion and dominated his heralded competitor. In later years, he insisted that the entire event was "far too grandiose" and that the rewards he received were disproportionate to his performance. Yet he admitted, "In law school, it made me. It attracted the attention of very important people and eventually opened countless doors for me."[20]

Despite his initial success in law school, he was still restless, even discontented. Between his first and second years in law school, Quigg evidently thought seriously about dropping out and changing careers. At Andover and during his undergraduate years at Yale, he had thoroughly enjoyed journalism, and he had never lost his enthusiasm for it. During the summer of 1934 he took a trip to the West Coast and pursued work at the *San Francisco Chronicle*, but he failed to receive a job offer. At the same time, he informed a friend that he was taking a course in accounting during summer school at Stanford University.[21]

Evidently, exposure to a single course in accounting snuffed out any possible interest in a career in that field, but Quigg retained a serious interest in journalism for several more years. He was facing other issues during the summer of 1934. On his trip to the West Coast, he was evidently out of touch with his family for weeks on end, and he sometimes failed to inform them where he was. Certain older family members considered such behavior by a well-bred young man selfish, thoughtless, and totally unacceptable. When the family finally located him in midsummer, his uncle Wilbur fired off an angry letter: "We have repeatedly tried to get you to tell us something of your plans so that we could get in touch with you if necessary, but you do not deign to help us. Will you please tell me what in hell is the matter with you that you think yourself above corresponding with poor mediocre souls like us. I will tell you what I think is the matter—you are spoiled rotten, for some unknown reason, and are as selfish as hell. ... You may be smart in your studies, but, if to be smart, one has to be like you, give me a dummy every time—a dummy might have some feeling."[22]

Quigg was beginning to rebel against controlling senior family members. He responded negatively to his uncle's venting of rage and frustration, enough so that his father's secretary, Harriett Thompson, attempted to intervene and smooth things over. A couple of weeks later she wrote to Quigg: "Your reaction to your Uncle Wilbur's letter is none of my business, I know, but I would like very much to be able to have you get a little different slant on it."[23] She mentioned that Jim Newton was one of the few people in the world Wilbur truly loved, and that her boss's health had been fragile during the summer. These factors might have touched off his uncle's explosion. Quigg wasn't quite ready to put the matter to rest. He replied to Miss Thompson, "That was a great letter that you wrote to me on Uncle Wilbur's behalf. I frankly am ashamed at myself that his outburst provoked in me only emotions of rage followed by amusement. My callous character unfortunately is left unimpressed by such tactics."[24] Quigg seemed determined to get in the last word with his parents as well. In his first letter to his parents following the "blowup," he included his uncle's letter with his own personal caveat: "At first I was sore. But that changed to amusement. I am surprised that after all his years in dealing with people he would write such a ridiculous letter, one that would make the ordinary man defiant rather than apologetic."[25]

Family tensions appeared to have been smoothed over by the middle of the summer. Evidently, Quigg wrote an ingratiating letter to his uncle Wilbur, since the latter wrote a gushing reply: "Next to your Father, I believe I am more fond of you than anyone else. You have made good in a big way and there is no limit to what you can do."[26] Quigg also began sending regular newsy letters home to his parents. More than anything, he insisted that he was having a productive summer. He claimed that his accounting course at Stanford would "hold me in good stead next year in the Law School." As if to counter his father's impression that he knew little of the real world beyond the hallowed ivy walls of Yale, he recounted venturing from Palo Alto and going into San Francisco to witness the city's general strike firsthand.

The San Francisco general strike during the summer of 1934 was a spectacular confrontation between management and labor. In mid-July, virtually forced into a corner by militant, confrontational employers' associations, the International Longshoremen and the Teamsters Union had led their members, followed by large numbers of other unions and their members, into a general strike. This not only involved considerable violence but shut down many of the city's services for days on end. Quigg wrote of ordinary citizens' fears over the possible spread of Communism, yet expressed mixed feelings about the strikers: "There are already thirty-five thousand people on strike with many more about to join the ranks. These men feel outraged. They feel that they have had a raw deal and that any damage they do is well deserved. So far they have stopped at nothing."[27] But Quigg did not reveal which side he favored. In another letter that hinted at his broadening interest in national and international issues, Quigg reported on drought conditions across the West and wondered if his father was still invested in May wheat.

Quigg turned twenty-three in the summer of 1934, and his letters sometimes conveyed the self-absorption typical of many young adults. In other respects, however, he was achieving remarkable maturity. Without question, Quigg was already practicing the superb interpersonal "networking" skills he had been developing at both Andover and Yale. After learning that Yale Law School dean Charles E. Clark was teaching at the University of Colorado at Boulder during the summer, he asked his father to look Clark up and perhaps show him around Denver: "Could you call him sometime or if you are driving into the mountains call on him in Boulder? He is a very reserved man and does not put up a good front, but he has a very brilliant mind, has written several books. I am sure you could get him going." He was also learning a willingness to own up to past mistakes. According to Quigg, his disagreement with Uncle Wilbur had been patched up: "He was very right in his criticism. It has all blown over now and a lesson learned."[28] For the moment, Quigg was willing to acquiesce in his parents' continued intimate involvement in his crucial life choices. A few years later, however, he would rebel against his father's blueprint for his life.

More Networking

Following his adventuresome and formative summer in California, Quigg returned to New Haven in the fall of 1934 and once again buckled down to study law. He was fortunate to be exposed to William O. Douglas, who would soon leave Yale to become a member of the Securities and Exchange Commission (SEC), in December 1935, chairman of that body twenty-one months later, and ultimately a member of the U.S. Supreme Court. While a law professor at Yale, Douglas revealed a genius for rising through the academic hierarchy through a combination of flashy intellectual brilliance, an almost inhuman capacity for hard work, driving ambition, and an uncanny aptitude for manipulating other powerful men into supporting his projects. Douglas was an enigma, presenting a bewildering variety of human traits. Early in his career, he alternated hypnotic charm and sometimes rude, even cruel treatment of other people. He presented a public image of a devoted family man, yet he largely ignored his children, was a serial philanderer, and married and divorced several times.[29]

In later years, Douglas had a significant impact on Quigg Newton's public career. Like Douglas, Newton would demonstrate an amazing capacity for vaulting quickly up a variety of career ladders. When Douglas died in 1980, one obituary described him as a man "who succeeded to a great extent in channeling his dissatisfactions into an amazing range and diversity of constructive pursuits. His insatiable curiosity took him all over the world to satisfy his urge to understand other peoples, to know their ways of life, their problems, their sufferings, their aspirations."[30] In later years, this description of Douglas would fit Quigg Newton as well. Although he never studied formally under Douglas, Arnold had introduced them, and they conversed fairly often. Douglas was impressed by young Newton and brought him into his orbit. Despite profound personality differences, Quigg was dazzled by Douglas's ability to cut to the heart of social and legal issues quickly, pinpointing their most relevant aspects, and he worked hard to develop the same skills.

Some of Newton's most important and character-shaping interactions with Douglas undoubtedly occurred during casual but increasingly intimate conversations. Although both men had been reared in the West, their family backgrounds had been totally different. Douglas had experienced a hardscrabble childhood. His father had died when Douglas was just six, and his mother struggled to put food on the table. Douglas was a puny youngster who compensated for his small physique by becoming the most brilliant student in his school. According to some sources, he had been a sheepherder, a freight hand, even a hobo. Several accounts claimed that he "rode the rods" from Chicago to New York before working his way through Columbia.[31] After a brief stint in corporate law, he became a teacher. Like his Yale colleague Thurman Arnold, Douglas believed that rather than emphasizing formalistic protection of the interests of the most conservative elements in the country, law should exert a positive influence for social change and legal reasoning should incorporate useful insights of the emerging social sciences, such as sociology and psychology. Douglas was deeply and passionately liberal in his social outlook.[32] Although Quigg may not have realized it at the time, Douglas's worldview almost certainly affected his own emerging views of justice and society. Throughout his years in public life, Quigg stood as a passionate defender of those less fortunate than himself.

By the end of his first year at Yale Law School, Newton had hit his intellectual stride. His grades dropped very slightly after his first year, but they were still remarkably consistent. For the three years of law school, his cumulative average was 78.2. He had averaged 79.5 as a first year student, and just over 77 during each of his last two years. All of his grades were either As or Bs, with the exception of Cs in business management and legal accounting, and property III. In the decades before the inflation of grades common to almost all graduate schools, these marks were highly meritorious. According to his official transcript, Newton graduated fourteenth out of a class of 105 men.[33] There were no women in his law school class.

As he entered his final year of law school, Quigg pondered what he would do after graduation and where he might settle down. He loved California; after his summer there in 1934, he briefly considered taking his final two years in law school in that state in order to prepare more effectively for the California Bar exam. His father had other ideas: he more or less assumed that Quigg would return to Denver and take a job in a highly respected law firm run by longtime family friend Jim Grant. Jim Newton had planted the seed with Grant, and the latter was prepared to offer places to both Quigg and his close friend Dick Davis. Davis had recently married Quigg's younger sister, Nancy. The prospect

of his whole life mapped out for him must have appeared very tidy—
and perhaps just a bit too confining to Quigg.

In the spring of his third year at Yale, Quigg received a very attractive short-term job offer from William O. Douglas. Not long after
Joseph Kennedy vacated the chairmanship of the SEC to become the
U.S. ambassador to England, Douglas had moved to Washington to
become a member of the SEC. As Douglas maneuvered to become SEC
chairman, he invited Quigg to serve as his secretary for a year following
his graduation from Yale Law School. Naturally, Quigg was flattered by
the offer and proud to share his "coup" with his parents. He wrote them
a long letter in which he claimed, "I haven't told him definitely yet that
I can not, but I have no intention of doing it." He then added, "I must
say next year in Washington is tempting."[34]

A few weeks later, he appeared far more inclined to accept
Douglas's offer. Virtually everyone he talked with at Yale, including several of his professors, believed he would be a fool to pass up the
opportunity to learn from such an inspired thinker. Quigg was torn
between taking the post and settling in comfortably in Jim Grant's
office: "It really depends in my mind how Jim Grant reacts to the idea:
in particular whether he is vitally in need of another man around the
office next year." Despite his initial disclaimer, he was leaning toward
taking the Washington job. He was definitely engaged in long-term networking, advising his parents, "The large offices are all anxious to get
lawyers with SEC experience and insight … a year in Washington in the
SEC would be likely to give me some lasting contacts with people who
are likely to be permanent fixtures around Washington. … Besides such
advantages as these there is [the] advantage of getting into a large active
environment of my own before returning to Denver." As Quigg's
thought process evolved, he reasoned that the disadvantages of delaying
his return to Denver were minimal. Although he would "miss out" on
some things happening around the city, "new things will be developing
all the time." His only real concern was that important people in the
Denver business and legal community might believe that he had "turned
completely eastern."[35]

Newton eventually accepted Douglas's offer. His father endorsed his decision, even while retaining the notion that Quigg would eventually return to Denver and enjoy a conventional career and life that he would help orchestrate. "Your Washington experience should prove invaluable in [Grant's] plans for you, and I would almost be willing to live my life again to have what he has in mind for your life." Jim once again reminded Quigg how fortunate he was: "I hope you have the sense to hit every opportunity you have *hard*. They may all come in bunches when you are young, but there are just so many in each man's life and he should avail himself of each one to the full extent of his ability. ... If you learn to appraise the real values of life and can know and associate with all kinds of people, you should have a wonderful life."[36] Although Quigg was an upper echelon graduate from a very distinguished law school, Jim Newton was still preaching to him.

Quigg attended his graduation from law school in June 1936 as his proud parents looked on. Jim Newton was right in one sense: Quigg's life seemed good, his future golden. Clearly he had pleased his parents. His father set up a family trust fund that permitted Quigg to draw a modest income.[37] With the prospect of an exciting job in Washington beginning in the fall, Quigg rewarded himself with a vacation to the South by automobile, during which he stopped off in numerous cities to visit friends from Yale and Andover.

One friend lived in Charlottesville, Virginia. In a letter to his parents, Quigg rhapsodized about the beauty of the campus of the University of Virginia and provided descriptions of some of the professors he met there. In the same letter, he provided vivid, if narrow pictures of the rural landscape through which he traveled. Quigg saw the South as a region not far removed from Reconstruction: "That was the impression I got all over the South. It seems to have changed very little and to have absorbed the civilization produced by the industrial revolution with great resistance. It appears to be unable to grasp just what has happened in the world, and to begrudge the encroachment of northern ideas."

If his analysis of overall social conditions and economic development was insightful in some respects, he still had considerable growing up to do. In his attitudes toward African Americans, he revealed an insensitivity that was all too conventional seventy years ago—even among highly educated whites. "The countryside in both North and South Carolina is surprisingly barren and unfertile. It is overrun with Negroes and seems to have acquired the slovenly Negroid touch. There are almost no well-kept farms or moderately sized farmhouses. Scattered all over are lots of funny Negro shanties, most of which have no doors or windows. ... Sitting and standing and lolling around each shanty are funny old ragged poverty-stricken Negroes, children that are poorly clad and old men and women who seem never to have lifted a finger to do anything."[38] As a twenty-five-year-old, Quigg had not yet developed the level of social awareness to understand how people less fortunate than he could appear to lack hope and ambition. Nor had he yet developed the depth of conscience he would demonstrate in future decades as a civic and educational leader and humanitarian.

While Quigg toured the South, his brother-in-law and former roommate Dick Davis returned to Denver to settle in at Jim Grant's law office. On occasion, Jim Newton meddled in even the minutest issues. Late in the summer of 1936, he urged Quigg to write a congratulatory letter to Dick for having become connected to Grant's law office. At the moment, Jim Newton was a bit uneasy about his son-in-law. "Dick is quite confused about life, but I am sure he will eventually land on his feet and also learn to take advantage of opportunities." He fretted that perhaps both Quigg and Dick had been given a bit too much too soon: "Opportunities, to some of you kids, are just a little more cake than you have had before, so try to be like a squirrel and stick some inside your jaw and keep it—don't throw it away."[39]

Following several weeks of leisure, lawn parties, and attending weddings of close friends, Quigg drove to Washington, D.C., to begin his work with the SEC. Quigg had, in fact, attempted to pack a bit too much activity into the summer of 1936. Realizing that sooner or later he would probably return to Denver and take up law, he had attempted to pass the Colorado Bar exam. He hired a tutor, who provided a few hours of preparation and advice. When the results came in, Quigg had failed the test. Jim Newton did not lecture his son. Instead, he attempted to give comfort, and, surprisingly, he blamed Quigg's failure on the alleged provincialism of local exam referees. Jim opened his letter by writing, "The bad news is out and I am happy to know that you can take it." He continued, "Without regard for the fact that you did not pass the exams, to me there is a terrific indictment of the law in Colorado to consistently flunk students of large eastern colleges—in fact, I might say, out-of-state colleges. It will eventually mean a localization of the Bar in Colorado, which, in itself, is very bad."[40]

Working for Douglas

Quigg was disappointed at the result, but not devastated. In deciding to take the bar exam, he had hoped for the best, but in retrospect, he realized he had tried to slip by with minimal preparation. Undaunted, he began his work with Douglas with enthusiasm. A good deal of his work at the SEC was routine. Corporations sent in registration statements, which were required to contain voluminous yet very specific information. One of Quigg's jobs was to make sure all the required information had been submitted. If the statements were in full compliance, Newton sent them to his chief for brief perusal before he provided his signature. Occasionally, there were questionable submissions by "fly-by-night" outfits, which required formal hearings. After hearings were completed, reports were sent to Newton or one of several other young lawyers working for the SEC. In these cases, Quigg's work became more interesting. Douglas relied on his young assistants to provide preliminary recommendations. Quigg could not recall ever being overruled by Douglas, but his mentor rewrote his opinions on several occasions. Newton gained further exposure to a brilliant legal mind at work. Quigg later recalled that Douglas was a prolific—and lightning fast—writer: "He would be able to do in one hour what took me six."[41]

The routine registration work for Douglas was not particularly challenging, but like many other bright young people present in Washington in the mid-1930s, Quigg experienced the excitement of being an entry-level New Dealer. He sensed that his work was fairly important. Because of the stock market crash and recent government investigations into huge profits earned by some of the nation's largest corporations during World War I, big business had suffered enormous damage to its public image.[42] Quigg was present during the early, experimental years of activity of one of the government's key "watchdog" agencies. He had a sense of being a witness and active participant in creating something new. Big government was an emerging reality, and Quigg wanted to learn everything he could about how it worked.

Other work for Douglas was much more interesting than the tedious but necessary SEC tasks of tracking down information missing from corporate filings. Douglas was a prolific writer, submitting numerous articles in learned journals, plus an occasional book. As Douglas developed his ideas, he needed to have Newton and other assistants look up legal precedents and other factual data to support his reasoning. Quigg spent a lot of time at the Library of Congress and in legal libraries looking up information to bolster his mentor's opinions. By the summer of 1936, Thurman Arnold had also hired on with the antitrust division of the Justice Department. Arnold was writing a book, and he too used Newton to track down specific information needed for his rough drafts.

Other Types of Networking in Washington

Quigg's free time provided equally critical opportunities for intellectual stimulation and personal growth. Shortly after moving to Washington, he found living quarters in a large house, which he shared with a dozen or so other up-and-coming young men. By pooling resources, they managed to rent a large house in a nice neighborhood; they even hired a cook. In many respects, it resembled living in a campus fraternity house. After long hours at work, the young men often gathered over food and drink, discussing issues of the day at great length. Quigg once again demonstrated uncommon leadership and networking skills in helping to turn casual "bull sessions" first into informal and occasional seminars, then into regular meetings, which occurred every fortnight and often lasted into the wee hours of the morning. "I got together other Yale people like myself and we had meetings on New Deal agencies and the laws they passed."[43] Inviting one Yale chum to attend, Quigg provided more details: "At these meetings, each person explains the work he is doing in his own department, a good way to get a broad although rather superficial picture of the entire setup in a brief period of time. The purpose of the meetings is to study the problems of government. No one, of course, does any studying. But the chief merit of the discussions is that the person describing his own work usually is expert in it and knows it from A to Z."[44]

These gatherings became important in the intellectual development of many bright young New Dealers. John Knox, then serving as a law clerk to James C. McReynolds, one of the Supreme Court's most reactionary members, recalled a friend taking him to the house, where he met Newton for the first time. "We entered the living room, where I was introduced to Newton. ... I noticed various groups of men standing around and chatting amiably in both the living room and a large adjoining room. I soon concluded that here before me was a glittering group of personalities the likes of which I had never before seen in Washington assembled under one roof." They included Charles Fahey, general counsel to the National Labor Relations Board, G. Mennen "Soapy" Williams, later to become governor of Michigan, and Travis Brown, an attorney with the Federal Trade Commission.[45]

In coordinating these seminars, Newton demonstrated a characteristic that typified his leadership style for his entire life: the ability to draw together groups of brilliant people who, consciously or otherwise, worked toward a common objective. This does not suggest that he and his friends always came to the most logical, or even sensible, conclusions about key public issues. For example, despite intimate exposure to several clerks working for Supreme Court justices, Newton did not appreciate at the time how dangerous and divisive President Roosevelt's 1937 "court packing" scheme was. Before the idea blew up in the president's face, Quigg wrote, "The President's message to Congress was inexcusably evasive but the plan itself is not so bad. ... It seems to me that all this talk about this plan being a threat to our Constitution and a threat to the theory of checks and balances is tom-foolery." Quigg was on more solid ground in predicting, "But whether it is a good plan or a bad plan, I have an idea it will have a terrible time getting by Congress."[46] In later years, Newton's political instincts would gradually become ever more acute.

Newton was also keenly aware of his opportunity to hobnob with more senior, experienced New Dealers. He recalled being on the fringes of a group including Thomas G. Corcoran, one of the most influential insiders helping President Roosevelt achieve many of his legislative triumphs. Without question, Quigg had already developed an uncanny ability to attract the attention of and win admiration from influential men who often worked behind the scenes to advance his career. His work with the SEC obviously impressed Douglas, whose positive opinion would soon affect Newton's life very directly. Douglas was a close friend of Palmer "Ep" Hoyt, managing editor of the *Portland Oregonian*, who would move to Denver to take over stewardship of *The Denver Post*. Douglas recalled talking to Hoyt about his protégé. "During the course of the year he worked for me, I had many long talks with him about his future. At the time, I believe he was toying with the idea of going to New York City to practice law. I told him then that I thought he had a bright political future if he would go back to Denver and get his roots established in the practice of law and then move into public life, heading for mayor, governor, or senator."[47] The future *Post* editor tucked Douglas's recommendation into the back of his mind; a decade later, his regionally influential newspaper would play a significant role in determining Newton's career path.

Quigg's year in Washington working for Douglas was by no means all work and no play. As young, educated, largely unattached, and attractive males in the prime of their lives in their mid-twenties, Newton and many of his Yale friends received countless invitations to some of the most glittering social gatherings in Washington. On occasion, Quigg was present at gatherings hosted by local icons, even those presided over by the incomparable Alice Roosevelt Longworth. Quigg had had various girlfriends, plus a serious relationship or two, but during his year in Washington, he basically played the field. On long weekends, he and a mixed group of friends might even slip up to Cape Cod for some fun and sunshine.

As his year at the SEC wound down, however, Quigg was aware that he needed to make some serious career choices. Sixty-five years later, he recalled that despite his father's firm and sometimes overbearing direction, he had no carefully thought out career plan, no firm sense of direction. He was not at all sure that he wanted to practice law on a full-time, or permanent, basis. He may have sensed that the summer of 1937 was a watershed period in his life. Quigg returned to Denver to sort out his options and perhaps open up some new avenues. He had been a dutiful son, and he had more than fulfilled his family's high expectations for his school years. Among other concerns, he may have sensed that he needed to establish independence from his father. That would be easier said than done, but Quigg was finally ready to take charge of his own life.

CHAPTER 4

SEARCHING FOR
SELF-IDENTITY

By the summer of 1937, Quigg Newton was approaching his twenty-sixth birthday. Until beginning his year of work with the Securities and Exchange Commission (SEC) with William O. Douglas, he had been supported by his family, and he had for the most part dutifully followed the firm and persistent guidance of his father. During his year at the SEC, Quigg lived on his own in Washington, and he thoroughly enjoyed his increasing independence. He found the social and intellectual climate in the nation's capital invigorating.

A single incident clouded his time in Washington. Jim Newton suffered a heart attack during a business trip to New York in the late fall of 1936, and Quigg commuted regularly to New York in subsequent weeks to visit his convalescing father. Although his mother temporarily moved east to be with her husband, Quigg still felt a major responsibility to help look after his father. Through Jim's secretary, Harriett Thompson, Quigg learned that his father suffered from depression, which he seemed unable to shake. Quigg sensed that Jim hid his feelings when he visited him. In December, he wrote to Miss Thompson: "This afternoon I go again to New York to see Dad. The times I have been there I have not noticed all this about Dad's mental depression. ... It seems to me that a certain amount of this is to be expected from a person like Dad. Even when he is well and engaged in his affairs, he gets terribly upset and depressed. ... I suspect that mother sees more of him and is more alert to his disabilities now than usual."[1] Jim Newton spent several months recuperating in New York before returning briefly to Denver in the spring of 1937. Later that year, he moved to California, where he purchased ranch land and became a gentleman farmer, raising avocados and citrus fruit with the help of hired hands. From then until his death in 1944, Jim and Nelle Newton spent several months each year in California.

Family Pressures

Although he enjoyed his year in Washington, young Newton felt restless, somewhat at loose ends, and uncertain of his future. The fact that he had failed his first attempt at passing the Colorado Bar exam gnawed at him, as did the thought of making another attempt. He apparently felt safer expressing his thoughts to his father's secretary, Harriett Thompson, than to family members. In an emotional outburst to Harriett, Quigg revealed some of his temporary frustration: "It's no use spending the whole of one's life studying for bars [exams]. There is too much else to do. That is the trouble with a lot of this present age. So damn much of our time is spent in detail, in meaningless statistics, in rigaramarole [sic], that we haven't time to think and acquire philosophy and breadth."[2]

Quigg was acutely aware that his father wanted him to return to Denver, establish a solid reputation as a lawyer, and live a thoroughly conventional life. Despite Jim Newton's initial concern, Quigg's brother-in-law Dick Davis was becoming solidly established in Jim Grant's law offices, and Quigg knew that his father expected he would sooner or later join Dick. Davis stated the situation bluntly in a letter to Quigg: "When I arrived here your Dad called and told me of their [his and Jim Grant's] understanding and that of course Jim wanted me *with you* (emphasis his), in there, and the rest of the well planned life that he has arranged for you. ... As I look it over it ... seemed to make another part of the setup in Denver, one more restriction on the scope of probable activity, one more reason why every aspect of your life would be certain and established. ... "[3] Although Dick truly wanted his good friend and former roommate to join him in practicing law in Denver, he refused to sugarcoat the existence of an environment Quigg might find oppressive. Instead, Davis provided revealing insights into what he considered a repressive local economic, social, and political climate.

In the fall of 1936, Colorado voters approved a $45 monthly pension to retired citizens over the age of sixty.[4] Conservative Coloradans considered the move economic lunacy, and some reacted almost hysterically. Davis recounted a visit to Quigg's uncle Wilbur a few days after the election. Wilbur apparently lectured him to the effect that he would be crazy to try to build a life in Colorado. According to Davis, Wilbur told him, "Now you will see another reason why you've made a mistake in coming to Colorado: unlimited income taxes. I must move, your father-in-law must move, and Boettcher and Co must move." Davis continued: "My reactions are slow at 8:30 and I didn't really appreciate the gravity of what he said but stood grinning at him and then when he lost breath said a little crudely, 'Where are you going to move to?' He then admitted it was a little soon to say."[5] Although Davis laughed off the incident as a predictable reaction by hidebound conservatives, his letter may have deepened Quigg's sense that gaining personal and professional independence in an economic, political, and social environment still dominated by Colorado's deeply entrenched old-guard thinkers would be a tall order.

By the summer of 1937, Jim Newton's health had improved, and he urged Quigg not to worry about him. Indeed, his father possessed sufficient energy at that point to insinuate himself even deeper in the lives of Quigg and Dick Davis. Although Quigg had prepared himself for a career in law, he still occasionally dreamed of a life as a journalist. His father asked him, "Have you any definite ideas of the future? Would you be willing to stake all your future in the political and newspaper game? Would you be willing to start a paper in Denver and stand or fall on its success?" Jim wouldn't let up; he kept hammering at his son: "Do you think of being a dillitante [sic] … playing in the train of some other man. … You are now 25 and must make a real decision. Learn to decide easily and quickly take the results as they come the good with the bad but decide quickly and decisively." Jim bluntly played the guilt card: "I feel I may not be here for very long and you should have the benefit of my experience."[6]

Not long afterward, Jim implied that he had been willing to go even farther to advance his son's journalistic ambitions. He informed Quigg that he had investigated the possibility of purchasing the *Rocky Mountain News*, but even if there were a remote possibility of a transfer of ownership, any potential deal had fallen through. Not easily discouraged, Jim was investigating the possibility of a "stockyards paper with a United Press franchise, plus a paper to be issued Saturday with stories and editorials of the best character possible." There might even be a "small radio hookup" connected to the deal. Jim thought it a "swell idea to … exert a degree of power necessary to satisfy our family pride to 'show off.'" Jim proudly informed Quigg that he had just "put Dick on my coal company board." Jim portrayed himself as willing and able to support his extended family, including his son-in-law, "without hurting the family income of $40,000, which amount ought to be enough to help you all over the rough road." Finally, he stated, "I'd like to have you all build houses and have a certain community expense which would allow you at least a fine place to live. … "[7]

No doubt, Jim Newton sincerely believed that he was being generous. But the two young men felt increasingly suffocated by his domineering presence. In a long letter to Davis in mid-July 1937, Quigg poured out his frustrations over his father's micromanagement of their lives: "You know as well as I do what's in Dad's mind, and what's there has been built over a period of many years and that it would be difficult to remove it at this point." He continued, "If Dad could only get it out of his mind that it is his responsibility to pave the way for you and me. If he could only realize that we don't want the way paved for ourselves—that what we get we want to get for ourselves, and that by all his effort he is helping to take the satisfaction that comes from achievement from both of us, he might see that he could more profitably spend his time living a happier and more selfish life." Quigg was still in Washington when he wrote the letter to Dick, who was directly under his father-in-law's thumb in Denver. As Quigg viewed the situation, "It seems to me, however, that a concerted effort must be made by you and me and Nancy to get both Mother and Dad out to California, for a year, if necessary, or more." Quigg confessed a certain feeling of angst, now that his year at the SEC was drawing to a close: "As the end approaches for me here I am beginning to have slight feelings of regret. ... somehow I dread the thought of starting anew, taking bar exams, etc."[8] Reading between the lines, one senses that Quigg was resisting the prospect of returning to Denver without any specific alternative plan of his own.

Quigg never did fully reconcile himself to his father's seemingly compulsive need to be directly involved in his affairs. Although Quigg eventually decided to return to Denver, Jim kept peppering him with questions and advice. In the spring of 1940, Quigg exploded: "The Mayor [Benjamin Stapleton] called me today to say that you were anxious for me to write letters. The same question has come up every time you have gone to California. I have not written any letters because I have not had time. ... I do not see why it is necessary to tell the Mayor to call me on personal matters ... whether I work at night or whether I don't, or whether I take vacations or whether I don't is up to me and not up to anybody else. Between you and Mother, it has already gotten so that whenever I go anywhere the fact that I work at night is thrown in my face."[9]

Feeling at Loose Ends

Yet any declaration of independence from familial control was still some distance in the future in 1937. As a young man actively involved in President Roosevelt's New Deal regulatory apparatus, Quigg was acutely aware of the Great Depression. Although satisfactorily situated at the moment, he was well aware of how difficult it might be to establish a solid foundation of a career in the midst of hard times. Quigg corresponded with former Andover and Yale classmates who were struggling with feelings of ennui due to either prolonged unemployment or being relegated to serving as errand boys for more senior, established family members. In the summer of 1935, Bill Sheldon, an Andover classmate still living with his parents in Woodstock, Vermont, wrote of being "at present a 'gentleman of leisure' which, quite frankly, is very trying. ... My life up here has consisted largely of reading, fishing, and helping Mother get the house in order."[10]

Dick Matthews, a Yale friend who lived in Berkeley, California, wrote that he had been "out of college one year" and that he hadn't "accomplished a damn thing. I've been into public accounting to satisfy my father." Attempting to break away, Matthews "worked [his] way out to India in a British freighter and back." The problem for Matthews was that he was back. "Way down below something says 'You've got something big to do'—then something else says 'but for God's sake get started.'" Matthews then turned his attention to Quigg, for whom he predicted great things: "What about you? ... You're going to be President of the United States and nothing is going to stop you. The pinnacle is calling for you. Take it. But do not sacrifice your joy for your ambition. Let them go hand in hand."[11] Two months later, Matthews wrote vaguely of trying to find something back East, perhaps in Washington. A girlfriend had urged him to come there, and he articulated his "desire to be completely free of any influence my father might have upon the course of my life from now on."[12] Matthews never really found his niche; he later committed suicide.

Quigg seriously considered a career outside of Colorado. He had spent the summer of 1934 in California seeking journalism opportunities there. Two years later, he wrote to Ben Lieb, a friend living in San Jose, "It would be hard to leave Colorado, and yet I have never had anything appeal to me the way the idea of going to California does. ... " Yet he continued, "I think the chances of its coming to fruition are mighty slim."[13] By the next spring, as his year with the SEC was drawing to a close, Quigg admitted to Lieb that even the more mundane facets of looking out for himself were giving him trouble. He wasn't any closer to deciding on either a career or permanent location, but at least he could ruefully poke fun at his situation: "For the first time I have been confronted with the problem of life, which I find to be more imposing than I ever thought it could be. Before graduation, you know, everything is easy sledding in that someone else always looks out for the details, such as paying the water rent and turning off the electric lights, so that costs won't run too high. Now that I have to look out for such things and, shamefacedly I must confess, I am constantly bothered by bill collectors."[14]

In the spring of 1937, Quigg briefly turned his attention to the possibility of settling in New York City and starting up a magazine publishing serious articles focusing on the workings of government. Vinton Lindley, another old school chum, worked for an organization named Vital Speeches of the Day, and Quigg thought Lindley could provide some useful contacts: "I thought it might be possible to get a few people like yourself interested and work up the details and then attempt to sell the idea to a magazine like *Time* ... or it might be possible to get some man interested who would be willing to finance such a magazine on a small scale." Quigg noted that he had also broached the idea with another friend, Mac Parsons. He had asked Parsons if he thought that the *Herald Tribune* might be interested in publishing it as "an adjunct to its newspaper."[15] If Lindley was interested and thought the idea had merit, he should feel free to float the idea by other mutual associates who might be better positioned to provide both financial support and other forms of clout.

Legal Networking in Denver

Despite repeated efforts to create a sensible plan for his life outside of the channel of his father's expectations, Quigg did not succeed. It is, indeed, difficult to let go of a well-oiled and welcoming network to strike out on one's own. After his year with Douglas, he swallowed his pride and returned to Denver, apparently resigned to meeting his family's expectations. Quigg moved back home to his parents' residence at 801 York Street, and he accepted a position at Lewis and Grant, starting at the extremely modest salary of just $100 per month. Perhaps the major reason for the paltry salary was that he had not yet passed the Colorado Bar exam. Quigg spent considerable time studying for the dreaded test, and he finally passed it on his second try on March 8, 1938. During his early weeks with Lewis and Grant, Dick Davis, who had joined the firm a year earlier, showed him the ropes.[16]

While doing routine legal work for Lewis and Grant, Quigg explored other interests. He wanted to put his experience with the SEC to good use, and he figured that with increasing amounts of government regulation of private enterprise, there would be a demand in law schools

for courses addressing new and highly complex regulatory issues. He
approached the University of Denver with the idea, and he soon found
himself working in the evenings, teaching classes in that field to young
law students. During his year at the SEC, he had accumulated suitcases
full of business documents and published decisions, so he had wholly
fresh materials to share with his students. Quigg recalled that he spent
many hours preparing for his classes. He called on Dick Davis for help;
sometimes, the two lawyers taught classes together. For three years, the
two young men spent three evenings each week teaching their course.
Quigg thoroughly enjoyed the experience, which marked the beginning
of a lifelong association with the University of Denver. It was stimulating but tough, "primarily because we had to assemble all our teaching
materials from scratch, there being no textbooks available."[17] University
administrators quickly noticed the bright, energetic young man, and
within a few months, Quigg was offered and accepted a position as secretary to the board of trustees.[18]

   Although grateful for the initial opportunity to enter the law field
under protected conditions, neither Newton nor Davis was content for
long to work under Jim Grant's control. On January 1, 1939, they
opened their own law office. Not surprisingly, they called the firm
Newton and Davis. Business was pretty slow at first. They did some routine work for the University of Denver that provided a monthly retainer
of $75, and Jim Newton steered some Boettcher and Newton legal work
in their direction. Without question, family connections helped the
young men. Several fledgling airline companies were starting up operations at the Denver Municipal Airport (later expanded and renamed
Stapleton Field), which had opened in 1929. Several of these companies
had raised capital through modest public stock offerings. As a senior
partner in Boettcher Newton Investment Company, which helped some
underwritings, Jim Newton once again provided help by guiding some
airline business to his son's firm. Quigg was soon invited to join the
board of Western Air Express.

   Capitalizing on their connection with the promising airline industry, just eight months after they formed their own firm, the partners

recruited another bright lawyer, Terrell Drinkwater, to join them. Drinkwater specialized in air law, and he had close connections with Bob Six, who was then organizing what evolved into Continental Airlines. In the late 1930s, Continental Airlines was rapidly expanding service into cities in the nation's heartland. Drinkwater could not handle all of the airline legal business himself; Quigg found himself negotiating with civic officials in numerous cities, particularly oil towns in Texas and Oklahoma. The partners also learned about labor law by serving as counsel for the Colorado Builders Supply Company, and they gained additional practical experience in antitrust law after taking on another major client, the Rocky Mountain Lumber Dealers Association. Although Newton family connections in the lumber business undoubtedly helped the young lawyers attract the latter client, hard work and perfect timing helped them gain an initial foothold in the fledgling airline business.

Within a few months after Newton and Davis struck out on their own, they were achieving recognition on their own merits. The firm pulled a major coup in being picked to represent the powerful Eccles family in a Utah case dealing with a disputed option to purchase one of the largest ranches in a remote section of that state. In August 1940, Quigg was elected to the board of directors of Denver National Bank.[19] Ever gregarious and energetic, Newton was constantly expanding his circle of acquaintances, some of whom would play important roles in his future career.

In December 1940, a year before both Newton and Davis left for duty in World War II, the firm added Arthur Henry to the partnership. This turned out to be a wise move. Henry, a few years older than his partners, had a draft deferment and kept the firm running during war years. Henry was an expert on Denver School Board operations, so he added that important line of legal representation to the firm's expanding menu of services.

In expanding their legal operations, Newton and Davis relied almost equally on their own ability and family connections. Quigg's year with William O. Douglas and the SEC provided him impressive expertise in New Deal regulatory law. Dick Davis nearly matched his associate in mastering this complex new field. The two young partners quickly established themselves as the men to see for corporate managers on the Front Range assessing the challenges of attempting to float new securities issues past the watchful eyes of government regulators.

Newton and Davis helped set up the Founders Mutual Fund and the Dow-Theory Fund, the first two mutual funds ever organized in Denver.[20] Newton worked on the reorganization of the Denver and Rio Grande Railroad, and he also assisted the Potash Company of America in setting up registration of securities with the SEC. Securities registration became lucrative business. In their first full year of operation, Newton and Davis each cleared $10,000—handsome incomes indeed for young lawyers still in their twenties during the Great Depression.[21] In the process, however, they learned hard lessons about collecting fees. Claude Boettcher had contested $47,000 in unpaid taxes demanded by the Internal Revenue Service; Quigg's firm won the case, and as was customary, he billed Boettcher for what he believed was a standard 10 percent. According to Quigg, Boettcher "hit the ceiling and didn't come down again until we cut the bill in half."[22]

As an up-and-coming, increasingly visible young lawyer, Newton was naturally a ripe target for entrepreneurs with "sure-fire investment opportunities." Quigg learned some hard lessons, and some of his earnings disappeared quickly. One scheme involved an inventor who introduced Newton to hydroponics, which was essentially the science of growing plants in liquid-based solutions containing the required minerals, rather than in soil. The conditions required for optimal growth of various plants involved elaborate procedures that were expensive to maintain. Years later, Quigg recalled, "We grew some beautiful luscious tomatoes, eggplants and cucumbers, but we went broke doing it." He also recalled investing some money with a Hungarian friend who was convinced that Colorado had an ideal climate for growing paprika. He convinced Newton to import special seeds from Hungary. Unfortunately, that particular growing season proved less than ideal, and another investment "got plowed under."[23]

Studying Public Policy

Despite Quigg's commitment to practicing law in the late 1930s, his primary interest was actually being channeled in other directions. From the time he was a student at Andover, his father had inundated him with correspondence in which he discussed economic, political, and social issues at the local, national, even global level. At one point, Jim Newton may have harbored political ambitions of his own. The local papers ran stories speculating whether he would seek the nomination for governor in the late 1930s. Jim may have been intrigued, but he was acutely aware that his quirky combination of conservative views on some issues and his liberal—even radical—positions on others made him a political maverick. In 1937, the Roosevelt administration appointed him the first chairman of the Denver branch of the Federal Housing Authority. Newton was gregarious and very well liked among his circle of friends, but he realized that a few considered him virtually a traitor to his class. He was astute enough to realize that his bluntness alone would almost certainly preclude any success as a political candidate.[24]

Whether or not Jim Newton's fascination with public policy issues and government was the root cause, Quigg shared those interests. From the time he returned to Denver after serving with the SEC, Quigg became involved in political issues. His primary focus was state government, and he educated himself about challenges on everything from the needs of disabled children to the financing of government operations.[25] The state legislature had hired a team of consultants to recommend reorganizing antiquated government procedures. Their recommendations, outlined in the Griffenhagen Report, attracted widespread interest.

In the summer of 1938, young Newton, not yet twenty-seven, became a key public speaker favoring adopting most of its recommendations. In midsummer, he stated in an address over Radio KLZ, "If there ever was a time in the history of the State of Colorado when it is necessary to take action, that time has come. We, the people, have a responsibility the like of which we have never seen before. That responsibility is to insist that the State be reorganized so that waste and confusion and ignorance and inefficiency can be eliminated, and let no man or thing stand in the way." Although he did not name specific people, Newton claimed, "One of the worst features of the antiquated fund system is that it allows little autocracies of governmental officials— little states within a state—to grow up, each pulling in its own direction, to accomplish a selfish purpose, instead of in one direction for the betterment of the state as a place in which to live."[26]

Examining the jerry-built structure of the state government system in detail, one can only shake one's head in wonderment that anything constructive ever got done. In 1939, there were 108 agencies, boards, commissions, and bureaus staffed by about 350 officeholders. There were twenty-five different means of choosing these officers, most of them beyond the control of the governor. The appointees controlled 231 separate cash funds. No wonder financial controls might have challenged the ingenuity of even the most skilled auditors.

Newton quickly assumed a key leadership role in promoting more widespread public awareness of the Griffenhagen Report. Within weeks of his radio address, he was sounding like a senior advisor in providing political advice on how to achieve its goals. He observed to one enthusiast of reorganization that "the real time to talk issues and get 'chummy' with the candidates is after the Primaries."[27] To another lobbyist, he regretted having to remove himself from key assignments in advancing the reform agenda because he was planning a vacation, yet he outlined steps that might be taken in his absence.[28] When he returned from his vacation, he continued to speak out on behalf of the Griffenhagen recommendations over radio and in front of business groups and civic organizations. In a report presented at the Colorado Legislative Conference in December 1938, Newton provided a lengthy technical analysis of the weaknesses of the state personnel system.[29] In a radio address in February 1939, he claimed that the intent of the Chicago consultants was not to discredit any current officeholders but to document how hamstrung they were by the unworkable, chaotic state government structure then in place.

The young lawyer and budding public servant kept pushing for a special session of the state legislature to enact the reorganization program.

In the summer of 1939, Quigg wrote to the senior author of the Griffenhagen Report that he hoped Governor Ralph Carr would promote the program.[30] However, Quigg still had a lot to learn about state politics. Griffenhagen informed Newton that the governor had told him personally that he didn't think the timing was right, and he would have to wait until 1941 to back reforms. Griffenhagen demurred, stating, "I don't think his chances then would be any better."[31] Even though Newton's efforts to effect reform in structure and administration of state government did not bear immediate fruit, he established a reputation for studying complex issues in depth and knowing his subjects thoroughly. Even more important for Quigg's long-range future, he was gaining notice from numerous highly influential leaders in the state, and even at the national level. These contacts would be key in his eventual decision to enter public life.

As an undergraduate at Yale, then later as a law student, Quigg had impressed his academic mentors with his inveterate curiosity, his desire to know about virtually everything. That included foreign affairs. In the late 1930s, when European powers and Japan were hurtling toward yet another catastrophic worldwide conflict, many Americans were isolationist, hoping against hope that the nation could avoid involvement in any future conflict. In fact, Dick Davis became active in America First, an organization promoting an isolationist response to the worsening European situation.

Whether or not the evolving world crisis was the root cause, Quigg sought out the same intellectual challenge he had encountered in Washington during his year with the SEC. He organized frequent informal discussions of foreign affairs with a few like-minded people, many of them from the University of Denver. Within a few months, the discussions had attracted considerable public interest and drawn in several influential local decision-makers. After Newton organized the Denver Committee on Foreign Relations, the group eventually gained recognition as a chapter in the national Council on Foreign Relations. In later years, Quigg was recognized as the founder of the Denver chapter, and he was honored by being named a permanent officer in the national organization. This was one of the honors he most treasured.[32]

Quigg's increasingly prominent public profile and his fascination
with international issues induced him to begin writing published articles
about contemporary issues facing the nation. By the fall of 1941, Japan
had been at war with China for four years, and Europe had been fighting
for two. In June 1941, Adolph Hitler had invaded the Soviet Union. As
the world fell ever deeper into its wartime morass in 1941, several of
Newton's articles appeared in *The Denver Post.* In his writings, Quigg
assumed the same position and often the same tone that his father had
used with him. This all-too-earnest young man, not yet thirty, lectured
readers about how, in his opinion, the nation should respond to the crisis.
He tapped out a steady drumbeat of proposals, many of them focused on
national defense. Once President Roosevelt narrowly convinced Congress
to back the Lend-Lease Program, which provided material aid to countries
fighting the Axis powers, Quigg urged his readers to support the program
wholeheartedly: "Now that the decision has been made, I believe we
should forget our differences of opinion and put our shoulders to the
wheel. Having dedicated our economy to the task of enabling Great
Britain to defeat Hitler, we should produce as only America can produce."[33] Newton was equally interested in the situation in the Pacific.
After hearing a public address by Paul C. Smith, editor-in-chief of the *San
Francisco Chronicle,* he wrote Smith in the summer of 1941 proposing that
Smith take him along as an assistant on an upcoming fact-finding trip for
Naval Intelligence to assess wartime situations in China and India.[34]
Nothing came of this initiative, but as a naval officer during the war,
Quigg would travel to South America and far out into the Pacific Ocean.

Courtship and Marriage
Although he was an intense, highly motivated, serious young man, Quigg
also enjoyed a good time, and he had an active social life. He was young,
strong, handsome, and from a fine family. Not surprisingly, he attracted
many young women. During his prep school years, and later at Yale, he
had several girlfriends. He experienced a serious relationship with a girl
from Rhode Island during his Yale years. Later, he was briefly engaged to
a girl from a well-known Denver family; he had even purchased a home

in anticipation of settling down with her. But none of these early romances worked out. Quigg may have unconsciously shied away from a final commitment because he wanted to avoid the type of domineering relationship his father had established with his mother. According to Newton, his parents' marriage was basically unhappy.[35] But Dick Davis, Quigg's close friend, was happily married to his younger sister, Nancy, and the young man may have contemplated the prospects of domestic bliss for himself. The time was certainly propitious for the appearance of the right girl.

Virginia Shafroth, born in 1920, was the granddaughter of former Colorado governor John F. "Honest John" Shafroth. Her mother, Abby Staunton Shafroth, was from a socially prominent family in Kansas City, and her father, Morrison Shafroth, was a well-known lawyer and a politician in his own right. Although never successful in his own bid for

The Shafroth family. Adults around the large table include Abby Shafroth (Ginny's mother), Quigg, Morrison Shafroth (Ginny's father), standing, an unidentified child, Ginny, and Ellen Shafroth (Ginny's sister).

political office, Morrison Shafroth ran some high-profile campaigns, including a run for the U.S. Senate as a Republican in 1924 against a Ku Klux Klan–endorsed opponent. The Shafroths were similar to the Newtons in background; in Denver, they moved in the same social circles. The Shafroths also had many friends back East. They usually summered at Osterville, on Cape Cod, and they knew the Joseph Kennedys in Hyannis Port. Just three years younger than the future president, John F. Kennedy, Virginia was acquainted with the Kennedy children and participated in sailing regattas and parties with them. Joseph Kennedy had close connections to Hollywood in the 1920s and 1930s, and he received copies of all of the "hottest" movies. The Kennedy children often showed current movies in the basement of their home, and Virginia was sometimes included in these gatherings. She was the same age as Kathleen "Kick" Kennedy, and the two became good friends.[36]

Joe Kennedy constantly pushed his children, particularly the boys, to compete in everything from sports to dinner table debates centering on important events. Virginia's parents also had high hopes that their children would excel at whatever they did. Years later, while in her seventies, Virginia recalled that her parents "had especially high expectations of me as the eldest child. Sometimes I felt the demands were too much, as when I fell off my Shetland pony and broke my arm and had to ride him again as soon as I recovered."[37] Virginia enjoyed competition; coached by her father, she excelled in tennis. She also liked field hockey, which her mother coached. Virginia worked conscientiously at both the piano and her academic studies. After graduating from the Kent School in Denver in 1936, she was admitted to highly competitive Vassar College, which her grandmother and mother had both attended. Just sixteen when she graduated from Kent, she delayed her entrance into Vassar for a year in order to take a trip around the world with her grandmother and a school friend. Virginia's grandmother chaperoned the journey. The admissions committee at Vassar permitted her to take the year off on the condition that she would keep a daily diary of her trip.[38]

Virginia Shafroth had been aware of Quigg for some time, albeit largely from a distance. Since he was eight-and-one-half years older, they did not know each other until one brief encounter in 1939, and then a second in 1941. With her world travel and her athletic and artistic talents, however, Virginia was a remarkably accomplished and interesting woman as a nineteen-year-old. Virginia first met Quigg on a hike up Longs Peak in the summer of 1939. Virginia's mother and the mother of Quigg's current girlfriend had arranged the hike. One of Virginia's roommates at Vassar also accompanied the group. Virginia recalled that Quigg spent most of his time helping her friend, who was terrified during the climb. Later, Quigg admitted that he was equally afraid. Virginia, however, was impressed with Quigg's concern about her friend.

More than two years later, they met again, and romance blossomed. By November 1941, Virginia had graduated from Vassar, and she was employed at Graland School in Denver, teaching music and assisting in sports and third and fourth grades. Quigg's older sister, Ruth, hosted a party that included the Shafroths. Ruth asked Quigg to take Virginia and a number of the younger guests to the Brown Palace for dinner and dancing, and once again, he and Virginia talked at length. The Brown Palace and its waltz orchestra was the crucible for their romance.

A few nights later, Virginia returned to the Ship Tavern at the Brown Palace with another male friend. All the tables were full. Quigg and Dick Davis happened to be there, and Quigg invited Virginia to join them. This time, they engaged in a heated intellectual discussion. America's involvement in the deepening world crisis was the topic of intense debate among citizens with any awareness of foreign affairs. At the time, Virginia believed strongly in the isolationist positions of the America First movement. Quigg was even more passionately committed to interventionism, which was promoted by the Committee to Defend America by Aiding the Allies. Quigg was intrigued by her willingness to stand up to him and argue her position. He was also attracted to Virginia as a woman, and a whirlwind courtship began. Just a few weeks later, the couple visited Winter Park for a weekend of skiing. On December 6, 1941, Quigg "popped the question" at the Arlberg Club in Winter Park. They discussed their future deep into the night. Virginia told Quigg that they could not be married until the following summer because she did not want to break her commitment to teach at Graland School for the entire academic year.

Pearl Harbor and Changing Plans

The very next day, December 7, all hell broke loose. Quigg learned of the Japanese attack on Pearl Harbor and left immediately for Denver; Virginia joined him that evening. Earlier in the year, Quigg's old school friend Charles Noyes had suggested to Quigg that the Lend-Lease Administration needed lawyers and that he should consider applying for work there. Quigg may have considered his friend's advice, but at the time, he had been very deeply engaged in his legal work at Newton and Davis and writing his newspaper columns and radio addresses about the necessity of preparedness, and so he put off action. But after learning about Pearl Harbor, Quigg acted quickly. From Denver, he phoned Noyes to find out if a legal job at Lend-Lease was still available. Apparently it was. Quigg also investigated wartime opportunities with the Office of Price Administration before accepting work with Lend-Lease.[39]

Within days, Quigg packed up and was off to Washington to take up legal duties there. His section's job was to review and either approve, reject, or modify contracts with corporations supplying products to the government.[40] Quigg summarized the work as routine, even rubber-stamp in nature, but slipups in contract wording could potentially cost taxpayers millions. During the dark weeks of the spring of 1942, as the United States and the Allies suffered one reverse after another in every theater of the war, Quigg was helping to direct critically needed supplies to Britain and the Soviet Union, where the Allies were grimly hanging on. Although he was not being shot at, Quigg had an acute sense of being involved in the hostilities. Allied strategists recognized how critical Lend-Lease was. German U-boats were blowing Allied freighters out of the water almost as fast as they were being filled with food and supplies. Some convoys were losing fully half of their cargo vessels.

While working for Lend-Lease, Quigg lived and worked in Washington under many of the same conditions he had experienced five years earlier during his year at the SEC: as a bachelor, with a large number of other young men. This time, his quarters were in Hockley House, a lovely turn-of-the-century home on Fox Hill Road in Georgetown overlooking the Potomac River. Katharine Graham, future owner of the *Washington Post*, described Hockley House as resembling "a second-hand Tara from 'Gone With the Wind,'" with lots of single rooms. It was owned by Theodore Wilkinson, an admiral in the Navy, and it served as wonderful lodgings for many rising young men like Quigg who were working in Washington. The intellectual seminars resumed. As Graham recalled, "No subject was taboo at Hockley. … All issues and events were discussed in great debates that often went on for days on end. … Insults were hurled as a matter of course. It was understood that the abuse and indignities, even ad hominem attacks, were fair weapons in arguing for your position, but in truth there were no real feuds or solid dislikes. … "[41] Virginia Shafroth recalled that the "butler" served marvelous mint juleps at their parties, including the day she and Quigg formally announced their engagement when she visited him in Washington during Graland's spring break.[42] The young men living at Hockley House worked hard, but they also knew how to have a good time when circumstances permitted.

As the United States had drifted slowly toward war over the previous two years, Quigg realized that it was highly likely that if the nation entered the war, his world could be turned upside down. By a narrow vote, Congress had authorized a peacetime draft in 1940, and in August 1941, the recruits' original twelve-month enlistments had been extended an additional eighteen months. Quigg would not necessarily have to serve in the military. He was a fit and single thirty-year-old; however, in the summer of 1941, his local draft board in Denver had ruled that men over age twenty-eight were still exempt from the draft. In late January 1942, Quigg's superior at Lend-Lease, Oscar Cox, sent a request to the Denver draft board for an exemption for him, based on the fact that "Mr. Newton is now working on three vitally important confidential assignments."[43]

But once the United States entered the war, Quigg sensed a moral obligation to serve in the armed forces. Unbeknownst to Quigg, his father once again intervened. Jim Newton actually began attempting to influence his son's military future more than a year earlier. Believing that Quigg would be a poor infantryman and that he would serve the country more effectively with his brain rather than his brawn, Jim figuratively pulled some rank of his own. The elder Newton was friendly with Admiral Harold Stark, chief of naval operations. Even as Nazi troops were overrunning France in May 1940, Jim was angling to line up a navy commission for Quigg.[44] Jim claimed that, should he be drafted, Quigg wanted to "be a private and work up to anything that may be within his ability." While expressing pride in Quigg's egalitarianism, he made it clear that, in this case at least, such youthful idealism should be trumped. Jim candidly admitted, "If he knew I was writing this letter to you, I am sure he would shoot me … , " yet he still pushed for a slot in navy intelligence for his son.[45] In March 1942, Jim asked Stark, "Would it be presumptuous for me to ask you to put me in touch with the Navy man who probably will have charge of Quigg's papers as they go through the mill?"[46] By that time, Quigg was engaged to Virginia Shafroth, and her uncle, John F. Shafroth, Jr., was a rear admiral in the southeast Pacific. Evidently, Quigg was not personally involved; he may not have been aware of these maneuverings.

But things changed soon after the Japanese attacked Pearl Harbor. Quigg was not simply a passive bystander; he took an active role in attempting to guide his military future. In late January 1942, he informed his friend Paul Smith, editor-in-chief of the *San Francisco Chronicle*, by then a lieutenant commander in the navy, that he would be interested in any navy assignment where he "could do the most good."[47] Quigg felt sufficiently informed about the bureaucracy of the navy that by mid-February 1942 he was advising friends back in Denver how the system worked. He wrote to one close family friend seeking a navy assignment: "I will be glad to contact the proper people for you, but it isn't as simple as that. Before you find a job that you are willing to take it might be necessary for you to contact a dozen or fifteen people."[48]

Instead of stateside duty, Quigg hoped for combat duty aboard a ship. By early March, however, he was resigned to the fact that such a request might not be granted. Still, he was hoping for some firm outcome of his future. After his papers were submitted in February, he waited for five weeks without orders.[49] Finally, on March 18, 1942, Quigg was sworn in as an ensign in the navy reserves. He learned that his wartime duty with the navy would involve legal work in establishing and maintaining the Naval Air Transport Service (NATS). Quigg's legal service for Bob Six and Continental Airlines was excellent background for his wartime work.

Virginia and Quigg had kept their engagement secret until the spring of 1942.[50] They planned a family wedding in Wianno, on Cape Cod, where Virginia's grandmother had a summer home and where her parents had also been married twenty-five years earlier. Quigg and

Quigg and Ginny's wedding on Cape Cod, June 6, 1942. Ginny's sister and maid-of-honor, Ellen Shafroth, and Quigg's best man and brother-in-law, Richard Davis, stand behind the newlyweds.

Ginny exchanged rings at St. Peter's Episcopal Chapel on June 6, 1942. The ceremony was officiated by Dr. Remsen B. Ogilby, who was president of Trinity College in Hartford and a friend of Virginia's mother. Ogilby's advice to the bride and groom was conventional, yet wise: always work out any disagreements before going to sleep.[51] Following the ceremony, the newlyweds welcomed extended family and friends at an outdoor reception at the summer home of her grandmother.

Wartime Service

There was a war on, so there was no time for an idyllic honeymoon. After a two-night getaway to a nearby beach cabin by sailboat, the couple hurried back to Washington, where they had to change living quarters several times because of an acute wartime housing shortage. While Virginia set up housekeeping, her husband immersed himself in duties for NATS. The young ensign quickly impressed his superiors. By the time Quigg had been at work for just a month, his section chief requested that he be promoted to lieutenant commander. He described

Ginny and Quigg on the beach during their brief honeymoon.

Quigg's duties in some detail. They involved "close liaison with other departments of the government and frequent conferences with the officers of those departments, and with the civilian officers of important airlines." An official NATS communication stated that Newton would "coordinate matters arising in Washington in connection with NATS contracts with commercial airlines, to maintain liaison with contract operators, other branches of the Navy and other government agencies in Washington on matters relating to such contracts; and to render assistance, where required, to the Bureau of Aeronautics and other bureaus and offices of the Navy Department in matters relating to termination of such contracts." Newton would be working with high-powered people both within the government and in the civilian sector, including generals, colonels, lieutenant colonels, and presidents and chief legal counsels of important corporations. His section chief based the promotion request on the fact that Newton's service to that point had been "eminently satisfactory" and that he needed the prestige of the higher rank to work effectively with those at higher levels.[52]

During his years with NATS, Quigg also served on the joint Army-Navy Air Transport Board. During this time, Virginia experienced an incident that could have created problems for her husband. Ginny had arranged to pick Quigg up at the Navy Department in their car. She had to make a phone call to Quigg from the entrance to tell him she was there. She entered an office where a man in uniform was using the phone, and he would not stop talking. As he droned on, Ginny shared her impatience. Eventually, a car pulled up and the driver addressed the man as "Mr. Secretary." He was none other than James V. Forrestal, secretary of the navy![53] Evidently, Forrestal had a sense of humor, or he quickly forgot about the incident.

Ginny and Quigg quickly fit into a routine in Washington. She learned the rudiments of cooking and keeping house and continued her interest in music. Ginny studied and taught at the Washington College of Music and also gave piano lessons there and at home. Although Quigg's work was necessary and undoubtedly important, looking back on his wartime work six decades later, he recalled his wartime service as basically a lark, even a "cushy" job, and that he essentially "did errands" for the top naval brass. "We had it made. I had this friend, Gilbert Kerlin, who had to log a certain number of hours in his plane every month. Since Ginny had family and a lot of friends out on Cape Cod, she would often go there ahead of me in the summer. Of course, I spent weekdays in Washington. On many Friday afternoons, Kerlin would meet me after work and fly me to Otis Field, nearby Osterville, where Ginny and Sally Kerlin met us with their cars."[54]

Quigg's duties included inspecting existing airfields and evaluating their suitability as transport bases. Newton and his team inspected dozens of airfields in the United States. The War Department had no idea how long the war might last or where the crucial battles might occur; however, it had to be prepared to develop supply bases in many exotic places. Therefore, Newton and his fellow inspectors toured the Pacific theater, and they visited numerous bases in South America. Quigg recalled that their plane would swoop into remote airfields. The crew would spend about two days talking to everybody, including civilians. They asked all sorts of questions and seemingly looked into every nook and cranny.

Quigg Newton as a naval officer during World War II.

During an extended five-week inspection tour in South America early in 1944, Quigg received a telegram when the group reached one of its stops in Brazil. It informed him that his father had died suddenly in Denver in the early morning hours of April 5. Even though Jim Newton was just fifty-eight at the time of his death, the news was not totally unexpected. Since his heart attack in 1936, the elder Newton had suffered from continuing health problems. According to one news account, he had been warned by his doctors that he had a "slowing" heart and that he should "reduce the tempo of his activities and take a well earned rest." Jim Newton was nothing if not stubborn, and he followed doctors' advice half-heartedly and grudgingly. The day before his death, he had lunched with University of Denver chancellor Ben Cherrington and his son's father-in-law, Morrison Shafroth. After dinner that evening with Nelle, he retired to his bedroom and died quietly sometime in the night.[55]

Although Quigg had sometimes resented his father's controlling influence, he felt a deep sense of loss. The two men had always been extraordinarily close. In his sometimes rambling letters to Quigg, Jim had probably shared more of his inner being than with any other human, even his wife. His ruminations dealt with his hopes, ideas, and many of his frustrations. Since Quigg was thousands of miles from Denver when he heard the news, and as there were wartime restrictions on travel, he was unable to attend funeral services.

Of course, life goes on, and Quigg and Virginia had started a family of their own. On September 17, 1943, their first of four daughters, Nan, was born. Although Quigg was now a family man, he would have preferred active duty and combat, like some of his friends experienced. In hindsight, it seems fair to speculate that he may have somehow, instinctively, sensed that he might eventually enter public life and that a combat record would greatly enhance his opportunities for attaining elected office.[56] In the spring of 1945, his section chief, Don Smith, took command of an aircraft carrier, the USS *Boxer*. Quigg saw this as his ticket to sea duty, and he urged Smith to take him along.[57] Smith wanted Quigg's services, and he sent paperwork requesting the transfer through a tortuous path up the navy's bureaucracy.

Nevertheless, Quigg's bid to leave NATS was denied. He was deeply involved in complicated contract negotiations with Pan American, and he would not be available until mid-April. But timing was not the only consideration preventing Newton from achieving his dream of sea duty. Ironically, his rapid rise in rank actually hurt his

chances. The commander of NATS noted, "Newton's lack of experience
and training on board a carrier ... and with his seniority of rank, subject officer should remain in his present billet for the best interest of
both the Naval service and NATS."[58]

Newton thanked Smith for his efforts on his behalf and repeated
his hope that conditions would change in upcoming weeks and permit
him to experience some combat duty. Like all Americans, however,
Quigg rejoiced in the fact that the war was winding down. Germany
finally collapsed in early May 1945. Although Japanese fighting men
were putting up furious resistance at strange-sounding locations such as
Iwo Jima and Saipan, time was clearly running out for them.
Knowledgeable military planners feared that the United States would
suffer hundreds of thousands of additional casualties if a mainland invasion of Japan was required. Detonation of atomic bombs over
Hiroshima and Nagasaki in early August rendered such considerations
moot, and the war finally ended when the Japanese surrendered a few
days later.

Newton would spend a few more months winding down his
duties with NATS before mustering out, but he faced a major crossroads
in his life. He had served nearly four years in the navy. Although he had
helped negotiate large numbers of contracts between the government
and service providers, he was out of touch with many facets of civilian
law. Should he return to Denver, bone up on the law, and join his partners at his firm? Without question, that would be the safest thing to do,
since he had a wife and a growing family to support. On the other hand,
both he and Ginny were adventurers. His father was no longer looking
over his shoulder and providing advice. Consciously or otherwise,
Quigg may have felt a sense of liberation from parental control. He and
Ginny were truly on their own. It was not characteristic of either partner to seek a routine, conventional lifestyle. Yet in the fall of 1945,
neither Quigg nor Ginny could have imagined the changes in their lives
that were just around the corner.

CHAPTER 5

Entering
the Public Arena

Although World War II ended in the late summer of 1945, it took Quigg Newton some time to finish his duties in Washington and prepare himself for reentry into civilian life. For more than three years, he had been engaged in negotiating contracts between commercial air carriers and the federal government concerning transportation, chiefly for navy personnel. The end of the war created considerable paperwork in contract modification or termination, and Quigg did not get out of the navy until late in 1945. The couple had decided to return to Denver, where Quigg would resume work with his old law firm and help a variety of civic organizations. He had served the University of Denver as secretary of the board of trustees, and that institution would probably welcome his resumption of those duties. By the end of the war, the couple had two daughters: Nan, then two years old, and Nelle, who was born on May 15, 1945. Both Quigg and Virginia looked forward to settling down close to their extended families.[1]

Return to Denver

But the couple was in no hurry to get back to Denver. They had never enjoyed a true honeymoon, being restricted to taking a long weekend after their wedding in wartime conditions during the summer of 1942. With the exception of weekends at Cape Cod, Quigg had been hard at work with the Naval Air Transport Service (NATS), and the couple hadn't enjoyed a real vacation. Since Quigg had had the foresight to order one of the last Buicks to roll off the assembly line in 1942, they were one of the relatively few American couples who still owned a decent automobile.[2] They returned to Denver for Christmas, left their two daughters with a caretaker, and drove with another Denver couple to Mexico. They viewed ancient ruins of Aztec temples and a vanished civilization, sunned, fished, played tennis, and simply relaxed. They returned to the United States via Carlsbad, California, where they looked over ranch property still owned by Quigg's family. In the early spring of 1946, they returned to Denver.[3]

During the war, Jim Newton had purchased a modest bungalow at 1941 South Fillmore Street for the young couple.[4] By the time Quigg and Ginny returned to Denver, however, they had already outgrown the two-bedroom house. Instead, they moved into a house at 75 Cherry Street, previously owned by Dick and Nancy Davis. There was an acute shortage of housing nationwide, exacerbated by expansion of war industries and movement of millions of workers into larger cities. The housing supply nationwide and in Denver would not fully catch up with demand until midcentury. The couple felt fortunate to be able to buy the house on Cherry Street.

If Quigg sensed that he was about to become an important figure in Denver, he certainly kept such thoughts to himself. In addition to resuming full-time responsibilities at the law firm, Newton quickly resumed his activities in civic affairs, most notably helping guide the University of Denver. In the minds of the board of trustees, the timing couldn't have been better. Millions of veterans were returning from war duty, and a large percentage of them were pursuing higher education, much of it to be funded by the GI Bill.

The trustees understood that they needed new blood to help administer the university in the challenging and rapidly changing postwar educational environment. John Evans, grandson of the territorial governor of Colorado and university founder, was retiring as president of the board. In a remarkable demonstration of their faith in Quigg's leadership and capacity for growth, just three months after Newton's return to Denver, the trustees voted to make him president of the board At age thirty-four,

Quigg was one of if not the youngest university board presidents in the country. Quickly sizing up the university's needs, Quigg stated that he supported the university's multimillion-dollar plans for expansion of its downtown and University Park campuses, informing reporters, "Almost every city which has any claim to greatness has a great university."[5] A slight variation of this comment became the board's well-publicized slogan in its successful fundraising campaign. Unbeknownst to Quigg at the time, he would be repeating variations of this concept for the rest of his life.

Ginny Newton became an adjunct to her husband in serving more-immediate human needs at the University of Denver. Sparing time from her homemaking duties, she volunteered several hours weekly to arrange temporary housing for new university faculty who were searching frantically for places to live. She and university officials voiced frustration when some promising young faculty had to turn down job offers because they could not find adequate living quarters.[6]

National Recognition

Newton was rapidly establishing himself, both locally and nationally, as a young man with a bright future. He also served as a board member for the Boettcher Foundation and the Colorado National Bank, and he was a trustee of the Grace Community Center. Additionally, he was active in youth welfare work. In his legal work, Newton was involved even more deeply than before the war with the expansion of airline service to Denver, an industry that would be crucial in shaping the region's postwar economy. In promoting airline service, Newton capitalized on contacts he had nurtured during his recent years with NATS; he was on a first-name basis with many leaders in the field, including Juan Trippe of Pan American and David Northrop, head of Northrop Aviation.[7] Quigg's hard work and uncommon commitment to public service earned him the gratitude of those he assisted and gained him widespread public recognition. The Denver Junior Chamber of Commerce (Jaycees) named him "Denver's Outstanding Young Man" of 1946.[8]

Winning this regional honor meant that Quigg's name was duly submitted to the selection committee choosing America's Ten

Outstanding Young Men of 1947. Back then, roughly 30,000 nomination forms were sent to local chapters of the Jaycees, so competition was extremely stiff. Newton was both surprised and deeply honored when he was informed that he had been named one of the Jaycees' ten "Outstanding Young Men" in the nation for 1947. Fellow inductees that year included Congressman Richard M. Nixon of California and Mayor De Lesseps S. "Chep" Morrison of New Orleans. The previous year, the Jaycees had chosen boxer Joe Louis, cartoonist Bill Mauldin, and the historian Arthur M. Schlesinger Jr., and two years earlier they had named Henry Ford II and future Supreme Court justice Abe Fortas.[9] Quigg was obviously moving in fast company, not just in Denver but at the national level.

Deciding to Run for Mayor

Certain hoary historical accounts and even some newspaper reports at the time claim that Newton's decision to run for mayor of Denver in 1947 came out of the blue. Although his campaign for the city's top office generated immediate enthusiasm and gathered momentum swiftly, his decision to run was hardly spontaneous. Like Joseph Kennedy's sons, Quigg had been well prepared to enter politics. He and his father had ruminated over local and regional issues for years. Understandably, early discussions had been one-sided, as Jim thoroughly dissected many issues in letters to Quigg beginning twenty years earlier when he was a student at Andover. Jim's frequent politically focused letters kept arriving while Quigg was a student at Yale, and they continued as long as Jim lived.

For the most part, Quigg shared his father's interest. More to the point, after graduating from law school and setting up his law practice in Denver, Quigg had become deeply involved in reexamining state government. Not content to be a behind-the-scenes student of government affairs, in 1940 and 1941 he carefully articulated his views on local and state issues in radio addresses and newspaper columns. Although a novice in political circles, Quigg had already gained respect and significant name recognition, particularly among powerful decision-makers in Denver.

Ben Stapleton's Vulnerability

If Jim Newton had been alive in 1947, it is unlikely he would have endorsed his son's decision to challenge Ben F. Stapleton. He and Stapleton had been cordial terms. Numerous influential old family friends, including Thomas Dines, were privy to Quigg's interest in local politics, but they assumed that if he ran for public office, he would initially seek a city council seat or run for the state legislature. Even some of Quigg's younger friends, including Henry Van Schaack Jr., thought he should move slowly.[10] Stapleton had first been elected mayor in 1923, with considerable assistance of the Ku Klux Klan. With the exception of a four-year term of George Begole between 1931 and 1935, he had sat in the mayor's chair ever since. He was seventy-seven years old in 1947. Critics, who nicknamed him "interminable Ben," argued that the five-term mayor had no more creative ideas and seemed to be running out of energy. Nevertheless, during his decades in office, Stapleton had built a formidable political machine, and experienced political observers considered him unbeatable.[11]

In hindsight, it is obvious that however powerful Stapleton appeared on the surface, he was increasingly vulnerable as he faced the prospect of running for his sixth term. During World War II, Denver and the surrounding region had attracted tens of thousands of new residents. After the war, many of them decided that they liked the Rocky Mountain region and they wanted to stay there. Stapleton and many of his cronies among the "Seventeenth Street Crowd" liked the "old" Denver, along with its dusty "cow town" image. They were comfortable, they were in charge, and they were extremely complacent. Some critics believed they were also arrogant. As his fifth term as mayor wound down, other observers suggested that Stapleton and his associates were simply overwhelmed by the challenges ahead. On a September morning in 1946, a reporter overhead him blurting out, "If those people [newcomers] would just go back where they came from, we wouldn't have any problems here."[12]

By the time Quigg and Ginny Newton returned to Denver, many critics of the status quo sensed that there was a new spirit afoot. It was

obvious that the newcomers were here to stay and Denver couldn't turn
back the clock. In particular, the daily newspapers began running stories
about long-festering problems in the region that needed to be addressed.
Under mounting pressure to take some action, the Denver City Council
had authorized the prestigious, nationally recognized city-planning firm
of Harland Bartholomew and Associates of St. Louis to conduct a study
of the city and provide recommendations. The Bartholomew and
Associates report was submitted in September 1946, and in polite language the consultants skewered the current administration: "It is
apparent that not all of the probable public needs of the immediate
future have been considered."[13] One *Denver Post* reporter suggested that
Stapleton had been grossly negligent: "During the war, other cities spent
years planning carefully integrated postwar programs. A year after the
war ended, Denver had no such plan."[14]

For many months prior to Newton's announced decision to run
for mayor, negative newspaper stories softened up Stapleton to the point
that he was an easy target. From the summer of 1946 forward, the overall tone of stories and editorials about Stapleton and his cohorts was
overwhelmingly critical. Some of the issues covered were relatively minor:
complaints about slow responses by plumbing inspectors providing
approval for housing renovations and inadequate and hard-to-read street
signs put up by longtime city parks commissioner George Cranmer. One
university professor remarked, "Street signs in south Denver are darn lies.
… Those triangle signs are turned so a stranger can't tell which street
goes which way. The fellow who put them up was probably raised out in
the country and had no experience with street signs." A few days later,
another newspaper editorial chimed in: "Recent installations in some
parts of the city have been extremely haphazard."

Not long after that, *The Denver Post* again scored both Cranmer
and the mayor, claiming that a "scientific survey" had shown that 80
percent of Denverites were annoyed by the "inadequate" signs and that
43 percent stated that they had "been lost at one time or another
because they couldn't find out where they were."[15] The triangular signs
proved almost uniformly unpopular, but the administration chose not

to replace them with more conventional horizontal signs until powerful business interests also demanded that they be changed.[16]

Traffic conditions in general were giving the Stapleton administration fits. Much of it was not of the administration's making, as Americans were snapping up cars as quickly as automakers could turn them out, and without wartime tire and gasoline rationing, more citizens were driving many more miles. Nevertheless, city hall received the blame. After a monumental traffic jam in the downtown area tied up traffic on a Tuesday afternoon in June 1946, *The Post* called for immediate action: "If the city's own traffic experts cannot diagnose the trouble and work out the remedy, Mayor Stapleton would do well to get somebody who can."[17]

Other automobile-related challenges, including inadequate downtown parking, compounded traffic problems. Although a few decentralized shopping areas were beginning to emerge, most Denverites still did their major retail shopping downtown. Many lawyers, doctors, and dentists also had offices there. Since there was very limited off-street parking, prospective shoppers and those with professional appointments spent frustrating minutes circling blocks and wasting gas looking for curbside spots. Public officials and private interests shared responsibility for resolving the gridlock, and late in 1946 the mayor's office and the chamber of commerce announced a comprehensive survey of the situation.[18] But nothing happened.

By the early spring of 1947, *The Post* took off the gloves and went after the city administration. Noting that traffic congestion had been "extremely critical" before the war, investigative reporter Robert Stapp chided public officials: "It was apparent that the problem would arise again as soon as restrictions were removed. In the face of that certainty, city officials made virtually no preparation for coping with the problem."[19] In subsequent articles, Stapp conceded that any solutions would be expensive to implement and it would be years before they were in place.

Unfortunately for Mayor Stapleton, investigative reporters were finding many other problem areas that city hall had allegedly been unforgivably lax in addressing. Although the cost of living has by 2006 increased approximately sevenfold since the late 1940s, pay scales were startlingly low. Newspaper stories recounted the plight of many city employees who worked for near-starvation wages. College graduates holding degrees in library science were earning a pitiful starting wage of just $125 a month; after five years, they might be advanced to $140. Library clerks received much less: $85 per month, or up to $110 if they were college graduates.[20]

But there seemed to be plenty of money in city coffers to assist the mayor's cronies. Brothers John and Thomas McCusker and Raymond C. Erb developed a 313-acre subdivision in the Valverde neighborhood. Sharp-eyed neighbors observed ten or a dozen city-owned trucks dumping gravel there, along with many city workers actively leveling the gravel at the site.[21] George Cranmer, city parks commissioner, claimed that the city's work was confined to a thirty-foot strip of ground just west of the McCuskers' property line.[22] But newspapers carried stories of these suspicious-appearing activities for weeks; their cumulative effect was to further chip away at the mayor's credibility.

According to some critics, the mayor's office was paying insufficient attention to public health. A series of articles and editorials exposed "shocking conditions in many of the city's eating places." One columnist complained of numerous "greasy spoon" restaurants and lamented that the city had no restaurant rating system. The national public health service already had such a system in place, and it would be relatively simple to implement tighter health inspections: "Mayor Ben Stapleton and the city council owe this to the city."[23] When city hall was slow to respond, a second series began to appear about two months later. Earl N. Pomeroy of *The Post* reported that public responsibility for restaurant sanitation basically rested in the hands of a single official, and all he did was issue a list of "recommended do's and don'ts" to restaurants.[24] A few days later, the president of the Colorado Restaurant Association announced he was "acting as an individual" to set up an investigative committee, which would supposedly be finalized by the end of the year.[25] Public officials remained silent, however, and the story largely disappeared from local newspapers. But in late April 1947, the director of the state board of health scored "improper food handling in restaurants and a general lack of cleanliness" as being directly responsible for a rise in communicable diseases in Denver and throughout the state.[26]

According to mounting numbers of news stories, Denver was becoming an increasingly dirty city, and the mayor seemed to draw the brunt of the blame. Citizens living near two city dumps complained that the facilities were eyesores and that they suffered from foul odors and smoke caused periodically by burning trash.[27] A more serious political problem for the Stapleton administration involved trash collection. The outbreak of a frightening postwar polio epidemic caused many citizens to be more acutely aware of potential health hazards. For the city's older residents, the polio scare brought back horrifying recollections of the international influenza pandemic of 1918–1919, which took 600,000 lives in the United States and up to 40 million worldwide. One problem was that trash collection was haphazard, not regularly scheduled. This meant that garbage often stood in cans outdoors, sometimes uncollected for days, even weeks. Although not directly blaming the polio epidemic on inefficient garbage collection, a *Post* editorial claimed that "there can be no doubt that garbage—some fed raw to hogs, the rest scattered up and down alleys to provide food and harborage for a citywide infestation or rats and mice—endangers health."[28] The newspaper chided the mayor and the manager of public health: "They have made 'So What?' the guiding policy of an administration."[29]

When city parks commissioner George Cranmer suggested that homeowners should purchase in-sink garbage disposals, *The Post* hit the roof. A visiting sanitary engineer had suggested to Cranmer that he was one of the "chosen few" wealthy enough to be able to afford this fledgling technology and that most citizens would have to rely on more-primitive means of disposal. The paper ran a withering editorial raising the question "Who Should Come First, Pigs or Housewives?"[30] Six weeks later, when Stapleton finally got around to calling for a survey of the city's health needs, Dr. Florence Sabin, chair of the governor's postwar planning committee on public health, caustically referred to this tepid commitment as a "miracle." Not long afterward, Sabin claimed that conditions in Denver

General Hospital's tuberculosis ward were "medieval." Among myriad problems, the hospital was filthy. According to one *Post* account, "Mice, scampering across the floor and along bedside tables, awake many of the patients at night. Those who sleep soundly frequently find mice have nibbled at packages of food or left droppings beside the beds. ... Cockroaches run around under the pan of water in which visitors wash their hands before leaving." Dr. Sabin called the facility a "public disgrace." Were conditions at the hospital a state or city responsibility? Public manager and superintendent of the hospital Carl Schwalb desperately tried to shift responsibility to the state. *The Post*, never inclined to give Stapleton the benefit of the doubt, weighed in against the city administration: "The general public can feel only shame that its elected and appointed officials are failing so unprofessionally in maintaining a ward which its tax moneys support for the ill and dependent."[31]

At times, it seemed as if *The Post* was waging a full-scale campaign to embarrass the mayor and his associates. Without question, editor Palmer "Ep" Hoyt, newly arrived from Portland, Oregon, believed the city needed new leadership. Thus, his reporters were encouraged to investigate poor service delivery and any improprieties by the denizens of city hall. In December 1946, staff writer Richard Dudman addressed yet another potentially explosive issue: public utility rates. The Public Service Company's twenty-year franchise was due to expire, and public hearings were being held to address future terms of renewal.

This time, however, Gene Cervi, who owned and ran his own newspaper, *Cervi's Journal*, took the lead in ripping the Stapleton administration. Cervi was also chairman of the Democratic state committee. At a public hearing before the city council, with 400 citizens in attendance, Cervi accused the company of using scare tactics and waiting until the last minute, then "holding a pistol at our head" in demanding unconscionably lucrative terms. He also charged the city administration with negotiating a sweetheart deal behind closed doors.[32] Further fuel was added to the controversy when reporters learned that George Cranmer was a large utility stockholder. *The Post* was soon back on the attack, demanding that Stapleton reveal the true facts. Specifically, the paper charged that the mayor had simply accepted the company's valuation of its property "without conducting any kind of an adequate, independent study to determine the fairness of the charges."[33]

But nothing involving the Stapleton administration made as negative a public impact as charges of widespread and varied abuses in the police department. During the last year of the mayor's fifth term, allegations of police malfeasance were in the newspapers almost daily. In late June 1946, both daily newspapers carried stories about mysterious deaths of prisoners in the city jail. In one case, a prisoner was allegedly struck by a blackjack three times while being booked. He died several hours later, but the coroner ruled that it was due to "natural causes."[34] Less than a week later, another man was arrested for public intoxication, booked, and then taken to the county jail. The next day he complained of feeling ill. Examined at Denver General Hospital, he was found to have a fractured skull. He died the next morning.[35]

One policeman was caught and charged with shoplifting; another stole linens from Denver General Hospital. Jail guards were caught accepting payment from prisoners for special services and supplying recreational drugs (mainly Benzedrine). A grand jury investigation of various police-related charges induced the district attorney, James T. Burke, to claim that the mayor, chief of police, and manager of safety were all adopting a "sedentary attitude toward the welfare of the citizens of Denver" and that they were shamefully "hiding behind skirts."[36] In a lengthy explanation of his campaign to clean up the police department, Burke stated, "Some of the finest [men] in the department are doing 'errand boy' jobs because they don't 'stand in' with 'the boss.'" He laid the cause of low morale and unrest in the department squarely on the mayor's doorstep: "Spies or stool pigeons working out of the mayor's office to check on the police department do not serve as a satisfactory substitute for good leadership."[37]

Three weeks later, the issue of corruption in the police department intensified when August Hanebuth, chief of police, refused to testify to the grand jury in the case of two patrolmen charged with burglary, on the ground that he might incriminate himself. The patrolmen under suspicion were still on the force and receiving full pay. Calling the situation "so shocking that it may prove impossible to restore public confidence in his department without removing [Chief Hanebuth] from office," *The Post* editorial tied his reluctance to talk directly to the mayor himself: "Because Mayor Stapleton exercises such close supervision over the police department, it is natural to suppose that the chief may have been acting under orders when he declined to testify. If he was not, the least the mayor can be expected to do is to direct Chief Hanebuth to waive all claims to immunity and talk freely or resign."[38] But the state's cumbersome legal system eventually provided protection for the mayor and his beleaguered chief of police. A compliant district judge ruled in January 1947 that Hanebuth did not have to testify, a decision that basically ended Burke's probe.[39] If the police chief and mayor quietly breathed sighs of relief, critics believed that the whole controversy reeked of politics as usual.

Mayor Stapleton may have felt relief at having dodged a potentially lethal bullet, but the papers kept taking potshots at the police. Around Christmas 1946, stories of police officers handling allegedly "private" traffic control for downtown merchants while they were on public duty and drawing full pay rankled many. In January, one city council member long at odds with Mayor Stapleton charged that the police chief had "whitewashed" police charged with drunkenness while on duty. When the National Western Stock Show came to Denver that same month for its traditional two-week stay, papers reported policemen doing such "flunky work" as opening and closing gates, strolling the grounds with night sticks on the ready, and keeping customers in line at the entrances to dining facilities. The implication was clear that their services might be more urgently needed on less-routine duty.[40]

As early as the summer of 1946, it was clear that Mayor Stapleton had worn out his welcome, at least among most of the region's journalists. Although Hoyt's *Denver Post* was his most outspoken critic, news coverage of the activities of the mayor's office by the other papers was decidedly unenthusiastic. However, *The Post* seemed overtly determined to drive Stapleton from power. Its opening salvo came in mid-September in an editorial titled "How'm I doing? ... Not so Hot, Ben." Reporting results from its own poll, the paper claimed that only 19 percent of those queried stated they would vote again for Stapleton, while 57 percent would vote against him. The editorial crowed, "It is fair to expect that, barring a miraculous flurry of housecleaning and reforming activity on the part of the mayor during the fall and winter, this opposition will be registered even more strongly in next spring's municipal election. ... Ahead we may see an indignant public breaking the twenty-year grip of the Stapleton machine."[41]

Candidate Quigg

By early fall 1946, it was already apparent that behind-the-scenes maneuverings to replace Stapleton were underway. Whose idea was it to encourage Quigg Newton to enter the race? The young lawyer had been active in studying potential reform of state and local government for nearly a decade. Various family members and friends had discussed his running for the city council or some other office. More than a half-century later, Newton recalled that the first serious talk about a potential run for mayor came up at a lunch meeting with his old SEC mentor, William O. Douglas, and *Denver Post* editor Palmer "Ep" Hoyt.[42] Prominent

local decision-makers also urged him to enter the race. Lawyer Louis E. Gelt weighed in: "A number of us who have become interested in obtaining better local government have been discussing the possibility of finding a young man, energetic, honest, capable, and with sufficient financial background to avoid concern over the meager emolument of the mayor's office."[43]

Henry W. Hough joined a quickly lengthening line of supporters: "I hope [rumors of your running are] true. Anyhow, it would be a mighty good idea for you to run for mayor. I'll be sure to do my bit to push, if you do."[44] The *Rocky Mountain*

Newton for Mayor campaign photo, 1947.

News did not want to stand by passively while Hoyt and *The Post* got all the glory for promoting a change in city administration. The *News* immediately picked up on swirling rumors and joined *The Post* in trying to push Newton into the race. Running an editorial titled "The Mayor Will Not Run," the *News* discussed Stapleton's possible successor: "It is a good thing to find civic leaders already talking about a young man of the caliber of James Quigg Newton for their next mayor." The editorial concluded with what almost amounted to an endorsement, some five months before Newton officially entered the race: "We hope that the wide-spread talk of James Quigg Newton for mayor is evidence that next spring the voters of Denver will have young, progressive native sons such as he to choose from for their chief executive."[45]

Quigg standing in front of the U.S. Supreme Court with his law school mentor, Justice William O. Douglas, and Bill Shafroth, Ginny Newton's uncle.

Newton did not formally commit himself to run for mayor until late February 1947. In the meantime, *The Post* in particular continued its campaign to embarrass and further weaken Stapleton. The embattled mayor was besieged from all sides by demands that he address urgent civic problems. One new media issue was low morale among city workers. In late October, Stapleton released a list of salary increases for city employees, most notably for firemen and policemen. The catch was that the raises would cost $768,000, and

Stapleton simultaneously raised taxes on retail sales. *The Post* jumped on the issue as further evidence of the mayor's incompetence. Claiming that the city would have a surplus of $1.1 million for fiscal year 1947, the editorial argued that a 1-cent tax would raise $3 million, or even more: "In deciding on a 1-cent city sales tax, Mayor Stapleton and the council are trying to get the city's hand deeper into the pockets of all the people of Denver. What they propose would be the worst tax gouge in the city's history."[46] While both major newspapers continued to release stories suggesting that his years as a useful public servant were over, Stapleton played a cat-and-mouse game concerning his possible candidacy for a sixth term. When rumors surfaced around Christmas that he had met with "the boys" at the City and County Building and had informed them that he would indeed enter the race, he blasted the stories: "I am not making up my mind at this time. ... Now please publish the truth."[47]

Quigg Newton finally confirmed the worst kept "secret" in Denver when he formally announced his candidacy for mayor on February 22, 1947, at 6:00 P.M.: "I am making this announcement at the insistence of many civic leaders, in the firm belief, arrived at after the most careful consideration, that Denver's greatest need is a new, alert and progressive administration." He then made a fateful declaration that would attract voters and greatly enhance his candidacy for local office but would eventually damage his hopes for further political advancement. "My mayoralty campaign will be conducted in a truly *non-partisan* basis, with no prior commitments whatsoever, disclosed or undisclosed, to any political party, to any group, or to any special interest" (emphasis added).[48] This was all boilerplate political rhetoric, except the pledge to run as an independent.

It became obvious that Newton had done his homework in the months between the first rumors of his candidacy and his formal announcement. He immediately spelled out a sweeping yet detailed thirteen-point program of what he would do if elected. Quigg offered to bring greater efficiency to city management by introducing "the best and most modern business practices." He promised uniform personnel policies and implementation of a modern civil service program in city hall. He would appoint a new police chief immediately, and he promised to

provide an up-to-date survey of the city's burgeoning traffic needs. One
of the region's most pressing needs was housing, and he offered to revise
an outdated and cumbersome building code, which allegedly wasted
millions of construction dollars annually. Newton complained that the
Stapleton administration had passed up opportunities to compete for
federal dollars for low-cost housing. In addition, he promised a "complete overhaul" of the health department and a cleanup of inadequate
sewage and garbage disposal operations. Newton would institutionalize
city planning, bring order to a chaotic and inefficient purchasing department, provide new recreational programs, and promote new industrial
development (particularly energy). He pointed out that the city charter
had been in place, unchanged since 1916, and it needed modernization.
Addressing the needs of minorities who had long been underrepresented
in public affairs, Newton promised to establish the nation's first official
city committee on human relations, which would deal primarily with
racial issues. Finally, he promised open and responsive city government:
"The business of the city has been conducted too long behind closed
doors."[49] The public must not only be informed about problems facing
city officials, but its input was crucial in helping solve them.

A Looming Landslide

Few if any discouraging words were heard among the region's newspapers. It seemed that every pronouncement Quigg made received full and
complimentary press coverage. Almost every journalist was on his side.
A week or so after he announced that he was running, a reporter for the
Rocky Mountain Herald wrote, "His only defect, as I see it, is his willingness to take on the job at all." Following a lengthy report on
Newton's background and impressive achievements and qualifications
for public office, the reporter gushed, "I think that when Quigg gets to
ringing doorbells and kissing babies—and he'll have a hard time holding down the female age groups because he's such a wonderful guy to
look at—he ought to pack a lot of dynamite."[50]

Bill Grant and Ralph Radetsky offered to help Newton run his
campaign. Grant was an old family friend and an active lawyer. Radetsky

was a brilliant young man who worked in public relations for *Cervi's Journal*. At the time, Cervi was a strong supporter of Newton, and he was willing to "loan" one of his top men for the duration of the campaign. This arrangement would lead to serious misunderstandings between Cervi and Newton. The newspaperman assumed that Radetsky would return after the campaign, but once elected, Newton hired him as his right-hand operative in the mayor's office. As one political historian noted, Radetsky emerged as "the key campaign coordinator and rapidly became the chief strategist and speech writer."[51] Cervi also assumed that if he provided enthusiastic support and Newton was elected, he would enter the inner circle of decision-makers in city hall. When neither expectation materialized, a serious rift developed between the two men. Cervi never forgave perceived slights, and he would be a thorn in Newton's side for decades.[52]

Other key campaign operatives included Andrew Wysowatsky, a key Democrat and a veteran of many political battles. Among his Republican supporters, Will F. Nicholson (who would succeed Newton as mayor) and Mrs. May Willis, secretary of the Denver Republican Party organization, were highly placed. In addition, leaders of both the Young Democrats and the Young Republicans joined his team.

Newton had the inestimable advantage of being a fresh new face with no previous political baggage. Although supporters were attracted primarily by Newton's youth, clean-cut image, and demonstrated abilities, another key attribute in the minds of knowledgeable political operatives was that he would very likely be able to draw upon family and influential associates for generous contributions to his campaign. Such expectations were not unwarranted. Within days of his announcement, Harry Combs and Lew Hayden of Mountain States Aviation sent him a check for $500, with the assumption that it would amount to approximately 2 percent of the $25,000 he would need to run an effective campaign.[53] Combs stated that both he and Hayden wanted to be more active in the campaign but felt constrained to act behind the scenes: "It ... seems to us that our open and public support of your candidacy would only serve to emphasize your 17th street bow tie college associations in the minds of the public."[54] In fact, this would be Stapleton's primary claim, which he repeated over and over in the campaign: that his young challenger was simply the unwitting tool of the Seventeenth Street crowd.

Campaign contributions were never a problem. From the law offices and investment firms on Seventeenth Street, family associates, and old friends from Andover and Yale, $50, $100, and even $200 checks poured in. Most gratifying to Newton, however, were the hundreds of $1 and $3 checks he received from so-called ordinary citizens he had never met. Newton was the front-runner even before he announced his candidacy. Research Enterprises, a polling organization, conducted 500 interviews in the third week of February and discovered that Newton already was the preferred candidate of 39 percent of those contacted. Stapleton trailed badly with just 15 percent.[55] The incumbent was undoubtedly hurt by the fact that other candidates included U.S. District Attorney Thomas J. Morrissey, who pulled much of the local Democratic organization that Stapleton did not control, and District Judge William A. Black, a conservative Republican.

In the last month of the campaign, it became painfully obvious that time was running out for the Stapleton machine. *The Denver Post* denied him any sort of a break. One of Stapleton's key campaign issues was that he had aggressively acquired more than sufficient water to ensure the city's future growth. In an editorial titled "The Record Debunks Ben's Claim to Fame," the paper attempted to poke holes in that argument, calling him opportunistic, claiming that his actions had little to do with the eventual completion of the Moffat Tunnel: "If it reflects any glory or credit on Stapleton he is welcome to it. It is largely a record of long delays and eventual success largely made possible only by federal funds."[56]

Political reporters basically ignored the other candidates and turned the contest into a two-man race between Newton and Stapleton. Sensing the latter's increasing vulnerability, *The Post* in particular continued sniping at every perceived Stapleton shortcoming. One facet of the newspaper's campaign was indirect attacks on the incumbent. Among the ballot issues voters were asked to approve was just over $14 million in bonds for a multiproject civic improvement program. Five weeks before the vote, *The Post* commenced a lengthy series of reports labeled "Your City Program Money" by veteran reporter Robert Stapp, examining each of eleven proposed improvements in detail. The items included construction of a new art museum and a concert hall and expansion and improvement of the library, civic center, Denver General Hospital, the airport, recreational facilities, and the zoo, plus construction of a new municipal stadium. There were several other minor projects.[57]

Although the reports acknowledged the necessity of most of the improvements, the general drift of the news coverage reinforced the impression that Stapleton had been asleep on the job for decades. For example, Stapp reported that the head librarian estimated that the facility required 187,500 square feet of space to adequately house existing books and exhibits and to permit expansion in the next few years. At present, however, everything was crammed into just 37,000 square feet. In discussing proposed improvements, Stapp also observed, "In the original memorandum submitted by the mayor to his advisory committee on civic planning, the zoo was omitted entirely from the list of projects to be considered."[58]

After dissecting each of the proposed projects in detail, Stapp charged that although "persons interested in the various projects were consulted," the makeup of the mayor's advisory committee of eighteen businessmen was "not diverse enough to represent all elements of the city's population." Other cities considering such a broad array of new construction efforts had advisory committees exceeding a hundred members. In his concluding article, Stapp called the $14 million bond issue "Hodge Podge Planning" and quoted Clarence Daly, chairman of the mayor's advisory committee, in a highly unfavorable light: "It's perfectly true, this isn't an overall plan and future bond issues probably will be needed to pay for other civic improvements. But there is no reason why these worthwhile projects should be rejected just because there are other things the city needs as well."[59] Readers were left with the distinct impression that the mayor and his cronies had thrown together an ill-conceived collection of projects at the last minute in a desperate effort to protect his flank.

In related newspaper accounts reinforcing a negative impression of the Stapleton administration, *Post* reporter L. A. Chapin charged that the city accepted lucrative bids for concessions without competitive bidding. Other articles by the same reporter charged that George Cranmer and his daughter profited personally from a five-year contract for a rent-free concession to operate Echo Lake Lodge in the mountain parks' system. Numerous other concessions in parks nearer to downtown had allegedly yielded large-gross revenues but exceedingly modest returns to the city. Although Chapin did not charge outright dishonesty or provable graft, once again the tone of the stories cast suspicion on the mayor's office of lax administration of important issues, which was very detrimental to the average taxpayer's—and voter's—interest.[60]

In the final weeks of the campaign, perhaps sensing the inevitable, some city employees began to jump ship. One anonymous public employee wrote to Newton that Stapleton was pressuring city workers for campaign contributions and that he had "spies and stool pigeons everywhere." He concluded, "It is a sad commentary on democracy when one's livelihood is in jeopardy because he dares to think and act honestly and hope for an end of this Municipal reign of terror."[61] In an effort to counter such pressures, Newton sent letters to many city employees reassuring them if he won the election they would keep their jobs if qualified to hold them and that there would be no clean sweep of officeholders. Newton wrote to one employee: "Whatever part you play in this campaign is a decision you must make for yourself, as a citizen of Denver. But let me assure you again, that, as mayor, I will not inquire into any employe's [*sic*] past political activity."[62] Visiting Stapleton's quarters a few weeks before the election, a reporter observed John Malpiede, the city electrician, trying to rally the troops. Malpiede was quoted as telling district captains, "If you fellows will stop wasting your time around the city hall, buttonholing people to find out who they are going to vote for, if you will get out into your districts and work, we still have a chance."[63]

Victory!

In the final days of the campaign, everything broke Newton's way and against Stapleton. Stapleton tried to score points with the claim that Quigg had been absent from Denver for most of his thirty-five years. In fact, in order to be eligible to run for mayor, a candidate had to be able to prove that he had been a taxpayer in Denver for two or three years. Fortunately for the challenger, several years earlier his mother had insisted that he pay personal property taxes on the piano in her house that he had bought from his grandmother's estate. By producing proof of the transaction, he technically qualified to run for the office.

Stapleton's intimation that Newton was a "carpetbagger" proved ineffective; many residents were newcomers or had been uprooted during the war, and this appeal failed to resonate with voters. Thomas Morrissey's supporters also resorted to ad hominem attacks, claiming that Quigg was the "second choice of Seventeenth Street."[64] A week before the election, Bruce Gustin, a veteran *Post* political reporter, noted, "Realization that Newton is the only genuine nonpartisan in the mayoral race drives the professional politicians to desperation."[65]

The mayor even managed to make a spectacle of himself in public. The minor-league Denver Bears opened their final full baseball season in old Merchants Park on South Broadway in mid-May. During the opening ceremonies, young congressman Richard M. Nixon tossed a soft pitch to Stapleton, who was supposed to strike it with his bat. The seventy-seven-year-old mayor gamely swung and missed, then fell, sprawled across home plate. An alert *Saturday Evening Post* photographer snapped the undignified image. Newton would not use the picture, but the magazine published a full-page photo of the event eight days before voters went to the polls, bearing the caption "Mayor Strikes Out." It was an apt metaphor for the entire Stapleton campaign.

The highly anticipated election finally arrived. Newton was swept into office by an absolute majority, with 79,695 votes. Thomas Morrissey was second, with 35,080 votes, and Stapleton finished a humiliating and distant third, with only 17,640 party faithful refusing to abandon the sinking ship. Two other candidates, William A. Black and William Dietrich, divided 6,000 votes. Newton's landslide total was 21,000 more than for all other candidates combined.

In the days following the election, accolades poured in. Quigg's victory generated sizeable stories in *The New York Times*, the *Christian Science Monitor, Look,* and other nationally prominent news organs. Quigg and Ginny received congratulatory letters and telegrams from hundreds of family members, friends, and supporters. Ben Loeblein wrote that "the people that voted for you will not be sorry that they elected you. I only wish one thing and that is that your Dear old Dad was still with us, so that he could see you take that mayor job over. … "[66] A well-connected lawyer friend in Washington celebrated Quigg's election: "For your information, all your friends around these parts take it for granted that, having done so well in this election, it will only be a short period of time before we will be calling you 'Governor Newton' or 'Senator Newton.'"[67] But a few old friends made sure he wouldn't get a swelled head. From California, Ben Leib, a friend from his days at Yale, wrote, "It has come to my attention that you have bamboozled the Denver voters into one of the greatest election stampedes west of the Alps. I have always had an uneasy feeling that you would do this some day to the people, after the time that you talked me out of the 21st hole at the Stanford Golf Course, and also several gallons of beer."[68]

As mayor-elect, Newton had no illusions about the hard work ahead. If he had, his future constituents did not allow him to bask in glory for long. Within days of his election, he began receiving dozens of solicitations for preferred placement in his administration and requests for city business. Elwood M. Brooks, president of the Central Bank and Trust Company of Denver, observed that his institution had a deposit of some $450,000 from the Stapleton administration. Rather than drawing interest on the deposit, the city was actually paying a fee for management of this account! Brooks wrote, "I assume this practice was instituted back in the dark banking days."[69] The banker undoubtedly assumed that a bright young mayor-elect would quickly discover and put a stop to such inefficient and costly financial mismanagement, and he wanted his institution to be on record as being on the right side of the issue from the start. Earl W. Mann of the city's water department informed Newton that he was "a Negro" and "echoe[d] the sentiments of ever [*sic*] lover of fair play and justice when I say we are brothers in the effort to make the people happier, and the sad less miserable." The long and the short of it was that Mann was "with you."[70] Wendell T. Liggins, minister of the predominantly African American Zion Baptist Church, wrote a letter "in recommendation of one of my fine friends and co-workers in our church who to my mind would be an asset in the employ of our great city in whatsoever capacity, commensurate with his ability, you might suggest."[71] Thus, as the cool days of May dwindled and the warm days of June 1947 began, the young mayor-elect realized that there was little time for self-congratulation. After decades of examining local and state government issues in Colorado, he was eager and more than ready to take on the task of running a vital, growing city.

CHAPTER 6

GRASPING THE REINS OF POWER

Shortly after Newton took the oath of office as mayor, a news photographer snapped a photograph of outgoing Mayor Ben Stapleton and his youthful successor posed before a picture window at city hall. Stapleton's left arm was draped casually over Quigg's shoulder, while the veteran politico's eyes were directed to a scene outside the window. The uninitiated might imagine that he was sharing inside secrets of running a large city successfully. The photo implied a cordial and orderly transfer of power, but appearances were misleading. Newton was not seeking guidance from his predecessor, and Stapleton essentially kept his files in his head. When Stapleton vacated the office and Newton sat in the mayor's chair for the first time, he was surrounded by little but empty drawers, a few filing cabinets, and numerous spittoons. Years later, Newton laughingly recalled that the first thing he did as mayor was to get rid of the spittoons.[1]

Quigg Newton and outgoing mayor Benjamin F. Stapleton. The photo implies a cordial transition, which did not in fact occur.

109

Taking over the Reins

As soon as Newton was sworn in, he got down to business. At the top of Quigg's list of campaign promises was to bring structure and professionalism to virtually every aspect of administering the needs of a growing city and region. There was no better place to start than with Denver's antiquated and inefficient personnel system. In Newton's view, hiring and firing had been guided not by the prospective employee's energy, education, and qualifications for preferred jobs, but by cronyism and political favoritism. In one of his first meetings with city employees, Newton previewed future personnel policies. He noted that there were as many separate hiring systems as city departments. Under Stapleton, each department head basically operated a private fiefdom. Although rumors had been rife about a wholesale cleansing of city hall once Newton took over, he reassured workers that nobody would be fired because of having worked for Stapleton, as long as they were "qualified for their jobs, capable of doing an honest day's work, [and] capable of loyalty to the principles of the new administration."[2] Newton promised to develop uniform standards regulating hiring, firing, sick time, vacations, administration of other employee benefits, and recommending promotions. Promotions and pay increases

Ginny and Quigg greet friends and well-wishers at a reception following his inauguration as mayor on June 1, 1947.

would be based on merit, not favoritism. Newton brought in Hugh Catherwood, a classmate at Yale, to oversee modernization of the personnel system. Catherwood had captained a landing ship tank vessel during World War II and had experience as a consultant in city government. To the dismay of only a few old Stapleton loyalists, a thoroughly professionalized personnel system was in place within a year.

A few of Stapleton's associates didn't understand the new culture, and they were soon weeded out of city hall. The following episode illustrates the changes taking place. Along with modernizing and professionalizing the city's personnel office, Newton and Catherwood also attempted to put some backbone in the city's moribund planning office by giving it a significant project. Although there had been a planning department for more than twenty years, it had generated few, if any, constructive ideas and possessed virtually no clout. That was largely because conservative business interests in Denver wanted full control, even veto power, over future development.

Newton challenged these interests, and he asked Maxine Kurtz, a young, energetic recent appointee to the department to prepare a "think piece" suggesting future city projects, emphasizing those that might be developed in cooperation with the movers and shakers in rapidly growing suburban areas. The document was to remain confidential until it could be fully aired in official meetings. Kurtz returned unexpectedly early from lunch one day, only to find a seasoned secretary reading aloud sections of the confidential document over the phone. Obviously, "insiders" were being given advance indications about where city officials were contemplating establishing new facilities. Clearly, such projects would greatly increase the value of vacant property.

The staffer promptly reported the incident to Newton, who wanted to fire the secretary on the spot. Kurtz suggested avoiding a direct confrontation and setting a trap instead. She proposed indefinitely suspending action on any project mentioned in the document. Presumably, the secretary's contacts would buy up property, anticipating a "killing" when the projects were announced. In the meantime, the secretary would be denied access to all other confidential memos. Years later, Kurtz recalled, "The Mayor liked that idea, and we put it into action. A couple of months later, the secretary suddenly informed me that she was going to retire at the end of that month. She didn't wait that long; over a weekend she used the key to her office, cleaned out her desk, and was never seen or heard from again."[3]

Most city employees, at least those who stuck out the transition, liked the quickened pace and the fact that Newton and his energetic protégés were creating an entirely new atmosphere in city hall. Newton was profoundly grateful to several capable, loyal assistants for assistance in bringing order out of chaos. None was more important than Ralph Radetsky, who was a year older than his new boss. A Denver native who had attended the University of Colorado and edited the student newspaper, Radetsky enjoyed a distinguished career in journalism and public relations. During World War II, he had served under Gene Cervi in the Office of War Information, and he had been involved with radio and press arrangements for the Bretton Woods international monetary conference, the world aviation conference in Chicago, and the United Nations charter session in San Francisco.[4] Before Newton's campaign for mayor, Radetsky worked closely with Cervi, helping produce Cervi's paper. As noted previously, Quigg had "borrowed" him from Cervi during the election campaign. Radetsky joined Newton's staff and quickly became his right-hand man.

Another key assistant was Bruce Rockwell. After Rockwell graduated near the top of his class from East High School, Jim Newton had helped him win a scholarship to Yale. Academic training was mixed in with military service, and Rockwell graduated just as World War II ended. With Newton, Rockwell received his baptism under fire, helping to handle some of the city's worst messes. He recalled being asked to help Quigg's new public works director, Charlie Berry, a tough and experienced contractor, straighten out that thoroughly demoralized department. According to Rockwell, before Berry assumed command, public works had been a "dumping ground" for dozens of Stapleton's party hacks, and the atmosphere in the department reeked of incompetence, indifference, and laziness.[5]

One of Newton's chief criticisms of Stapleton was that after several terms in office, he had become very remote from the city council, many department heads, and particularly his constituents. Quigg resolved to change that by conducting weekly meetings with the city council. Stapleton had called such meetings infrequently; the few that did take place were essentially "rubber stamp" affairs, where council members basically ratified decisions that had already been made in Stapleton's office.[6] Newton, in contrast, informed council members that he considered that body a branch of government equal to the mayor's office. He did, however, reserve the right to set a prearranged agenda. In addition, he stated that he would hold *two* news conferences daily, one in the morning for the afternoon papers, and one later in the day for the morning paper. Reporters had been fortunate if they could see Stapleton once in two weeks; they often had to settle for a few mumbled words from one of his aides. Such open access granted by Newton was unprecedented in Denver. The downside was that the news conferences consumed valuable time and energy; within a few weeks, he stopped doing them twice daily.

Newton learned that there were certain issues over which he had little, if any, control, yet constituents somehow expected him to work miracles. Some of the most sensitive cases involved city personnel. In one case, Quigg received an anonymous letter from a "group of constituents in the blocks of 1500 and 1600 South Josephine" complaining about repeated drunken excesses of a high-ranking department head, who allegedly was often "so drunk he [had] to crawl up the terrace into his yard and house." The letter continued: "[We] and our children have to listen to violent arguments with threats by him to kill his wife and children because of his philandering with his secretary, who we understand is a city police officers [*sic*] wife." The writers complained, "We have watched him prowl the neighborhood with a flashlight at night. Why? We don't know." Pleading that "the wife is being slowly driven out of her mind," the writers begged Newton to take the matter in hand: "We feel, Mr. Mayor, that something should be done and that you are the man to do it."[7] Unfortunately, there is no record of Quigg's response, if any.

Charter Reform Considered

Although Newton made many shrewd moves in his first months in office, he also learned some hard lessons. Among his campaign issues was a promise to overhaul the antiquated city charter, adopted originally in 1904. But even as voters overwhelmingly elected him, they only narrowly approved a ballot initiative to draft an entirely new charter. Newton actually would have preferred to work within the existing charter, gradually revising its provisions as situations warranted. But the people had spoken. Moving quickly, Quigg created a slate of twenty-one respected citizens to draft a proposed new charter. Rather than stack the convention with supporters who thought the way he did, he included people representing a comprehensive range of views. They went right to work. After sixty days of concentrated effort, the delegates submitted a simplified and streamlined document that, among other things, created a runoff election system, a merit system for all city employees under which the mayor lost hiring and firing rights, mandatory competitive bids on city contracts, modernization of the city's antiquated accounting procedures, limitations on political activities by city employees, and significant salary hikes for certain city officials.[8]

One political historian stated that, unfortunately for the mayor, "there were ... a few sharks in the lagoon of civic harmony," who quickly "formed a school."[9] City auditor William H. McNichols Sr., attorney Victor Miller, a "concerned citizen" and self-proclaimed defender of the taxpayers named James Renner, and key representatives of the Library Commission and the Board of Water Commissioners were determined not to yield power to a political neophyte. As the November date of the referendum on the proposed new charter approached, Newton grew increasingly ambivalent over whether to endorse the end product. For the record, he sided with acceptance.

Speaking live over the radio four weeks before the election, Quigg said, "I have no hesitation in stating that it represents not only a big forward stride for Denver, but also a substantial advance in the science of democratic city government. I believe that by adopting this charter we will establish in Denver a system of modern municipal government that will become a model throughout the United States."[10] Privately, he thought that the revisions might be too extreme and that they could well have unintended consequences. He had no objection to raising salaries of other city officials; in fact, many high-level officials were so poorly paid he had trouble attracting qualified individuals to fill slots. However, the new document would have raised his admittedly paltry mayor's salary above the current level of $6,000 per year. Thus, he believed that his active public endorsement of the new charter could be interpreted as a conflict of interest.

On November 13, 1947, voters narrowly rejected charter reform by approximately 5,000 votes. A few of Newton's associates analyzed the reasons why it failed. If there was a consensus, it centered on the idea that he had, perhaps, attempted to fulfill one campaign promise too quickly. One observer claimed that the new mayor had identified himself too closely with a particular slate of delegates. They represented an impressive cross-section of interests in the region, but did not produce a document providing uniform improvement: "The result was that the Convention, with your help adopted a compromise charter between people with wide differences with the argument that it was the best the people would support."[11] In a speech to the Yale Law Club a year and a half later, Newton ruminated that he and his administration might have come across as dewy-eyed reformers in those first few weeks: "Yet we did not pretend to be, or want to be a 'reform' government. ... The people ... don't like the cold, objective sternness of reform governments. Every once in a while they like to

The hardworking young mayor at his desk during his first term.

throw the rascals out, but they don't like to replace them with saints, because saints are just plain uncomfortable to have around." Suggestive of his political maturation after his first two years in office, Newton allowed, "We may, at the end of four years, find that impartial, objective government—no matter how attractively it is garnished for serving—is still an unappetizing cold fish."[12]

Early Political Lessons

The new mayor made a few other political miscalculations in his first months in office. With the approach of the Christmas holidays, city workers traditionally decorated the City and County Building with bright and highly festive Christmas lights. Thousands of local citizens enjoyed driving down Broadway Boulevard at night just to gaze at the spectacle. Newton believed that the decorations were in bad taste and far too garish, and he ordered that the display be toned down. Newspaper columnists provided biting criticism of his autocratic decision-making, and the mayor received an avalanche of angry letters from outraged citizens. Needless to say, Quigg promptly learned an indelible lesson, and the bright lights went back up immediately.[13]

Over the years, numerous reporters described Newton as a dedicated and sober-minded executive who approached his responsibilities in a serious manner. Although there is truth to this assessment, Quigg had an uncanny ability to poke fun at himself at appropriate moments. It seemed that the city's leading politician could find trouble in the most unexpected circumstances. In one radio talk, Quigg recounted a visit to Denver by Roy Rogers, a midcentury cowboy movie hero loved by millions of American youngsters. Evidently, Rogers was being welcomed at one part of city hall, and a police cordon was posted outside an exit to escort the star to his next appointment. Newton innocently left the building, only to be quickly engulfed in a swarm of confused children. Moments later, Rogers emerged from a nearby door. Someone in the crowd recognized him, and hundreds of kids stampeded down the sidewalk in pursuit of their idol. Tongue-in-cheek, Quigg recounted how his appearance disappointed many future constituents: "I do blame those who were in charge of his visit. Certainly his studio publicity department has had experiences of this sort before. ... [P]eople may well assume—and I among them—that the studio prefers the type of publicity which comes from disorder, the type which says: 'Fans Mob Movie Star.'"[14]

Salaries and Taxes

One of the most vexing issues for the mayor was the fact that salaries of public officials were absurdly low. Shortly after taking office, Newton ordered a review of salary schedules; his staff's report showed that public officials' salaries in the Queen City had not been raised since 1916: "And as for public employment, Denver's salaries for city officials are by far the lowest of comparable cities."[15] The mayor's salary in 1947 was just $6,000, and one source claimed that he spent three times his official salary to support his family.[16] Newton's own low pay did not concern him as much as it did Ginny. Quigg realized that unless appropriate action were taken, attracting and retaining capable public servants would become next to impossible. During his run for office, his campaign managers had managed to accumulate a small surplus, and Newton apparently used portions of it to supplement salaries of a few key officials informally.[17] But following any such unorthodox strategy over the long-term was obviously impossible; it would potentially create a minefield of resentments, not to mention charges of secret "slush funds" and rank favoritism.

By a variety of temporary expedients, Newton managed to raise salaries of key personnel to competitive levels. He realized that if the city were to be run effectively, he had little choice but to make numerous "exceptions." Late in his first term as mayor, twenty-two public officials on his staff made more money than he did. In March 1951, the head of the public health department earned $11,700, almost twice Quigg's salary.[18] In the mayoral election of 1951, voters finally agreed to support more realistic salaries for public officials. Although Newton suggested in 1948 that the mayor's salary be increased to $10,000, an independent salary survey three years later determined that it should be increased to $14,000.

Years later, when preparing to leave the mayor's office in 1955, Newton cited increases in wages and benefits for city workers as one of his proudest achievements. Salaries for virtually all public employees had been doubled, and in some cases nearly tripled. Workers on the lowest rungs on the public-service ladder enjoyed the largest percentage increases. For example, food service workers who had earned $62 per month in 1946 earned $171 over the same period in 1954. Comparable figures for practical nurses were $73 and $187. In 1946, many employees worked forty-eight hours, and almost all others worked at least forty-four. By 1955, the work week for all nonmanagerial employees was firmly set at forty hours. Every public employee enjoyed eleven paid holidays, up from just five such days off in 1946.[19]

Despite his youth and lack of political experience, Newton was not reluctant to tackle potentially sticky issues—including some that he might have easily sidestepped. During the national housing crisis accompanying the enormous dislocations of World War II, the Office of Price Administration (OPA) had controlled rents that landlords could charge. When the OPA was dismantled a year after the end of the war, mayors in most of the nation's cities were faced with the thorny political and ethical issue of whether to institute and enforce local rent controls. Many landlords hoped to recoup revenues lost because of federal price controls, and they jacked up rents whenever and wherever they found legal loopholes in hastily drawn up local rent control guidelines. Newton chose to stick up for some of the city's poorest and relatively powerless citizens: the marginally employed and often elderly people who lived in some of the city's hotels. A few local residents, evidently anticipating a political double-cross, gave Newton almost no time to act in their behalf. Shortly after being sworn in, Quigg received a letter from one constituent claiming that she was about to be thrown out of her house because she couldn't pay her rapidly rising rent. She complained that while Newton was running for office, he had made lots of promises but was now forgetting about them: "[It] seems as soon as the oath of office is taken the promises are taboo."[20]

It is unlikely that this particular voter's letter alone stirred Quigg to action, but he was aware that rent controls were a highly sensitive issue. A

month later, he released a statement that charged some hotel operators
with gouging helpless residents: "Denver for many years has had one of
the most acute housing shortages in the United States. The primary effect
of the partial decontrol [of rents] in Denver is being felt by the permanent
residents of hotels." While praising "the vast majority of hotel operators
who were keeping rate increases at reasonable levels," Newton insisted,
"The city has an obligation to protect the many residents of hotels who
are in danger of being homeless because of their inability to pay increases,
which in some cases are as high as 300 percent."[21] In response to the crisis,
Newton introduced two ordinances that extended eviction notice periods
from ten to thirty days and held rent increases to a maximum of 25 percent over rents that prevailed on June 30, 1947. He also voiced regret that
the city had no authority over rents charged in the dozens of "tourist
courts" that were outside of the city limits.

Virtually every individual who has ever been responsible for
administering public funds would agree that taxpayers almost invariably
believe they are paying more than their fair share and that far too much
of their hard-earned money is being squandered irresponsibly, if not with
criminal intent. Although a political neophyte when elected, Mayor
Newton showed the instincts of a veteran in directly addressing the "fairness" issue in regularly scheduled radio broadcasts to the public. Quigg
astutely implied that local citizens might have cause for complaint, due
in part to the appallingly sloppy record keeping of his predecessor.

In one early radio talk, he noted that the city owned between
25,000 and 40,000 small parcels of land that for one reason or another
were not on the tax rolls. The implication was clear: there had been ram-
pant political favoritism on the part of the Stapleton administration.
Thousands of pieces of land had been bought and sold, and responsible
officials casually admitted that they simply kept track of the exchanges
informally. Newton recalled interviewing a veteran city employee who
stated, "It's this way, Mayor. ... I always figured that the more I kept in
my head, the harder it would be for anybody to fire me, and I think it
worked out pretty well. Everybody around my office has to come to me
for information, and I usually know the answers. They all depend on

me. Matter of fact, I've just about made myself indispensable." Newton
didn't fire him, but he insisted that a modern inventory of city property
be implemented. In addition, he promised either to sell the parcels to
generate revenue or make sure that all unsold parcels were put back on
the tax rolls.[22]

The new mayor realized the acute sensitivity of the issue of the
fairness of property tax assessments. For starters, he hired a capable executive, Harvey Wilson, as manager of revenue. According to Bruce
Rockwell, it took Wilson about two years to modernize tax collections.[23]
Newton repeatedly addressed assessments in his public addresses. In his
radio talks, Quigg brought up the issue, directly or otherwise, at least
once a month. He announced revision of the system by which tax
appraisers would assess property in the future. He explained that he had
personally attended the opening session of the city's training of household appraisers. There were approximately forty-five persons in the class,
about half of them new employees. Newton explained that they were
not political hacks; they had passed written exams demonstrating that
they were fully qualified to do their jobs.

In his appearance before the group, Newton provided specific suggestions about how they should comport themselves when they visited
taxpayers' homes. Quigg reflected upon the fact that household appraisers were "generally not very popular," in part because the public had the
impression that they were rude and made arbitrary appraisals that were
very difficult to challenge. He was acutely aware that, in the minds of
many citizens, the impression the appraisers made directly affected his
administration: "As appraisers, you men will be in direct touch with virtually every taxpayer in the city, and to a great extent the policies and the
character of the entire city administration will be judged by the impression you make." He urged the men to get off on the right foot in their
interviews with homeowners: "Do not go into a house with the assumption that the taxpayer is dishonest, because that is a false assumption and
a dangerous attitude. You will find that the great majority of the people
will cooperate fully with you *if you succeed in convincing them that they are
receiving the same treatment as their neighbors*, that everyone is being taxed

according to the same uniform standards, and that there is no special privilege or favoritism for anyone" (emphasis added).[24]

From tax collections to confrontations between management and labor, Newton was not afraid of taking on tough issues. Early in 1950, the *Rocky Mountain News* gave Newton high marks for intervening in a threatened milk strike. A *News* editorial observed that many public officials would have sidestepped the issue as being outside of their area of responsibility or that they might plead that they were unfamiliar with the issue. Newton, however, got both sides together and eventually jawboned a truce.[25]

Radio Talks

In his commitment to maintain an "open" administration, Newton started weekly thirty-minute appearances on radio KLZ every Sunday afternoon. The show, titled *Mayor's Mailbag*, wasn't aired live; rather, it was taped. Quigg had extensive experience in formal debate at Yale, and he had delivered numerous public talks on reforming local government in the early 1940s. Thus, he was comfortable behind a microphone. In question-and-answer sessions reminiscent of Franklin Roosevelt's famous "fireside chats," Newton would quote directly from letters written by constituents, citing their complaints or concerns, and then explain how his office or the appropriate city agency would address the problem. In a few cases, he explained why situations were beyond his or the city's control. The show was, by most accounts, quite popular. If he did not always satisfy constituents, many Denverites who held negative feelings toward local government had a sense that their individual concerns were at least being recognized for the first time in years.

Perhaps most important, Newton *humanized* city government. Listeners were almost certainly charmed when Quigg recounted receiving a letter from a mother of two young boys in England, a country still suffering severe postwar shortages of many commodities. For weeks, the boys had been pestering her to try to get them some bubble gum, a newly emerging and highly popular treat for youngsters. The boys and their mother had sat down with an atlas and selected Denver as a place where they might find it. The mother wrote to Newton, "As I know nobody in America, you are the unfortunate recipient of this letter." In their appeal, the boys had sent along a small box of English sweets, which the mother estimated was about forty cents' worth. Quigg was so affected by the appeal that he recounted it during a Sunday talk. He told his listeners, "I know the Edwards family can't listen to this broadcast, but it is being recorded, and a record containing this section will be sent to them—along with a box of Bubble Gum and six American candy bars. I am happy to comply with your request, Clinton and Teddy, but I hope your parents won't hold me responsible for what may happen after you once get going on Bubble Gum—and I hope it won't cause any international complications. The gum is being sent you with the best wishes of all of the youngsters in Denver. ... "[26]

Regular listeners could not help but gain a sense of the mundane nature of many demands and requests that the mayor received. Although Newton was a modern, forward-thinking leader in a dynamic, growing metropolitan region, some of the issues he had to deal with retained a small-town flavor. One of the most frequent complaints of citizens concerned regulation of pets, particularly dogs. It seemed that correspondents either loved them or hated them; there was no apparent middle ground. Newton recalled one persistent citizen who regularly complained about dogs running wild around his neighborhood. After several complaining letters, Newton invited him to visit city hall, but the man didn't take him up on it. Instead, he kept writing nasty letters. As Quigg recounted, the most recent incident concerned the "disgraceful sight" of "a large group of male dogs in pursuit of a lone female dog—a situation for which he clearly considers me personally responsible."[27]

In another Sunday talk, Newton confessed that when it came to regulating dogs, neither he nor any other city leader could win. He recounted talking to a councilman who told him that the only issue that he was really nervous about was dog control. The veteran politician recalled voting for an ordinance calling for strict regulation of pooches, then being kept awake all night by angry phone calls from constituents calling him a dog hater. Some time later, he voted *against* a dog control regulation, and he was bombarded with equally angry calls charging that he had "no respect for private property, no regard for flowers and lawns." Someone even threatened to "come out and rip up his garden and lawn."[28] Newton wisely tried to take a middle-of-the road approach, advocating a modern system of licensing dogs.

At times, being very accessible had its drawbacks. In the middle of the twentieth century, most urbanites probably felt less threatened physically than they do today. Most politicians felt safer as well. Newton allowed his home telephone number to be listed in the directory! At times, constituents called him with complaints at all hours of the day— and night. Ginny Newton recalled answering the phone once at about 3:00 A.M. The caller was being kept awake by airplanes departing from Stapleton Airport. She demanded that Newton close down the airport immediately so she could sleep in peace.[29]

Relatively early in his first term as mayor, Newton recounted an incident that demonstrated his quickly developing political instincts. A particularly insistent resident was pressing hard for construction of a municipal swimming pool in his neighborhood. The man had lived in Denver for fifty years, and he presented the mayor with facts and figures to support his request. Newton agreed that he had presented a well-supported case and then invited the man to take a ride with him to examine numerous other projects competing for relatively scarce city revenues. Following the outing, the man conceded that his neighborhood's project should probably wait until the next bond issue. Quigg praised his companion, noting, "That's the kind of citizenship—the kind that is based on understanding and a picture of the needs of the entire city—that makes my job much easier, whenever I encounter it."[30]

Over several years of Sunday talks, Newton provided his listeners with a running commentary that provided a wonderful sense of the myriad common, everyday issues that consumed his time. In one radio address in the summer of 1948, Newton devoted half of his time to reviewing the city's mosquito control policies.[31] In addition to ongoing complaints about swimming pools, there were numerous demands for improved mainte-nance and staffing of other recreational facilities. There was continuing controversy over sanitation in Denver's restaurants. Motorists who received parking and speeding tickets often protested that the police should spend their time pursuing *real* criminals. On one occasion, such complainers included the mayor's extended family members. Ginny's uncle, Admiral John F. Shafroth Jr., returned to Denver while Quigg was mayor and received a speeding ticket on his way back to the airport. He mailed the summons to his brother, Morrison Shafroth, Quigg's father-in-law. The admiral obviously felt that the mayor should "fix" it. Morrison in fact called Quigg and offered to pay half the fine if Quigg would put up the other half.[32] Unfortunately, there is no record of Quigg's response.

Family Life

Although being mayor raised Newton's visibility both locally and nationally, he tried to ensure that his deep involvement in public life did not unduly disrupt his family life. He was, of course, a young father. The oldest two daughters, Nan and Nelle, had been born in Washington during World War II. While he was mayor, two more daughters were born. Abby entered the world on February 7, 1948, and Ginna arrived on June 14, 1950. When Newton was first elected mayor, the family lived at 75 Cherry Street, but as the family expanded, the couple needed a larger home. They decided on a roomy, comfortable house at 712 Corona, which was very centrally located. The drawback was that it was also quite old, requiring extensive renovations, including new plumbing, rugs, and wallpaper. Murphy's Law prevailed, as everything that could go wrong seemingly did. The couple was scheduled to move in during February 1949, but they had to wait until May of that year.[33] Fortunately, it was worth the wait. The new home was quickly filled with laughter, music, friends of the children, and assorted pets.

Newton was not an early riser, since he often put in late hours. He was usually out of bed by 8:00 A.M. After a quick breakfast with his family, his chauffeur would pick him up and deliver him to his office by about 9:00 A.M. Following a full day's work, during which lunch often consisted of a sandwich at his desk, he might return home by 6:00 P.M. to shower and change clothes before departing for some official evening function.[34] Ginny recalled that when Quigg was elected, they agreed that she would usually accompany him during evenings out, as long as she was spared from civic responsibilities during the day. For her, daytime was usually devoted to raising the children and giving music lessons. Four or five nights a week, the city's first couple was on display at some important gathering. Since Quigg's driver worked an eight-hour day, the couple drove themselves to after-hours events. Evenings out almost always involved dinners, and Quigg and Ginny were almost always seated at the head table. More often than not, the mayor was expected to speak.

Given his hectic schedule, Newton did not have a lot of time to spend with his daughters. Having been born in 1943, Nan, the oldest daughter, remembered the mayoral years quite well. Both of her parents were serious-minded people. Because of her father's long workdays, she almost never saw him fully relaxed and remembers him as being quite remote. Instinctively, she realized he was an important figure, although he downplayed the significance of his career. Still, Nan remembered feeling a bit different from her friends, that her father was almost like the king of Denver. That realization made her feel special, almost like royalty. She watched him conduct Sunday afternoon talks to his constituents after they switched from radio to television.

Both of her parents were incessant readers, and they encouraged their daughters to read. In addition to providing music lessons, Ginny Newton frequently read to her daughters, and on some occasions, Quigg would read to the girls during his few evenings at home at bedtime. Nan recalled that he read classics such as *Little Women, The Wind in the Willows,* and *Little Britches.* She realized that her parents were in solid agreement that it was their responsibility always to push their daughters to excel. Since their mother spent far more time with the girls than their father did, she was the primary disciplinarian. Quigg never laid a disapproving hand on any of the girls, but they recalled dreading his lectures about good behavior and what their parents expected of them. Perhaps, as his own father had imparted to him, Newton had definite expectations about how his children should order their lives.[35]

The busy mayor pauses for an evening reading to daughters Nelle and Nan (ca. 1947).

Ginny practicing piano with Nelle and Nan (ca. 1948).

Nan's younger sister, Abby, born in 1948, recalled being about four or five years old and riding in a car with one of her friends, who innocently threw some blades of grass out the car window. Abby immediately admonished her, saying that she couldn't do that because her daddy had to clean the streets. Abby recounted another occasion when her older sister, Nan, was in grade school and studying about animals. Her teacher informed the class that female horses were called mares. According to Abby, her sister piped up in class, "Oh, my daddy's a mare!"[36]

Ginny Newton recalled a number of interesting evenings out. More often than not, Governor Lee Knous was also included. Knous usually preceded Newton to the podium to deliver some remarks, usually including a joke. Since he appeared before different groups, the governor slipped into the habit of almost always telling the same joke. One night, Quigg was scheduled to speak ahead of Knous, and Ginny urged her husband to steal Knous's joke.

But Quigg wouldn't do it, even on a dare. As long as he was in public life, Newton prided himself on preparing original speeches for almost every occasion. He would sometimes toss ideas out to Ralph Radetsky or another trusted aide, who might actually craft the words.

Usually, the first couple was seated together, but on one large and important occasion, Ginny and Quigg were seated apart, each accompanied by a different dinner partner. The mayor was seated at the head table next to a lovely blonde actress, and Ginny was at a regular table with other guests. Because he hadn't had time to review his remarks, Quigg was worried about how his address would come across and was, therefore, concentrating wholly on the speech he was about to deliver. He appeared utterly unaware of his dinner partner's charms. Ginny's companion piped up, "Boy, you must really have him on a tight leash!"[37]

Investing in Television
During his years as mayor, Newton found the time to become a part-time businessman once again. In the past, Quigg and his father had often discussed the future of radio and the communications industry. In

Ginny photographing Nan, newly arrived Abby, Quigg, and Nelle (ca. 1949).

1952, there was still only one television station in Denver, KFEL, which had burst upon the scene in the summer of 1948, broadcasting shows from ABC, CBS, NBC, and Dumont. Newton requested his top aide, Ralph Radetsky, to explore the possibilities of obtaining a television license. Bill Grant was also involved from the earliest days. Quigg believed there was plenty of room for more stations, and Radetsky's detailed report reached the same conclusion.

Because of an antitrust conflict of interest, NBC was forced to sell one of its radio stations, KOA. Newton believed that if he and his associates purchased KOA, they would have a leg up on any potential competitors in bringing another television station to the city. Newton had received a $100,000 payout from a life insurance policy his father had purchased, and against the advice of his father-in-law, he decided to invest the entire amount in television. But he and several friends, whom he had asked to join his bid, worried that, even as a group, they didn't have sufficiently deep pockets to swing the deal or to bid seriously if rivals showed serious interest.

Newton and his friends nevertheless entered negotiations, and just as the action was heating up, he received a phone call from Bob

Quigg and several business associates brought Denver's second television station to Denver in the early 1950s. A key partner in the deal was comedian Bob Hope (front row, seated, far left). Mayor Newton's top aide, Ralph Radetsky, is wearing glasses and standing directly behind Hope. Quigg is seated in the front row, far right, with his close associate Bill Grant seated next to him.

Hope. The famous entertainer knew all about Quigg, whom he had good-naturedly nicknamed the "Mayor of Boy's Town." He had also talked to Quigg at a banquet in Denver. Hope asked Newton if he wanted a partner in purchasing KOA. Quigg answered a delighted, "Yes!" and Hope and the Newton group formed a partnership named Metropolitan Television Company.[38]

Obtaining a license from the Federal Communications Commission (FCC) was an enormous challenge, in part because a competing group emerged. They were supported by none other than Colorado's Democratic U.S. senator "Big Ed" Johnson, who testified on their behalf. However, Newton's consortium hired an FCC lawyer from Washington to present their case. In addition, Radetsky knew the communications business extremely well, and he was masterful at preparing witnesses to testify. Their witnesses emphasized what Newton's associates would do in terms of community service.[39] Negotiations were lengthy and difficult, but the mayor's group eventually prevailed. With Hope's support, KOA and NBC reached an agreement to broadcast its shows, the first of which was on Christmas Eve 1953.

Quigg's partner Bob Hope also helped the second-term mayor promote airline service in Denver in the early 1950s. Hope (on stairs with cowboy hat), assorted Hollywood celebrities and airline officials, and a beaming Quigg (far right) are helping promote Continental Airlines.

Newton's direct involvement in commercial television occurred deep into his second term as mayor, more than a half-century ago. Today, any such activities by an elected official would likely be construed as being in direct conflict of interest, but they were very common back then. More to the point is that Newton never used his position as mayor to improve his own financial interests, and nobody ever accused him of doing so. In his own mind and those of an overwhelming number of citizens, Quigg and his partners were performing a welcome public service in doubling overnight the amount of entertainment and information available through television. Long before KOA broadcast its first offerings, Newton had gained his constituents' trust, and for the most part, their deep affection. In large part, he had done so by repeatedly demonstrating forward-looking, inspired leadership in his city and the region.

Quigg's television and "Hollywood connections" brought visits to the Mile High City from numerous movie celebrities, including Roy Rogers and Errol Flynn (shown here with the young mayor in 1947).

CHAPTER 7

∽

REGIONAL VISIONARY

Throughout his eight jam-packed years as political leader of the Queen City, Quigg Newton dealt with many complex issues. Most, if not all of them, were a consequence of rapid change and growth. When the new mayor assumed his duties in the summer of 1947, Denver was obviously primed for a major growth spurt. According to Newton and most contemporary experts in the workings of regional political, economic, and social development all across the nation, there was an urgent need for coordinated decision-making at both local and regional levels. With the exception of the Public Works Administration, the Works Progress Administration (WPA), and a few other federal government projects, for nearly two full decades, urban development and most civic improvements had been postponed or cancelled—first by the catastrophic financial consequences of the Depression, then by strict limitations on building during World War II.

Population Growth and Regional Cooperation

Rapid change was in the air when Quigg stepped into office. Some of the changes, including the decentralization of regional population, affected the manner in which future decisions would be made. In 1940, Denver had contained almost four-fifths of the population in the surrounding region: more than 322,000 out of a total of just under 408,000 citizens. The populations of Jefferson and Arapahoe Counties were just over 30,000 each, and Adams County was home to just over 22,000 dwellers. When politicians in Denver made decisions, suburban governments generally reacted. By 1950, the city's population had increased to almost 416,000, but the surrounding suburban areas had achieved far greater growth. Jefferson County was home to almost 56,000 residents, followed closely by Arapahoe County with over 52,000. Adams County had almost doubled in size during the decade, boasting more than 40,000 residents at midcentury.[1] While Denver was still the biggest kid on the block, Newton understood that its days as a regional bully were over. Population growth presented wonderful economic opportunities, but it also brought increasingly complex challenges and problems. Quigg understood that from that point forward, regional issues would have to be addressed cooperatively by numerous government entities.

Newton was a firm believer in formal city planning. Although Denver had established a planning office in the 1920s, key decisions affecting the city's development during the Stapleton administration were made by a handful of well-connected developers, with little or no input from civic-minded professionals who might have coordinated them. Shortly after taking office, Newton solicited advice from nationally renowned planning experts, including Charles W. Eliot. Eliot concluded that unless public officials took the initiative, central Denver was threatened with slow strangulation by automobiles. For example, the central business district was under siege by mounting traffic and inadequate parking; new shopping areas in outlying areas threatened its core businesses. He also warned that unless city hall acted, there would be needless and expensive duplication of many municipal services throughout the region.[2]

Across the country, many big-city politicians were attempting to solve regional problems by annexing as much of the surrounding areas as possible. For decision-makers in the inner cities, incentives for aggressive annexation were obvious, highlighted by the irresistible lure of a greatly expanded tax base. Affluent suburbs that possessed well-developed government structures and adequate public services usually resisted such efforts. Newer suburbs possessing few informed civic leaders, those lacking adequate sources of water, and industrial areas with poorly developed public services, often succumbed to takeover efforts. Although Newton would have preferred annexation in many cases, he realized very early in his first term that, for the most part, key decision-makers in surrounding areas were staunch advocates of independence and aggressive efforts to force them inside Denver's tent would generate little but ill will.[3] Cooperation would be better than confrontation.

In February 1948, Newton invited representatives from several surrounding communities to meet with Denver officials to discuss common problems. Initial talks led to creation of the Tri-County Commission, dedicated to addressing the most critical issues involving Denver and the suburbs, most notably distribution of precious water to the rapidly growing region.[4] The commission established six committees to study specific problems: water issues; health and sanitation; fire and police protection; building, planning, and zoning; legislative matters; and educational and cultural issues.[5] One committee focused on the new Valley Highway (now Interstate 25) that was in the earliest planning stages. The Tri-County Commission met formally on an annual basis, and it eventually became the Denver Regional Council of Governments.[6]

Dealing with Developers

During the election campaign, Newton's supporters had exploited the widespread perception that Stapleton had been a compliant tool for many of the old line, firmly established banking and business interests in the city that basically wanted to keep things as they were—and under their control. Retaining such an attitude in 1947 would have been counterproductive. As Newton recalled, "Denver had been discovered—and we knew it." Outside investment was going to happen, whether or not the old elites liked it. Although Quigg's own family had close ties to many of the city's leading decision-makers, he sensed an opportunity to channel creative new ideas and help attract millions of dollars of outside capital.

Newton was no Babbitt, however, pursuing economic growth for its own sake. He thought hard about how active a role he and his office should play in civic boosterism. In one Sunday afternoon radio talk to his constituents, Newton stated forcefully that he would not simply sell out to big corporations. "Uncontrolled, haphazard growth does not always mean progress. There are some industries which would be inappropriate for Denver and for which Denver would be inappropriate. The first responsibility must be to achieve an economy which will provide steady employment for our present population."[7] Decades later, he recalled that he believed that if Denver provided an attractive enough business environment, effective corporate managers would *find* the region and decide to set up facilities in the region by themselves.[8] That was a realistic attitude at the time. Although he did not court big business on bended knee, when important eastern financiers such as William Zeckendorf committed to major investments (in his case, the Courthouse Square project) in the region, Quigg made it his business to get to know them personally.[9]

Newton and his aides certainly made sure that pertinent information highlighting the advantages of the Front Range region reached the hands of businessmen considering operations there. His office staff helped assemble brochures describing Denver's superlative physical setting, educational opportunities, regional parks, recreational amenities, sports facilities, and other attractions. Their efforts to discover just which amenities were most important to entrepreneurs considering establishing corporate quarters in the region also helped Newton and his associates prioritize future civic projects. They learned that expanded airline service, efficient movement of traffic, added cultural attractions, and modern public health facilities were high on the lists of considerations for top corporate managers.[10] This feedback helped Newton and his associates decide which challenges to address first.

Newton's experiences with air transportation, both before and during World War II, inspired him to think hard about future economic prospects for air freight and passenger travel, along with international business opportunities created by newly emerging aircraft technology. When Newton became active in the American Municipal Association (AMA), he became very friendly with Mayor De Lesseps S. "Chep" Morrison. New Orleans had extremely strong economic ties to South and Central America. Braniff Airlines was opening up new routes between the United States and South America. Early in 1949, Quigg and Ginny Newton were invited by the airline to join a select group of big-city officials on a 13,000-mile-long "goodwill" tour of South America. Morrison was organizer and host of the group, and he may also have helped open up Newton's eyes to the possibilities of Denver expanding its international business.[11] The trip started in New Orleans; Morrison provided lavish entertainment, highlighted by the Mardi Gras parade through the city. Later, when Quigg was president of the AMA, the organization met in Denver, and he reciprocated with a party at the spectacular outdoor Red Rocks Amphitheatre.

If Denver was to develop into a major international destination, the city would have to accommodate the new jet aircraft technology that was emerging. When the Denver Municipal Airport (later renamed Stapleton Airport) was opened in 1929, its location in the far north-eastern corner of the city seemed remote. By the end of World War II, however, residential and industrial expansion had occupied much of the adjacent land. Newton and his associates were challenged by the dilemma of whether to tackle a long-term project of building a brand-new airport even farther from the central business district or renovating Stapleton Airport to handle new jet service.

During the Newton years, air passenger travel at the airport expanded rapidly, from just over 200,000 passengers in 1947 to almost 500,000 in 1954.[12] Newton recalled that although his gut instincts pushed him in the direction of promoting a new airport, sober deliberation convinced him that the technology of jet airplane service was emerging so rapidly that airport needs were changing with dizzying speed. It would be prudent to wait until knowledge of future airport needs evolved more thoroughly before making such a huge commitment.[13]

Federal Government Facilities

Newton was certainly not reluctant to help promote Colorado and the Denver metropolitan area as a preferred site for the new military academy that was to educate future officers for the newest branch of the armed services, the U.S. Air Force. The Air Force Academy, opened in

1954, was located fifty miles south of Denver, just north of Colorado Springs. Political maneuverings to attract the facility began years earlier. Quigg informed radio listeners early in 1949 that he was in close contact with Colorado's representatives in Congress, doing everything possible to promote the state's chances of landing the plum. According to Newton, Texas was the primary rival.[14] If Colorado was selected, the massive new facility would pump tens of millions of dollars into the state's economy annually.

Other prime growth fields included aeronautics, defense contracting, and space exploration. In fact, Newton would do far more in promoting these industries in the region after he became president of the University of Colorado late in 1956, but he helped plant many earlier seeds of success. Aerospace giant Martin Marietta opened a huge facility in suburban Littleton to build Titan missiles the year after Newton left office. In just a few more years, numerous other important, newly emerging "clean industries" in high-tech fields would establish operations in the metropolitan area. Newton's successors would reap much of the credit, but his vision helped pave the way for these important economic coups.

In hindsight, the introduction of certain other government installations into the Denver metropolitan area was less fortunate. The Rocky Flats nuclear testing site, located about fifteen miles northwest of downtown, is a case in point. Many early twenty-first century Americans now consider such facilities as nothing less than environmental catastrophes: hideously dangerous, toxic-waste generators whose cleanup will take generations and cost taxpayers billions.

Why would any politician in his right mind not oppose the federal government establishing such facilities close to an American city? One must remember that the Cold War was in full swing fifty years ago. Almost all Americans, including local public officials, were far more trusting of the federal government back then. In addition, construction and maintenance of Rocky Flats brought hundreds of new, high-paying jobs to the region. As Newton recalled, "I wasn't closely involved in the process of bringing Rocky Flats to the area. It was a state-level issue. But federal government experts told people it was safe and that building the facility was a key link in the national defense effort. Who had the scientific expertise to challenge them?"[15]

Mayor Newton was considerably more puzzled by various civil-defense recommendations flowing from the desks of bureaucrats in Washington. Along with other big-city mayors, Newton dutifully appointed a director of civil defense, George Berger, a World War II veteran and at the time president of the Colorado National Bank. Yet Newton voiced considerable concern that the federal government was loading far too much responsibility for civil defense upon cities without providing any financial assistance to carry out its recommendations. In December 1953, Quigg complained that to meet the government's minimal standards for preparation for a nuclear attack, Denver would have to spend $1.5 million for communications centers, auxiliary fire equipment, and the like, "and we don't have $1.5 million."[16]

When Newton attended the AMA meeting in November 1954, he listened to civil-defense experts outlining elaborate plans for "protecting" cities against the most catastrophic possible outcomes from attacks. Prevalent thinking at the time held that wholesale evacuation of cities was more feasible than attempting to provide viable shelter for those close to the most likely target areas.[17] By the end of Newton's second term as mayor, the city's defense plan basically consisted of converting all major streets radiating from the downtown area to one-way streets, directing the maximum numbers of vehicles as far away from the city center as possible. One reporter suggested, "Lateral movement of traffic would be restricted, at least until the major portion of traffic got out of town."[18] He failed to consider how panicked citizens attempting to merge onto the major arteries from side streets might be persuaded to wait patiently at intersections while their more fortunate fellow citizens fled to outlying locations.

Looking back on the city's midcentury civil defense response a half-century later, Newton recalled having had an acute sense even at the time that there was no effective defense against nuclear weapons.[19] But he understood that no responsible politician could publicly acknowledge the impossibility of defending against an enemy attack. At best, such preparations might help prevent a few thousand additional deaths. But Newton understood that at the height of the Cold War, jittery citizens needed to have a sense that they, and their public officials, were taking appropriate steps to protect the city.

Traffic and Transportation

But most citizens did not want to pay much attention to civil defense; they had more-mundane concerns. Newton clearly understood that if he didn't address his constituents' immediate problems, his honeymoon would be very brief. In 1947, the most obvious regional problems included deteriorating streets and highways, rapidly mounting traffic congestion, and inadequate parking. During the last years of the Stapleton administration, the region's increasing traffic congestion had been shrouded by the fact that the number of privately owned vehicles had remained relatively constant. During the Depression, the number of cars owned by Americans remained flat, and production of private automobiles had been suspended during World War II. In the first two years following the war, as the nation's factories reconverted to peacetime production, automobile output surged, but supply remained far behind demand.[20]

Nevertheless, many citizens had long been frustrated by the fact that even when they could get behind the wheel, they were often forced to drive at a snail's pace. Stapleton's inability, or unwillingness, to tackle traffic problems had negatively reinforced his image as an inefficient, even indifferent, leader. Without question, traffic in Denver was a mess, and many people found it difficult to get around. Part of the problem was a decaying public transportation system. Like mass transit companies in many other American cities in the immediate postwar period, the Denver Tramway Company, which had received virtually no infusions of capital since the 1920s, operated a rickety fleet of streetcars, "trackless trolleys," and buses. Much of the equipment was old. Patrons had stoically endured mass transit during economic hard times in the Depression and under severe gasoline and tire rationing in World War II, but they couldn't wait to escape crowded, inconvenient, and uncomfortable mass transit facilities.[21] As Newton recalled, "We started with the old tramway company. We wanted to get rid of the overhead electric wires that were very unsightly. I supported converting to diesel buses, although I realized there were pollution problems involved. I knew we couldn't expand rail transit out into the suburbs. It was too expensive. In fact, I advocated removal of the rail lines that existed."[22]

From the day he assumed office, Newton had taken a hard line against granting the Denver Tramway Company rate increases *in advance* of improvements in service. He pressured the company to commit its promises of "modernization" to paper before the utilities commission granted any hikes in fares.[23] In Newton's view, improved service meant diesel buses. Conversion to buses would probably have occurred regardless of the mayor's views. On June 3, 1950, electric trolley service ended in Denver. There was a nostalgic last ride, a public closing ceremony, and a commemorative plaque. Mayor Newton officiated, calling conversion to all-rubberized mass transit "the most significant step taken in the development of Denver's transportation system since the horse car appeared on its streets in 1871."[24]

Given the fact that in the early twenty-first century, dozens of American cities, Denver included, are spending billions of dollars to revive rail transit in their most heavily traveled corridors, it is tempting to criticize Newton for presiding over the dismantling of the city's original system. In many cities, including Denver, light-rail lines are being built over the former rights-of-way of the original electric trolley lines. In fairness, Newton was neither more nor less enlightened regarding mass transit than his contemporaries governing the nation's other cities. In the two decades following World War II, there were virtually no major additions to street railway lines, even in the nation's largest and most densely settled cities. Across the country, electric trolley lines were being ripped out and buses, usually powered either by diesel or electricity, were replacing electric trolleys.[25]

As historian Mark H. Rose has ably demonstrated, public transportation policy at the national level was geared toward road building, in order to move the automobile and commercial trucks more efficiently.[26]

Private investors sought newer and far more-attractive opportunities than those offered by outdated mass transit companies. Although some cities were subsidizing daily operating costs of mass transit lines during Newton's years as mayor, almost no public funds were being poured into the renovation of electric rail lines, let alone laying new track and purchasing new streetcars.

Newton was acutely aware of national trends in transportation policy, and he intuitively sensed that close association with electrified mass transit would be a losing proposition for any city mayor, particularly in a region as sprawling as Denver. By the time Quigg was sworn into office, thousands of shiny new Fords, Plymouths, and Chevrolets were appearing on city streets. He understood that his constituents would be assessing his response to traffic ills with a critical eye. In fact, more than half of all comments in a suggestion box he set up in city hall involved traffic issues.[27] In Newton's words, "People's mobility was crucial. People wanted relief from traffic jams. ... Rapid movement was a key to maintaining Denver as a viable, growing community."[28] Within days of assuming office, Newton's parks manager, Thomas P. Campbell, assessed the pitiable condition of the city's streets. He pointed out that "most Denver streets have no actual foundations but are horse paths which have been covered with asphalt or oil mat." Campbell estimated that simply renovating the city's severely potholed streets would cost $2 million.[29]

Consequently, one of Newton's early moves as mayor was to hire an energetic, imaginative traffic engineer. After an extensive search, his choice was Henry A. Barnes, a traffic engineer from Flint, Michigan. Two months after being sworn in, Quigg brought Barnes to Denver for a personal interview. Newton quickly sensed that Barnes was his man, but he realized he would have to handle his announcement very carefully since he was already under pressure from some elements in the Denver community for bringing in too many "outsiders" to administer the city's affairs. Barnes recalled being forced to "hide out" at the Brown Palace for several days, his career in limbo, until Newton finally found an appropriate moment to make his appointment public. As his days of inactivity dragged on, Barnes got so fed up that he almost gave up and skipped town.[30]

When Newton finally made the announcement, Barnes sensed immediately that he was in the hot seat and that every move he made would be subjected to minute scrutiny. Barnes experienced his first lesson in local politics when he recommended converting several two-way streets into one-way streets to speed up movement of traffic to and from the downtown area. One problem was that some of the streets affected happened to pass through neighborhoods of some of the city's more prominent residents, including the mayor's. Quigg supported his engineer's initiative, even over his own wife's concerns. Ginny complained to Quigg that the street on which they lived was designated to be one-way, but her objections were futile.[31]

Many people were upset, and some of them took out their frustrations on Barnes, not the mayor. In one public meeting, Barnes was surprised when an elderly resident piped up, "Mr. Traffic Director ... sixty-eight years ago I drove my horse and buggy west on Eighteenth Street, and I don't need any smart-aleck traffic engineer from Michigan to tell me that I can't drive that same horse back east, on the same street, tonight, if I want to." Barnes was so flabbergasted he couldn't muster a reply. He was even more amazed when the city council rejected his suggestion to convert the avenue in question to a one-way street.[32]

He also learned that traffic engineers would be held responsible for any snafus involving the flow of traffic to and from Red Rocks Amphitheatre. Although George Cranmer's WPA–funded creation was an aesthetic tour de force, access was highly problematic because it was served by narrow, winding roads, and parking was very limited. In his autobiography, Barnes recalled that maintaining smooth traffic control at the site during frequent well-attended public events tested his patience and ingenuity and consumed massive amounts of time.[33]

Perhaps his most famous innovation in Denver was the so-called Barnes dance. At regular intervals at downtown intersections, motorists were all held by red lights, while pedestrians were permitted to cross streets in any direction they chose, even diagonally. During the transition, on at least one occasion Barnes himself stood out in the middle of a busy intersection and directed traffic. Motorists sometimes grumbled, but pedestrians and many downtown merchants were enchanted; the system is still in place a half-century later. Barnes's achievements in Denver attracted national attention and enhanced his career. After several years in Denver, he moved on to Baltimore, and eventually to New York City, where he headed traffic operations for many years.

By the end of Newton's first term, Barnes had convinced key civic leaders that some one-way streets were critical for more-efficient traffic flow. However, downtown parking problems proved to be a tougher challenge. Although most city streets were laid out in conventional north-south and east-west directions, the downtown streets, dating from gold-rush discovery years, were laid out at forty-five-degree angles from the conventional pattern. Seventeenth Street, for example, ran from north-west to southeast. This anomaly confused some new Colorado drivers. Although downtown streets were roughly average in width for big cities, the fact that authorities permitted on-street parking greatly restricted traffic flow, particularly during rush hour. As in many other American cities, public officials had experimented with elimination or strict regulation of parallel parking on downtown streets, only to arouse intense opposition from merchants, who demanded unrestricted "convenience" for patrons of their stores.[34]

One obvious solution was to build more off-street parking facilities: either open lots or multistory garages. A few property owners demolished obsolete structures and converted land to parking lots, but such solutions were usually temporary. A long-term answer appeared to be parking garages. The problem was who would pay for them. Merchants and downtown employers looked to city hall. Newton and his staff studied the situation promptly; they unveiled a report in July 1947, indicating that the downtown area needed a 40 percent increase in available parking slots.[35]

Late in the same year, Denver voters approved a $4.5 million bond issue to finance purchase of land and construction of off-street parking facilities. But convincing lending institutions to underwrite the bond issue tested the ingenuity and persuasiveness of Newton's top financial advisors, because city officials refused to commit revenues from parking meters to pay off the bonds. Nobody could provide believable estimates of future revenues, and lenders insisted that loans be paid off entirely from fees collected at the new parking sites. Despite mounting frustration about the glacial pace of negotiations, Newton insisted that details must remain secret "in order to prevent land speculation and unfair windfalls for a few property owners."[36] City officials eventually persuaded two prospective underwriters to submit bids, but many months elapsed before the financial details were ironed out.[37]

In hindsight, Newton concluded that although his administration made an honest effort to tackle downtown parking problems, they weren't very successful.[38] By the time he left office in 1955, the city had built three parking garages and cleared three vacant lots for off-street parking that, combined, could hold 1,665 vehicles if filled to capacity.[39] This gesture could not stop the commercial flight to outlying areas, or even slow it down. By the mid-1950s, it was already apparent that retail merchants were beginning to search for large expanses of decentralized real estate upon which to establish large-scale shopping malls, allowing patrons to park for free, close to stores. The Cherry Creek Shopping Center, located at University and First Avenues, opened in 1953, followed by the University Hills Shopping Center on South Colorado Boulevard in 1955. By then, plans were also underway to open up another huge complex in Lakewood.[40]

In contrast to their ongoing struggles to ease traffic flow in the downtown area, by the end of his second term in office Newton and state-level traffic engineers could point with pride to two major achievements facilitating flow of traffic in the region: completion of the Valley Highway and the Boulder Turnpike. Following passage of the Federal Aid Highway Act of 1944, "road engineers both in Washington and in the state highway departments, focused attention on blocking out coordinates for the interstate system."[41] For more than two years, the Stapleton administration had achieved little progress in formalizing plans to apply for potential federal funds to assist construction of a superhighway through Denver. When he took over as mayor, Newton was determined to break the logjam and see that the city received its fair share: "If we fail now to proceed with the Valley Highway, to take advantage of the liberal financial aid available from state and national funds, we may find ourselves in future years confronted with an even more serious problem and no funds at all with which to solve it."[42]

One major hurdle was disagreement over where the highway should be built. A route straight down Broadway would serve the largest number of vehicles, but costs of property condemnation and building a highway using proper design standards would be prohibitive. Others promoted a highway straight down Colorado Boulevard, but such a route would be too remote from downtown to permit easy access.[43] When Newton entered office, state engineers had already laid out a proposal to build the planned route on a north-south axis along the South Platte River (its present location).

The plan had generated some heated opposition. One citizen complained, "The proposed route traverses the slum part of the city, squeezes through North Acoma and Bannock Streets in Globeville and surely will not make a good impression on tourists. ... "[44] This Denverite proposed two alternative routes, a north-south route down Federal Boulevard and an east-west highway along Forty-Sixth Street (basically the I-70 corridor today). Following conferences with state and federal highway engineers, Newton endorsed the state engineers' plan for construction of a route along the South Platte River, stating that he was "convinced that competent men laid out the Valley Highway route after considerable thinking and much study."[45]

Technically speaking, the Boulder Turnpike was also a state project. Denver city officials were minor role players in the complicated process of turning this much-needed highway into reality, but they were vitally interested in the outcome. The idea had been floated by a Boulder planning committee a year before Newton assumed office in Denver, and the state legislature approved the project in principle on April 30, 1947. Although the project was approved, it would have to be entirely self-sustaining through tolls collected. Two years later, after intense political maneuvering, the state finally agreed to provide 30 percent of construction costs plus interest. Following an unsuccessful state supreme court challenge by opponents, the legislature authorized a $6.3 million bond issue. Groundbreaking took place in October 1950, and the seventeen-mile toll road opened for travel on January 19, 1952. The new road cut eight miles off the previous route from Denver to Boulder, and it was successful from the start. Between 1952 and 1967, nearly 47 million vehicles passed through the tollbooths, roughly five times the total number originally predicted by engineers. By the fall of 1967, the road had paid for itself, and it became a free public highway.[46]

Although planning for long-term regional traffic movement needs was crucially important, most voters reacted more immediately to street conditions in their own neighborhoods. Two crucial issues were the repair of axle-jarring potholes and the cleanliness of streets. It may not have been entirely coincidental that Newton was elected in late May, when the Stapleton administration was ineffectively trying to patch up Denver's streets, which had been heavily battered during the winter. Taking advantage of mild weather, within days of Newton's inauguration repair crews were out in force, tackling the worst of the thousands of potholes impeding smooth traffic flow. It is perhaps testimony to the effectiveness of Newton and public works director Charles Berry's handling of street repair challenges that neither major Denver newspaper mounted any sort of publicity campaign regarding poorly paved streets during the eight years Quigg was mayor. To be sure, the reporters commented on specific projects and sometimes urged more rapid progress, but in general the mayor and his staff received high marks for their handling of street repairs.

Street Cleaning and Trash Collection

Keeping streets clean was a more complex issue. During the Stapleton years, trash collection had been extremely haphazard. Many citizens burned combustible refuse in large incinerators in their backyards. Not only was the practice dangerous, but it added greatly to the air pollution that was beginning to generate significant public concern. At midcentury, few homes had garbage disposals, and residents routinely put out large amounts of trash in garbage cans, either in back alleys or out in front of houses. Nobody wanted to keep smelly garbage indoors, so garbage stored outdoors in cans often fermented for days, attracting rats and other vermin. Sanitation problems, or at least proliferation of noxious odors, became even more problematic during summers. Some citizens failed to dispose of trash in secure packages or covered garbage cans.

Complicating the issue was the fact that rowdy teenagers some-times amused themselves by tipping over trash cans. During windy weather, loose papers and wrappings often littered entire neighborhoods. Newton's response was twofold. In his Sunday afternoon *Mayor's Mailbag* talks, he informed citizens that trash would be picked up on prearranged days so citizens would know when garbage trucks would arrive. Then he reminded citizens of city ordinances that prescribed how garbage was supposed to be set out for collection: "I do not think that compliance with that ordinance imposes an unfair burden for anyone. Certainly we intend to be reasonable about it. We are not demanding that everyone immediately replace his present trash can with the type described in the ordinance, but we shall do everything that we can to see that when replacements are made, the proper type of receptacle is obtained."[47] Newton intuitively knew that he had to proceed very gingerly, sensing it would be political suicide to impose draconian measures against citizens who failed to comply with city regulations.

Despite his informed and sensitive response to garbage collection issues, Quigg failed to convince all of his constituents that he was man-aging the appearance of local streets effectively. One Sunday, he read aloud a complaint from a constituent: "I am writing as a private citizen and without the knowledge of my husband. In fact, he especially asked me not to write when I threatened to do so at one o'clock in the morn-ing. ... But I am getting worn down by the street cleaners scraping their shovels at midnight, or at one or two o'clock in the morning on 7th and Corona Streets, once or twice a month and waking us up with the scrap-ping [sic], as last night with the yelling across the street for Joe to 'go between the cars,' for Bill to 'get another shovel,' and similar observations. I, for one, would much rather have 7th and Corona Streets somewhat less clean than be awakened at all hours by the cleaning."

It turned out that the letter writer was Newton's own wife! Attempting to maintain marital harmony, the mayor looked into the matter, only to decide that night cleaning would have to continue. High daytime traffic volume made it far more difficult, dangerous, and expensive to complete street cleaning during normal working hours: "I know of no large city in the United States which is successful in keeping its streets cleaned without having crews work at night, and I am inclined to feel that there are some 'big city noises' which we just have to accept as part of the price for living in the big city."[48] Quigg judiciously declined to reveal whether his handling of the matter satisfied Ginny. It is easy to imagine that the incident was a lighthearted joke between the two.

Newton demonstrated considerable political acumen in demonstrating to his constituents that he was on top of day-to-day management issues and was always looking for ways to increase the efficiency of city workers. In Denver, one constant threat to any mayor's image is how well the city handles snowstorms. In the winter of 1949, the city experienced several heavy snowfalls, and numerous constituents complained about the response of street cleaning crews. Newton carefully explained his options. Obviously, weather predictions a half-century ago were far less scientific and precise than

Denver's official first couple ducks low at a square dance in 1950.

they are today. Back then, the National Weather Service might be able to indicate that a storm was coming, but predicting amounts of snowfall was far trickier. Newton pointed out that the decision of when to send out snow removal crews was always something of a hit-or-miss gamble. Ideally, crews would start cleaning streets when about three inches of snow had accumulated. But if only four or five inches fell and the weather remained relatively warm, the sun and nature might melt the snow almost as quickly as crews could shovel it aside. In such a case, tens of thousands of dollars would be wasted. On the other hand, if the mayor delayed sending out crews until the snowfall was very heavy, it would be far more expensive and take far longer to make the streets passable: "It's a case of too much too soon, or too little too late—and it isn't easy to guess them right every time."[49]

Public Health

Other serious issues attracted Newton's attention. During the year preceding the election campaign of 1947, *The Denver Post* had published a series of feature stories deploring the state of public health and conditions at Denver General Hospital. Newton had capitalized on the negative attention the Stapleton administration had received. As mayor, he faced the daunting task of attempting to bring order to a chaotic public health situation. According to the memoirs of Maxine Kurtz, a longtime city planner, "A common saying around Denver at the time was that you go to Denver General Hospital to die. … " Following an inspection tour shortly after Quigg became mayor, she provided a nightmarish description of the facilities: "[One] new area devoted to inpatient care surrounded a multistory open space that would have been a great chimney in the event of a fire. But we all had to agree that the worst housed activity at the hospital was the welfare department. Its working area was in a tunnel connecting two buildings. That tunnel was located in the subterranean bed of Cherry Creek, so there always were several inches of water covering the floor. The desks were raised by blocks under the legs, and wooden platforms provided places for the social workers' chairs. However, clients had to sit with their feet in the water, and the employees always were overshoes because they had to walk around in the course of their work."[50]

During his two terms as mayor, and for many years afterwards, initiatives to improve the delivery of health care services were among Newton's most important achievements. Most of these occurred during his years as president of the University of Colorado, and later as president of the Commonwealth Fund. However, Quigg made an excellent start in attacking the local public health mess by appointing Dr. Solomon Kauvar as manager of health and welfare. He agreed to take the job for a year. According to Newton, Kauvar "transformed the organization" and "concluded an agreement with the Colorado Medical School whereby the medical school would provide staffing for the Denver General Hospital meet[ing] the same standards the medical school used for its own staffing."[51] When Kauvar's year expired, Newton replaced him with Dr. Florence Sabin. This was another inspired decision. Although she was seventy-six at the time, Dr. Sabin was still an energetic and highly respected public servant who had shepherded a number of important health bills through the Colorado legislature. She was equally effective working for the city. According to Denver historian Thomas J. Noel, "She began a citywide X-ray and treatment program that by 1950 cut the city's tuberculosis rate in half, and launched a campaign to remove rats from alleys and dumps and to teach public health."[52]

Law Enforcement

Despite the embarrassing controversy surrounding Police Chief August Hanebuth's conduct during Stapleton's last year as mayor, law and order had not been a particularly thorny issue during Stapleton's long reign. These issues did not plague city hall during the Newton years either. Newton made a point of personally addressing every graduating class of police cadets. He would inform them that they were very much in public view and that their conduct had to be above reproach. He stressed repeatedly that mistakes in the line of duty could be forgiven, but involvement in any corruption would result in strict disciplinary action.

There may have been more corruption within the city council than in the ranks of the police force. Newton recalled a city councilman who was rumored to be soliciting bribes involving liquor licenses. One applicant agreed to make a payoff and then tipped off the mayor's office. With the assistance of the police, Newton's aide, Ralph Radetsky, wired up the room to record the transaction. When the money passed hands, several police emerged from hiding places and arrested him. Caught red-handed, the councilman tried to bluff his way out of the arrest. Although Newton and his associates thought they had an airtight case, the defendant hired skilled lawyers and lucked into drawing a sympathetic judge. Newton was shocked when the trial ended in an acquittal. However, subsequent public pressure against the councilman became so intense that eight of his fellow councilmen arranged a more extensive investigation of the case, which was headed by rigorously honest former Colorado governor Ralph Carr. An emotional and highly charged three-day hearing was held, and it was announced that a decision would be forthcoming within two weeks. An hour before the results were to become public, the councilman submitted his resignation. Quigg and his allies finally felt vindicated.[53]

Some issues confronting public officials appear timeless. A perennially divisive issue was conditions in the city's jails. Responsible officials pleaded that as the prison population increased, the jails were filthy, overcrowded, and unsafe. In the early 1950s, local prison inmates protested overcrowding and a perceived lack of exposure to any meaningful activity. Early in 1954, the county jail warden informed manager of public safety Leonard Campbell that 569 men were crammed into space that was "adequate" for only 327 inmates.[54] As every experienced politician knows, the expenditure of public funds on prisons is never popular, as voters invariably grumble about "coddling" of prisoners and images of "country club" jails. Progress in easing overcrowding in the prisons would be elusive; a half-century later, it remains an unresolved and contentious issue.

Housing

Another major challenge was public housing. As noted, Quigg's father, Jim Newton, had been the first director of public housing in the late 1930s. The postwar period marked a severe housing shortage in Denver. Virtually all contractors focused on building *new* housing for the "deserving"—returning war veterans and other members of the rapidly expanding American middle class who could afford modest monthly mortgage payments on single-family homes. Much of the older existing housing had been overcrowded for years, if not decades. Throughout the Depression and World War II, and for a year or two after V-J Day, much rental property had been allowed to deteriorate. The reason was simple: landlords could almost always find tenants, who had little choice but to pay inflated rents even for deplorable facilities. This situation was hardly unique to Denver; it existed in big cities nationwide. But most citizens not directly affected by slum conditions acted on the principle of "out of sight, out of mind."

Similarly, the housing shortage was not just a local issue but a national concern. In response, Congress passed the Federal Housing Act in 1949 to help public officials deal with the rapidly deteriorating housing situations in inner cities. Although Denver's slum conditions were not nearly as grim as those in older eastern cities such as New York, Washington, and Philadelphia, Newton not only believed that helping the city's most disadvantaged citizens secure decent housing was a moral imperative, but he was determined Denver should get its share of federal funding available for this endeavor. In one radio address, Newton informed listeners that the Federal Housing Act was no panacea: "It is a new program and a good deal of experience will be necessary before it can operate to the greatest public benefit." But Quigg voiced hope that the federal government would "impose the minimum of restrictions on the manner in which cities proceed with urban redevelopment." He concluded, "I have no doubt Denver should participate in this program."[55]

Securing federal funding was difficult enough, but administering the grants was equally challenging. According to the law, one unit of substandard housing had to be torn down for every new unit constructed.

Displacement of some families from what middle-class "experts" labeled "substandard" housing uprooted them from the only homes they had ever known, as well as from their neighborhoods. Sometimes, tenants had to be evicted forcefully from even the most dilapidated rentals. Not all public officials handled evictions sensitively, and misunderstandings were common. Nevertheless, by 1952 Denver's urban renewal efforts led to construction of 3,240 new units in thirteen new projects.[56]

Civil Rights

Some citizens forced out of homes by urban renewal felt alienated from the decision-making process. From the beginning of his first term, Newton made conscious efforts to enhance local citizens' collective sense of being involved in Denver's government. On many key issues being debated in his office and by the city council, he appointed citizens' committees to study the issues and provide input. Newton took these citizens' groups seriously; a few even became permanent. One of the most influential was the Mayor's Committee on Human Relations, created in August 1948 and chaired by Paul Roberts, dean of St. John's Episcopal Cathedral. Roberts's committee dealt primarily with civil rights issues. In the late 1940s, Denver was still basically a segregated city. If Mayor Ben Stapleton had shed the notoriety of being connected to the Ku Klux Klan twenty-two years earlier, his administration still sanctioned discrimination and exclusion. For example, although African Americans were permitted to use the city's swimming pools, their hours were strictly limited to the day before the water was changed, and they were not allowed in the water with whites.

Although the *Brown v. Board of Education of Topeka, Kansas,* decision was still six years in the future, in 1948, Jackie Robinson had recently broken the color barrier in Major League Baseball, and Newton was determined to modernize race relations in Denver. Bolstered by the advice of Paul Roberts, Quigg appointed Native American Helen Peterson as Denver's first director of human relations. Peterson, an energetic and gifted administrator, remained on Newton's team for almost seven years, eventually resigning to accept an appointment as director of the National Congress of American Indians.[57]

Peterson headed a permanent committee of eleven citizens. The budget was tiny, just $8,500 in its first year, and the commission's office was supported by contributions from local businessmen. Initially, the "staff" of one and one-half persons consisted of Peterson and Muriel Swayse, the latter working half-time. Its chief function was to investigate allegations of discrimination within city government. The committee also handled similar complaints at recreational facilities, charges of police brutality, and other confrontations having racial overtones.[58]

When interviewed about the commission's achievements forty years after she left, Peterson recalled Newton's role in almost reverential terms. In her view, Quigg was an indispensable catalyst for change. "He lent dignity, purpose and direction and support for human relations efforts officially … " She elaborated: "All levels were attracted by Quigg Newton. He was identified with socially prominent wealthy old line families. Consequently, a great many of them felt comfortable with his leadership and were involved."[59] When elite volunteers possessing clout gave time and expended effort in areas ranging from investigating police treatment of minorities to monitoring public health, progress occurred. Although the civil rights groups did not transform race relations in Denver overnight, Newton received high marks from virtually every representative of the region's long-ignored minority communities.

A newspaper comparison of images of Quigg in 1947 and 1951 suggest that the duties of office matured him. Yet he bore his responsibilities gracefully.

Reelection and the National Stage

In the spring of 1951, Newton's four-year term as mayor was drawing to a close. Despite his emerging interest in other ventures, there was never any serious question of whether or not he would run for a second term. Quigg believed that important, unmet challenges remained, and he still enjoyed the enormous variety of problems he had to deal with in running the city. His team of key advisors and department managers was in place and working harmoniously, and his relations with the media remained positive and cordial.

One of his few visible and outspoken critics was Councilman Clarence M. Stafford, who decided to run for mayor. There were three other minor candidates in the race. There were more registered voters in Denver in 1951 than there had been four years earlier, but there was little suspense in the campaign. Voter turnout declined by nearly one-fourth, or 33,000 ballots cast. Once again, Newton won in a landslide, drawing a little over 67,000 votes. Stafford received less than half of that amount, just over 32,000 votes. The three other men in the race divided about 6,000 votes. Newton's winning total in 1951 was approximately 12,500 fewer than the total he attracted four years earlier.[60] About the

Newton family Christmas card photo, 1950. The girls, left to right, are Nan, Abby, Ginna, and Nelle.

only suspense during Quigg's reelection campaign involved a ballot issue determining whether Denver voters would agree to raise the salaries of several public officeholders, including the mayor. Local voters approved the raises by a slim margin of approximately 1,400 votes. During his second term, Newton would receive an annual salary of $14,000.[61]

By midcentury, Newton was becoming a national figure. Quigg's campaign for mayor in 1947 had attracted widespread attention, in part because of his extreme youth and the fact that he decisively defeated a legendary, seemingly permanently entrenched "machine" politician. Quigg's personal administrative style was energetic and enthusiastic, and he provided constituents and the newsmen covering him convincing evidence that he was constantly on the job. Press coverage was over-whelmingly favorable. At times, it almost seemed that he was inundated in national recognition and honors. Selection as one of the U.S. Junior Chamber of Commerce's Ten Outstanding Young Men came in 1947, the same year he was elected mayor. As mayor, Quigg joined the AMA, and he regularly attended the organization's conventions to interact with other city mayors and learn firsthand their approaches to common urban problems.

By the end of his first year as mayor of Denver, Newton had already assumed a position of leadership in the AMA, which represented the interests of 9,500 cities and towns. In late December 1948, for exam-ple, he gave a national address, aired over CBS, informing listeners about the activities of the organization. Quigg explained the association's recent formal response to the age-old conundrum of cities in many states being hog-tied in their efforts to collect and wisely spend sufficient tax revenues by uncooperative, even antagonistic state governments. He deftly avoided political controversy by praising Colorado's "enlightened" attitude toward the city of Denver, but singled out Washington, D.C., where local citizens had almost no control over how their affairs were financed and administered, as a political anomaly at the opposite end of the spectrum. Newton mentioned several other cities where hardworking and effective mayors were unfairly thwarted in conscientious efforts to do their jobs by confrontational state legislatures. He reminded listeners that "in a nation generally preoccupied with international and national problems, there is a tendency to forget about local government and to assume it will take care of itself."[62] While conceding that a few old-style political machine mayors might prefer "not to operate in the limelight," Quigg argued that most urban problems would prove more tractable when local citizens were directly and actively involved.

As a leading member and national spokesman for the AMA, Newton formed fast friendships with some of the organization's most influential members. Close friends included De Lesseps S. "Chep" Morrison of New Orleans, who had been elected president of the organization in 1948. Quigg may have been more surprised than his peers when he was elected as president of the AMA. Like his predecessors, he served a one-year term between 1950 and 1951. Among the many honors he received during his lifetime, it was one of the most cherished.[63]

Presiding over the association was not simply a ceremonial honor. It led to a rather strange encounter with J. Edgar Hoover and agents of the Federal Bureau of Investigation (FBI). In the early 1950s, McCarthyism was approaching its peak, and public officials at every level were being subjected to all sorts of "loyalty tests" and investigations of even the most intimate facets of their personal lives. In the same convention when Quigg was elected as the organization's president, the AMA passed a resolution critical of what its members viewed as the FBI's unwarranted prying into the lives of public servants. As president of the organization, Newton received a visit from an FBI agent who wanted the names and particulars of which mayors introduced and were most active in pressing the resolution. With the consent of his peers, Newton stalled and eventually refused to provide details. The agent's report concluded that "Newton was quite vague and evasive."[64]

Evidently, Newton himself was not thoroughly investigated by the FBI. In the early months of President Dwight D. Eisenhower's first term, however, before Senator Joseph McCarthy was finally censored by the U.S. Senate, an investigator for the FBI sent a memo to an unnamed presidential assistant concerning the mayor. It stated that although Newton had never been subject of a probe, FBI files did contain a pamphlet titled "American Council Institute of Pacific Relations, Membership, Spring, 1938." The memo stated: "According to a July, 1952 report of the Senate Subcommittee on Internal Security, the Institute of Pacific Relations (IPR) has been considered by the American Communist Party and Soviet officials as an instrument of Communist policy, propaganda and military intelligence, disseminating and seeking to popularize false information including that originating with Soviet and Communist sources." The memo provided no details of Newton's degree of involvement, if any, with the organization.[65] If President Eisenhower ever saw the report, he evidently was not unduly alarmed at the prospect that Quigg might be a card-carrying member of the Communist Party—or a covert sympathizer.

Still, Newton may have felt more welcome in Washington, D.C., when President Harry S. Truman was in office. As president of the AMA, he was invited in 1950 to head up an investigation of organized crime in the United States. Although Quigg was honored by the summons, he was genuinely surprised, since Denver was not known as a crime-ridden city. It is interesting to note that some of the problems addressed at the conference appear almost innocent by today's standards. For example, the conference tackled the problem of how to control slot machines and prohibit interstate shipment of the devices and how to discourage the dissemination of racetrack betting across state lines.[66]

Newton's Legacy as Mayor

After seven years as mayor, Newton felt that he had achieved most of his objectives, and he was beginning to tire of the job. In 1954, he ran in the Democratic primary for nomination for the U.S. Senate.[67] As mayor of Denver, he had been an independent, however, not a Democrat, and his bid failed. Quigg announced in January 1955 that he would not be a candidate for reelection as mayor; he was a "lame duck." Almost immediately, tributes to his achievements as mayor began pouring in. Dozens of columnists across the Front Range praised Quigg's initiatives during his eight years in office. Roscoe Fleming, a respected veteran reporter for *The Post,* spoke for the vast majority in asking, "Who has been our best mayor?" Comparing Robert Speer, Ben Stapleton, and Quigg Newton, Fleming placed Newton above both Speer and Stapleton: "I nominate Quigg Newton. … Denver in the past eight years has had better government than I previously thought could be. Actually, Denver could lay claim to being the best governed American

Breakfast at the busy Newton home, 1952. The girls, left to right, are Ginna, Abby, Nan, and Nelle.

local unit during that period." Fleming concluded, "What I like best about him, I think, is his manifest belief that it is a privilege to serve his fellow-men; and not, as too many of our public men seem to assume, the other way around."[68] In a single eloquent sentence, Fleming revealed one of the key touchstones defining Newton's career—and his life.

There were a few critics. Following their parting of ways early in his first term, Gene Cervi never forgave Newton. When there were initial rumors that Newton would run for the U.S. Senate, Cervi dismissed him as "a Tom Dewey among Democrats." He claimed that Quigg was "coldly impersonal toward the public in general" and that he was "not exactly a good public relations risk for a press agent." Considering Newton's radio and television appearances and frequent

The Newtons on vacation at Cape Cod (ca. 1953). The girls, left to right, are Abby, Ginna, Nelle and Nan.

press conferences, such views appear misguided. When Quigg announced he would not seek a third term as mayor, Cervi provided a generally negative assessment of his administration. He conceded that Newton had done well with downtown traffic, parking, and in bringing about a merit system for city employees. But he claimed that Newton "flunked dismally on water. ... In short, Denver is out of water—and the Newton water board is to blame."[69] Cervi's dislike of Newton was so deep that he was still taking potshots at the former mayor more than a decade after he left office.[70]

The long-term impact of Newton's eight years as Denver's first citizen can perhaps be assessed best by historians. Lyle W. Dorsett, who provided an extremely favorable assessment of Ben Stapleton, called Newton "a vigorous young Navy veteran who symbolized a fresh era for Denver—one dominated by youthful optimism and growth." In contrast to Cervi, who felt that Newton fell down on the job of bringing water to Denver, Dorsett argued that Newton and his successor, Will Nicholson, were actually *too effective* in acquiring water: "The role that these mayors played in creating this regional disaster [unchecked suburban sprawl] was significant, but they did not act alone. Citizens of the City and County of Denver overwhelmingly endorsed the expansion crusade."[71] It should be noted that Dorsett wrote this in the mid-1970s, shortly after Coloradans had rejected the Winter Olympics and

QUIGG NEWTON

DEMOCRATIC CANDIDATE

FOR

U. S. SENATOR

Quigg Newton for U.S. Senate campaign poster, 1954.

during a period when Colorado's "pro-growth" policies were under vigorous attack by environmentalists and many other concerned citizens. Writing in the mid-1990s, two decades after Dorsett's book appeared, noted Denver historian Thomas J. Noel claimed that Newton "imagined a great city" fifty years ago. He was referring, of course, to Mayor Federico Peña's popular slogan from the 1980s. Noel provided a lengthy laundry list of Newton's accomplishments, concluding that Newton and Robert Speer were the city's two greatest mayors.[72]

As his second term wound down, however, Newton wasn't concerned with how future columnists and historians would assess his years in office. In his mind, he had done all that he could do as mayor, and it was time to move on with his life and career. Quigg had run a spirited if unsuccessful campaign for the U.S. Senate as a Democrat, and some friends and associates thought he might be in line for a cabinet position—should a Democrat win the presidency in 1956. But he needed to provide for his family, and he had many other responsibilities. As is so often the case in the lives of capable, creative, and energetic individuals, an intriguing new opportunity appeared at just the right moment.

CHAPTER 8

DEAD END

No individual who has experienced a full, involved life can look back and seriously believe that it was free of mistakes. That was certainly true of Quigg Newton. Looking backward from the vantage point of ninety-one years, Newton did not dwell on mistakes; he did mention several forks in the road where he might have taken another direction, presumably with equally interesting outcomes. If he made one decision he regretted, it was running for the U.S. Senate in 1954. "I was nearing the end of eight years as mayor, and I was getting stale. I wanted to do something else. I enjoyed public life, and I thought I would enjoy the intellectual issues in the Senate. But I shouldn't have run for the Senate. I didn't know the political game. Some of the folks I had appointed couldn't even support me."[1] What he meant was that he had served Denver as a nonpartisan mayor. Newton knew the political game all right, but his expertise was primarily at the local level. When he attempted to enter the political arena at the state and national level, he quickly realized that he was at a major disadvantage in not being affiliated with either major party. In short, he had no solid political foundation. A final obstacle was that many Colorado Democrats had another candidate in mind.

Like every other major commitment Newton made in his life, his decision to run for the U.S. Senate was neither spontaneous nor casual. Quigg had, in fact, been thinking beyond the mayor's office for some time. In order to be a serious candidate for another significant office, he had to join a major political party. On July 2, 1953, more than a year before nominating conventions, Newton registered as a Democrat. This would prove to be a momentous decision. His father, Jim Newton, had been a Republican, albeit with some rather unconventional views for a member of the GOP. When Quigg joined the Democrats, some of his Denver Country Club friends and associates were shocked and dismayed at what they considered his apostasy, his abandonment of what for them were fundamental values of men of his class. After Newton lost his bid for the Democratic nomination, several associates insisted that, had he become a Republican, he would almost certainly have been nominated and elected to the Senate.

"Big Ed" Johnson Bows Out

Newton's registration as a Democrat was linked to the political career of three-time Democratic senator Edwin C. "Big Ed" Johnson. Johnson, a highly influential and popular former governor, had been elected to the U.S. Senate in 1936 and was nearing the end of his third consecutive term. Johnson enjoyed thorough respect of his colleagues in the Senate. Although he was seventy, he appeared healthy; many political pundits considered his renomination and election for a fourth term as almost inevitable. Early in the spring of 1954, one columnist expressed the view that odds were ten to one that he would run again. As one newspaper columnist put it, "Around here [the Senate] nobody voluntarily goes back to Pocatello."[2] Although Newton was by that point "making speeches around the state," the columnist believed that he intended to run either for the House of Representatives or governor of Colorado.[3]

Johnson had promised that he would make a decision about his future in the Senate no later than April 2. True to his word, the incumbent released a clear statement that he would not seek a fourth term in the "world's most exclusive club." Newton seemed to have had advance information about Johnson's decision. Evidence to that effect was the fact that Quigg informed reporters that he was "sorry to learn" of Johnson's decision not to run again; his comment was made twenty minutes *before* Johnson made his announcement back in Washington.

Why did "Big Ed" retire? He was a very enthusiastic baseball fan who had been a linchpin in reviving the minor league single-A level

Denver Bears in 1947, after they had been in hibernation since 1932. In 1954, he helped the Bears gain promotion into the AAA-level American Association.[4] Rumors had circulated for months that Johnson might quit the Senate to assume a position helping run baseball, either at the major or minor league level. In his public statement, however, Johnson denied any intention of becoming a baseball executive. He claimed that the chief reason for leaving the Senate was that after eighteen years, his wife was tired of living in Washington. The couple's family and grandchildren lived in Colorado, and they wanted to spend more time with them. He would fish, play some golf, and generally relax. "A long time ago, Senator Alva Adams told me that retirement is man's most difficult decision. I have found it so." There was immediate speculation that the Colorado Democrats would "draft Ed for governor." Johnson replied with a grin, "I am not taking any of that seriously." But when pressed by reporters, Johnson refused to say that he would reject a draft.[5]

Initial Maneuverings

Political pundits immediately speculated about who would enter the lists as candidates to replace Johnson. The day following Johnson's announcement, local newspapers identified Newton as a possible candidate, along with former congressman John A. Carroll and Charles F. Brannan, who had been secretary of agriculture under President Truman. For the time being, Newton was noncommittal about running for the Senate, stating only his deep admiration of Johnson as "an outstanding servant of the people."[6] Carroll was not so reticent, announcing that he would be a candidate for the Senate just two days after Johnson decided to vacate the office. There had been bad blood between Johnson and Carroll for a number of years, however, and political insiders did not expect Johnson to give the former congressman any encouragement.

In contrast, Johnson admired both Brannan and Newton, but he was clearly warmer toward the mayor. He called Brannan a "fine man," but he extolled Newton at some length: "Mayor Newton is a great guy and he has a lot on the ball. The Democratic Party would make a mistake if it didn't cultivate that young man. He's a very good man. He's the kind of man that ought to be placed in high office. The nation could use men like Newton." Asked about Carroll, Johnson bit his tongue and stated, "He has a lot of ability and a lot of talent; there isn't much more I can say." Officially, however, Johnson declined to endorse any candidate for the position, stating that the people of Colorado were perfectly capable of making up their own minds without his interference.[7]

Even before announcing that he would seek Johnson's seat, Newton received enthusiastic encouragement from one of *The Denver Post*'s most respected veteran political reporters, Bruce Gustin, who stated, "Of all those mentioned as possible candidates, Mayor Newton is far and away the ablest and best fitted. And the U.S. Senate is where he could be used to best advantage."[8] From the moment Johnson spoke highly of him, reporters pestered Quigg incessantly regarding his future plans. For a few days, the mayor held them off, responding simply, "No comment." Just days before Quigg announced he would seek Johnson's seat, he claimed, "I am mayor of Denver and have plenty of problems in that job. I have no political plans *at this time*" (emphasis added). Denver papers reported that Newton was "considering" running for the U.S. Senate.[9]

Even fifty years ago, political scenarios often evolved with breathtaking speed. Just five days after Johnson's formal announcement and only three days after Carroll notified reporters that he planned to run, Newton officially threw his hat into the ring. In his customary fashion, Quigg took the high road, expressing hope that both he and Carroll, "whom I have always held in high regard," would receive designation from delegates to the upcoming state Democratic convention. Newton publicly welcomed any and all challengers for the position: "I hope he and other possible candidates share my conviction that an energetic primary campaign is good for the state and for the party." He then asked rhetorically, "Am I qualified to represent Colorado in the United States Senate? I believe I am. Will the voters of Colorado concur in that belief? I cannot know." Newton listed reasons why they should place their trust in him: "During my seven years as mayor of Denver, I have encountered in one form or another almost all of the basic issues affecting the economic, social, and political welfare of the people of Colorado and the United States." Newton expressed the opinion that, whatever the outcome of the primary, "however vigorous it may be—we will close ranks for party victory in November." Although his words were high-minded, Quigg astutely attempted to protect his flank. He understood that his recent registration as a Democrat was a serious handicap, and he realized that his opponents would almost certainly attempt to exploit it. Newton stated, "Although my formal identification with the party may be of comparatively recent date, my dedication to its principles is of long standing."[10]

Not surprisingly, Newton's announcement drew praise from his friends and supporters. Denver attorney Bill Grant, who was his campaign manager when he ran for mayor, stated, "I have great respect and high regard for Quigg Newton and will help him in any way I can. I think it's going to be a tough battle for both sides." Grant sounded a note of caution in adding, "It's very hard to tell about a primary or to gauge what chances a mayor of Denver has in running for anything." Newton's longtime aide, Bruce Rockwell, expressed similar thoughts. He labeled himself an "ardent supporter," adding, "I think his chances for election are excellent and that he would make a marvelous senator for Colorado."

Republican governor Dan Thornton attested to Quigg's character, noting that he and his wife had "a very fine relationship with Mayor Newton and his whole family. We're very close friends." Thornton proved to be a prophet when he added, "It certainly shows one thing, though—there's going to be some competition in the Democratic primary." But it quickly became obvious that Newton had ruffled some feathers as mayor and not all observers statewide were enthralled with the prospect of his candidacy. Felix L. Sparks, former district attorney for Delta County, observed, "The Denver water situation will hurt Mayor Newton on the Western Slope. He made a bad impression when he went to Grand Junction recently to discuss water and then closed the door on the subject."[11] Sparks believed that Carroll definitely had an edge over Newton on the Western Slope, but he believed that the party's potential delegates from the region would be willing to listen to Newton's detailed proposals and keep an open mind.

Following Johnson's announcement, Charles Brannan had indicated that he wouldn't decide whether or not to enter the Democratic primary until July. Ultimately, Brannan decided that mounting a serious bid would be too demanding, and nothing further was heard from him. State Senator Lew Williams of Norwood eventually entered the campaign, but he was never a serious contender. The race quickly settled into a two-man contest. Respected *Rocky Mountain News* reporter Robert L. Perkin wrote evenhanded background sketches of both candidates. John Carroll was a formidable opponent. He was in many ways the direct opposite of Newton. Whereas Newton was born into a world of privilege, Carroll was from a working-class background. Ten years older than Quigg, he was born in the Lincoln Park area on Denver's near west side. He was one of many children, and his father drove an ice wagon. His early memories emphasized hard physical work, from lugging fifty-pound blocks of ice for his father, serving as a Western Union messenger, and riding the rails over to Palisade, Colorado, to pick peaches for a dollar a day.

Although Carroll did not see combat in World War I, he dropped out of school to join the military as a sixteen-year-old, and in World War II he served in North Africa, Corsica, Italy, and France. Between the wars, Carroll burned the candle at both ends as a Denver policeman by day and a law student by night. As he worked toward his hard-earned law degree at Westminster Law School, Carroll's interest turned to politics. He became a protégé of Senator Edward P. Costigan, a New Dealer and liberal Democrat. In keeping with both his blue-collar background and natural instincts, Carroll ardently supported the cause of labor, and he earned the respect of other disadvantaged elements, initially in Denver. In the Democratic landslide of 1936, he was elected district attorney for the city. Before he returned to the military during World War II, Carroll lost a primary campaign for governor in 1940. Following the war, Carroll was twice elected to Congress, first by a narrow margin in 1946 and then by a landslide two years later. Carroll attempted to reach the United States Senate in 1950. Although he won the Democratic nomination, the tide had turned against liberals, both in Colorado and across the country. He ran a good race, but he lost to Republican Eugene Milliken by about 25,000 votes. Carroll was determined to wipe out that bad memory in 1954. Only Newton and a Republican opponent in the fall stood in his way.

Newton must have realized from the beginning that he was a decided underdog. For the first and only time in his life, Quigg faced a disadvantage in the "networking" game. Carroll, a lifelong Democrat, was much more experienced, and he had far deeper connections to party regulars—not just in Denver but around the state. Over nearly a quarter of a century, he had been helping to build a party organization, either to promote his own candidacy or those of others. He was well known and generally well liked. Yet Carroll had what many considered as flaws. Some critics claimed he was one of the most predictable politicians in the country. Others believed that, overall, his political positions were far too liberal for the times; they argued that he might be able to win the Democratic nomination, but that he would be a weak candidate in the general election. A few simply dismissed him as a "pinko." Critics stated that his campaign style was a bit stodgy, his words invariably deliberate and measured. The latter could be considered either a strength or a handicap. Although he might not possess charisma, he was unlikely to make serious mistakes by uttering some impulsive or poorly thought out remark. Perkin didn't pass judgment on Carroll; his story basically set out the facts.

Perkin's parallel sketch of Newton's background was equally even-handed: noncommittal and nonjudgmental. At the end of his account of Newton's achievements to date, he noted, "Almost everything interests him; his boredom quotient is extremely low. He has a seemingly inexhaustible store of intellectual patience and perseverance. He's an inveterate question-asker, and he has a special talent for the board of directors sort of approach to problem solving."[12] Perkin may have uncovered some of Quigg's political strengths *and* weaknesses. Possessing a low boredom quotient would well serve any candidate who needed to engage day after day in the same campaign rituals, shake thousands of hands, and deliver virtually identical speeches dozens of times. At the same time, if it appeared to voters that he took a "board of director" approach to issues and problems, he might come across as a bloodless bureaucrat. Voters in Denver knew him well, but he was by and large a stranger elsewhere in Colorado. Quigg would need to project the same warmth and compassion in public before large groups that was so evident in most of his one-on-one personal relationships.

Shortly after Newton entered the race, another columnist writing for the *Durango Herald* considered the relative strengths of both candidates. He noted, "Newton has no old party sores to heal; he has no party factions to overcome; he has suffered no defeats and they say that 'nothing succeeds like success.'" He concluded, "Thus, it's a political veteran with many political scars against a fresh newcomer."[13] Newton may have been a newcomer to Democratic Party ranks, but he did have some fences to mend. Former Denver mayor Ben Stapleton had died in 1950, but a number of his old associates were still around, and some of them carried long-festering wounds. If Newton expected to mount a serious challenge, these suspicious men, and many more like them, would have to be courted and coaxed into his camp. At a minimum, they had to be neutralized.

Newton's biggest challenge was building his own party organization. Hundreds of jobholders in city hall felt enormous loyalty to Newton, but they were, officially at least, nonpartisan. Over more than two decades in politics, Carroll had developed cordial relations with many of the powerful leaders in the statewide Democratic Party. With some old family ties to Pueblo, Newton hoped to attract support in Colorado's third largest city, but he faced formidable opposition in that bastion of labor. It would be a tough fight. Two weeks into the contest between Carroll and Newton, Philip "Tiger" Muhic, Pueblo County Democratic chairman, declared, "I am for John A. Carroll, who has been a Democrat ... I'm for 100 percent Democrats, not seven-month Democrats. But I'll be for whoever wins the primary."[14] Quigg faced opposition from party leaders, not only across the state, but even within his supposed stronghold, Denver. In some of Denver's precincts, the captains, and most of the regulars at party caucuses, were in Carroll's hip pocket from the beginning. In the initial enthusiasm of declaring his candidacy, both Newton and many of his supporters almost seemed to discount the difficulties in overcoming this huge disadvantage.

One of Newton's biggest challenges was reversing a vague but negative impression he had created on the Western Slope during contests over water. Denver had grown rapidly during his years as mayor, and the Front Range had needed to divert increasing amounts of water from the Western Slope. As Denver's mayor, Quigg sometimes found himself in conflict with farmers, ranchers, and key decision-makers on the Western Slope. Newton's campaign strategy was to emphasize that as mayor of Denver, he had acted in an honest, direct, forthright manner in pursuing the *city's* best interests. If nominated and elected to the U.S. Senate, he would represent the entire state, and he would carefully protect Western Slope interests.

During an early May speech in Glenwood Springs, and with Carroll sharing the same stage, Newton indicated that he might be in the "doghouse" on the Western Slope, but promised, "If I am elected to the senate, I would do the same kind of job for the state as I have tried to do for Denver."[15] Speaking at a Jefferson-Jackson Day dinner two days later in Craig, Newton expressed the wish that, "like a magician," he could make water issues disappear—but that wasn't likely to happen. He predicted that the Western Slope would experience a period of "fabulous growth." In response to any implication that a big-city mayor couldn't really understand rural issues, Quigg observed that, as mayor, he had dealt with problems at all levels of government, from local, to state, to the national stage.[16] He claimed that the allegations that elicited his response had come not from Western Slope sources, but "certain quarters" in Denver itself wishing for his defeat.

Senator Ed Johnson was officially on the sidelines during the primary campaign, but privately he supported Newton, offering him detailed practical advice. Early on, Johnson identified Newton's biggest challenge: attracting delegates who would back him at the state convention in July. "Visit personally every Eastern Slope county. Usually the same people go to the State Convention year after year as delegates. Visit as many of the prospective delegates as possible in each county and work on them." He suggested starting with an initial letter, "cold turkey," asking them for support. Johnson advised Quigg to minimize speeches: "This is not a time for oratory. It is a time for 'pussy footing,' personal visiting with party leaders and *delegates*" (emphasis his). Johnson suggested that Newton confine his speeches to short radio addresses and that they not be too partisan at this point: "Be a democratic statesman." If Quigg won the primary, he could then modify his strategy for the general election.

If Johnson was pessimistic about Newton's chances, he kept his thoughts private. He told Quigg that Lew Williams's decision to enter the primary "cut Carroll's vote on the West Slope by 5,000 votes, and that, for purposes of the state convention, Williams had '*taken the West Slope Country off your back*'" (emphasis his). Still, he warned Newton that if he was to make a serious bid for the nomination, he had to get moving: "You are not working hard enough and you are shooting at the moon instead of Newton delegates to the July 24 convention." Johnson then urged Quigg to warm up to the irritating little things that candidates for office traditionally had to do: "Women voters will love it if you pay a tribute to your wife and a *lavish one*. Pull out all the stops on wife and babies. Say you married a fighting Democrat and she converted you long, long ago. Tell 'em you could not live with that woman without accepting her political views, etc. Pull that a few times, and the taunts will cease" (emphasis his).[17]

During his years as mayor, Newton had maintained a modest-sized war chest of contributions from friends and business associates, banks and corporations, plus dozens of small donations from city workers and average citizens. In 1953, contributions in Denver and across the state amounted to approximately $60,000.[18] Running a campaign for the Senate would be a very expensive operation, however, and he needed some heavy contributors to step forward. Quigg's brother-in-law, Dick Davis, conducted the fundraising campaign, but he encountered significant difficulties, even among longtime associates and family friends. In response to a solicitation letter, Mahlon Thatcher, chairman of the board of the First National Bank of Pueblo, informed Davis, "I fully agree with you as to his integrity and fidelity to his convictions, but feel that he leans farther toward New Deal philosophy than I can go along with."[19] Equally influential, Denver investor Tyson Dines, an old-line Denver blueblood, voiced similar concerns. After stating his personal affection for Quigg, he expressed outrage that he had not joined the Republican fight "in stopping the drift to Socialism and in correcting at least some of the evils with which the Democratic Party has burdened the country." Dines insisted that Newton had "joined ranks with those whom I feel have undermined our constitution and jeopardized our freedom." Dines would not support Quigg's campaign; he would even vote against him if he was nominated.[20]

As the campaign entered its final weeks, money became an increasingly worrisome issue, and Davis adopted a strategy of requesting support from Republican-leaning friends based on the notion that Newton was a far less dangerous, or "liberal," Democratic candidate than Carroll would be. Davis did not put it in so many words, but he implied that they should help Democrats nominate the lesser of two evils. To one distant family member, Davis wrote, "I know that you would be surprised and pleased at the number of our good Republican friends who have come to realize that they have a vital stake in the outcome of the Democratic primary, regardless of party, and that they can ill afford to let Carroll beat Quigg. ... Many of our friends have finally decided that they cannot run the risk of having a labor Senator to represent them and have come forward with substantial help. ... "[21]

Thomas K. Younge, partner in a law firm in Grand Junction, worried that the likely Republican nominee, Gordon Allott, could not defeat Carroll. Younge conceded that of the three candidates, Newton was "the best qualified." He believed that it would be "disastrous" for Colorado if Carroll were elected. However, he was deeply disturbed that Newton, "a man of very commendable family background was attempting to curry political favor by taking a stand opposed to his own class," and he told Davis he could not provide any financial support.[22]

Newton received a good deal of advice on how to deal with the "Johnny-come-lately" tag he received from some Democrats. His father-in-law, Morrison Shafroth, had run unsuccessfully for the Democratic nomination for the Senate in 1930. The individual who defeated him, Edward P. Costigan, was then a newcomer to the party. Shafroth had worked in the trenches among the party faithful for years, and he recalled resenting Costigan. Yet he acknowledged that Costigan had been a brilliant senator, even a national treasure: "I believe that everyone will agree, including myself, that the nomination and election of Senator Edward P. Costigan brought to the Democratic Party and the State of Colorado a vision, a breadth of viewpoint, a new outlook, and a general attitude on public affairs that has seldom been equaled in the entire history of the State." He added paternally, "I believe you will do the same."[23] Equally important, Shafroth recalled that complaining about Costigan's recent conversion and taking on a "poor me" attitude toward him hadn't swayed voters. Shafroth was clearly suggesting that if Carroll or his supporters kept repeating the "newcomer" charge against Newton, he could perhaps turn it to his advantage by discussing the stellar contributions of other recently converted Democrats in the nation's past.

Shafroth even wrote out suggestions for a speech the candidate might use in the future. Shafroth's draft recounted in detail how William Jennings Bryan, a three-time Democratic candidate for president who had been defeated each time, strongly desired to make yet another try in 1912. The battle for delegates had been bitter. After interminable wrangling and forty-six ballots, however, the Democrats finally nominated political newcomer Woodrow Wilson. Describing Bryan as "an old warhorse who had battled the battles of the party for many years," Shafroth noted that he had acquired many enemies, and his name had become associated with "so many issues to which the public exhibited an iron-clad resistance." Shafroth clearly implied that Quigg's quest bore strong parallels with Wilson's: "Wilson coming newly into the party without the scars, bitterness and animosities and petty divisions that had been aroused in previous campaigns was able to sweep the country. ... Had the nomination been made on the length of service to the party, Bryan would have been nominated and probably defeated in the general election."[24] In fact, although Quigg did not follow Shafroth's suggestions to the letter, he did stress that his lack of "battle scars," compared to Carroll's, would be a significant advantage for Democrats in the general election.

Newton was beginning to grasp the reality that rounding up convention delegates was a decidedly uphill battle. Mike Pomponio, a longtime district captain and Democratic power broker in North Denver, had not yet decided which candidate to support, but he set up a dinner at his restaurant for Newton to meet other district captains. Unfortunately, nine captains failed to show up, including several of the most powerful men in the party.[25] By late June, the *Rocky Mountain News* reported that, lacking control of the regular party organization, Newton was trying to create a parallel organization. Bruce Rockwell, an administrative assistant during Newton's first term as mayor, returned from his public relations job with Colorado National Bank to help set up an organization and try to recruit delegates. Tom Currigan, a future mayor of Denver, also worked in that capacity.[26] Establishing a rival organization without permanently alienating regular Democrats would prove to be a very tricky and ultimately impossible task. Although increasing numbers of Newton buttons began appearing around city hall, the candidate and his advisors realized that strong-arm tactics, or connecting job security to political "loyalty," would backfire. In early July, a story in the *Rocky Mountain News* reviewed city hall politics in past elections. The reporter claimed that the late mayor, Ben Stapleton, had once estimated that each of 4,000 employees "was good for ten votes." Despite the fact that Newton insisted that he was continuing to manage the city on a nonpartisan basis, the reporter claimed that Newton was building his own political machine, and he flatly stated, "City workers have had it made clear that they are expected to vote for Newton."[27]

Despite some reversals, Newton and his newly recruited political operatives were learning the game of rounding up delegates to the state convention. At the Democratic county assembly in early July, the Carroll and Newton camps both pulled out all the stops in attempting to manipulate each election district into choosing delegates who would vote as a bloc for their candidate, despite much more evenly divided support within given districts.[28] Following the assembly, Carroll supporters predicted that the city would support their candidate by an 80 percent margin, but Newton backers claimed the split was more like fifty-fifty. In order to receive a line on the Democratic ballot for the September 14 primary, a candidate had to receive at least 20 percent of delegate votes at the state assembly. That amounted to just over 300 votes. Newton revealed that he had learned something about politics when he predicted that after "a hard uphill battle," he might get 400 votes. Privately, Newton was hoping to do much better. At the state convention, after all the votes were counted, Carroll earned an absolute majority with 760 votes and Newton received 503. Lew Williams, the third candidate, attracted only 238, and thus he did not gain a place on the ballot. Although Carroll had won the initial face-off, Newton gained a strategic victory when the state election commission decided that rather than placing Carroll on the "top line" of the ballot—a place most politicians perceived as a distinct advantage—the two candidates' names would appear side by side.[29]

After the state convention, the candidates had just over six weeks to make their final pitch to Colorado voters, and it would be an all-out sprint to the finish. Quigg did receive some "in-kind" assistance in moving quickly around the state. Ginny Newton recalled that Harry Combs, an old Yale friend and future president of Gates Learjet, had started an aircraft company, and he frequently flew the couple from town to town to make campaign appearances. More than once, they landed in farmers' fields.[30] Despite help from generous friends, by the end of July, Newton could already sense that his chances were beginning to slip away. For starters, coverage of his campaign in the *Rocky Mountain News* was taking on a distinctly negative tone. When Newton delivered an important televised campaign "kickoff" speech in early August, the paper stated that he "formally opened his campaign … on a disappointing note." The *News* added, "Stepping off with the four-station television address labeled 'A Statement of Convictions,' he spoke only in the broadest and most general terms." The *News* story accused him of clouding the issues and presenting vague homilies, finally concluding, "To take his measure as a possible United States Senator, the voters must know specifically where he stands and what he believes."[31]

Negative Campaigning

Both Democratic candidates could take heart in the results of a *Denver Post* poll taken a month before the statewide primary predicting that *either* man would defeat Gordon Allott, the Republican candidate, who was unopposed. Even there, however, Carroll had the edge, as he outpolled Allott by nineteen points, whereas Newton's margin was just thirteen points.[32] As the campaign entered its final stretch and Newton sensed that his candidacy was in trouble, he began resorting to ad hominem attacks against Carroll. A month before the primary, leaders of the Committee for Industrial Organization, the American Federation of Labor, and the Railroad Brotherhood all officially endorsed Carroll. In a speech delivered on August 18, Newton blasted Carroll as a tool of labor: "The record of my opponent on labor issues, and on all national issues in which labor has an interest is crystal clear. What the leaders of organized labor want, he wants. He is committed—by his 100 percent record, by his all-out statements, and by his long-standing obligations—to the position that the leaders of organized labor are always right." Quigg presented himself as a moderate on virtually every issue, implying if not specifically stating that

his opponent was an extremist. On the labor issue, Newton pointed to his record as mayor of Denver to prove that he had the "friendship, the support, and the confidence of the working people."

Yet in the same speech, he also claimed that the Taft-Hartley Act, despised by almost every labor leader, had a few good points along with many bad ones,

In all likelihood, Ginny is out of the picture directing the Newton daughters' music ensemble (ca. 1954). Left to right: Abby, Nan, Nelle, and Ginna.

and he stated that he had opposed the closed shop in Denver and would continue to do so: "The closed shop should remain outlawed. No worker should be deprived of the right to work for reasons which may have nothing to do with his ability on the job or his willingness to join a union." Newton stated, "Labor and management are wholly dependent on each other and must work together as a team."[33] Newton's moderation on the labor issue may have won him a few votes from more-conservative Democrats in the primary; yet it suggests that, for all intents and purposes, he conceded the labor vote to Carroll.

In explaining his "attack strategy," Newton insisted that he was simply trying to set the record straight. Although Quigg's verbal offensive was by no means vicious, Carroll expressed outrage and disappointment that the campaign had degenerated into name-calling: "The people of America are sick, tired and disgusted generally with smear campaigning." He continued, "[I]n the past week, whether born of fear, disappointment or desperation, we seem to have entered a phase of name-calling and mud-slinging." Attempting to present himself as the more high-minded candidate, Carroll pleaded for party unity: "We are not campaigning in the Deep South. The winner in the primary contest cannot thereby be regarded as the virtually certain winner in November." But Carroll warned, "If the campaign should degenerate into a mud-slinging campaign, it will be necessary for us to fight fire with fire."[34]

Carroll got off a few zingers of his own. He charged Newton with "riding a Trojan horse crammed with Republicans ambitious to take over the Democratic Party."[35] That did not stop Newton, who decided to review Carroll's voting record in Congress in detail. Quigg labeled his opponent a "rubber stamp" politician who always looked to the party's most radical elements for guidance on how to vote. Newton claimed that in his first term, Carroll had voted the straight "party line" 91 percent of the time, and that during his term between 1948 and 1950, Carroll had a "100 percent rubber stamp vote." Newton claimed that as mayor of Denver he had promoted a wide variety of projects advocated by liberal Democrats, "but I never have aligned myself with or agreed with the party extremists in the East who see nothing but evil in business and nothing but good in labor."[36] The same day, Carroll retorted that Newton's attack was not only "juvenile and immature," but was the work of a "frightened and desperate candidate." Carroll insisted, "Colorado Democrats won't be fooled by the 'lifting' of certain pages in the Carroll record for political convenience and ignoring the complete record—a record that bespeaks leadership, I say proudly not rubber stampism."[37]

Negative attacks increased on both sides. Newton may have believed that his one hope was to paint Carroll as an extremist who would have little or no ability to attract disaffected Republican voters in the general election. Defending himself against Carroll's rhetoric, Newton stated, "The hackneyed Trojan horse charge was characteristic of Mr. Carroll's consistent attitude through the years that any Democrat who does not go along with his left wing position is necessarily a Republican reactionary." In the same speech, Quigg charged that Carroll had divided the Democratic Party into two factions: "left-wing Democrats and middle-of-the-road Democrats. The left wing faction is the John A. Carroll faction. The middle-of-the-road is led by U.S. Senator Ed C. Johnson." Not surprisingly, Newton allied himself as closely as possible with Johnson's image, insisting that only a candidate with his perspectives would be able to work effectively in the Senate by cooperating with moderates in both parties. Carroll was having none of it. He replied acidly, "The mayor is a spoiled boy, and he's apparently in a violent tantrum." Although political polling a half-century ago was not nearly as sophisticated or accurate as it is today, Carroll and his managers firmly believed they had a comfortable lead among likely voters. He added, "There's nothing any one of us can do except perhaps to take him to the woodshed Sept. 14 and whale the devil out of him."[38]

The last two weeks of Newton's campaign appeared very disorganized. In his speeches, he seemed to be moving back and forth across the political landscape, searching for some issue or combination of issues that would ignite a spark in the minds of voters. Quigg devoted one entire speech to farm issues. Quigg acknowledged that, being raised in an urban area and being a big-city mayor, he was "not an expert on farms, on farming or on the farm problem." He pledged that if elected senator, however, he would "work to help hold the legislative gains farmers have made in the last two decades and work for improvements."[39] With his military service and his long-term interest in foreign policy challenges, Newton was undoubtedly more convincing when he devoted an entire speech to these issues alone. But he failed to clarify where he and Carroll parted company on foreign policy.[40]

In another speech, Newton tackled problems facing the nation's elderly citizens. After presenting actuarial statistics revealing rapidly escalating numbers of Americans of retirement age and acknowledging that meeting their old-age needs would become an increasingly contentious issue, Newton launched into a philosophical discussion of the importance of valuing the nation's elderly and making their lives *meaningful*: "Most of all—old people want to feel that they still matter to somebody—they are important to their family and community—and that they are not merely being tolerated."[41] Quigg's words provided invigorating, fresh, and deeply compassionate insights, but just how they connected to the everyday, pragmatic concerns of Colorado electorate in 1954 was anybody's guess. On certain issues, Newton sounded as visionary and disconnected from reality as former Democratic vice president and party maverick Henry A. Wallace.[42]

Unfortunately for Newton, investigative reporters who researched some of his statements about Carroll's voting record as a congressman uncovered discrepancies in at least one of his claims. James Daniel, a Washington correspondent for the *Rocky Mountain News*, stated that Newton's charge that during 1950 Congressman Carroll had followed a 100-percent "party line" vote was erroneous, perhaps caused by an inadvertent misinterpretation of language in the *Congressional Record*.[43] The dispute was largely a matter of semantics, but it forced Quigg to spend valuable time backtracking and defending his statements in the last week of his campaign. Newton's campaign received another jolt when a former city attorney in his administration defended Carroll's record and claimed that Newton "[was] forced by his ghost writers and political advisors to mouth untruths against John Carroll."[44]

As the campaign headed into the homestretch, Newton continued to pound away at the idea that Carroll was a "tool" of big labor. Carroll deftly countered Newton's words, implying that his opponent was in fact criticizing workers themselves. The mayor had to backtrack to explain that he was criticizing a few powerful labor leaders who, in his view, were attempting to dictate to the rank and file how to cast their votes.[45] In a televised address five days before the primary election, Newton appeared to be missing some of his fire. He stated that one of his purposes in joining the Democratic Party and running for the Senate was to act as a party healer, one who might draw dissident elements closer together: "It was my hope at the time that I might in some way be able to help in bringing them together, in restoring unity to the party. That hope is not altogether gone, but it has faded." Was Quigg conceding the outcome? Not at all. He continued, "I want no part of the arrogant intolerance that goes with the Carroll attitude that parades the false label of liberalism. The true liberal is the man who has some respect for those who disagree with him and is willing to sit down and try to work out differences of opinion."[46]

Looking back on Newton's campaign for the Senate a half-century later, Bruce Rockwell, one of the mayor's most influential campaign volunteers, recalled that he had sensed almost from the beginning that his candidate would lose. Newton had no viable party organization, and he simply had too many obstacles to overcome.[47] For the uninitiated, however, there may have been some suspense even in the last week of the campaign. The weekend before the primary, the *Rocky Mountain News* published a so-called poll showing the candidates literally neck and neck, each carrying 23 percent of the vote, with a 41 percent margin for error! The story was an apparent spoof written by a veteran staff reporter.[48] A serious poll published two days before the election showed Carroll with roughly a five-to-three edge among likely voters.[49]

Facing Defeat

Primary day finally arrived on September 14. There was little suspense at either campaign headquarters. Newton's supporters were holed up at the Albany Hotel, Carroll's two blocks away. As precincts around the state began to report, Carroll jumped out to an early lead. Carroll took roughly a three-to-two lead as the votes were tallied, a margin that held throughout the evening. By nine o'clock, Bill Grant, Newton's campaign manager, knew that the issue was settled, and Quigg prepared to concede. Publicly, the mayor took the outcome well as he mingled among dwindling groups of supporters: "Cheer up. A little loss is good for us. We learn from our mistakes." Quigg's father-in-law, Morrison Shafroth, added, "We mustn't be too discouraged; it's part of politics. Just remember, Abraham Lincoln was beaten when he ran for the first time."[50]

When queried about the Senate race almost a half-century later, Newton quickly acknowledged that it had been a mistake. During the first few months, he believed he might win. Polls suggested that, in the first few weeks, he actually did lead Carroll. Knowledgeable political operatives in his camp realized that the tide was running against them by the early summer, however, and that he was unlikely to win. Naturally, they did not confide their feelings to the candidate. Perhaps a month before the election, Newton himself sensed that it was a hopeless cause. Quigg recalled that the last two or three weeks before the election were quite depressing; he was going through the motions of what he sensed was a failed effort. For the last weeks, he couldn't sleep very well. His greatest disappointment was his failure to carry much of the labor vote. He believed that, as mayor, he had treated labor well, and workers did not demonstrate their gratitude. Newton was not used to failure, and it hurt deeply.[51]

In the aftermath of the primary, the defeated candidate received comfort from many quarters. Two days after the count was in, Ed Johnson wrote a long handwritten letter to Newton analyzing the campaign. He praised Quigg's effort, but reminded him that Carroll had enjoyed a huge head start. Had the Democrats chosen Newton, Johnson believed, "You would have won hands down in the general election." Like Shafroth, Johnson believed Newton still had a bright future in the Democratic Party.[52] Kenneth C. Penfold of the Associated Alumni at the University of Colorado wrote, "It is difficult for me to comprehend how the Democrats in Colorado could be so stupid to have elected your questionable opponent in place of you. … My faith in the Democratic citizens of Colorado has been shaken badly." Penfold then shared a view many citizens held at the time: "I can't help but feel that you would have been the next U.S. Senator from Colorado had you chosen the Republican Party."[53]

Ben Cherrington, regional director of the Institute of International Education in Denver, blamed Newton's defeat in part on his advisors' strategy during the last half of the campaign: "[You] possess a quality which was not allowed to stand out in the campaign. It is a quality which not many men in public life possess, but when they genuinely do have it, historians usually refer to them as statesmen and common people erect monuments in their memory. I refer to the quality of magnanimity."[54] Finally, another supporter wrote, "My greatest concern is that you do not allow this experience to cause you to lower your sights. There is a desperate need in high lawmaking bodies of this nation for persons with your ideals and comprehension of problems."[55]

In the fall of 1954, however, Newton was in no mood to dream of a future in politics. He might still have considered running for a third term as mayor, and some speculated that he would do so. But Quigg sincerely believed that he had effected most of the programs he believed were key to the city's future and that it was time for him to turn over the reins of local government. Mostly, though, he was becoming bored in the position. If he hoped to evolve as a productive public citizen and human being, he believed he needed a new challenge. Quigg also had a wife and four daughters to support, and he sought new challenges.

Following his loss to Carroll, Newton provided a routine endorsement of his rival's candidacy, but Carroll did not seek much assistance from him during the general election campaign against the Republican nominee, Gordon Allott. Bruce Rockwell believed that this was largely because Carroll didn't believe that Newton, lacking a significant party organization, had much to contribute to the campaign.[56] Although he suggested otherwise in public interviews, Newton was still interested in political service. Following the general election, he wrote letters offering unspecified services to numerous victorious Democratic senators, including

Lyndon B. Johnson (Texas), Theodore F. Green (Rhode Island), Strom Thurmond (South Carolina), and Paul Douglas (Illinois).

Landing on His Feet

Newton didn't realize it at the time, but his political career was over. Fortunately, an exciting new opportunity awaited him just around the corner, or at least in New York City. At about the time he announced he would not seek a third term as mayor of Denver, he received a call from Paul Ylvesaker of the Ford Foundation asking if he would be interested in interviewing for a public relations position with that prestigious organization. It is highly unlikely that Quigg was surprised to receive this feeler, since he had networked skillfully, nurturing deep roots into the East Coast establishment ever since his years at Andover a quarter century earlier. His selection as one of the Jaycees' Ten Outstanding Young Men in 1948 plus his election as president of the American Municipal Association in 1950 had provided him further national visibility.

Newton had also been chosen in 1951 to serve as a trustee of the Yale Corporation, the managing body that reviewed general university policy and advised the university's president. That placed Quigg in very

The Newton family in Riverdale, New York, (1955) during Quigg's service with the Ford Foundation.

elite company. Fellow trustees included some of the nation's most influential decision-makers, including President Truman's secretary of state Dean Acheson, Ohio Republican senator Robert A. Taft, Prescott Bush of Texas, and Roger Blough, president of United States Steel. Although he was mayor of Denver and lived almost 2,000 miles from New Haven, Newton took his duties as a trustee very seriously, and he almost never missed the monthly meetings. Quigg seemed to know everybody of importance in positions of authority. He was on a first-name basis with supreme court justices, U.S. senators, key university presidents, top-level business executives, and even Vice President Richard M. Nixon.

Newton only served four years of his six-year elected term at the Yale Corporation. After he joined the Ford Foundation, he resigned from the Yale Corporation. Since the Ford Foundation had extensive dealings with the university, Quigg feared that serving both institutions simultaneously might involve conflicts of interest. He made his decision against the advice of high-level men in both organizations, and he later regretted having done so. Newton felt enormous loyalty to Yale for his entire life, and he felt deeply privileged to serve his alma mater. Quigg's years as a trustee involved some very complex freedom-of-speech issues. He served during the height of McCarthyism, and universities and their faculty across the country faced demands to prove their loyalty to the United States, its traditions, and most of all, its form of government. Newton was deeply impressed at the integrity of men such as Roger Blough, an economic conservative and a staunch Republican, yet a fierce defender of the right of professors to express liberal, even radical, ideas.

In June 1955, Newton watched as his successor as mayor, Will F. Nicholson, was sworn in. Then he and his family departed for a leisurely cross-country vacation, ending up at the Shafroth family summer home in Cape Cod. Good friends in the New York City area helped the Newtons find a spacious home on an estate in fashionable Riverdale, located on the east bank of the Hudson River, about thirty minutes by train north of the city.[57] As Quigg took up his duties at the Ford Foundation in the early fall, Ginny set up housekeeping, enrolled the girls in schools, and taught music at the Riverdale Country Day School.

In 1955, the Ford Foundation was less than twenty years old, and it faced major organizational challenges. It had been incorporated in Michigan in January 1936, funded by bonds, stocks, cash, and real property donated by Henry Ford and his son, Edsel. Early gifts, in relatively small dollar amounts, benefited Michigan charities for the most part. The foundation was being run by good-hearted amateurs. Following World War II and the death in 1947 of the patriarch, Henry Ford, the foundation received tens of millions of dollars of new assets and suddenly became one of the largest private foundations in the country. The directors realized that recruiting professional management and establishing long-term goals were critically important. They moved into sumptuous offices at 477 Park Avenue in New York and undertook a major study of how best to reorganize. The study was presented to the directors in 1949. The directors failed to modernize the organization overnight, and in the mid-1950s, the foundation was still haphazardly doling out relatively small grants with no discernable overall focus. Hiring Newton was part of the foundation's effort to modernize and establish professional management.[58]

When Newton reported for work, the Ford Foundation was dealing with yet another major infusion of capital from the Ford family. Most of the new assets were Ford Motor Company stock, and foundation officials wished to sell off a good deal of it to diversify its holdings. As the newly hired manager of public relations, Quigg received letters from executives at securities companies hoping to acquire some of the foundation's business—even before he reported for work.[59]

Newton threw himself into his new work with his customary gusto. The challenges and possibilities inherent in the position excited him. Since he was extremely well connected with the nation's mayors and had solid connections with governors, U.S. senators, and other high-level public officials, the foundation asked him to develop ideas ranging across "the whole gamut of public affairs—advancing the science of government, strengthening processes, testing new theory and techniques, broadening citizen participation, initiating and promoting programs of civic education, and taking a creative stance toward the whole field. ... "[60]

Some relatively small grants caused public relations problems. The foundation had given money to the Fund for the Republic, headed by former University of Chicago president Robert M. Hutchins. The organization's purpose was to study strengths and weaknesses of democracy, and some reactionary public officials thought this amounted to treason. The House Un-American Activities Committee was raising questions about whether or not the Fund for the Republic was a Communist front organization. Although the foundation refused to withdraw support, Newton wisely sensed that the organization should put itself firmly at arm's length from any investigation and that Hutchins could ably handle external pressure himself. Quigg's instincts proved correct. The Ford Foundation had also provided funding for a study of the effectiveness of the jury system in America. The recipients had engaged in some highly unorthodox initiatives, such as bugging jury rooms and judge's chambers. Newspapers revealed details, and public criticism was intense.[61]

Another grant that attracted a good deal of public attention was a $200,000 initial award, with a potential payout of $1.5 million over five years, to researchers in Wisconsin to "study the handling and final disposition of criminals from the time they land in police court until final action has been taken by the highest courts in the land."[62] This was hardly a routine commitment. Conspiracy theorists and reactionary critics might interpret such a grant as a calculated attack against the criminal justice system.

Thus, Newton was tossed into a pressure cooker immediately. As had been the case when he was mayor of Denver, Newton sensed that he was operating in a fishbowl in Manhattan, but the bowl seemed quite a bit larger and contained more dangerous obstacles. Evidently, Quigg passed all his tests. His work in public relations was so outstanding that his superiors quickly promoted him. Within six months of moving to New York, he became a vice president of the foundation.

After becoming a vice president at the Ford Foundation, Newton stressed his view in a confidential internal memo circulated among top level administrators that the organization faced a number of public relations minefields. They included its special tax status: "In this atmosphere of increasing public attention, the Foundation is an obvious target. It is, for example, the most conspicuous product of tax exemption for philanthropic purposes—hence the prime target for those who attack the exemption theory." Newton also noted that when the foundation awarded funds to organizations reexamining traditional American values, "the mere act of re-examination may provide criticism from those who tend to regard the status quo as sacrosanct." Newton believed that when making any award, foundation officers needed to be acutely aware that "one ill-advised major grant could destroy all the public confidence and good will engendered by the bulk of our program." He stressed, "A policy of tailoring all of our actions to fit the prevailing mood or convictions would, in fact, be a modification both of the Foundation's program and of the concept of the foundation role upon which that program is based."[63] In other words, the foundation would sacrifice its integrity by craven submission to short-term public opinion.

With acquisition of huge chunks of Ford Motor Company stock in the mid-1950s, the Ford Foundation became the largest private foundation in the world, surpassing even the Rockefeller Foundation. Back then, most of the grants awarded were still in the $25,000 to $100,000 range. Even a half-century ago, these were quite small by major foundation standards. Newton realized that if the Ford Foundation hoped to upgrade its image and operate in a truly professional manner, it should focus on providing much larger grants to major institutions. When Newton arrived, the foundation had a large staff administering large numbers of small grants. In Quigg's mind, this was an inefficient use of personnel. Rather than monitoring dozens, even hundreds, of small awards, Newton believed that the foundation, and the public, would be better served by it making a smaller number of large awards that focused on more-sharply defined areas of public interest. An added advantage of such a strategy would be that foundation personnel could monitor the awards more closely and provide guidance and assistance where they were needed.[64]

Newton by no means redirected the foundation by himself in his eighteen months with Ford; rather, he helped refine ideas that were already percolating among its leaders. One of Newton's greatest strengths was networking, and he quickly formed close working relationships with many of the most influential policy makers at the nation's leading private universities. During his time on board, the Ford Foundation made a series of grants to many of the larger private universities in the country that permitted them to enhance their academic programs in a variety of ways. University presidents were encouraged to stretch their imaginations concerning how the funds were used, but one $50 million grant, allocated on a dollar-for-dollar matching basis by participating institutions, was earmarked for enhancing faculty salaries.

The foundation also awarded $20 million for scholarships for particularly promising undergraduates. Another major program area was upgrading of numerous private hospitals around the country. The foundation pumped some $500 million into universities and hospitals. Newton worked particularly closely with the hospital grants. Although mandates concerning what type of awards hospitals might pursue were extremely broad, hospital administrators whose grant applications focused on ways to provide services to citizens previously excluded from health care networks tended to receive most favorable consideration.

Although Newton had temporarily left Colorado, the editors of Denver's dailies believed that the ex-mayor's activities in New York would interest readers, and they occasionally sent reporters east to do follow-up interviews. On separate occasions, two respected Denver journalists, Max Goldberg and Robert L. Perkin, conversed with Newton in his comfortable office at the Ford Foundation. Newton basically gave the same story to both men. He loved his job, and he enjoyed the challenges of living and working in the pressure cooker of New York. He stated that his family was enjoying life in Riverdale. Ginny had settled in and was teaching at nearby Riverdale Country Day School, and his daughters were making new friends in the suburb. Quigg mentioned that he had no intentions of spending the rest of his life in New York, however, and that both he and Ginny hoped to return to Denver "some day." He told Goldberg that "when I return I shall participate in those things which I am interested in most, 'politics and government.'"[65] Interviewed by Perkin early in 1956, Newton admitted that another run for public office might be the catalyst for returning to Colorado, but he "couldn't say" when that might occur. Yet he would definitely return to the Mile High City: "Denver is our home. Our roots are deep there. Ginny's and mine. We want to get back when the time comes. There's no substitute for Denver."[66]

When Quigg talked with Perkin in February 1956, he may have been vaguely mulling over thoughts of eventually running for a seat in the House of Representatives, making another try for the Senate, or running for governor of Colorado. Even he couldn't have imagined the circumstances in which he would return to the state just ten months later. In the fall of that year, Newton received feelers concerning whether he would be interested in becoming president of the University of Colorado. Intrigued, Newton permitted his candidacy to move forward. In a vote in their October meeting, divided four to two along party lines, the regents decided to offer him the job. After talking over the situation with outgoing university president Ward Darley, Quigg agreed at the end of October to assume the reins at the university.

Although Newton had only been at the Ford Foundation for a year and a half, he had made a big impact, and his highest-level associates were disappointed to lose his services so suddenly. John J. McCloy, former assistant secretary of war and an entrenched member of the East Coast establishment, wrote to another associate at the foundation, "It is a real job that he is undertaking because the University of Colorado has a real potential, but it is very unfortunate we have to lose him."[67] Newton understood, correctly, that in accepting the presidency of the University of Colorado, he was stepping into an exciting intellectual challenge. If Quigg had any idealized, romantic notion of stepping into a comfortable, if challenging, intellectual atmosphere, however, he was seriously mistaken. He was, in fact, signing on for what would become a wild six-year ride.

CHAPTER 9

THE HALLS OF ACADEMIA

Just months after going to work for the Ford Foundation, Newton received the first inkling that he might return to Colorado much sooner than he or his family expected. The University of Colorado was searching for a new president. The incumbent, Ward Darley, had experienced three trying years as head of the institution; in June 1956, he formally notified the regents that he wanted to return to his primary interest, medical education. He had accepted an offer to be director of the Association of Medical Education in Evanston, Illinois, and he planned to begin work there in January 1957. Thus he would only stay at the University of Colorado until the end of the fall semester.

In fact, several months before officially informing the regents of his future plans, Darley had indicated privately to Quigg that he was feeling uneasy as president at the university, and he was clearly sounding Quigg out regarding possible interest in becoming his successor. Newton had just been made a vice president at the Ford Foundation, but he must have expressed immediate interest. In early December 1955, Darley wrote, "I am pleased that this promotion will not stand in the way of a proposition which I hope will be in your hands in a few weeks."[1] Weeks turned into months, but by the late summer of 1956, Newton was under serious consideration to replace Darley; according to some sources, by late August he was the leading candidate.[2]

The University of Colorado had experienced considerable turmoil under Darley's watch. Darley served during the height of the McCarthy era. In recent years, the university had been deeply divided over the propriety of loyalty oaths and the firing of several popular and dynamic professors because of alleged ties to the Communist Party and/or other suspected communist front organizations. There had been other fractious issues, including a divided vote by the regents to require social fraternities to renounce racial discrimination clauses in their charters. The day-to-day challenges of running the university were also becoming more intense. In the decade following the end of World War II, the university had grown very rapidly. It was saddled with an inefficient and thoroughly outdated administrative structure that, in the words of several university historians, had "produced organizational chaos."[3]

Taking the Helm

Why would a major state university seriously consider hiring as its leader an individual without a Ph.D. and no formal academic background? Two key factors made Newton attractive. Given the administrative challenges negatively affecting the university and considering Newton's experience in modernizing city government in Denver, a majority of the regents believed he would handle this key challenge extremely well. In addition, at midcentury, the importance to universities of gaining external grant support for faculty research and for institutional development had never been greater.

In terms of population and economic development, Colorado was a rapidly growing state, and university enrollments were expanding quickly. Fifty years ago, the University of Colorado did not yet enjoy a reputation as an important research university. As a vice president of the Ford Foundation, Newton brought to the table an insider's knowledge of how the external funding process worked. To university leaders aware of such quickly expanding opportunities, Newton's familiarity with the process more than compensated for his lack of academic credentials. They may also have assumed that since Newton didn't possess a conventional academic background, he would not interfere in faculty matters. A third, less-crucial consideration in Newton's favor was that, unlike many potential candidates already in academic positions, he would be able to assume the post in the middle of the academic year.

Newton was both flattered and pleased by the attention, and he was intrigued by the opportunity from the start. He learned that the job would pay $20,000, a major pay cut from his salary with the Ford Foundation. But living costs in Boulder would be far lower than in New York, and the university would provide housing and cover all entertainment expenses. At the same time, Quigg could not help but be aware that when his name was submitted for consideration, the thought of offering the presidency to a nonacademic individual aroused considerable concern among some faculty. At the time, Newton was not fully aware of how strongly Dayton David McKean, dean of the graduate school, wanted the position. In fact, McKean, who had written a biography of Jersey City's notoriously corrupt and extremely powerful political boss Frank Hague, was an intense student of manipulative politics.[4] McKean was lobbying hard for the presidency, and he had already lined up two faculty committees from various schools and colleges to support his candidacy. One committee included nine deans. The other was a group from the faculty assembly. At this crucial juncture, however, McKean made a major strategic blunder. Typically, faculty committees provide complex responses to relatively simple issues. Such was the case with McKean's support groups. In late October, they reported to the regents that the new president "should be a man of academic stature with university experience in administration, teaching and research."[5] This would obviously exclude Newton. Rather than forcefully making the case for appointing McKean, however, they attempted to prove to the regents that they had considered numerous viable candidates; they duly submitted lists of a half dozen or more possible appointees.

As it turned out, the majority of regents were concerned that overly lengthy delays in moving to replace Darley would mean the loss of the most attractive candidate. Prompt action was crucial. At least one decision-maker raised the possibility of appointing an acting, or interim, president, but the idea generated little enthusiasm. Another idea circulated was the notion of creating a sort of dual-headed administration, with two men hired at identical salaries. McKean would presumably be in charge of faculty matters, and another individual selected by the regents would handle all other facets of running the university. Although the two faculty committees backing McKean voted 8-4 to support such an arrangement, it never advanced any farther. Cooler heads reasoned that grafting such an unorthodox management setup onto an already unwieldy administrative structure would be a recipe for disaster.[6] They wanted the new president to be fully in charge and wholly accountable.

At a contentious meeting on October 27, the regents voted 4–2 along strict party lines to offer the presidency to Newton. All four Democrats voted in favor of the motion; the two Republicans, Charles D. "Jim" Bromley and Virginia Blue, were opposed.[7] President Darley immediately informed Newton of his selection by phone. Not surprisingly, Newton did not accept the post immediately. Although Ginny was enthusiastic about returning to Colorado, the girls were in school and had established new friendships, and leaving the East Coast in mid-year could be stressful for them. In addition, Newton learned that his selection was a contentious issue; he wanted to visit the campus and talk with each regent individually before making a final decision. One of the chief reasons Darley had resigned was that he was tired of campus politics. Quigg arranged to talk over campus issues with the departing president at Chicago's Midway Airport. Darley stressed that because Newton had been mayor of Denver for eight years, he would soon learn the political ropes at the university.[8] Thoroughly methodical as always, Newton took what he perceived as every possible precaution before committing himself. Despite his best efforts, however, it appears unlikely that at the time Quigg fully grasped the depth of frustration among many university leaders and personnel caused by his selection.

For example, Newton wanted to learn why Regent Charles Bromley was so opposed to him. As mayor of Denver, Newton and his staff had done some business with Bromley, a lawyer from Littleton, and he had little grasp of what the regent might have against him. Quigg talked with his father-in-law, Morrison Shafroth, who voiced his belief that once he took over as president, Quigg would be able to get along with Bromley.[9] But on this occasion, Shafroth's instincts were off target. Imploring Quigg to take the job, Leonard Kinsell, a personal friend from Lakewood who considered himself well informed about university politics, similarly assured him that any difficulties with regents Bromley and Blue could be overcome. While expressing regret that the two Republicans "would stoop to place [your] selection on a partisan basis," Kindsell stated, "I am reasonably sure that the choice of the regents will be unanimous before you make your final decision."[10] Unfortunately, neither prediction came true. Although Blue soon departed from the board, Bromley would become increasingly bitter and constantly opposed to Newton's initiatives throughout the six-plus years Quigg served.

The weekend following notification of his selection, Newton flew from New York to attend the Colorado-Oklahoma football game, visit the campus, and talk with principal decision-makers. Quigg met with a faculty committee for approximately two hours. He recalled that it was a loose, informal session and that only about a dozen faculty were present. He had expected some flack because he lacked an academic background, but apparently nobody questioned his intellectual credentials. Newton didn't pretend to be a scholar, and he certainly emphasized what many faculty wanted to hear. One of his chief talking points was that faculty salaries were far too low, and one of his highest priorities would be to raise them dramatically.[11] Evidently, his visits with regents Bromley and Blue were at least superficially cordial. Shortly after his campus visit, Newton announced that he would accept the position.

Denver's daily newspapers were generally enthusiastic about Newton's impending return. *The Post* tabbed him a "Man for a Big Job," stating that he "possesses all the important qualifications a man should have to pilot Colorado's largest educational institution during the years of growth and development that lie immediately ahead." The *Rocky Mountain News*, which generally took positions opposite those of *The Post*, reported considerable internal opposition to Newton's appointment but indirectly supported the move: "The fact that a man is a first class educator is no proof that he is a good administrator and quite often the opposite is true." The *News* stressed that Newton's experience with the Ford Foundation could dramatically increase the university's fundraising potential: "That experience undoubtedly taught Newton where the big money for educational programs is and how to get it, and he is accustomed to think in big terms."[12]

Outgoing president Ward Darley hoped Newton would assume his duties quickly. A week after Quigg accepted the job, Darley wrote, "I want you to make the move back here as soon as possible. The situation as far as the legislature is concerned is such that this is important. Further, now that my successor has been chosen, I feel that the longer I stay on the job, the less acceptable my leadership is going to be." Darley continued, "Finally, from our own personal standpoint, Pauline and I are really at the end of our rope, and we are anxious to be relieved of our responsibilities at the earliest possible moment."[13]

Not surprisingly, once Newton announced his acceptance of the job, congratulatory letters poured in from family members, old friends—even complete strangers. Newton was warmed by such positive encouragement, and he was grateful for sound advice from experienced university people who warned him about the pitfalls ahead. Laurence M. Gould, president of Carleton College in Northfield, Minnesota, wrote, "[T]here is no more complex or difficult task in American life than being president of a college or university." Being a "superlative business-man" was by no means enough: "Beyond that you must have the endurance of an elephant, the patience of an ox, the vision of an eagle, the diligence of a beaver, the adaptability of a chameleon, the complacency of a camel, the cheerfulness of a cricket, the wisdom of an owl, the innocence of a lamb, the tenacity of a bulldog, the strength of a lion, the brass of a monkey, the presence of a peacock, the charm of a domesticated deer, the epidermis of a rhinoceros, and above all, the digestion of a boa constrictor. Nothing short of these will qualify you fully."[14]

John Banks, an old Denver associate from the mayoral years, tried to inject some humor into the equation, writing, "That presidency will be 'duck soup' for you. All you will have to do is satisfy the regents, keep the faculty happy, keep on good terms with the general assembly, and have a winning football team." Tongue firmly in cheek, Newton replied, "Ginny and I especially enjoyed the very consoling words that the presidency will be 'duck soup.'"[15] Flashing his own sense of humor not long after he took over as university president, Newton puckishly classified his priorities as "football for the alumni, sex for the students, and parking space for the faculty."[16]

To former advisors and mentors, Newton revealed some doubts and a few reservations before taking over the position. Informing Supreme Court Justice William O. Douglas of his decision to accept the job, Quigg wrote, "I am not too confident of my ability to lead an educational institution, but I shall certainly do my utmost to continue the fine tradition at the University of Colorado, and, if possible, to enhance its scholastic standing."[17] In a letter to former Andover teacher Arthur B. Darling, Quigg admitted, "I have a few qualms about my new position because of my dearth of academic background," then added, "but there are some aspects of it that tie in very well with my past experience."[18] Finally, in a letter to Louis T. Benezet, president of Colorado College in Colorado Springs, Newton wrote, "I will need a great deal of assistance in the years ahead, especially from my colleagues in the academic world in Colorado." Sounding a bit like the former vice president Theodore Roosevelt when he took over the presidency after William McKinley was assassinated, he continued, "Ward Darley has set an excellent precedent in the cooperative relations he has maintained with all the institutions of higher learning in the state. I will do my best to do the same."[19] Like young Roosevelt, who almost immediately challenged McKinley's modus operandi, Newton would reexamine almost all of his predecessor's objectives.

A few months after taking over duties from the departing Darley in December 1956, Newton had an opportunity to participate in a two-week seminar for new university presidents offered by Harvard University. The "case study" approach emphasized concrete examples of the types of issues that could entrap the naïve or unwary, and Quigg believed the experience was very helpful. Harvard also ran a parallel seminar for university presidents' wives, which Ginny attended.[20]

Despite the baneful impact of McCarthyism on intellectual freedom a half-century ago, in many other respects, American colleges and universities existed in a far more insulated, even innocent, atmosphere than they do today. Students were certainly less confrontational. When Newton took over the reins at the University of Colorado, most male students sported crew cuts and wore jeans or chinos, loafers, and button-down striped or madras shirts. A few even wore sports jackets and neckties. In cold weather, they added cardigan sweaters and perhaps navy pea jackets. At fraternity parties, they listened to the Kingston Trio, then cranked up Elvis Presley, Buddy Holly, and Little Richard. In a far more innocent age, one of the biggest campus issues was controversy over a recommendation by the Associated Women's Students Senate that all females abide by a dress code. The organization actually issued a policy statement urging women to wear modest skirts and loose sweaters rather than more "informal" attire (namely, "revealing" shorts and/or tight blue jeans and sweaters).[21]

Settling into Boulder

After the New York schools were closed for Christmas vacation in December 1956, Ginny and the girls flew from New York to Denver, arriving just in time for the president's Christmas reception. Ginny's suitcase had been lost en route; she had to borrow an evening dress, plus

Newton family Christmas card from Boulder, 1957. The girls, left to right, are Nan, Nelle, Ginna, and Abby.

shoes that were too small. Her feet hurt, so she soon slipped them off and stood shoeless in the receiving line. She was relieved that nobody noticed. One of her first tasks was getting the four girls settled into Boulder's excellent public schools. Ginny also took on the role of a president's wife in doing a lot of entertaining. There were formal gatherings of large groups at the president's house, and Quigg regularly brought guests home for lunch. Fortunately for the Newtons, many female students vied for the privilege of living in a garage apartment adjacent to their house and receiving free room and board in exchange for frequently supporting the Newton girls' activities, such as getting their breakfasts and driving them from one activity to another after school. The family was very pleased that the university provided an excellent housekeeper, Evelyn Moore. She stayed with them during their entire time in Boulder, and she took over all cooking and serving obligations, and even shopped for groceries.[22]

Ginny Newton had prodigious energy, but she certainly could not have run the household by herself. Between April 1960 and April 1961, some 2,688 people were entertained at the president's house on eighty-two different occasions.[23] Most guests who came through the doors delighted the couple; a few were endured. The Newtons greatly enjoyed welcoming luminaries such as Eleanor Roosevelt and Margaret Mead, who provided stimulating conversation at dinner parties. On occasion, two or more celebrities would generate "competitive" discussions.[24] Ex-presidents and future presidents were also guests. The Newtons were charmed by former president Harry Truman, who was interested in their two pianos. He asked which one was better, and promptly tested both of them. Richard Nixon was a great sports enthusiast. He watched a football game from the Newtons' box, and then stayed for a reception at their home. Nixon talked at length about the game, and he recognized many of the players by name.[25]

Despite all the demands of motherhood and filling the role of a university president's wife, Ginny found time to begin taking courses in psychology.[26] She explained at the time that, being mother to four daughters, insights gained in her courses might help her understand their needs and differences. As she recalled, "I had four daughters who couldn't have been more different from each other. I decided to find out why, and I started with a course in educational psychology." After getting her feet wet with undergraduate-level psychology courses, Ginny quickly advanced to graduate-level offerings, and her academic work became a top priority on her growing list of commitments. Newspapers quickly picked up on the image of an attractive woman in her late thirties whizzing around the campus on her bicycle. As Ginny explained it, she was involved in so many activities that she was constantly in a hurry. In addition to playing tennis, riding her bicycle provided good exercise. The only downside, according to Ginny, was that her daughters were embarrassed by a mother who rode a bicycle, which was not being done by most mothers at the time.[27]

Ginny stuck to her studies, eventually earning a master's degree in social psychology at the University of Colorado, followed by a Ph.D. at New York University. Ginny by no means lived in the shadow of her husband. Six months after the family's arrival in Boulder, she was elected vice president of the Baseline School Parent Teacher Association. In addition, she was serving on the board of trustees for her undergraduate alma mater, Vassar College. Ginny also kept playing piano and giving music lessons, often in exchange for art, music, and tennis lessons for the girls. She studied during daylight hours when the girls were in school. Ginny regularly attended evening university functions and productions with Quigg.

Faculty Salaries and Other Issues

Newton wasted little time wading into the serious business of running a university. One of the first issues he confronted was deplorable faculty salaries. Just three weeks into his duties, Quigg responded to a legislative report that underscored the seriousness of the situation. The Colorado legislature's own detailed study revealed that from 1940 to 1954, college teachers' salaries had actually *dropped 5* percent in real purchasing power. "In contrast, lawyers have had an increase of ten percent in purchasing power, industrial workers forty-eight percent, and physicians eighty percent." Newton observed that many citizens had a romantic notion that instructors and professors taught primarily for "their love of their profession."[28] The *Rocky Mountain News* published a story revealing that instructors at the University of Colorado were even more poorly paid than Denver public school teachers. Including all faculty, from instructors to full professors, the average salary at the university was about $6,600.[29] Salaries at Boulder were in the bottom third for all state universities and in the bottom quarter of those in western and northern states.[30] Although Newton was appalled at the situation, he emphasized the fact that the university was losing its best professors either to private industry or to other academic institutions offering far higher salaries. The situation was dire. Newton stated, "New Ph.D.s with no experience other than their graduate training are starting in the Denver area in industrial or government positions for from $7,200 to $8,200 a year, and get $8,000 to $9,000 if they are willing to go to either coast."[31] However, local college enrollments were mushrooming. The university needed to recruit ninety new faculty before September 1957. Quigg urged the legislature to ratchet up faculty salaries—and fast: "Bluntly, we asked for an average salary of $7,500, but we want $8,000."[32]

One of the chief reasons the regents hired him was that Newton was acutely attuned to the rapidly evolving world of institutional research. If the University of Colorado hoped to attract the nation's best and brightest minds, it would have to offer much more than pedestrian salaries and a pristine mountain environment. Newton realized the importance of creating an exciting intellectual climate, and there were some traditions to build on. A few years before Quigg arrived, sociology professor Howard Higman had founded the World Affairs Conference, which one observer has described as "a week of intellectual brawling."[33] A hundred or so visiting scholars, politicians, business executives, artists, musicians, and assorted crackpots were invited to spend a week on campus exchanging ideas. The visitors were thrown together in disparate groupings "by design" and had almost no time to prepare any remarks. Many panelists were assigned topics about which they knew almost nothing; they had to think fast on their feet. Although often hosted in homes of Boulder residents, participants received no honorarium; most people were honored by their invitations and gladly paid their own expenses. Students, faculty, and townspeople were free to come and go, attending whichever sessions caught their fancy. The event was unique.

As one reporter wrote, "Most academic conferences are highly orchestrated and specialized events. In contrast, CU's affair was an "assault on bad ideas of all kinds, including the genteel traditions of the academic conference. ... an outlandish and unpredictable gathering of unlike minds, an intellectual free-for-all."[34] During the early 1950s, when threats of McCarthyite "witch hunts" hung over most college campuses, Higman loaded the conference with leftist intellectuals, many of whom were unwelcome as speakers anywhere else. Newton admired Higman's courage. It was just the type of unconventional initiative Quigg admired and approved. He and Ginny thoroughly enjoyed the annual conference, and the Newtons and Higman soon became good friends.[35]

Newton introduced traditions of his own. Just as he had conducted his administration as mayor of Denver, Newton stressed that his office door was always open. Some entrenched senior faculty felt threatened by Quigg's hiring of high-priced "heavyweight" outsiders as department chairs and top-level administrators and the growing emphasis on research. But most faculty appreciated his openness and the opportunity to communicate directly and frequently with the university's top officer. Students also enjoyed interacting with a leader who could often be found casually strolling between buildings on campus. Beginning in April 1959, Quigg initiated the first "President's Forum," a regularly scheduled open meeting including himself and his assistants, numerous top-level deans, student leaders, and any faculty and students who wished to attend. The *Boulder Daily Camera* announced that topics for discussion included "religion on the campus; long range planning; the University's reputation and purpose; future plans for holidays and length of vacations; University expansion and building programs; and the registration and advising procedure." The meetings were to be left open for other topics as well. The paper noted that in the past, student leaders "had expressed frustration at an apparent lack of administration understanding of student views."[36]

As university president, Newton had to confront numerous challenges simultaneously, and some issues posed dilemmas during his entire time in the office. Faculty salaries created ongoing problems. During his six years as president, Quigg was extremely successful in raising faculty salaries at the university across the board. He made it very clear from the start that salary increases would be based not on rank or seniority, but primarily on proven merit and potential for future research that would provide visibility for the university. Newton arrived on campus with a coherent and deliberate strategy for rapidly improving the university's research reputation. One option was to urge department heads to commit resources to attractive salary offers for bright newcomers. To a limited extent, some departments did so, but following that strategy alone would take years to nurture "homegrown" talent. In a highly competitive academic marketplace, promising young scholars, who spent years at the University of Colorado conducting basic research, might, in turn, be recruited by richer institutions as soon as the fruits of their research blossomed and made them highly visible. In order to jump-start the university's quest to enter the ranks of major research universities, Newton also urged department chairs to recruit numerous established "stars."[37]

There was no way Newton could sugarcoat his salary policy, nor did he make any effort to do so. At Yale, faculty salaries were secret, but at the University of Colorado, they were published. Some entrenched faculty in Boulder hadn't turned out books or significant articles and papers for years; nevertheless, they had enjoyed small but predictable raises year after year, and they were comfortable with an essentially egalitarian salary structure. During the Newton years, the biggest annual raises went to established senior scholars who brought in outside grants and maintained and expanded their research programs and to energetic newcomers with promising research agendas. Not surprisingly, when Newton almost immediately brought in several demanding, challenging deans and department chairs from major research universities, some long-term faculty felt devalued. They believed he was attempting to convert the university into a "Harvard or Yale of the West." They reacted predictably by resisting and complaining of unfair treatment. Years later, as Newton candidly stated, "If anything, we felt a need to recognize outstanding people and we *created* a lot of salary gaps, between good and mediocre. I got a lot of grief over salaries."[38]

Early in 1961, a campus representative for the American Association of University Professors complained to the regents that "I think it is fair to say that the Faculty, perhaps mistakenly, is beginning to feel that too many unilateral decisions are being taken by the administration, and that in some instances the work and [salary] recommendations of Senate committees are being by-passed." The speaker believed that good teaching was being downgraded and that for salary purposes, little mattered besides research. He articulated an "old school" view in being offended that the administration did not "trust" internal faculty committee recommendations for tenure and promotion, but instead began requiring external recommendations regarding the quality and quantity of a candidate's research.[39] For several years, Quigg managed to sidestep these types of criticism fairly easily. Toward the end of his presidency, however, when critics charged that the administration discriminated against conservative-leaning faculty when determining annual raises, relatively subdued rumblings of discontent became an uproar.

Modernizing the University Administration

Another issue Newton needed to address immediately was the university's unwieldy and inefficient administrative structure. Quigg had streamlined Denver's government and delivery of many social services. He proved equally effective in restructuring the university and enabling administrators to prioritize problems and then respond more quickly and effectively to resolve them. A good example of this was when Newton created a new position, hiring James Doi as director of institutional research. Doi's office basically broke almost every traditional university practice into its smallest parts, determining first of all whether each ongoing task was necessary, and, if so, how procedures for dealing with given tasks could be streamlined.

Needless duplication of effort bothered both Newton and Doi. The president asked Doi to pursue opportunities to coordinate the University of Colorado's efforts with those of other colleges and universities in the region. Doi and his assistants also helped Quigg assemble hard data to present to the legislature in support of requests for additional funding. The office examined issues affecting faculty morale, including salary equity, fringe benefits, parking, office space, and other working conditions. In the late 1950s, construction of several new buildings was underway. Coordination of architectural design and effective distribution and utilization of new space were all issues requiring the department's close analysis. When undergraduate enrollments inexplicably dipped in the fall of 1958, the president wanted to know why, and he asked the director to study the issue.[40]

No amount of managerial streamlining could protect the president from certain mundane chores. Every university president is burdened with some tasks that by logic should be delegated to subordinates but nevertheless require personal attention. Such is often the case when influential friends and alumni request personal attention in tracking the performance of less-than-motivated young family members. One of Newton's close relatives had a son attending the university, and he was struggling. He evidently asked Quigg to try to get to the bottom of why his son, along with one of his close friends, was performing poorly academically. Newton did turn the matter over to an acting assistant dean, who in turn investigated the situation and reported directly back to him. The episode had a happy ending, as the young man's grades improved markedly.[41] Quigg undoubtedly received dozens of similar requests each year. They all had to be dealt with, sometimes personally. If they did not consume large amounts of his time, they were distractions nevertheless.

Exploring New Frontiers in Science

Although certain mundane chores may have occasionally tried Newton's patience and worn him down, truly significant events energized him. Nothing excited him more than important intellectual breakthroughs, particularly in science. On October 4, 1957, the Soviets electrified the international scientific community by successfully orbiting *Sputnik*, the world's first manmade satellite. Newton recalled that on the evening following the launching of *Sputnik*, Walter Orr Roberts, director of the

High Altitude Observatory (HAO), telephoned the Newtons to come up at once to listen to the distinctive beeping made by the satellite in flight.[42] For American policy makers and university educators, the Soviet achievement was a wake-up call to begin a crash program to upgrade scientific research. This was the type of challenge that Quigg loved. The following year, Congress established the National Defense Education Act, which poured tens of millions of federal dollars into advancing all aspects of education, particularly science and mathematics. Research budgets at the National Science Foundation were similarly beefed up, and Congress also created the National Aeronautics and Space Administration in 1958.[43]

National policy makers wanted to jump-start creation of a new generation of bright scientists capable of helping the United States regain worldwide leadership in scientific research. Quigg's mind locked in on the fact that the University of Colorado was located in the midst of a huge region without a major research university. He fervently believed that the citizens and business and political leaders in Colorado should first recognize and then capitalize on that fact. In Newton's mind, the situation represented an enormous challenge and also a remarkable opportunity for institutional development, one that might not occur again for decades. In stating his case for dramatic increases in funding for the university to state legislators and in other appropriate situations, Quigg frequently shared his favorite Shakespearean quote:

> There is a tide in the affairs of man
> Which taken at the flood, leads on to fortune;
> Omitted, all the voyage of their life
> Is bound in shallows and in miseries
> We must take the current when it serves
> Or lose our ventures[44]

His message was crystal clear: strike while the iron is hot; ride the crest of the wave, or forever regret not capitalizing on lost opportunities.

Beyond vastly expanded public support for higher education in Colorado, Newton envisioned a three-pronged program to position the university to respond to the stark Cold War realities challenging the nation. First, whether a public or private entity, the university should be a key factor helping to attract new scientific institutions to the Boulder and Denver region. Second, university administrators and faculty must work together to generate grant proposals tapping the millions of dollars in new federal research funding suddenly available. If the first two objectives were met, Newton believed that more brilliant, motivated, and energetic faculty and students would flock to the university. That outcome was Quigg's third objective.

Throughout his years as university president, Newton tirelessly promoted his dream of creating an important research institution to those who would listen, but particularly to businessmen, state legislators, newsmen, and anyone else in a position to affect public policy in Colorado. Some scientific institutes were already in Boulder. When Newton assumed his duties, the HAO, a nonprofit research laboratory, had established headquarters on the Boulder campus in 1947 and had an observation station in Climax, Colorado. While serving as mayor of Denver, Newton had provided assistance to Walter Orr Roberts, one of the nation's leading atmospheric research scientists, who was then being investigated by the Federal Bureau of Investigation for alleged ties to the Communist Party and with befriending others so charged. Roberts had been denied a top-secret security clearance, which threatened both his career and personal reputation. Whether or not Quigg's endorsement of his character and reliability was a major contributing factor, Roberts soon thereafter gained his security clearance. A close friendship developed between the two men and their families. With his career back on track, Roberts had taken over as director of the HAO.

In 1960, Roberts was offered the position as head of a new national laboratory, the National Center for Atmospheric Research (NCAR). Roberts discussed this dazzling career opportunity with Newton. Roberts wanted to accept the offer, but only under the condition that NCAR be located in Boulder and that the HAO become an integral part of the new institution. Newton persuaded the regents to permit the HAO to leave the university and join NCAR, and Quigg and other university officials in turn helped persuade the legislature to acquire NCAR's spectacular 500-acre site just below the Flatirons in southwest Boulder. During planning and construction of the NCAR laboratory complex in the foothills, NCAR occupied office and laboratory space in various buildings on the campus.[45]

Other situations demonstrated that Newton did not shy away from associating with high-profile scientists with "pink" reputations. In 1960, the university hired Frank Oppenheimer, brother of atomic physicist J. Robert Oppenheimer, "father" of the A-bomb. Frank Oppenheimer held a Ph.D. from the California Institute of Technology, and he was a highly respected researcher in his own right. He had worked with his brother at Los Alamos, and he had taught at Stanford and the University of Minnesota. After having admitted joining the Communist Party in 1937, however, he was fired from Minnesota, and he was teaching high school science in Pagosa Springs, Colorado. Despite the threat of controversy, Newton approved hiring Oppenheimer, and he joined the university as a visiting lecturer in the fall of 1960.[46] Newton publicly acknowledged that Oppenheimer *had* been a Communist, but emphasized that he had ended his association with the party more than twenty years earlier. Nevertheless, several angry alumni peppered Quigg's office with unsigned letters calling Oppenheimer a traitor and questioning his judgment.[47]

Another scientific initiative involving the University of Colorado was establishment of the Joint Institute for Laboratory Astrophysics (JILA), originated in April 1962 by agreement between the National Bureau of Standards (NBS) and the university. Once again, Newton was in the center of the negotiations. University physicist Lewis Branscomb had received an annual federal grant of $500,000 for three years to set up a laboratory for interdisciplinary research in atomic and radiation processes in hot gases. This research involved experiments vital to critical areas of national defense. Branscomb initially met a stone wall when he attempted to secure federal funding for university buildings to house the required laboratory space. The sponsoring agency funded research, but not bricks and masonry. Fortunately for Branscomb, Newton was extremely supportive of his initiative, and Leo Hill, vice president of finance and a creative individual with considerable banking experience, negotiated a complex but entirely legal million-dollar loan from a state escrow account.[48] Although the JILA facilities at the Boulder campus were not finished until 1966, the support of Newton and Hill had been critical to the enterprise.

Newton made other significant commitments to scientific research. Just before leaving the presidency, Ward Darley had earmarked $18,000 in planning funds to explore possibilities of establishing a cyclotron and nuclear physics laboratory on the east campus in Boulder. Darley had also requested $250,000 from the state planning board for construction of a new building. That was where matters stood when Quigg assumed office. In order to receive serious consideration for the project, physicists at the university had to secure the endorsement and some matching funding from officials at the Atomic Energy Commission (AEC). At the time, physicist David A. Lind was preparing a personal pitch to officials in Washington. Years later, Lind wrote to Newton, "I still remember vividly the trip that you as President of the University and I as senior investigator made on March 11, 1957 to present the plans and argue the case for support of a research facility of this type."[49] The two men received seed money from the AEC, which led to state funding and larger federal grants in the future. The building was completed and the cyclotron was up and running before Quigg left the presidency.

In 1961, *Denver Post* reporter Wayne Johnson presented a retrospective assessment of the university's emergence as a scientific research center. He quoted Dr. Fred Brown, director of the NBS: "In 1954 there was opposition to our moving to Boulder. People said we were going to an 'intellectual Siberia.' You don't hear that any more." Newton received high praise for helping recruit outstanding men, particularly in the sciences, including Walter Orr Roberts, Frank Oppenheimer, George Gamow, and many others. In terms of funded research, the administration's aggressive recruiting was beginning to pay off. In 1959, university researchers garnered less than $1 million in external funding. The next year, researchers generated more than double that amount. But Newton was by no means content to rest on these achievements. Salaries at the university still were well below average, ranking ninety-sixth in the nation and only ninth among thirteen state universities in the West. Newton wanted to create fifteen "special professorships" that would pay $17,500 per year. The top academic salary at the university at the time was just $13,500. According to Newton, "Good people—students and professors alike—tend to go where excellence already exists. Good men follow good men, and money for research also follows good men."[50]

Modernizing the Medical School

One of the most significant achievements during Newton's six-plus years as president was upgrading and vastly expanding the University of Colorado Medical School. The institution had a long history, dating back to the early 1880s. When Quigg took over his new duties late in 1956, the medical school was housed in bleak, cramped, and functional but unimpressive quarters in east Denver. The core structure of the medical school dated from 1924. The facility played an important role in the university's commitment to public service in the region by providing free medical care for indigent patients. Although teaching was a key function, medical school personnel conducted relatively little original research. Most of the doctors staffing the hospital were experienced private practitioners in Denver whose chief interest was providing direct health care. Many of them were firmly established in the city's social hierarchy, and they had no interest in upsetting the comfortable status quo. Although the medical center was a decent regional school, the institution was almost invisible nationally.[51] Under Ward Darley's leadership, the university had created a ten-year plan for expanding and upgrading the medical school.[52] With his departure, however, the plan was basically on hold, and some farsighted and ambitious faculty and university leaders believed that its basic assumptions and premises needed to be reexamined.

Both as mayor of Denver and as a member of the Yale Corporation, Newton had faced numerous opportunities to consider the needs of indigent patients and potential roles university teaching facilities could play in providing vital services. As vice president at the Ford Foundation and as a member of the board of the Commonwealth Fund, two private foundations that provided significant funding for university initiatives in expanding delivery of medical services and advancing research, he had devoted even more time and attention to such matters.[53] Later in his career, Newton would become even more deeply committed to the public service function of university hospitals, but in the mid-1950s, he focused on the idea that urban medical schools would attract far better and more ambitious students and faculty if they developed reputations as research institutions. Shortly before Quigg was hired as president, Dr. Gordon Mieklejohn, head of the department of medicine and chair of the search committee, hired a rising star, thirty-eight-year-old Dr. Robert J. Glaser, as dean of the institution. Glaser had received his medical doctorate at Harvard, and he arrived from highly respected Washington University in St. Louis.

Glaser immediately invited Newton to become involved in deliberations about refocusing the efforts of the medical school. Many university presidents, particularly those new to their jobs, might have bypassed such invitations because they were not experts in medicine and might feel overwhelmed by other challenges. In Newton's case as well, the medical center was thirty miles from his office in Boulder and attending meetings would consume large amounts of his time. None of these considerations deterred Quigg. Not only did he accept Glaser's invitation, but he committed himself to expanding his knowledge about the complex challenges facing medical education, medical research, and maintaining a public service function. Much to Glaser's delight, Quigg emphatically rejected a passive, or largely ceremonial, role, quickly becoming an integral part of the decision-making process. Glaser was particularly pleased that Newton took the time to interview bright young doctors he was trying to recruit for the faculty. In many cases, Glaser believed, the fact that the university's president was willing to recruit junior faculty confirmed the importance that the university's leaders attached to medical education and was a vital factor persuading attractive candidates to accept positions at the medical school.[54]

During Newton's presidency, the medical school significantly expanded and modernized its physical plant and placed its operations on a more businesslike basis by beginning to collect fees from patients who were covered by medical insurance.[55] Although the medical school improved local delivery of health care, its most impressive advances were in medical education and research. Ambitious doctors competed effectively for external research grants, and the volume of funding from the National Institutes of Health and other sources expanded rapidly. Together, Newton and Glaser negotiated a grant from the Eleanor Roosevelt Institute to fund a basic cancer-research program.

One of Glaser's first recruits to the medical school faculty was Dr. C. Henry Kempe, a rising young researcher in his mid-thirties who came from the University of California, San Francisco. Kempe was deeply disturbed by the prevalence of child abuse, a widespread phenomenon that was largely unexplored up to that time. With enthusiastic support from both Glaser and Newton, Kempe authored many pioneering papers concerning various aspects of child abuse and neglect. In 1961, Kempe arranged a national conference of the American Academy of Pediatrics that focused on the battered-child syndrome. Kempe established a center for further studies of child abuse at the medical center. Under his leadership, other bright investigators moved to Colorado to participate in an exciting and rewarding new movement.[56] They included Dr. Henry Silver, who would enjoy a long and distinguished career at the medical school. In addition to his interest in child abuse, Silver initiated significant improvements in streamlining and modernizing the delivery of health care services.[57]

Newton's role in upgrading the medical school was crucial. Dr. Glaser recalled that, although he had no medical training, Quigg was a marvelous facilitator. He had a unique ability to listen quietly then ask penetrating questions at opportune moments. Another of his great strengths was team-building, which he utilized to benefit the entire university. One of Quigg's first key recruits was Oswald Tippo, who took over a newly created position as university provost. Tippo played a crucial role in Newton's mission to beef up the scholarly output of faculty at the Boulder campus, Tippo and Newton in turn helped recruit able department heads, who usually managed to set aside their egos and work well together. Tippo was just as committed to the medical school as was his boss. Both men regularly attended meetings at the school. What Glaser most cherished was their work in helping to create an espirit de corps within the institution, a condition that in Glaser's view had not existed previously. Newton also devoted considerable attention to promoting the medical school among state legislators. Quigg had the sense to downplay pure research when addressing legislators directly. According to Glaser, a key element in his sales pitch for rapidly expanded state funding was the idea that the citizens of Colorado deserved the very best medical care, which necessitated thoroughly modern medical facilities.[58]

Family Life

Looking back on his six-plus years as president at the university almost a half-century later, Newton recalled them as some of the best years of his life. Despite the excitement, cosmopolitanism, and fast pace of New York City's atmosphere, he and his family truly felt most at home in Colorado. Living on the campus and interacting with faculty, administrators, and students was very exciting. But the couple also faced the challenge of raising four daughters. The Newtons were less than thrilled when their oldest daughter, Nan, wanted to become a cheerleader in junior high school in Boulder. She had, in fact, begun practicing on the lawn outside their house. They decided to send her to Graland, a private school in Denver, and later the Milton Academy in Massachusetts. During most of the Boulder years, the younger girls still attended public schools there. With support from female undergraduates in tending to the needs of her daughters, Ginny managed to make considerable headway on her graduate work in psychology. In addition, the whole family enjoyed the bracing and constantly changing weather in Boulder, along with its spectacular scenery. Ginny was an enthusiastic tennis player and played regularly. Once a week or so, she coaxed Quigg onto the court, where he got some vigorous exercise and competed with her on fairly even terms. Newton also rode horseback at the Shafroth farm west of Denver. By the summer of 1958, Quigg claimed that he had become "an addict" of the activity and that he had been in the saddle three times in the previous two weeks.[59]

Regardless of how much the family enjoyed the atmosphere in Boulder, they usually managed to take an annual vacation, usually in August, and almost always at the Shafroth family summer home on Cape Cod. They drove back to the cape, sometimes visiting friends along the way. In the summer of 1958, the girls were all in summer camps, so Ginny and Quigg took the trip alone with no itinerary, starting from Boulder and driving through Canada. Newton eagerly anticipated being disconnected from pressing responsibilities for a few days: "We have chosen no definite route and shall just set out from Boulder with a map, picking our way as we go. We have never done this together, so it should be much fun."[60] As the couple headed east from Boulder, Quigg may well have recalled scenes from thirty years earlier, namely summer 1928, when, as a sixteen-year-old, he enjoyed the marvelous adventure of delivering a new automobile to his mother after driving alone from Detroit to Denver.

As the summer of 1958 wound down, nights on Cape Cod were growing cooler, and Quigg and Ginny anticipated their return to Boulder. They had many reasons to be optimistic. At that point, Quigg had only been on the job as president of the university for a year and a half, and in some respects, he was still enjoying a honeymoon period. He was helping to bring many positive changes to the university: a modernized and efficient administrative structure, an improved and expanding medical school, millions of dollars of research grants and new scientific institutions, rapidly increasing faculty salaries, and many other improvements. There had been grumbling over some of his initiatives, and a few alumni fretted over alleged "Communist influences" on campus, but for the most part, dissension would remain below the radar screen for the remainder of the decade. By the early 1960s, however, Newton would have to contend with many new problems and challenges. The last three years of his presidency were marked by exhilarating triumphs, along with profound disappointments.

CHAPTER 10

STORM CLOUDS OVER BOULDER

When Newton accepted the presidency of the University of Colorado late in 1956, his appointment was generally heralded; yet, it was also controversial. The rapid changes he and his top-level advisors introduced made some longtime university loyalists uncomfortable. During the first three years of Quigg's leadership, groundbreaking achievements occurred in rapid succession and attracted almost uniformly favorable publicity. During that period, Newton's initiatives generated some criticism, both within and from outside of the university. For the most part, opposition to his leadership was muted, and it flowed largely beneath the radar screen. But the last three years of Quigg's term in office brought a seemingly constant stream of confrontations. When universities become embroiled in controversy, presidents, as the most visible authority figures, usually become lightning rods for public criticism. By late 1962, a seamy football scandal and public fear that Communism pervaded the Boulder campus made Newton's position so precarious, he felt he had little choice but to resign.

The Football Mess

As Newton began work at the university, friends and well-wishers had warned him, only partially in jest, that failure to field winning football teams consistently might eventually lead to big trouble. Ironically, Quigg's first encounter with the football program at the university generated only pleasant memories. Two weeks after taking office, he and

Ginny accompanied coach Dal Ward's team to Miami, where they played in the Orange Bowl on New Year's Day 1957 and defeated Clemson, 27–21. Newton enjoyed football and had played the game in prep school, but his interest in "big-time football" was skin deep. Although Quigg and his family regularly attended home games at Folsom Field, close observers sensed that he did not agonize over the results. Newton's primary focus was elsewhere.

He was trying to lead the university into the "big time" intellectually at the national level. Given his Ivy League background (where there are no athletic scholarships and varsity sports are not taken very seriously), Quigg may not have fully realized how ardently many alumni and certain regents desired to propel the Buffaloes into the big time in intercollegiate athletics. The university had joined the Big Seven Conference in 1947 and had hired Dal Ward to lead the football team. By the time Newton arrived, Ward had been the head coach for nine seasons. His teams had won approximately two-thirds of their games. Alone among coaches in the Big Seven Conference, Ward still ran a single-wing offense, which many "expert" alumni considered obsolete. Although his teams competed effectively, they had not yet won a conference title, and most importantly, they had not yet defeated the University of Oklahoma.[1]

Ward's 1956 team had a record of seven wins, two losses, and a tie. Although losing to Oklahoma, the team finished second in the Big Seven and had won the Orange Bowl. Evidently, the taste of big-time success further whetted the appetites of football-obsessed alumni and helped set Ward up for failure. In 1957 and 1958, the Buffaloes finished with a combined record of 12–7–1 during these two years, but that was not good enough for many fans. Newton apparently learned of some misgivings, and he visited with Ward about the football situation once or twice following the 1958 season. Evidently, neither man fully sensed the determination of highly influential alumni to force change. In a secret session at their monthly meeting at the University Club in Denver on January 23, 1959, after only ten minutes of deliberation, the regents voted 5–1 to dismiss Ward. Further adding to the mystery, athletic director Harry G. Carlson was never consulted. Whether or not

Newton was taken by surprise, he did not publicly oppose the decision. To reporters, he stated laconically, "Today's action was taken after very thoughtful consideration over a period of time."[2] Quigg did not elaborate, announcing only that he was appointing a committee to begin the process of choosing Ward's successor.

Reaction around the state and on campus to Ward's abrupt ousting was explosive and almost universally negative. Chet Nelson, a respected veteran sports reporter for the *Rocky Mountain News*, opined, "It is inconceivable that six men, our elected Regents, went into a regular meeting and decided to fire the coach by a 5–1 margin." Nelson implied that sinister forces were behind the move: "Has a self-appointed maker (or makers) of kings infiltrated the Board of Regents?" Nelson was pretty sure he knew which regent masterminded the coup: "If the regents approve the new coach as stupidly as they fired Ward, chaos will prevail quicker than you can say Jim Bromley." Nelson was also outraged at the unorthodox procedure used in dismissing the coach: "It is ridiculous that the university's athletic director, Harry Carlson, a dedicated man for more than 30 years service, was not consulted in the firing of a coach two months after the season ends."[3]

All of the football players who were interviewed rallied to their popular former coach's defense. Sherm Pruitt, chosen most valuable player by his teammates, observed, "Coach Ward is a fine man and a fine coach. If it had not been for him and his staff, I would not have been at CU." Star quarterback Boyd Dowler ripped the regents: "I just can't see how five or six people can think they know so much about the situation up here, especially when it refers to athletics. Dismissal of Ward sure wrecks the recruiting … and I know I would sure not come to school here under the circumstances."[4] Ward expressed complete shock, but he maintained his composure, at least publicly. He wished that the decision had come immediately following the season. Although he was a tenured professor in the Physical Education Department, he was concerned that several of his assistants would have difficulty finding new positions, since most movement in the coaching ranks of football programs happened in November and December.[5]

Although Newton may have been surprised by the regents' sudden move, he understood that the sooner a new coach was named, the sooner the furor would die down. Thus, he wasted no time in establishing a committee to select Ward's successor. Local newspapers published numerous rumors about who would succeed Ward. At various points in time, such well-known coaches as "Slinging Sammy" Baugh of Hardin-Simmons, former Notre Dame coach Terry Brennan, and Dartmouth coach Bob Blackman were rumored as front-runners for the position. But just seventeen days after Ward was let go, Everett "Sonny" Grandelius, a twenty-nine-year-old assistant at Michigan State University, was offered the position. His knowledge of the game, a short stint as a National Football League player with the New York Giants, along with his fiery enthusiasm and energy impressed the selection committee and the regents, who voted unanimously to hire him. Newton offered him the job at a salary of $14,000 per year, $1,200 more than Ward had received.[6]

Grandelius promptly accepted the position, but he commenced work under inauspicious conditions. Although most of Ward's players eventually remained on the team, Grandelius attracted few serviceable recruits in the spring of 1959. Under the circumstances, the fact that the Buffaloes had a 5–5 record during the 1959 season could be considered an impressive achievement. In fact, Grandelius's aggressive coaching, featuring a wide-open passing attack, excited both players and fans, who quickly forgot the fiasco of the previous winter. They sensed that far better results were on the horizon, and they weren't disappointed. During the 1960 season, the team compiled a 7–3 record, defeated Oklahoma for the first time in school history, and finished second in the conference. But the crowning glory of the Grandelius regime was a seemingly magical season in 1961. The Buffaloes, led by All-American lineman and future Rhodes Scholar Joe Romig, won nine games, went undefeated in the Big Eight, and were ranked seventh in the nation. Although the team lost 25–7 to Louisiana State University in the Orange Bowl on New Year's Day 1962, to the outside observer, all seemed well in the Buffalo corral.[7]

Beneath the surface, however, were all the ingredients of a major scandal. In the words of Colorado sports historian James Whiteside, "Even as the accolades poured in … NCAA [National Collegiate Athletic Association] and university investigators were uncovering the dark reality behind Sonny's bright season. NCAA investigators began looking into the CU football program in August 1961, and in November a preliminary report cited evidence that twenty players had received illegal financial help. With Grandelius's knowledge, boosters had set up a slush fund to help players with living, travel, and other expenses. The players picked up their payments at a Boulder drugstore."[8] The secretary of the board of regents, Don Saunders, loved football, and he was Newton's "eyes and ears" concerning football matters.

Newton actually received hints of the brewing scandal in the early spring of 1961. He recalled feeling personally violated, as the drugstore where payments were allegedly made was directly across the street and within sight of his family's residence on campus.[9] In March 1961, Newton directly queried Grandelius and several assistant coaches, who denied that anything was amiss. On March 20, Newton sent official "reminder letters" to members of the coaching staff, the director of athletics, and the conference faculty representative stating the following: "I want to re-emphasize that absolutely no deviations from the rules will be tolerated and that any coach or staff directly or indirectly contributing to a rule violation will be considered to have nullified any agreement pertaining to his future connection with the university."[10] If he thought these steps had settled the matter, he was sadly mistaken.

In hindsight, it now appears clear that Grandelius's tactics should have raised red flags almost from the moment he took over the program. In mid-September 1959, Colorado State Senator Herrick Roth wrote to the coach, "By pure coincidence, I happened to view the Goldberg TV show on which you were a panel guest last Saturday evening and noted your comments with regard to football financing and recruiting at the university. Your comment that everything is now alright in regard to some of the recent questions first raised on the financial budget by Senator Locke and later raised by myself with regard to matters of general educational endeavor, in addition, has left me somewhat puzzled inasmuch as no direct communication has ever been sent to the university on the matter from any interested legislators, to the best of my knowledge, and therefore no replies or comments regulating to satisfactions have been received."[11] Roth described himself as an enthusiastic fan of spectator sports; thus, he may have been more attuned to the possible whiff of scandal than most responsible public officials. Roth sent a copy of the letter to Newton's office, and Quigg might have picked up the scent of impropriety sooner.

Joint investigations by the university and the NCAA moved forward during the fall of 1961. The final report by the NCAA did not become public until the early spring of 1962. Once the truth unfolded, however, the regents voted to fire Grandelius, and they simultaneously attempted to deflect criticism from themselves. Although they acknowledged the pressures of big-time college football, they stated that such forces "[were] more often exerted by over-zealous football enthusiasts than by the institutions themselves." In the words of sports historian Whiteside, "The regents' claim that 'there has never been such pressure on Coach Grandelius from either the administration or the Regents' was either self-deceiving or incredibly disingenuous."[12]

As had been the case when Ward was fired three years earlier, all sorts of self-appointed "experts" flooded both the president's office and the media with "suggestions" directed toward various parties involved in the decision, many of which were manifestly unhelpful or anatomically impossible. Large numbers of football-loving, flask-toting alumni with boys-will-be-boys attitudes were furious that the scandal had been exposed rather than simply swept under the rug. They loved the pageantry of big-time football and the thrill of victory. Some of Quigg's good friends and even family members criticized the coach's ouster. Not surprisingly, a few extremists at the other end of the scale argued that intercollegiate athletics had become so corrupt that the university should simply eliminate them altogether. John Farrell, the editor of the student newspaper, suggested that "if President Newton and the regents are really interested in 'doing the right thing,' as they say they are, they must do more than sack Grandelius. They must disarm the high pow-ered athletic program which he operated as it had to be operated [in order to win]."[13]

The sanctions imposed by the NCAA were stiff, but they might have been even more severe had the university failed to investigate itself. The university was placed on two years' probation, and the team could not appear on television or in any postseason contest. The conference declared nine lettermen named in the NCAA report ineligible for the following season. Since all were seniors, the decision ended their colle-giate football careers. Many players still on the roster felt they had been abandoned, and some were bitter. The coaching situation was totally up in the air. Who in his right mind would step into the breach and pro-vide leadership? Certainly no big-time football coach.

Rocky Mountain News sports reporter Chet Nelson, the very same individual who had protested so vehemently against the firing of Dal Ward a few years earlier, voiced the frustrations of many fans who wanted big-time football in Colorado, at any cost. He even lambasted Newton for having investigated his own program. Evidently, Nelson would have pre-ferred that university leaders wait until caught red-handed by the NCAA: "Kansas and Oklahoma took their medicine from the NCAA like men, not like the namby pambies we have here at CU. ... Colorado must forget about athletics and go in for checkers and bridge, challenging Colorado Women's College and Loretto Heights."[14] Attempting to reestablish order to the chaotic situation, the regents finally replaced Grandelius with alumni director William E. "Bud" Davis, who manfully agreed to under-take a nearly impossible task on an interim basis. Davis had been a scrub on one of Dal Ward's first teams, then a successful high school coach in South Dakota and Colorado, but he had no college-level coaching expe-rience. Player reactions ranged from shock to incredulity. Team captain Ken Blair reacted viscerally, threatening a player revolt: "You've got your-self a coach, now get yourself a team."[15]

Few coaches ever faced a more daunting situation. A cloth figure was suspended by rope from a tree in the front yard of the Newtons' home on campus. It was unclear whether it represented Newton or the coach, but since Newton was out of town when the incident occurred, Davis took responsibility. As Davis recalled a few years later, "I believe I may be the first coach in the history of intercollegiate football [to] be hung in effigy *before* he got the job."[16] Fortunately, Davis was self-effacing and had a sense of humor. The day before the 1962 season opened, the student newspaper, the *Colorado Daily*, editorialized, "Tomorrow night should see the first in a long series of losses for the University of Colorado's Golden Buffaloes, termed the 'vanishing herd' by one sports columnist." Many predicted that the team would not win a single game. In fact, the team lost 62–0 to Oklahoma and 57–0 to Missouri. To Davis's credit, against overwhelming odds he held his over-matched team together, and they managed to win two games, including a season-ending 34–10 upset of heavily favored Air Force Academy. To his great relief, early in 1963 Davis turned over coaching duties to a young University of Oklahoma assistant, Eddie Crowder, who, for better or worse, would eventually return the football program to glory. By the time the Buffaloes once again emerged as a football powerhouse, however, Newton would be long gone from the president's office.

In hindsight, handling the football mess was one of the very few instances in his presidency where Newton failed, at least initially, to provide truly decisive leadership. His biggest mistake may have been going along with the abrupt firing of Dal Ward. Part of the reason was that football-loving alumni, whose most vocal representative among the regents was Charles D. "Jim" Bromley, appeared so insistent on pursuing athletic dominance, even ahead of academic greatness. Perhaps Newton believed that if he went along with Bromley on this matter, he could secure greater cooperation on issues closer to his heart. His usually astute instincts may have been clouded by the fact that he was devoting enormous amounts of political capital persuading the state legislature to increase university funding, and he understood, at least at some level, that its response would be positively influenced by a winning record in major sports.

Having attended Yale for seven years and having served that university's corporate board for another five years, plus having been a trustee at the University of Denver, Newton had never been exposed to the dark side of big-time intercollegiate sports, at least up close and personally. To his credit, despite failing to respond to hints of improprieties raised by state senator Herrick Roth in 1959, Quigg immediately launched a probing internal investigation when the first concrete rumors of scandal surfaced. That was a major reason that the NCAA did not impose even more draconian sanctions against the athletic program. When it became apparent that Regent Bromley was intimately tied to alumni providing cash payments to the suspended players, however, Newton avoided exposing his activities.[17] Unfortunately in this case, Newton's usually astute judgment of men failed him. Rather than showing gratitude, Bromley quickly emerged as Quigg's avowed enemy. In hindsight, Newton realized that he should have openly exposed Bromley and his shenanigans to the press and public.[18] Years later, Don Saunders, Newton's administrative assistant, ruefully characterized the "football nuts who resented the Board's decision by a five-to-one vote to fire Grandelius" as "free-loaders who held the jock-strap aroma of the locker room in higher regard than the honor and integrity of the university."[19] The entire unhappy episode clearly left deep scars on many people, including the university president.

Red Baiting in Boulder

The unfolding football mess was just one of many problems besieging the institution, and Newton, during the early 1960s. By then, he and his top-level administrators felt themselves under constant attack by conservative forces in the city of Boulder, the state, and the nation. Almost from the beginning of his presidency, Newton was subjected to charges of hiring and protecting former Communists and supporters of various left-wing causes. His support of the Physics Department's hiring of famous Robert Oppenheimer's brother, Frank, in 1959 brought a storm of criticism from some alumni and citizens. One anonymous "alumnus" wrote, "Newton now has Oppenheimer to lecture on physics at CU. Has he tried to get Castro to lecture on Latin America?" Another letter writer, identified only as a "100 percent American," wrote "I should think that the parents of the students would object to having their sons

and daughters exposed to that *traitor* Robert [*sic*] Oppenheimer. The
colleges get *redder* and *redder*. He should not be allowed to be in the
country" (emphasis his).[20] The president of the First National Bank in
Fleming, Colorado, complained to Regent Dick Bernick, "As an alumnus I find it hard to support Mr. Newton's never ceasing demands for
additional funds with which to attract the ilk of such peoples as
Oppenheimer, Higman and Jesser. I know that I am not alone in this
matter, and I think it is high time that the Regents asserted themselves
before the reputation of this fine University is damaged beyond
repair."[21] Newton staunchly defended Oppenheimer: "He has demonstrated to our complete satisfaction that he is an outstanding scientist,
an inspiring teacher, and a man of high integrity and loyalty to his country, and fully deserving of membership on our faculty."[22] Newton was
equally forthright in defending other professors accused of holding
unorthodox and unpopular views.

Some faculty members were also becoming restive, albeit for other
reasons. As noted, many tenured senior faculty felt threatened by the
growing emphasis on research and publication. One faculty representative
of the American Association of University Professors stated to the regents
early in 1961: "On Faculty relations to the Administration, I think it is
fair to say that the faculty, perhaps mistakenly, is beginning to feel that too
many unilateral decisions are being taken by the administration, and that
in some cases the work and recommendations of Senate committees are
being by-passed." Specifically, the speaker lamented "the decision to apply
all funds available for salary increases to merit increases ... [effecting] the
downgrading of *teaching* ... (emphasis his)." He was also upset that tenure
and promotion decisions were based increasingly on assessments of candidates' research by external reviewers, stating, "I must concur with Faculty
opinion that the requirement of recommendations is probably unjustifi-
able and even worthless." The writer expressed uneasiness over perceived
loss of faculty autonomy: "You don't *administer* university faculties; they
are *self-administered*" (emphasis his).[23]

A handful of highly visible, outspoken conservative faculty kindled
a growing feeling that they were somehow being persecuted. One of the

more publicized incidents revolved around a deep conflict between Edward Rozek, a conservative political scientist, and Howard Higman, a liberal sociologist. Higman and Newton had, in fact, become personally close. Although Higman never earned a Ph.D., he was both a brilliant teacher and a creative scholar. More importantly, he had close associations with many famous people around the world, both within and outside of academia. As noted, Higman almost single-handedly organized and masterminded the first weeklong World Affairs Conference, which grew in significance under Newton's watch and continues to this day. When Higman was promoted to professor despite not having his Ph.D., however, some faculty and alumni believed administrators were guilty of rank favoritism. From their perspective, Newton and his top advisors were willing to bend rules for those they considered most deserving.

Higman had given a talk at a luncheon in Boulder in late April 1959 on American higher education, and Rozek, who was in the audience, made numerous acerbic comments. Rozek claimed that friends of Higman had characterized him as a McCarthyite, even a fascist. In later discussions with a *Rocky Mountain News* reporter, Jack Gaskie, Rosek may have alleged that Higman ruled the Sociology Department and that he had fired one scholar who was later "hired by a more respectable institution." In a letter to Newton explaining the situation, Rozek alleged that he had been misquoted, that he had called it a "*very* respectable institution."[24] Yet other faculty and witnesses claimed that Rozek *had* indeed charged at *earlier* public gatherings that conservative, or "anti-Communist," faculty were regularly persecuted and that McCarthyite methods were employed to discredit them, forcing them to leave the university.[25]

Rozek, in turn, denied these claims, and the situation was never resolved. Although Rozek was awarded a promotion and tenure, his resentment against the administration festered. Two years later, allegations surfaced that he and another faculty member had met secretly with legislators, spelling out serious discrimination against conservative faculty by administrators. Although he conceded that any faculty member had the right to meet with their state representatives, Newton also believed that such conversations would seriously damage the university's budget negotiations with the legislature. He held a private meeting with the two men, after which he expressed "full confidence" in their claim that no inflammatory issues had been discussed.[26] Clearly, Newton aimed to defuse a no-win situation for all sides; he hoped to put the matter to rest, but Rozek would be heard from again in the near future.

Unfortunately, increasing numbers of legislators were convinced that the university had become an incubator for dangerous radical ideologies. Colorado Senator Earl A. Wolvington of Sterling was an erstwhile critic of the university in general and of Newton in particular. Newton and Wolvington had experienced recent clashes. In the fall of 1959, the senator had come to the "defense" of a student whose parents claimed that their daughter had received a failing grade from a professor because her paper advocated a conservative political position. Newton asked Kenneth Clark, dean of the College of Liberal Arts and Sciences, to look into the situation. Evidently, the student was persuaded that the reasons for her low grade were wholly unrelated to her political views, and she retracted her complaint. That did not, however, mollify either her parents or Wolvington. In fact, the senator sent a letter to Newton bristling with righteous indignation: "I am more alarmed now than I was initially. Either she has now been completely brainwashed or has had the fear of God instilled in her. Certainly I can see no reason for her parents to fabricate such a story and furnish me that information." Wolvington flatly accused Newton of attempting to muzzle an impressionable student. He concluded, "I would ask that neither you, Tippo, nor Dean Clark again call Miss Hamil into your office or offices."[27]

Newton's troubles with the senator were just beginning. In November 1961, Wolvington wrote a "Dear Quigg" letter to the president, threatening dire financial consequences if the university maintained its so-called Communist sympathy. "If this trend isn't stopped, I would venture a guess that the legislature will be extremely reluctant to, and probably will not, appropriate the additional millions you requested from the Joint Budget Committee last Wednesday."[28] Apparently, any reply from Newton failed to satisfy the senator. A few weeks later, he took the floor at the state capitol and harangued against Newton for thirty-five minutes. Wolvington claimed that Newton's administration had been "generally bad" and that faculty morale was "now the lowest it has ever been." Some of Wolvington's charges were simply silly. He was particularly offended that "you need only to go into the Student Union on any warm day to see boys in beards and girls in short-shorts and bare feet." In addition, Wolvington provided further evidence of his own small-mindedness in his negative attitude toward the "distinguished professor" program.[29]

The *Colorado Daily* fanned the embers of conflict by printing a mocking response from a writer identified only as "Sage King," which included the following doggerel:

> Oh, if we could only rule
> That corrupt, immoral school,
> We would show them what
> Is best for all them kids
> We would have a lot more courses
> Teaching them how to saddle horses
> And box socials where
> The boys could make their bids.
> All the girls would study sewing,
> Canning fruit and petunia growing.
> And we'd put their dresses
> Back down to their feet.
> We'd require agriculture
> Husbandry and horticulture
> And the boys will all wear ties
> Won't that be sweet?[30]

Despite the ridicule they attracted on campus, Wolverton's charges struck a nerve, chiefly among narrow-minded reactionaries who resented the so-called pretensions of the university's leadership and feared change. In many small towns across the state, conservative newspaper editors picked up on his attacks against the university and its president. The Buena Vista *Republican* voiced qualified support for the senator from the eastern plains, claiming that the regents (except for Bromley) had closed ranks around Newton: "Lo and behold, Ol' Quiggy is an A-OK boy. We are confident that were Senator Wolvington called upon to offer specific proof of his charges he could do so. But this won't happen. The whitewash has effectively been applied and the incident is closed, simply because Newton was not sufficiently wounded to arouse the blood-craze in the pack of wolves now feeding on the Colorado body politic."[31]

In his drive to enlarge and modernize the university and bring it into big-time academics, Newton had created the new position of provost shortly after he arrived. Oswald Tippo, a Harvard-educated botanist who had served at the University of Illinois and most recently at Yale, filled the slot. Conservative Coloradans who had been comfortable with the status quo grumbled when the Newton-Tippo team almost immediately began hiring easterners with prestigious academic reputations as department heads. Newton and Tippo also hired several "distinguished professors" at salaries of $17,500. According to Wolvington, these professors were too "busy keeping themselves distinguished to do much teaching." He continued, "The teaching is done by lowly instructors and assistant professors. ... The distinguished professors get the credit and the Legislature gets the bills."[32] Complaints about the professors' supposedly "inflated" salaries usually topped the list of objections to the appointments.

By early 1962, however, Newton's growing legion of critics were complaining that salary decisions were increasingly based on political orientation of faculty: that liberal Democrats and those with "radical" outlooks received the lion's share of annual salary raises, while Republicans and those with conservative leanings were left with the dregs. One "study" claimed that in biology, Associate Professor John W. Marr had earned $8,250 in 1960–1961. He was allegedly a Republican and he received a $700 raise for the following year. His colleague Sam Shushan, a conservative Democrat, received a $600 raise from $7,300 to $7,900. However, "left-wing" Erik K. Bonds, who had allegedly "attacked the Army in public letters and interviews with the *Colorado Daily*, had received a $1,900 raise to $9,500. All three men were associate professors.

The same story could be told in chemistry. Three professors received widely varying raises. Joseph D. Park, a "moderate," received a $1,250 raise, whereas two "left-wing" members, Stanley Cristol and Harold F. Walton, received $4,250 and $3,425 respectively. In history, the salary gaps were smaller, but the pattern remained the same. Professors James G. Allen and Karl Swisher, two Republicans, received raises of $500 and $825, respectively. Professors Robert G. Athearn and Fritz Hoffman, both identified as "left wing," received increments of $1,800 and $1,825, respectively. The anonymous author of the memo concluded, "This is how the taxpayer or the parents of the students are used to support the left-wingers at the C.U. campus. The professional qualifications of the faculty members are secondary to their political views. Many professors are losing faith in the democratic processes which permit this kind of injustice to go on unchecked. Is there any hope that the Legislature is going to investigate CU?"[33]

Senator Wolvington aired broad-based charges against the university in general and Newton in particular in another rambling, half-hour speech in the legislature on January 26, 1962. Newton and his top-level advisors evidently were taken aback by charges of left-wing favoritism in salary decisions, which would take some time to examine in detail.[34]

But one member of the Joint Budget Committee felt compelled to address other charges, one by one. A few days after Wolvington's outburst, he replied. Against charges that university budgets were out of control, he stated that Colorado ranked twelfth out of thirteen comparable state universities in funding per student. He claimed U.S. Department of Education figures revealed that deans' salaries at CU were "well below average paid in the public universities of 10,000 enrollment or more." Against charges that full professors were overpaid, Newton replied, "In comparison with other good state universities Colorado pays its lower ranks better than it does the full professors on its staff." Furthermore, it was simply untrue that distinguished scholars

shirked teaching. Of three individuals singled out by Wolvington, two
offered high-enrollment freshman surveys. The third, although not
teaching freshmen, "has one of the heaviest teaching loads carried by any
professor. ... " Indirectly addressing charges of salary favoritism being
based on political orientation, that they were "at the whim of the president," Newton revealed that salary recommendations were first made by
departments, then reviewed by deans, then the provost, and finally sent
to his office. Newton's ally concluded, "I am embarrassed that the floor
of the Senate would be made a forum for a general attack on the student
body of the University."[35]

By late 1961, however, Newton's opponents were throwing daggers
from every direction. One of his most constant and vitriolic critics was
Mrs. E. C. Pickett of Boulder, who, among other charges, complained,
"Large-scale brainwashing and downright misrepresentation were
employed as the administration sought to sell the university's goal of
'greatness.'" She repeatedly aired charges that the university was infested
with "reds." Pickett stated, "It is significant that CU has never, so far as
we know, ever hired a former Nazi or a former Fascist to teach. Yet it has,
and still does, employ former Communists." She claimed that they even
infested courses such as freshman English composition, "where probably
not one 'greenie' [freshman] in a hundred has ever heard of the Party
background of the person advising him." Pickett contended that when
"left-wingers and their 'liberal cohorts' represent more than 80 percent
of a university's social science faculty, you no longer have education but
indoctrination." She contended that the university had become "a
thoroughly hostile environment for faculty members and students holding opposing views."

Pickett also claimed, "The present CU administration has become
increasingly bold in its discrimination not only against conservatives but
also against middle-of-the-roaders and honest liberals who refuse to join
the 'club.'" Pickett obviously didn't think that students had the sense to
discriminate between fact and fiction. She claimed that the administration
cynically manipulated impressionable students: "Last year, uninformed
students lobbied for the budget, and received a tuition increase as their

reward. Will they be duped again by the administration?" Judging by student senate action, the answer is yes." Pickett engaged in almost gutter-level language, stating, "The CU administration's attitude toward the public and taxpayers can only be regarded as snotty."[36]

The *Colorado Daily* immediately defended the administration. Columnist John Farrell wrote that "some people choose to view every [challenge to democratic ideals] as part of a larger conspiracy. The John Birch Society does this on the national scene; the Mrs. Picketts do it here in Boulder. … The fact that professors disagree with her about the possibility of going back to the 'good ol days' leads her to conclude that they are Communists or their dupes." Farrell challenged Mrs. Pickett to be more specific: "[She] must have come up with some names of these nefarious Reds. But we are given no names, just warned that these Caspar-like Commies are lurking in our midst, plotting to turn us into dupes." He continued that "she conceives a fantastic plot of conspiracy and political skullduggery that will keep you on the edge of your seat." He concluded, "This is the kind of thinking that kindled the flames during the Salem witch hunts."[37]

The Barry Goldwater Controversy

If there was a single incident that most negatively affected the administration's connection with its wider constituency, the general population of the state of Colorado, it would be a rapidly escalating brouhaha surrounding a campus speech delivered by Senator Barry Goldwater (R-Arizona). The campus chapter of the Young Republicans invited the senator to visit on March 3, 1962. The colorful, opinionated right-wing Goldwater attracted 3,000 listeners, who jammed into Macky Auditorium. Controversy ensued almost immediately. According to conservative sources, approximately twenty-five Young Socialists stormed into Macky and occupied front-row seats that had been reserved for dignitaries. Representatives of the group later insisted that they had taken the seats by prearrangement and that Goldwater himself had agreed that their members would be permitted to raise the first three questions following his speech.[38]

Although there were some boos and catcalls during Goldwater's talk, there was also considerable applause. The major controversy erupted over how Goldwater was treated in the question-and-answer session following his speech. As promised, Young Socialists dominated the floor for the first few minutes. Almost all witnesses agreed that several of their "questions" basically turned into long-winded political "statements," which elicited shouts of "sit down" and "oh, come on" from the audience. They also agreed that the Young Socialists unfurled a banner over the balcony that read "Tippecanoe and Goldwater Too."[39]

Yet disparate sources indicated that neither the speech nor its aftermath appeared controversial at the time. Reginald Howard, Boulder County chairman of the Republican Party, indicated in a telephone interview that he personally had "kind of enjoyed the experience" and believed that the meeting was "good exposure for all concerned." According to Aurora *Star* editorial writer Ken Bundy, who was present at a $100-a-plate Republican fundraiser the next day, Goldwater stated that he had "enjoyed the tussling with college students at C.U. and Denver U during the day. The daily press gave you the idea that the students at C.U. were rude instead of political." Even the *Rocky Mountain News*, which by then had taken a consistently critical stance toward the Newton administration, quoted Goldwater as saying, "This is the first instance in speaking to approximately 200 different schools and colleges where I have ever found an organized Socialist group, and *I very much enjoyed their questions*, and their obvious lack of knowledge of what they were trying to discuss" (emphasis added).[40] Shortly after the speech, Newton phoned the senator to "apologize if the Senator felt he had been mistreated at his appearance at the university." According to Newton's internal memo, "Senator Goldwater said the heckling had *not been particularly offensive*, that politicians are *not unaccustomed to demonstrative audiences*" (emphasis added).[41]

If Newton believed that one phone call would resolve the issue, he was mistaken. Evidently, Goldwater's conservative friends saw an opportunity to make political capital and embarrass the university. If the senator had not been offended by his treatment during the speech, he was definitely offended by statements in the student newspaper, the *Colorado Daily*, which were brought to his attention. Six days after his appearance, he wrote to fellow Republican Senator Gordon Allott (Colorado) that he had been handed three different issues of the paper, "each one succeeding the other, and each one more vitriolic in its attack on me. Frankly, the issue which was represented as being the last and, as I recall it, published on the day of my arrival constituted *the most concentrated attack on my character I have ever witnessed*, and this includes the press of Russia and the *Daily Worker* published in New York" (emphasis added). Clearly, Goldwater's letter to Allott was intended for prominent public display. He closed by stating, "I do not offer this as any objection to the treatment afforded me. *I merely express it with more than mild surprise that I would find these conditions on a Western campus*" (emphasis added).[42]

Newton realized that the situation was spiraling out of control and it was time to consult independent campus groups for input on how to proceed. The University Board of Publications investigated the matter and reported that the *Colorado Daily*'s coverage of Goldwater's talk "had been generally fair in its handling." Similarly, the Faculty Senate Committee on Student Affairs concluded that the conduct of the Young Socialists amounted to neither "abuse nor vilification" of the senator. Newton tried to defuse the issue in a letter to Goldwater in early May. He informed the senator that he was "much disturbed at the report that you had been treated discourteously during your visit here." Newton offered to sit down with Goldwater during a planned visit to Washington on May 9, when he "would welcome the opportunity to spend a few minutes with you if you can spare the time." Attempting to cover all of his bases, Newton invited Allott to join the meeting, if a mutually convenient time could be arranged.[43]

If any such meeting took place, ruffled feathers were not smoothed and tensions simmered beneath the surface. Summer vacation came and went, and another school term began in September. With the beginning of the new school year, another newspaper appeared on campus. The *New Conservative* was run by two unusually able, experienced students who, henceforth, not only printed right-leaning stories but generated incendiary fodder for other dailies around the state that were targeting Newton and the liberals. The new paper had an annual budget of $25,000, which dwarfed that of the *Colorado Daily*. Nobody was quite sure of the source of its funding; Newton believed that Joe Coors, the arch-conservative regional brewer, and the John Birch Society were its primary supporters.[44]

The arrival of the *New Conservative* coincided with the explosion of the next two bombshells, both detonated by columnists for the *Colorado Daily*. On September 21, editor Gary Althen wrote an editorial addressing the unfolding football scandal in which he expressed the hope that the football team would lose all of its games. The article represented sincere if somewhat self-righteous disgust with what he and many students believed was overemphasis on big-time athletics. But many alumni, and more particularly Regent Jim Bromley, were furious at the overt lack of "loyalty" to "old CU." In a supplement to the same day's issue, sociology student Carl Mitcham wrote a lengthy review of Barry Goldwater's book, *The Conscience of a Conservative*. Mitcham unquestionably engaged in an ad hominem attack rather than a careful examination of the senator's ideas, stating, "Barry Goldwater is a fool, a mountebank, a murder [*sic*], no better than a common criminal."[45] Predictably, most alumni initially paid more attention to the attack on their cherished football tradition than that against a U.S. senator; it took four days for anyone to raise a red flag about the Goldwater piece. But on the fifth day, conservative Coloradans brought Mitcham's review to Goldwater's attention. The senator demanded a public apology, and the controversy became front-page news in the state's press.

Once again, Newton apologized to Goldwater and asked the university's Board of Publications to investigate whether action should be taken against editor Althen. The board refused to exonerate him, warning him that he "had been guilty of printing libel and that libel could not be justified on grounds of freedom of the press, academic freedom or student inexperience." Evidently, it took hard convincing, but Althen, who had already written a halfhearted apology to Goldwater, was pressured into writing a second "more profuse" disclaimer. The board then agreed not to fire Althen as editor and sent its own apology to the senator. Only Mitcham was publicly unrepentant; he wired Goldwater to the effect that he meant what he had written, and he dared Goldwater to sue him. On September 28, a week after the controversy began to unfold, the regents delivered yet another apology to Goldwater, along with an announcement that it had ordered a study to be made of the *Colorado Daily* and its role at the university.[46]

Even with a sheaf of apologies in hand, Goldwater demanded unconditional surrender. On October 1, he wrote what could only be considered an insulting and confrontational letter to Newton, which he clearly intended to make public. Somewhat disingenuously, Goldwater claimed, "It isn't what was said about me or who said it. It was the fact that it has now become obvious that this type of attack is the rule rather than the exception at the University of Colorado." Directly confronting Newton, Goldwater concluded, "I must because of this, then, come to the conclusion that you either do not know what is going on at the university, or you don't care, and in charity, I will presume the former. To put it briefly, *I doubt that you have the interest or the concern to be in the position you hold*" (emphasis added).[47] Newton was in Washington when Goldwater's letter was released in full, and his executive assistant, Don Saunders, indicated that he would have no immediate comment. Colorado Senator Gordon Allott also joined the attack, however, accusing Newton of "lax administration" of university affairs and demanding, in effect, that he muzzle Mitcham, Althen, and "*correct administrative functions which would permit this sad affair to occur*" (emphasis added).[48]

By then, Newton had had more than his fill of sanctimonious admonitions from right-wing politicians. In one of his finest moments as president of the university, he let Goldwater know that the apologies were over: "What remains now is the simple fact that you do not like the way our university is being run. My first impulse was to reply, as politely as possible, that I did not consider it any of your business. But, on reflection, I do not think that would be accurate. The real issue does involve you, because you have made yourself a symbol of the suppressive forces which are waging an all-out assault on the university." Newton was just getting warmed up: "We have a genuine democracy of ideas on our campus ... and the fight has been against those who—like yourself— believe the function of a university is to indoctrinate, rather than educate, to control thought rather than to stimulate it." Newton con- cluded, "The cry you raise has a very familiar ring to us: 'You must silence those who do not agree with me!' We have heard it from the John Birchers, from the Wolvingtons, from the Rozeks, from the Eakins, from the Bromleys, from the local Goldwaters. It is always the same: 'Our way is the only American way. All others are un-American and sub- versive. You must silence those who do not agree with us!'" But Newton would have none of it, at least not for the moment. He concluded his letter with a dramatic challenge: "Senator, I shall not silence them."[49]

For a brief, shining moment, it appeared as if Newton's stirring rejoinder might carry the day. Public opinion wavered; some felt that Goldwater had gone too far and that the president had shown both courage and superior judgment in confronting him. Unfortunately, the apparent "victory" proved Pyrrhic. The young men of the *Colorado Daily* were still up to their old tricks. On the very day Newton's letter to Goldwater was released, Mitcham wrote and Althen published yet another rambling analy- sis on the contemporary American political scene in which he took a potshot at ex-President Dwight Eisenhower: "It was hard to keep from laughing at the old futzer's grammar." Once again, there was little reaction at first. None of Newton's enemies brought it up for several days. The pres- ident even talked to Althen a day or so after Mitcham's characterization of Eisenhower appeared and allegedly "made no complaint at the time." A few days later, however, editor Jack Foster of the *Rocky Mountain News* splashed the "story" across headlines, "Eisenhower Called an Old Futzer," and Newton was again under fire. Privately, Quigg described Althen to one fac- ulty member as "an albatross around my neck."[50]

By then, Newton was fed up with repeatedly defending young journalists' rights to express their opinions, whether or not they were well thought out. Quigg may also have felt that the seemingly endless con- troversies were seriously compromising the university's larger missions of teaching, research, and service to the state. Without question, he was under enormous, unrelenting pressure from the press, conservative alumni, the state legislature—even the governor and politicians in Washington. The constant bombardment of demands from outsiders was distracting his administration and sapping morale of those around him.

Newton would soon discover just how isolated he and his top staffers were. During the second week of October, he asked the Board of Publications to fire Althen, but that body refused his request. Newton then persuaded a group of student leaders to urge Althen to resign voluntarily. Allegedly, after an all-night session, the editor decided to stand his ground. The Faculty Senate then became involved. By substantial majorities, it tabled a motion to recommend firing Althen, along with another motion to censure him. Many students and faculty were mystified and upset by Newton's abrupt reversal of his position on First Amendment rights. In Newton's defense, his critics in the university community were not the ones being hounded from virtually every direction to "do something" about the "mess" in Boulder. Evidently, a majority of faculty at Boulder were still on his side. Fearing that their lack of support might precipitate Newton's resignation, during the meeting in which it backed Althen, the Faculty Senate also passed a motion expressing "confidence in the president's ability to handle the case in the future."[51]

By then, however, Newton had reached the limits of his endurance and his patience. On October 17, two weeks after his public defiance of Goldwater, Newton called Althen into his office and told him he was fired. Among other considerations, the president and his supporters believed that Althen's irresponsibility was causing irreparable harm to the university by making it a constant target of public wrath. Not surprisingly, many students and faculty were upset with the decision, believing that Newton had caved in to the barbarians. They noted that since the dawn of American history, newspapers had indulged in name-calling and that campus newspapers had been among the most noteworthy exemplars of that tradition. In summarizing the whole untidy affair, one former University of Colorado faculty member wrote in *The Nation,* "The campus had rendered a verdict, but the outside world demanded a victim, and Newton threw Althen to the wolves."[52]

Newton's many friends around the country reassured him that he had borne up well under excruciating and unrelenting pressure. One supporter, trying to bolster Quigg's spirits, wrote, "A client of mine is a close friend of Goldwater and doubts that Goldwater really believes all of the guff he puts out, but does so in the belief that it will get him the most political mileage."[53] However, Newton's experiences with Goldwater and freedom of the press issues clearly compromised his effectiveness as leader of the university and caused him considerable personal anguish.

Despite all of the troubles Newton experienced during his last three years as president of the university, he did experience numerous ego strokes and thrilling moments. In late April 1961, he received the following telegram from President John F. Kennedy: "I would appreciate it if you would join me, Henry Alexander and six or seven others on Thursday, May 4, at 5:00 PM in my office to discuss application of concepts in new approach to foreign assistance outlined in my recent message to Congress."[54] Quigg understood that the president wanted to hear his views on foreign aid. He made the trip to Washington, and when he was ushered into the Oval Office, the "group" consisted only of himself, the president, and George Woods, a prominent New York financier representing First Boston Corporation. After Quigg briefly stated the case for the federal government increasing foreign aid, Woods took over, arguing basically that private industry initiatives could more effectively help revive foreign economies by stepping up their levels of investment. Newton recalled that the meeting lasted about thirty minutes.[55]

Bromley's Broadsides

By mid-October 1962, Newton faced other festering problems, and he was seemingly under fire from all sides. None was more vexing than his quickly deteriorating relationship with Regent Charles "Jim" Bromley, an association born in mutual distrust and one which had been spiraling downhill for many years. By 1962, Bromley had a long history as a university regent. He had served between 1928 and 1934, then two more terms from 1950 until 1962. He was preparing to run for yet another elected six-year term.

As previously noted, Bromley had been one of the two Republican regents who opposed hiring Newton as president of the university. At the time, Bromley claimed that he simply wanted to ensure that the selection process was not unduly hasty and that all viable candidates for the position received full consideration. Relations between the two men never improved. Bromley had been the main force behind the firing of Dal Ward as football coach in 1958, and he remained a strong supporter of Sonny Grandelius until the very end, even amidst the ever-increasing stench of the football scandal. In the summer of 1961, Bromley escalated tensions by charging publicly that one of his legal clients had revoked a legacy of $2 million, which would otherwise have been given to the University of Colorado, because Frank Oppenheimer had been hired. When challenged to give specifics, however, Bromley refused to identify the mystery "donor," claiming that "the stature of the man was so great that there was no need to question the validity of the information and there was no possibility that the statement was made for suspect purposes."[56]

Bromley's "loss" on the Grandelius issue ignited his increasingly bitter public break with Newton. From March 1962 forward, Bromley unleashed a vicious, unrelenting assault against Newton and virtually everything he stood for as leader of the university. In late March, he charged that many meetings of the regents were secret, or "closed," meaning that no reporters or outside visitors were allowed in the room. The implication was clear: those running the meetings had something unsavory to hide. The *Rocky Mountain News* snapped up the bait and published an editorial on March 20 demanding that the meetings be open. Newton observed that Bromley had, in fact, "participated in closed meetings without any hesitation during the last six years and found no objection to them—*particularly when he was pushing for the firing of Ward ... and McKean*" (emphasis added). Bromley abruptly terminated his attack on closed meetings. In the spring and summer months, the regents continued to conduct closed meetings in which sensitive issues were discussed, and Bromley continued participating in them.[57]

Squelched on that issue, Bromley withdrew from the spotlight for several months. However, he was up for reelection in November, and he dreamed of a landslide victory. Borrowing a page from the late Wisconsin senator Joseph McCarthy, he pressed forward with a battery of charges against Newton the next summer. Evidently, Bromley hoped to keep his adversary so busy defending himself that he and his top administrators wouldn't have any energy left over to persecute conscientious conservatives on campus. Some of his charges were new, but most had a distinctly familiar ring. In a speech to a Republican women's club in Broomfield on August 28, Bromley described the university as "a terror-ridden autocracy where an intimidated faculty lives in constant fear of offending a tyrannical school president." Bromley charged that, "Republicans not only are a minority on the faculty, they are a decided minority." Although he conceded that, when interviewed for positions, nobody asked faculty recruits about their political affiliation, "They [Newton and his supporters] have a way of screening applicants. The administration gets full details of an applicant's background, but they only present to the regents a summary and their recommendation."[58]

The day following Bromley's attack, all of the other five regents defended Newton. Phillip A. Danielson of Boulder took direct issue with Bromley: "I think what Jim Bromley is trying to do is divert attention from his own votes in favor of crooked football and in favor of segregated fraternities and sororities." Albert E. Smith, a regent from Julesburg, agreed that Bromley, not Newton, was the problem: "There have been no witch hunts except the one Jim is making. … This is terrible to have a regent do this. … Faculty morale is at an all-time high, not only because of its academic freedom but because of the growing academic status of the university."[59] A few weeks later, *The Denver Post* published an editorial titled "Bromley Has Been Regent Long Enough." The writer documented numerous examples of when the regent's public statements were directly contrary to positions he had taken in private.[60]

Although polling techniques were not as sophisticated forty-four years ago as they are today, Bromley's friends and supporters sensed that political tides were in his favor and that he was riding a powerful wave of public frustration with the university. Large numbers of voters did not understand Newton's emphasis on upgrading the faculty and pushing research. Many of these same constituents were perplexed that, despite rapidly increasing public support, radicalism appeared to be growing on campus.

Even a mild heart attack on September 28 did not slow Bromley down. If anything, forced rest solidified and intensified his visceral hatred of Newton. By late October, with the election just two weeks away, Bromley's pledge to "oust Newton" was the cornerstone of his campaign. In a speech read for him by his friend and fellow attorney, Joe Myers at the Lincoln Club, Bromley claimed, "The University of Colorado was a great institution before the present president was appointed, and it will be a much greater one shortly after he leaves, and to this end I pledge my utmost effort." Lest there be any doubt, Myers read Bromley's pledge: "Jim will introduce the resolution asking for the president's resignation in the firm confidence that the resolution will be seconded by Dr. Atkins."[61] Myers's reference was to Dr. Dale Atkins, a medical doctor and fellow Republican, who was also running for regent.

The last weeks before the election coincided with tumultuous international events, most notably the Cuban missile crisis. The hysterical messages of doomsayers carried a greater than usual aura of plausibility. That may also have helped the rise of a conservative movement, at least in Colorado. In the election held on November 7, both liberal Democrat U.S. senator John Carroll and Democratic governor Steve McNichols lost to Republican opponents. In the regents' races, Bromley led the field with a total of just over 300,000 votes. Atkins was second, with 293,451, and Newton supporter Fred M. Betz Jr. lost his bid for reelection with 275,507 votes.[62]

Quigg Newton was a tolerant, instinctively gentle, forgiving human being who seldom, if ever, held grudges. But from that point forward, his feelings about and attitude toward Jim Bromley conveyed deep personal revulsion. In a regents' meeting in early January 1963, the two men exchanged verbal blows over a motion to fire the chair of the Chemical Engineering Department. For a number of complicated reasons, a majority of the faculty in the department wanted the chair replaced. After considering all of the evidence, Newton and his top advisors supported them and asked the chair to step down. The issue came up at the January regents' meeting. Although numerous members of the department attended the meeting and stated their case for his removal, the chair himself refused to speak, referring all comments to his attorney, who was also present. Not surprisingly, Bromley defended the chair and turned the inquiry into a sweeping indictment of the administration. He accused Newton of "rewarding his friends and punishing his enemies." Quigg bristled, "That's an intolerable charge." Bromley retorted, "If you want to leave the room, leave it." Again, Newton stated that Bromley's behavior was "simply intolerable. I know no other university in the United States that has to face up to this kind of thing."[63]

More than a year later, after Newton had left the university, Bromley once again made newspaper headlines because of a drunk driving accident. Newspaper accounts revealed that it was his third automobile accident in three years.[64] In the latest incident, Bromley drove through several yards and rammed a couple of parked cars in an east Denver neighborhood. Needless to say, although apparently uninjured physically, the regent was embarrassed at the negative publicity. For one of the few times in his life, Newton expressed delight in another human being's misfortune. Writing to Don Saunders, his former administrative assistant at the university and a trusted friend, Quigg stated, "I guess there isn't much to say about it except that it is too bad it didn't happen two years ago *and also too bad it wasn't more serious.* He is really a very evil man and ought some day to get his come-uppance, but I doubt if he will" (emphasis added).[65]

Stepping Down

With victories by two severe critics in the regents' contests in November 1962, Newton sensed that his opportunities for advancing new and challenging initiatives at the University of Colorado were dwindling. In his mind, this meant that his effectiveness as a leader was severely compromised. Quigg spent a few more weeks testing the waters, but it was clear that from that point forward he was looking for a graceful exit. In an interview forty years later, Newton recalled that the main reason he delayed announcement of his resignation was that he wanted to help his top-level associates find good positions elsewhere.[66]

As postelection pressure against him mounted, Newton heard from many friends, both within and outside of the university, voicing their loyal support and urging him to stay and fight. An administrative colleague at Colorado College argued that Newton had strong support from less vocal, yet more informed people: "I hope that you know how bitterly most of the reasonable people in this state, of whatever political conviction, resent the unfair, untrue and distorted attacks upon you and upon the University of Colorado. ... Keep up the good fight and please know that the faculties at all institutions in this state and other administrators are right behind you."[67] A member of the English Department in Boulder urged him to look above the littered landscape of calumny and hatred: "The malice and hostility of little men, within and without the University, is the inevitable price of real achievement and should be properly discounted and dismissed. You have won not only the respect but also the affection of those of us who have come to know ... how tolerant and sincere, how diligent and wise you have shown yourself."[68]

Newton may have been warmed by such expressions of support, but they did not sway his deliberations. On December 5, 1962, Quigg announced that he planned to step down as president of the university at the end of the current academic year. This would give the regents adequate time to recruit and hire his successor. After his announcement, a barrage of newspaper editorials appeared lamenting Newton's "forced" decision and providing ringing endorsements of all he had done in the six years he had served as president. Houston Waring, editor of the *Arapahoe Herald* and *Littleton Independent* and one of the most thoughtful and deeply respected journalists in the Rocky Mountain region, commented, "The thinking people of the University of Colorado, and that means over 99 percent on the campus, are dismayed at what has happened to their institution." Laying the blame for Newton's ouster directly on the shoulders of Edward Rozek, whom he called a "paranoic professor," Bromley, and the *Rocky Mountain News*, Waring charged that this small but powerful cadre had "destroyed the academic climate that makes a university attract brilliant faculty members and dedicated students."[69]

After the immediate buzz of his resignation quieted somewhat, Newton also heard soothing words from former university president Robert L. Stearns: "I cannot blame you for the step you have taken, but I deplore many of the critical comments which have been made by unthinking people." Stearns added that "yours had been a distinguished administration. Your contribution and that of your administrative staff have contributed immeasurably to the growth and stature of the university and in time to come future generations will rise up and call you blessed."[70]

Reporters who covered the story at the Boulder campus uncovered an avalanche of angry student commentary over the situation. A female philosophy student believed that Newton was virtually forced to quit because "everybody is afraid of new ideas ... because parents are afraid of what we'll turn out like if we're exposed to anything but the tried and true." A twenty-two-year-old male student from California stated that "at one time this used to be known as the play school of the West. ... Today, you've got to work and work hard. The faculty is more interested in teaching you, too." Several students expressed fear that the university would hire a "yes man" and that "faculty freedom would be 'strangled' by the new administration."[71] Many faculty members worried that much of what Newton had tried to accomplish would be lost and that large numbers of the most accomplished faculty would leave for greener pastures.[72]

Newton's last six months as president of the university were anticlimatic, involving largely housekeeping details. In due course, many of his most valued and trusted associates, whom he had brought to the university, also left for other positions. In early March, Provost Oswald Tippo announced that he would be moving on to "a post in another university in the East" (it turned out to be productive stints, first as provost at New York University, then later as president of the University of Massachusetts at Amherst). The student senate expressed its anger over Tippo's resignation, laying it at the feet of Bromley, "a man seemingly intent on reducing the stature of the university." The senate resolution stated, "Dr. Tippo had worked to give the people of this state something they do not deserve and could not appreciate, a fine university dedicated to a liberal education for the youth of the state."[73] Dr. Robert Glaser, dean of the School of Medicine, also timed his departure to coincide with Quigg's. Glaser moved on to become a professor of medicine at Harvard University and president of Affiliated Hospitals Center, Inc., in Boston.[74] Others joined the exodus. The early 1960s were boom times in higher education, and superior researchers in particular regularly attracted lucrative and appealing job offers.

One of the qualities that many of his associates most admired in Quigg was his willingness to stand up and take the heat when he might have deflected it. Years later, Tippo fondly recalled the camaraderie that existed within the administrative hierarchy when he and Newton served together: "I remember we'd say to him, 'Quigg, there is no reason that *you* should get all these barbs. I am the academic officer. Why don't you let me take the blame for things that happen in the academic area?' 'Oh no,' he said, 'I'm the president. I'm the one who takes it.' And yet, when it came to praise, he always praised us. You would lay down your life for a guy like that."[75]

Unfortunately, "housekeeping" still involved nasty confrontations with Bromley. In an early January 1963 regents' meeting, the two men clashed over the fate of the chair of the Chemistry Department. During the meeting, Bromley stated that Newton's decision to continue in the presidency until June was the "second most disastrous thing that has happened to this university in the past six years." The "worst thing," Bromley later stated, "was the appointment of Newton as president."[76] Incredibly, relations between the Bromley and the embattled president deteriorated even further. One observer described the February 1963 regents' meeting as a "sordid free-for-all," where "supposedly educated men shouted personal invectives that would make a sailor blush." He continued that "there were threats of physical violence."[77] Several years later, one administrative official aptly summed up the nightmare events of 1962 and 1963: "We did more than just disrobe ourselves in front of the public; we disemboweled ourselves. The University could not have done a more complete or messier job had it committed hara-kiri on the steps of Norlin Library."[78]

By that time, Quigg was undoubtedly counting the days until he could step down. In early April, he wrote to a friend at Dartmouth College, "The whole business here has been a nightmare and ... there have been evil forces at work beyond the slightest question. ... "[79] At times, he simply gave in to voice frustration and depression. To another supporter, he wrote, "The key to much of our trouble was one of our Regents who led the attack *and unfortunately the other Regents, with one exception, failed to stand solidly behind our program*" (emphasis added).[80] Fortunately, Quigg's ordeal was almost over. To his great relief, the February regents' meeting marked his last public confrontation with Bromley.

In May, Newton had to put down a brush fire of protest when Norman Lincoln Rockwell, head of the American Nazi Party, spoke on campus. In previous years, Quigg might have defended even the most objectionable campus visitors, but in this case he did not. Since Rockwell had already spoken, freedom of speech issues were moot. When Rabbi Milton H. Elefant of Boulder's B'nai B'rith Hillel Foundation voiced his objections to the speech, Newton tried to soothe the rabbi, observing that Rockwell's appearance had been cleared with a staff member in the office of the dean of students. Newton acknowledged that Rockwell's application should have been reviewed (and by implication denied) by higher authorities: "I am sure the rules on outside speakers should be tightened up. ... "[81]

In Newton's last weeks in office, tributes to his and Tippo's leadership poured in. A few days before he departed from the presidency, Newton received a heartfelt letter from Mrs. Edward Kingery of Boulder: "I feel a profound sense of regret over your resignation. Your leadership at this University has directed the institution to a deeper and broader realization of its potential for greatness. The emphasis you place on academic freedom has been a key part of this leadership and has struck a responsive note in my own thinking. ... To my mind some of your political opponents have exhibited an incredible ignorance of the true function of a University as 'the conscience of a society,' to use your own term."[82]

Quigg responded, "I want you to know that your letter was one of the finest statements that I have received. It evidences a very clear understanding of what we were trying to do at the University. ... "[83]

The Faculty Senate passed a resolution referring to the departure of Newton and several of his top associates that stated, "We deeply regret your resignations. ... We deny that your resignations were in the best interests of the university, and we deplore the circumstances under which they occurred."[84] Three-fourths of the faculty signed the resolution, and at least one who refused to sign stated that it was because he felt that the resolution was far too mealy-mouthed and filled with pious platitudes. He assured Newton, "If an effective expression of appreciation of your valiant efforts in behalf of the university and our regret at your departure is forthcoming, I shall be delighted to sign it."[85]

Newton's day of departure, June 30, 1963, finally arrived. He could take an enormous amount of satisfaction at his administration's achievements. Between 1956 and 1962, total enrollments at Boulder increased from 9,844 to 12,300; the number of graduate students jumped from 859 to almost 2,100. Financial aid for students more than doubled during that period, from just $250,396 to roughly $680,000. Average faculty salaries increased 74 percent, from $5,628 to $9,765. Despite Newton's sometimes contentious relationship with the legislature, the university's annual budget also doubled, from $20.5 million to $40.7 million. New campus construction, including the Medical Center, amounted to just under $24 million. Brand-new or vastly expanded institutions included the Institute of Behavioral Sciences, the Joint Institute for Laboratory Astrophysics, the Computer Center and the Institute of Computer Science, the National Center for Atmospheric Research, and housing for and acquisition of a cyclotron, provided by the Atomic Energy Commission.[86]

More than any other president before or since, Newton helped thrust the University of Colorado from its comfortable niche as a good but basically undistinguished regional institution dedicated mostly to undergraduate teaching into a prominent state university taken seriously by leading academics around the country. Just as he had helped transform the university, Newton essentially furthered much of the work he had helped start as mayor of Denver. He had a clear vision of the Front Range becoming a scientific research corridor, even a national center for research, utilizing the combined academic strengths of the University of Colorado,

Colorado State University, the Colorado School of Mines, Denver University, Colorado College, and the brand-new Air Force Academy. Just as scientific research communities were emerging around Chicago, Boston, and San Francisco, Newton envisioned a similar nucleus forming around Denver and eventually stretching from Fort Collins to Colorado Springs. His vision placed him years ahead of most other leaders in the region. Major research institutions and industries moved into the region, and most of them stayed: the National Bureau of Standards, IBM, Hewlett Packard, Martin Marietta, Ball Brothers Research, and others.[87]

After Newton announced his resignation, many wondered what type of a leader could be persuaded to step into such a volatile situation. The various groups involved in selecting Quigg's successor finally settled on Dr. Joseph R. Smiley, a distinguished scholar in French literature and most recently president of the University of Texas at Austin. University leaders placed a premium on hiring a nonconfrontational facilitator who could soothe ruffled feathers. Smiley seemed to fill the bill, and many observers predicted a lengthy "honeymoon" for the new president. Although university events temporarily receded from daily headlines in the mid-1960s, conservatives finally established full parity on the Board of Regents. Joe Coors landed a place on the six-man board, joining Bromley and Dr. Dale Atkins; predictably, they soon created headaches for Smiley.[88]

With deeply conflicting emotions, Newton presided gracefully and eloquently over graduation ceremonies at Boulder. In his farewell address at the spring commencement, he received several standing ovations, including one from graduating students. Despite all of the recent pressure and turmoil, Quigg stated that his six and a half years as head of the university had been "the best years of his life." Certainly, both he and Ginny had found the experience enormously stimulating; their girls had settled into Boulder, and they had done a lot of growing up. As he and his family departed from the university in the summer of 1963, they looked forward to more adventures and more challenges. They were again headed east, toward New York City, where Quigg would head up the Commonwealth Fund and Ginny and the four girls would continue their formal educations.

CHAPTER 11

MEDICAL VISIONARY

After the prolonged conflict with critics at the University of Colorado, the Newtons looked forward to an extended break. After Quigg and Ginny took a vacation to the Caribbean, the family headed to the Shafroth family retreat in Osterville on Cape Cod. They stayed at Cape Cod through August.[1] At the end of the summer, they relocated to New York City. In December 1962, when Quigg announced his impending resignation from the university, he also confirmed that he had accepted an offer from the Commonwealth Fund, a venerable private charitable organization in New York City, to become its third president. In fact, the offer from the Fund had been on the table for several months before Newton finally accepted it.

"Old-school" networking ties once again played a key role in the evolution of Newton's career. Several decades earlier, Steven V. Harkness, one of John D. Rockefeller's original partners, had died and left his considerable fortune to his widow. In 1918, she established the Commonwealth Fund with the simple directive "to do something for the welfare of mankind."[2] Like Newton, Malcolm P. Aldrich, the second president of the Commonwealth Fund, was a Yale graduate. Aldrich had also been a member of Skull and Bones at Yale, and although older than Newton, the two men became well acquainted during World War II while Quigg was serving as a liaison officer for the Naval Air Transport Service. Aldrich persuaded his younger friend to become a member of the board in 1951, when he was beginning his second term as mayor of Denver.

At the time, Quigg was developing an intense interest in medical care delivery to disadvantaged Denver residents, and the Commonwealth Fund was directing much of its effort to improving medical education. The connection was natural, and Newton took his duties as a director of the Fund seriously. In fact, in the early 1950s, he was also serving as a member of the Yale Corporation. As Yale University was the recipient of considerable support from the Fund, Quigg felt that it was a conflict of interest to serve both organizations. But the fact that he was on the Ford Foundation's payroll played an even larger role in his decision to resign from the Yale Corporation in 1955.

In terms of size, the Commonwealth Fund was a second-tier charitable organization. When Newton assumed the presidency, its assets were valued at $86.5 million. When he resigned his position twelve years later, its assets were $99.9 million, but with a book value of roughly $130 million.[3] The Fund was dwarfed by giants such as the Rockefeller and Ford Foundations, but it still awarded between $6 and $7 million in grants annually. When Newton assumed the presidency of the Fund, its primary focus was providing grants to institutions, primarily university medical schools, to improve medical education.

Family Life during the New York Years

After a restful summer, the Newtons moved into the famous Dakota Apartments at Seventy-Second Street and Central Park West for about a year, then purchased a seven-room apartment at the corner of Fifth Avenue and Ninety-Eighth Street and settled in. The permanent apartment was on the tenth floor and faced onto Ninety-Eighth Street, but one room had a direct view onto Fifth Avenue. Ginny had plenty to do in setting up a household and getting the girls enrolled in various schools. But she was also a career woman with her own goals. Having earned her M.A. in social psychology at the University of Colorado, she looked for work in New York. She was introduced to Professor Martin Hamburger of New York University. Hamburger had National Defense Education Act (NDEA) fellowships available, and he needed a research assistant. In order to qualify for an NDEA fellowship, a student had to be a Ph.D. candidate, so Ginny signed up for the doctoral program at NYU. While taking courses and writing a dissertation under Hamburger's direction, she took a position with the City of New York and was involved with several projects, including work with inner-city schools, and then counseled high school dropouts from East Harlem. Ginny Newton finished her Ph.D. in 1971.

During the years in New York, the Newton girls were moving through high school and college. Nan went to Bennington College in Vermont, which she loved. Later, she studied music at Indiana University. Nelle graduated from high school and then attended Pace College briefly. Abby went to Putney School in Vermont and then attended the University of Wisconsin, where she had a front-row seat as a witness to some of the nation's most violent antiwar activities. Ginna, the youngest, attended Putney School, but she also dropped out for a time. Abby and Ginna in particular were caught up in the aura of rebellion. It was a difficult time to be a college student.

As the two youngest girls explored radical ideas in the late 1960s, Quigg and Ginny had the good sense to let them find their own ways in life, but they engaged in countless family discussions about controversial issues at the family dinner table. On one occasion, Quigg and Ginny became involved in an antiwar demonstration themselves. There was a large parade down Fifth Avenue, and they went outside to watch from the sidewalk. It wasn't long before they became so swept up in the moment that they, too, joined the march.[4]

Abby had some of the most vivid memories of the early New York years. When her parents moved to Manhattan, she was fifteen and enrolled at the Putney School. Abby recalled one of her initial visits home. She was walking down a street with her laundry bag slung over her shoulder, and a truck driver yelled out, "Hi, Abby!" Her name was stenciled in large letters on the bag, making her an easy target. In Boulder, which in the early 1960s still had a "small-town" feel, she was used to greeting people on the street. But if she did that in New York, strange men sometimes followed her. She learned to look straight ahead and to avoid making eye contact on the street.[5]

The Newtons and their daughters frequently found refuge from assorted stresses away from the city. During many weekends and summers, they retreated to a cottage on a large estate in Cold Spring Harbor on the north shore of Long Island owned by one of Ginny's college classmates. It was about an hour outside of the city by train. The cottage was about a half-mile up a hill from the bay.

Settling in at the Commonwealth Fund

Quigg took over his duties at the Commonwealth Fund on September 1, 1963. Since its offices were at Fifth Avenue and Seventy-Fifth Street, once the family moved into their large apartment on Ninety-Eighth Street, his "commute" was a mere twenty-three blocks south on Fifth Avenue, a short bus ride. In some respects, running the Commonwealth Fund was a welcome change from the university environment. Although his years at the university had been exciting and enormously stimulating, Quigg had been surrounded by competitive and often strident individuals who, when they did not get their way, sometimes laundered their differences with administrators in public. In the plush, carpeted offices at the Commonwealth Fund, people conversed in quiet, cultured voices. He had a small staff that basically made sure the officials' decisions were implemented smoothly and efficiently. Newton recalled that sitting behind a desk waiting for others to ask him for money was a strange and fascinating experience: "It was a different world. I was giving away money ... picking the best causes within a prescribed area of medical education. It was like moving from a battlefield to a safe haven. Other people were on the front line. As university president, I was the one going to the legislature, hat in hand. Now, I was the guy on the other side of the desk."[6]

In typical fashion, Newton was far too self-effacing. He did not simply relax behind his desk in a comfortable executive chair and wait for proposals to cross his desk. He networked aggressively, using his previous experience and contacts to solicit imaginative and innovative grant proposals. Several men who served as his vice presidents, including Dr. Robert J. Glaser, also relied upon their extensive contacts within the medical community to identify institutions and individuals working on the most-promising projects. One of Quigg's great strengths as an administrator from his earliest days as mayor forward was his willingness to delegate authority. Although Newton might personally guide a proposal from a close and trusted medical associate through the labyrinth of approval, in most cases he gave staff members wide latitude in decision-making.

Occasionally, unsolicited proposals came in. Newton and his staff encouraged potential grantees to submit initially a brief one- or two-page proposal. If a preliminary proposal looked promising, one or more staff members would meet with candidates to discuss their ideas in more detail. If a project passed that screening, Fund officers invited candidates to submit formal proposals. The next step would be discussion by the staff of the most-attractive proposals at weekly meetings. In most cases, Newton and his top-level assistants only examined personally those proposals the staff identified as "probable" given their intrinsic quality, compatibility with the Fund's mission, and the amount of money available for funding in a given period of time. With few exceptions, those were the only pro-posals the board considered. When proposals reached the board of directors at their scheduled meetings, approval was usually a formality.

Travel for Business and Pleasure

In seeking the most exciting funding opportunities and conducting on-site visits to projects already being supported, Newton was away from the city several days a month. While conducting official business, Quigg almost always traveled first class. Most of his trips were routine, but because the Fund sponsored a number of projects for the improvement of teaching and research in medical schools in foreign countries, he enjoyed several extended visits abroad, accompanied by Ginny. One of their most memorable journeys was a five-week-long trip around the world late in 1966. The highlight for the couple was attending a conference at the Christian Medical College in Narangwal, about 200 miles northwest of New Delhi, India. American personnel helping train Indian doctors were being housed in a half-dozen or so "village houses." The director informed Quigg that most of the people attending the conference would probably have to be put up in tents, but that he might be able to arrange for him and Ginny to take over one of the "houses" in the village. As he stated to Newton, "The ruggedness of the experience has, in most such excursions to the subsistence level of living, depended on the weather. We have picked a time of year when conditions should be ideal. We guarantee a memorial [*sic*] experience."[7]

There were certainly other high points during the trip. Before attending the Narangwal conference, the couple stopped off in Beirut, Lebanon, for four days so Quigg could evaluate Fund-sponsored projects at the medical school at the American University of Beirut. Newton spent a day with university personnel, and then he and Ginny arranged to spend most of the remainder of their time on guided tours of ancient archaeological discoveries.[8] Following several days of "roughing it" at the Narangwal conference, they visited New Delhi, where Quigg attended the Third World Medical Education Conference. Heading home, they visited Bangkok, Thailand, for two days and Hong Kong for the same length of time. Before heading back to the States, they traveled to Sydney, Australia, for a week, where Quigg conferred with several local doctors who had received either Harkness Fellowships or Fund support for various projects. On the journey home, they stopped off for three days of relaxation at the Royal Hawaiian Hotel in Honolulu, Hawaii.

During the Commonwealth Fund years, the couple took several other trips abroad, not all related to business. In early 1968, they made another memorable trip to South America, visiting Rio de Janeiro, Brazil, and Santiago, Chile. They also visited Peru, where they marveled at the wonders of Lima, Cuzco, and Machu Picchu. Ginny recalled that during their visit to Machu Picchu, the weather at the famous Incan stronghold atop rugged mountains was dreadful. Although Ginny might have preferred seeing only part of Machu Picchu, Quigg insisted on fighting the elements, walking around the ruins to see all of it.[9]

Reexamining the Fund's Mission

One of the primary reasons Malcolm Aldrich had pushed for Newton to take over the presidency was that Quigg was a generalist who had extensive contacts in many important fields, including academe, medicine, law, business, and politics. Newton realized that, given its modest size relative to giant foundations, the Fund needed to exercise sharp judgment in awarding grants to make the maximum impact with comparatively limited funds. Although possessing an informed layperson's interest and knowledge about medicine, Newton believed he should hire persons trained in medicine to help guide the decision-making process. He originally wanted to bring his close friend Dr. Robert J. Glaser along with him from the University of Colorado School of Medicine, but Glaser had just accepted an appointment at Harvard and the Affiliated Hospitals in Boston. In fact, following a move to Stanford University and involvement in the Kaiser Foundation, Glaser did come on board in 1970. Colin M. McCloud, another medical doctor Newton recruited, served as vice president of the foundation between 1966 and 1969.[10] Both before and during McCloud's period of service, Quigg also relied heavily on Glaser's advice regarding many proposals submitted to the foundation.

Newton and Glaser believed that one of the greatest mistakes leaders of any charitable organization could make was to focus all of their efforts into one narrow field and lose touch with society's overall concerns and direction. Therefore, they regularly invited leading civic leaders, businessmen, judges, lawyers, social scientists, an occasional politician, and other highly informed people to one-day seminars at their offices at Harkness House. A dozen or more "outstanding professionals" would sit around a conference table and give a day of their time to participate in "freewheeling discussions" of current social, political, and economic issues. Not only did these discussions prove highly stimulating to the foundation's leaders, but they helped them pinpoint promising new areas for long-term future support.[11]

After becoming president of the Fund, Newton conducted an intensive study of both its traditions and previous grants. Wealthy people setting up charitable organizations almost invariably have definite opinions about how their money should be spent, and directors of funds usually share those views. Newton had served on the board for a dozen years before his appointment as president, and he knew the

Fund's internal culture well. In addition to Harkness Fellowships, the
Fund had focused a good deal of its effort to supporting medical
research. Although its objectives were admirable, in the mid-1960s
Newton believed a new focus might be appropriate. In the previous two
decades, the National Science Foundation (NSF) and the National
Institutes of Health (NIH) had poured hundreds of millions of dollars
into medical research. Between 1955 and 1960, for example, the annual
NIH budget for medical research skyrocketed from $81 million to $400
million.[12] In a post-*Sputnik* era when supporting scientific research was
in high fashion and universities and medical schools were rapidly expanding, other huge private foundations were also jumping on the bandwagon
and pouring tens of millions of dollars into medical research.

In addition, by the time Newton took over as president of the
Fund, medical education was becoming increasingly rigorous and much
more highly specialized. Before World War II, after medical school most
doctors served an internship of approximately one year and then went
directly into practice. In 1940, more than three-fourths of the nation's
doctors were general practitioners, and most set up private offices. By the
1950s, most doctors were serving three or more years in hospital residency *after* an internship. By the late 1950s, medical students were
bypassing general practice in droves. A Cornell University study showed
that between the first and fourth year of medical education, the percentage of students intending to become general practitioners plummeted
from 60 to 16 percent, while those planning to specialize increased from
35 to 74 percent.[13] Addressing this phenomenon a decade later in his
chairman's address at the Association of Medical Colleges in 1969, Dr.
Glaser sardonically intoned, "By and large, medical school administrators
and faculty members adhere to what has come to be known as the Willie
Sutton principle. Sutton, when questioned as to why he robbed banks, is
said to have replied, 'That's where the money is.'"[14]

Glaser and Newton shared a strong conviction that, although medical knowledge was expanding rapidly, neither medical schools nor private
hospitals were paying sufficient attention to medical needs within their
communities, particularly those of the uneducated and indigent. Quigg

specifically identified this issue late in 1964. In a list of recommendations to the Fund's board, Newton wrote, "There continues to be a distinct lag between the discovery of new knowledge and its translation into better medical care. ... " He also wanted to place far more emphasis on *preventive* medical care; more attention to this generally neglected sphere of health care could lessen the incidence of costly hospitalization for millions of patients.[15] Although a majority of Americans were covered by private health insurance through employers, large segments of the population were not. Medical care was becoming one of the nation's biggest enterprises. Between 1950 and 1970, the number of persons employed in medicine more than tripled, from 1.2 to 3.9 million. Medical expenditures rose from $12.7 billion to $71.6 billion annually, and from 4.5 to 7.3 percent of the gross national product.[16] Although much of the rising cost of health care was inevitable, justified by the high price endemic to the development of new drugs and "heroic" medical procedures, the increasing complexity of the entire health care delivery system was deeply frustrating. Long before most American leaders had given the problem much thought, Quigg grasped the fact that it was also becoming an explosive and highly divisive public policy issue.

Newton lived in New York at this point, and he was a close observer of growing civil unrest among the disadvantaged elements of American society. American cities were entering a harrowing period of violence, and both Newton and his wife saw it coming. Ginny worked directly with severely disadvantaged inner-city youths who saw little reason to have faith in the American system. The couple often discussed the ramifications of the unequal distribution of the benefits of American capitalism. Many youths were products of broken homes, where health care was a priority ranking well below rent, food, and other more immediate necessities.

"Democratizing" Access to Medical Education and Services

Obviously, the Commonwealth Fund could not address all of society's problems, but Newton believed it could make an impact in two general areas. After extensive discussions with public policy analysts, various highly informed friends and other trusted associates, and many doctors around the country, Quigg came to the conclusion that many medical schools could better serve society by providing more direct medical service to people in their communities, even at the sacrifice of some research. As a corollary to this view, Newton believed that a key factor inhibiting the diffusion of medical services was that many *routine* medical services were attended to by doctors and that less highly skilled individuals could handle most simple, ordinary procedures. In effect, the often narrowly specialized skills of many doctors were not required in the vast majority of their contacts with patients. Within the culture of the medical profession, however, many patients had been conditioned to believe that unless they saw "the doctor," they weren't receiving competent medical care. Despite the rapid expansion of health care services, there was a severe "doctor shortage" in the United States. By the late 1950s, hospitals were seeking more than 12,000 interns annually, but medical schools were producing fewer than 7,000 each year. Increasingly, foreign-born doctors were filling in gaps in American hospitals.[17]

Both Newton and Glaser sensed an opportunity. Glaser had experience with American industrialist Henry J. Kaiser's system of health care, which had begun developing health maintenance organizations (HMOs) for the general public in the mid-1940s. The Kaiser program featured *teams* of health care providers.[18] In the 1950s and early 1960s, Newton and Glaser, along with several key individuals at the University of Colorado Medical School, had begun developing parallel ideas. These men and a handful of women believed that if patients could be persuaded that medical providers without M.D.s could handle routine needs, efficiency would greatly increase, doctors would be relieved of unchallenging cases, and costs could be significantly reduced. The expertise of specialists could thereby be more efficiently utilized, which in turn would also help alleviate the "shortage" of doctors.

With a few notable exceptions, these principles characterized the focus of the Fund's grant awards during Newton's twelve-year tenure as president. For example, Henry K. Silver, a professor of pediatrics, and Loretta C. Ford, a professor of nursing, both at the University of

Colorado Medical Center (UCMC), received a three-year grant of
$254,000 from the Fund in 1966 to develop a program for training
pediatric nurse practitioners (PNPs). Public health nurses with master's
degrees "were trained to recognize conditions requiring a physician's
attention; routinely, guided by physicians, they carried out normal pediatric procedures, including physical examinations, medical histories,
laboratory tests, immunizations, and family counseling on nutritional,
behavioral, and other matters affecting child health and development."[19] The key idea was that nurses could become *independent*
decision-makers, providing primary health care. Newton, Glaser, and
their colleagues in Colorado understood that the vast majority of children moving through pediatric clinics were healthy, that they really did
not need to see doctors. Silver and his associates found that the program's graduates could handle roughly three-fourths of all pediatric
outpatients and that "most parents found the combined care acceptable,
or even preferable." Two Commonwealth Fund historians concluded,
"The gamble that Newton and his board of directors took in supporting
this program at its inception paid off handsomely." The initial grant
helped prepare more than 150 PNPs at the UCMC, "as well as more
than 2,000 PNPs across the United States."[20]

A closely allied program also initiated by Dr. Silver was the Child
Health Associates Program. This initiative basically prepared *undergraduates*, who, in a five-year program, received two years of premed
education, plus three years of intensive professional education at the
UCMC. The last three years included two years of study in basic medical sciences, plus one internship year. By 1974, twenty-three associates
had graduated from the program at UCMC. A follow-up study showed
that because of their more focused training, second-year associate students had the same level of knowledge in clinical pediatrics as senior
medical students. A further study revealed that "diagnoses were not significantly different in more than 97 percent of 143 cases seen separately
by child health associate interns and practicing pediatricians." The
Commonwealth Fund and the Carnegie Fund shared the underwriting
of Silver's initiative. The graduates were able to serve between 65 and 95

percent of patients "usually seen by pediatricians" at one-third to one-half the cost. Perhaps most noteworthy, many PNP graduates were working in rural and other areas that had "a desperate need for primary health care." A third program initiated by Silver and underwritten by the Fund involved school nurse practitioners (SNPs), specially trained medical providers who "served as the first line of defense in identifying and managing the basic health problems of children in [their] school." The SNPs worked with teachers, helping them deal with students with psychological and behavioral problems. This initiative had a significant impact nationally. By 1976, when Newton left the Commonwealth Fund, roughly four dozen nurse practitioner programs were established across the United States, with more than 3,000 SNP graduates.[21]

Advocacy of training medical assistants to do much of the routine, largely repetitive "heavy lifting" in health care was not confined to the Commonwealth Fund or the UCMC. Other foundations became involved, often after the basic concept had been established. The Commonwealth Fund, however, was recognized as a leader in this realm. At Duke University, after an initial grant from the Joshua Macy Jr. Foundation to get the program started in 1965, the Commonwealth Fund joined forces with both the Rockefeller Foundation and Carnegie Foundation to support a "physicians' assistants" program. These professionals assisted doctors in performing electrocardiograms, urinalysis, cardiac monitoring, renal dialysis, respiratory support, and other procedures. By the early 1970s, physicians' assistants' contributions were so widely accepted that the Nixon administration committed $15 million to further training of physicians' assistants through the Comprehensive Health Manpower Training Act. By the mid-1980s, there were fifty-four accredited training programs for physicians' assistants. That there were more than 16,000 people with this training by then is testimony that they were in high demand.[22]

Further promoting the same general principal, the Commonwealth Fund provided a $425,000, three-year award to Cornell University in 1972 to help establish a program to train surgical assistants. Dr. Paul A. Ebert, chairman of the school's Department of Surgery, believed that such personnel could greatly relieve the pressures on surgeons created by large-volume, comparatively routine procedures. Under direct supervision of sponsoring surgeons, candidates could assist in operating rooms, intensive care units, and elsewhere. Less "formalized" than other programs, the surgical assistant initiative depended on individual recruitment. Surgeons could work closely with ambitious nurses or other paraprofessionals they selected themselves. In some cases, previous surgical experience in military units might qualify a candidate for consideration.[23]

Sex Education

Newton took pride in these efforts to "democratize" medical education and provide more professional opportunities for individuals who, in previous generations, might well have been excluded from medical careers. Not only thousands of women, but many upwardly mobile black, Hispanic, Puerto Rican, and other ethnic youths forged viable careers, albeit often on the lower rungs of the medical establishment ladder. Newton also pushed the Fund into more controversial areas, including drug abuse and sex education. Although Quigg was in part a *facilitator*, a key individual who helped connect investigators advancing worthy ideas with the funds needed to pursue their objectives, he also thought deeply about medical issues himself. In the mid-1960s, he was genuinely puzzled that, in a society seemingly obsessed with sex, very few doctors received any formal training in sex education in medical school. They were supposed to deal confidently and authoritatively with patients despite the fact that they ignored a core element of their well-being.

Newton and several key investigators wished to introduce this vital subject into the curricula of most, if not all, medical schools. In 1965, the Commonwealth Fund committed an initial $50,000 to the Sex Information and Educational Council of the United States (SIECUS). Basically, the initial grant helped the SIECUS network with other institutions and individuals interested in the same issue. Dr. Mary S. Calderone, a physician with a master's degree in public health, headed up the effort and set up a national conference for lay and professional leaders focusing on the possible content of sex education programs; a workshop for teachers, administrators, and health officers; and a system to edit, produce, and distribute SIECUS publications. In the same year, the Fund awarded the Bowman Gray School of Medicine at Wake Forest University (one of the few medical schools in the country with a sex education program already in place) $180,000 over a three-year period "to develop an experimental teaching program in mental health, family life, and human sexuality."[24] A follow-up grant of $121,000 in 1967 allowed Bowman Gray to offer summer training sessions for faculty from other medical schools.

Newton and the board at the Commonwealth Fund were excited by the potential benefits of such awards. In 1968, they awarded the University of Pennsylvania $143,774 to set up a Center for the Study of Sex Education in Medicine. In 1969 and 1970, the center received follow-up grants totaling almost $549,000, and it became "a clearinghouse for the production and distribution of teaching materials needed to help keep medical school programs current in this rapidly expanding body of knowledge."[25] Between 1968 and the time Newton left the Fund in 1976, several other medical schools, including Stanford University, the University of California at San Francisco, Columbia University, and the University of Minnesota, had also received funding to develop or enhance programs in sex education. Although the Fund was not the only organization supporting sex education in medical schools, it was a recognized leader. In 1968, only thirty of the nation's medical schools offered any formal instruction in the field. By 1975, almost all medical schools, a total of 106 in the country, had either established such programs or were setting them up. By then, the Commonwealth Fund had invested $1.5 million to support sex education.[26]

Equal Opportunity in Medical Education

During the early years of Newton's watch, Vice President Colin M. Mc-Cloud, M.D., helped direct considerable support from the Commonwealth Fund for the improvement of educational opportunities for minorities in the United States. During a period of explosive civil rights controversies, McCloud had Newton's full support. A bit of background is in order. In the first half of the twentieth century, the Julius Rosenwald Fund had been a primary supporter of advanced education for blacks, but its resources were exhausted by 1949. Between 1949 and 1961, the Commonwealth Fund contributed $140,000 to National Medical Fellowships, Inc., an organization devoted to helping minorities become doctors. Although the Fund remained interested in advancing minority opportunities in medical schools, by the mid- to late 1960s, federal grants were filling much of the need.

When federal funds began drying up during the Nixon administration, the much larger Robert Wood Johnson Foundation stepped into the breach. The combined efforts of private foundations and federal grants helped triple minority enrollment of first-year students in the nation's medical schools from 2.6 percent to 7.5 percent between 1968 and 1975. With other institutions basically "covering" scholarships, McCloud and Newton became interested in helping one of the nation's most well-known black medical institutions enrich its academic program. In 1967, the Fund awarded Meharry Medical College in Nashville, Tennessee, a $700,000 grant to develop a program in basic sciences. Once again, larger foundations followed the Fund's lead; in 1972, the Robert Wood Johnson Foundation provided a five-year $5 million grant to Meharry—the largest ever awarded to the college.[27]

The Fund could not support every initiative suggested by even the most prominent representatives of minority interests. In May 1965, Newton had an interview with Roy Wilkins of the National Association for the Advancement of Colored People, who urged the Fund to underwrite efforts to examine the adjustment problems that rural blacks experienced when moving to large metropolitan areas. Wilkins believed, and Newton concurred, that they were ill equipped to deal with the challenges they encountered. Newton listened respectfully, but he had to inform Wilkins that the Fund was basically focusing on medical education and that it could not diversify its support to any greater extent.[28]

One unstated but obvious reality in awarding funds was that applicants from the most prestigious universities usually had a decided advantage. Men with Ivy League backgrounds dominated the board of directors. Newton's predecessor, Malcolm Aldrich, had gone to Yale; Vice President Robert J. Glaser had equally strong ties to Harvard. Newton and his colleagues acknowledged that, on occasion, worthy proposals sometimes came from unknown individuals from lesser-known institutions, and the Fund occasionally supported such initiatives. A good example was a $19,000 joint grant with the Carnegie Foundation to an applicant from the University of Florida who was attempting to greatly improve rural health care by establishing numerous ambulatory clinics in lightly populated areas in northern Florida. Several years later, the recipient wrote a gushing letter to the Fund in which he reported that the $19,000 in seed money had been critical to the success of his endeavor; subsequently, he and his associates had raised another $1.7 million from other foundations. He concluded, "The Commonwealth Fund should be proud that at one critical time in the history of a community's health project being developed by a totally unknown medical school professor in an eight-year-old medical school, it was able to contribute $19,000—and what a significant $19,000."[29]

Still, the overwhelming majority of the Fund's awards went to elite institutions. As two historians noted, "The leaders ... preserved the Fund's 'trickle-down' concept of philanthropy. As in the support of programs in medical education and medical research, the Fund's policy assured the education of excellent students who could migrate to other universities to found programs that would train additional qualified individuals in their fields."[30]

Confronting "Real World" Problems

However, applicants from prestigious institutions would not receive support from the Fund if they insisted on remaining in their ivory towers. Newton and Glaser pushed medical schools hard to provide more tangible services in their local and regional communities. In the mid-1960s, the Fund helped the Harvard Medical School establish the Harvard Community Health Plan. Under the direction of Dean Robert H. Ebert, the Harvard Medical School used a 1966 planning grant of $125,000 to begin exploring the *social* aspects of disease and how the school might reorganize its departments to respond to the needs of local residents. In a follow-up application for additional support, Ebert provided words that were music to Newton and Glaser's ears: "There must be a major shift in emphasis within these institutions from the present preoccupation with the problems of the individual patient to the broader social and preventive issues of health care."

In 1967, the Fund awarded Harvard another $600,000 spread out over three years to help bring Ebert's vision into reality, embodied in a Center for Community Health and Medical Care. In the late 1960s and early 1970s, Harvard's outreach program was so successful it was expanded to several other nearby communities. Centers were set up in Boston, Wellesley, and Cambridge, and the program acquired a patient clientele of 150,000 within a decade. By then, larger foundations had taken up much of the load on helping provide critically needed financial underwriting. Once again, the Commonwealth Fund's relatively small initial grant had essentially provided the initial momentum for a highly worthwhile endeavor.

During the 1960s, the Commonwealth Fund awarded Harvard and Massachusetts Institute of Technology (MIT) $1,255,000 in two separate awards to help establish a joint effort to apply the latest theoretical advances in the sciences to concrete medical problems. Newton and his associates envisioned establishing both physical structures and administrative reorganization that would encourage some of the nation's most brilliant scientists to engage in collaborative teaching and research. Again, the awards to Harvard and MIT were made with the understanding that the universities would basically use their support as seed money to help develop their original ideas and gain access to additional sources of funding. Harvard and MIT met these expectations, raising another $8 million in the five years following the initial Commonwealth Fund awards. As he departed from the Commonwealth Fund in 1975, Newton wrote, "I believe this joint enterprise is on target in what we hoped would be accomplished."[31]

Another innovative award helped Yale University establish a trauma center. Jack W. Cole, head of Yale's Department of Surgery, was disturbed by the fact that many accident victims, particularly those in automobile collisions, died before medical technicians could even begin to treat them. Cole originally envisioned emergency response units attached to local hospitals and supported by helicopter airlifts for injured victims. If the time between injury and initial response medical treatment could be significantly reduced, Cole believed, many more lives could be saved. He had received very modest donations from a handful of small foundations, $1,000 here and $3,000 there. The Commonwealth Fund committed $2 million to Yale's program, and the payoff was enormous. Private citizens' groups provided important ideas and support. The Connecticut state legislature also cooperated in passing legislation in the early 1970s that helped coordinate emergency medical services in southern Connecticut. The Yale trauma center developed new procedures for treating burn victims, emergency obstetrics, and other conditions, but its primary focus was on in-transit prehospitalization procedures. Connecticut became one of the nation's leaders in developing procedures for training Emergency Medical Technicians (EMTs). Once again, the Fund's significant early support for a promising initiative was crucial in convincing larger foundations to make bigger grants. By the early 1970s, the Yale trauma center was also receiving support from the NIH and other sources of long-term funding.

Rescuing Battered Children

Given the explosive social and political climate of the 1960s in the United States, it is hardly surprising that Newton and Glaser were deeply concerned about increasing levels of violence. One doctor Newton deeply admired was C. Henry Kempe, chairman of pediatrics at UCMC. Kempe had long been interested in the effects of violence in early childhood and its deleterious long-term effects on the young victim's physical and psychological development. Kempe's influential book, *The Battered Child*, was published with support from the Commonwealth Fund; the book went through numerous editions.[32] Newton and Glaser shared Kempe's conviction that expanded knowledge in this area might help medical professionals learn how to ameliorate the psychological trauma that caused earlier victims of youthful violence to perpetuate vicious cycles by engaging in similar acts against their own children.

Kempe was convinced that child abuse, ranging from simple neglect to extreme physical abuse and incest, was not confined to the poor but permeated all classes of society. In 1971, the Fund awarded Kempe a three-year grant of $278,142 to enable his child-abuse team at UCMC to add several new dimensions to its role as a national model for research into this harrowing but promising new field. Kempe used the money to help medical experts work directly with the parents of abused children, establish short-term safe havens (day care nurseries) for youthful victims of abuse, and to conduct "follow up research on the current status of the large population of abused children who had been cared for at the center."[33]

The Washington, Alaska, Montana, and Idaho Program

Although most of the Fund's efforts to improve health care delivery focused on urban areas, a notable exception was the Washington, Alaska, Montana, and Idaho (WAMI) Program, which began in the late 1960s. Those four states contained nearly one-quarter of the nation's landmass but just 6 percent of its population in 1970. From the standpoint of delivering medical services, one of the major challenges facing the region was a lack of easily available medical training. The only state-supported medical school in the Pacific Northwest was at the University of Washington in Seattle. Not only was it extremely difficult for ambitious students living in remote regions and dreaming of careers in medicine to gain access to the required training, but many communities found it extremely difficult to attract and retain competent doctors.

Several high-level administrators at the University of Washington Medical School approached Newton with a preliminary proposal aimed initially at *decentralizing* premed education in twenty-eight "feeder" colleges and universities. It was an intriguing initiative. The applicants believed that many faculty at other regional institutions were fully capable of providing core courses required of all medical students and that coordination of their efforts could help the medical school train large numbers of qualified students more efficiently.

They also believed that selected faculty from the University of Washington could augment these courses so that students at the state universities in Alaska, Montana, and Idaho could take a full first year medical curriculum on their "home" campuses. In the second year of their medical training, students came to Seattle and trained at the University of Washington Medical School. In their third year, students would gain practical field experience by enrolling in a so-called community phase of the WAMI program, during which they would spend six weeks in community clinical unit training under guidance of a physician in an outlying rural community in one of the four states. Faculty from the medical school visited these units at least once each six weeks to monitor students' progress. In addition to arranging periodic visits from faculty at the medical school, coordinators of the WAMI program also established a telephone hookup between outlying clinics and faculty at the medical school. Practitioners in remote areas could place "hotline" calls to the medical school for diagnostic advice in complicated cases. The telephone network got plenty of use; by the late 1970s, the medical school was fielding nearly 10,000 calls each year.

Coordinating such an ambitious program had the potential to create a political and logistical nightmare. It involved dozens of faculty, four groups of university regents, four state medical societies, more than two dozen college and university administrations, four state legislatures, and many other bureaucracies. Despite all of these potential obstacles, evolution of the WAMI program was remarkably smooth. The Commonwealth Fund provided a three-year seed money grant of slightly less than $1 million under the assumption that the applicants would generate long-term support from other sources. In the first year under the WAMI Program, the University of Washington was able to expand the number of medical students admitted from 102 to 175. By the end of the first decade of operation, the performance of first-year medical students outside of Seattle was comparable to those of students on the main campus. Equally important, increasing numbers of medical school graduates were setting up practice in smaller and more remote cities and towns.[34]

Hospice Experiments

One Commonwealth Fund initiative in which Newton took great personal pride was its support of the nation's first hospice in New Haven, Connecticut. One of the most depressing realities of American medical practice was that although many hospitals were well prepared to perform complicated surgery and deal with serious illnesses, little thought had been directed toward dealing with patients who were obviously terminally ill and had just weeks to live. Often, patients and their families were told hospitals could do nothing more for them and they were going to have to make alternative arrangements for care. In too many cases, administrators in nursing homes were reluctant to accept such patients, in part because their personnel lacked experience in adequate pain control, and dying patients usually required more intensive assistance from already overworked and underpaid staff. Few patients could be treated effectively at home because physicians seldom made house calls. In countless cases, families of terminally ill patients were strung out both financially and psychologically.

In the early 1950s, Cecily Saunders, who was setting up the Saint Christopher Hospice in London, made the first of many visits to Yale. Her interest in and dedication to hospice care eventually inspired Florence S. Wald, dean of Yale's nursing school, to give up her position and devote her efforts to establishing a similar institution in New Haven. It took years to convince the medical establishment that such a venture was not only desirable but a necessity. Doctors are—by instinct, training, and oath—dedicated to keeping patients alive, even if they have to resort to "heroic"—and hideously expensive—procedures. Accepting death and the hard truth that their procedures were often contrary to the desires of terminally ill patients, and even threatened the financial stability of many of their families, was anathema to many powerful doctors. Thus, progress was initially slow. But Wald and several associates began a two-year study of local medical facilities and their policies regarding dying patients.

The Fund was not the first organization to assist them. They received initial funding from the U.S. Public Health Service and the American Nurses Foundation. Although interested in the project from

the mid-1960s forward, Newton and Glaser did not became significantly involved financially until the early 1970s, by which time Wald
and her associates had compiled detailed recommendations of what
needed to be done.[35] They had determined that roughly two-thirds of
terminally ill patients wanted to die in their homes. Thus, any hospice
funded should provide extensive home care, in addition to actual beds.
Although bricks and mortar were an important part of their long-range
program, Wald and her colleagues realized that they needed to convince
mainstream doctors they were providing a vital service and that the hospice must become "an integrated part of the health care system." In
addition, they envisioned a volunteer program linking its home care
services to community groups and a "forum" to educate concerned citizens about the needs of terminally ill patients.[36]

The Commonwealth Fund provided key support in the early
1970s. Although its $100,000 grant was small compared to much larger
awards by organizations such as the American Cancer Institute, which
awarded $1.5 million, it was crucial. According to Wald, "The role that
the Commonwealth Fund took was unusual and in a way daring because
by the time we asked for its help we had separated ourselves from Yale
… the then deans of Divinity, Medicine and Nursing were in agreement
with this decision and were supportive, but it did take the trust of
Commonwealth."[37]

Funding for Research

Although the majority of the Fund's effort was directed toward improving education of medical students and the actual delivery of medical care
to the general public, in several instances, Newton and Glaser remained
interested in encouraging pure research. Shortly after Newton assumed
the presidency of the Fund, Yale President Kingman Brewster wanted to
conduct a comprehensive study of the direction of the medical school in
response to rapidly changing conditions in American society. The Fund
underwrote the study in 1967. Among other ideas, Kingman's committee concluded that Yale was well positioned to advance the frontiers of
knowledge in human genetics.

Although several faculty members were interested in further developing the field, they were scattered across the campus. In this case, Brewster essentially desired money for bricks and mortar, to establish facilities to bring the researchers together. In 1975, the Fund awarded $2.5 million to Yale, largely for that purpose. It was the second largest grant that the Fund made under Newton's direction. Some of the money helped create faculty positions and establish joint appointments with other departments. In this case, the Commonwealth Fund did not insist that other larger foundations make more substantial awards. Instead, Newton took the lead in making the largest single private foundation award to Yale. In the words of Dr. Leon E. Rosenberg, chair of the new department, "The results [of the grant] breathed vitality into what was previously a paper organization."[38]

Another Fund initiative, seemingly devoted to pure research, was actually based on addressing some of the most difficult problems facing contemporary society. The mid-1960s had marked the emergence of civil rights and urban riots. The following years brought the upheaval and "police riot" at the 1968 Democratic National Convention, Woodstock in 1969, increasingly violent anti–Vietnam War demonstrations, and the Kent State "massacre" in 1970. A report by Fund staffers noted, "Recent years have recorded unprecedented waves of riot and insurrection in our cities and campuses … and profound alienation among youth manifested by life styles of hostility, distrust, and drugtaking. Finally, the extent and degree of violent crime have made fear and disquiet a widespread feature of American community life."[39]

Investigators at Stanford University's School of Medicine wanted to study factors causing aggression and violence. Dr. David A. Hamburg, head of the Department of Psychiatry, directed the undertaking. Hamburg proposed to conduct clinical studies of the evolutionary basis of violent human behavior, primarily by examining the "intricate threat-and-attack behavior patterns of chimpanzees, man's closest living relative." His team would also explore the role of early life experiences in humans in the development of human aggression, problems of stress and conflict in early adolescence, and the impact of environmental stress on human behavior.[40]

In 1970, the Fund awarded Stanford $505,686 spread over a three-year period. Some of Hamburg's work essentially piggybacked on that of his colleague and collaborator, Dr. Jane Goodall, begun a decade earlier, on aggressive behaviors of chimps in their natural habitat. Hamburg's team also set up laboratory courses for undergraduates in Stanford's Human Biology Program, plus advanced courses on the psychobiology of human aggression and other topics. Combined, the courses enrolled about 500 undergraduates each year. Among other initiatives, some of them loosely connected to their mission statement, the team also conducted drug counseling on campus, peer counseling with disadvantaged youths, studied therapeutic alternatives to jail time for adolescent offenders, and surveyed the contemporary state of knowledge of the evolution of human hatred and violence.

Officers at the Fund believed they were getting a lot of "bang" for their bucks, and Newton and his associates agreed to provide a follow-up grant of nearly $320,000 to Stanford in 1974. Quigg was thrilled to witness experiments in person. During a visit to Hamburg's facility at Stanford, he was transfixed by chimps showing "fiendish cleverness" in putting together any and all objects available to build ladders up the concrete walls of their cages. Hamburg and Goodall provided a joint presentation to the Fund's directors. Later Newton conveyed his fellow board members' satisfaction with the project in a letter to Hamburg: "I am especially pleased because we have never tried anything like this before. The members of the board who were present were delighted. ... For the first time, they have heard one of our grant recipients describe a project in vivid terms. In other words, you have started a precedent, but I am afraid it will be hard for anybody else to follow you."[41]

Harkness Fellowships

One of the most time-consuming tasks Newton undertook as president of the Fund was administration of the Harkness Fellowship Program. This was a sort of reverse Rhodes Scholarship Program. Gifted applicants from England, Australia, New Zealand, and several European countries competed for Fund support to study and travel in the United

States, usually for two years. Successful applicants had most of their living and travel costs covered by the Fund. When Newton arrived, the program funded between thirty and forty promising young leaders/scholars per year. Expenditures to maintain the fellows totaled almost a $1 million annually, roughly 14 percent of the Fund's allocations for all projects. To some members of the board, the Harkness Fellowship Program exemplified the most idealistic, cherished traditions of the Fund.

Newton and his associates enjoyed the camaraderie of exchanging perspectives on the qualities of various applicants with their colleagues at prestigious medical schools overseas, and they believed that "goodwill" created by hosting brilliant young foreigners would exert long-term payoffs. During the 1960s and early 1970s, however, several external developments led them to reassess the underlying rationale for and purposes of the Harkness Fellowship Program. When the program was started in the 1920s, some of the countries from which fellows were recruited were poor, and there were few indigenous sources of support for able and highly ambitious young scholars. But in the decades since World War II, the national economies of certain countries, particularly France and Germany, and to a lesser extent the British Empire, had experienced remarkable recoveries. A view emerging within the Commonwealth Fund held that, if the program was truly valuable, individuals, institutions, and foundations within those countries should provide more, if not all, of the support. In Newton's view, "There are now literally thousands of opportunities for young people from England and Western Europe to visit, work and study in the United States and to learn about the American culture. We are now living in an age of rapid communication of all kinds, including travel. We are also witnessing a proliferation of multinational corporations and international agencies which station their foreign employees for considerable periods of time in America. Under these circumstances, why should a foundation be spending a million dollars a year to add 37 more such opportunities to a multitude that already exists?"[42] In other words, the Harkness Fellowship Program had lost its distinctiveness.

A closely associated view was that the "goodwill" toward the United States, allegedly created by a two-year residency, was extremely difficult to measure. In most cases, Harkness fellows were in their late twenties and early thirties, and few would achieve positions of influence for a decade or more. In addition, during the 1960s, civil rights unrest, mounting urban violence, and increasingly strident anti–Vietnam War protest were generating significant strains of anti-Establishment feeling within the country and growing anti-Americanism abroad. Newton did not share the view of a few board members that they were sometimes subsidizing fellows who would return to their home countries with implacable anti-American attitudes, but he could understand their frustration.[43]

Not long after he took over as president of the Fund, Quigg and his colleagues broached the idea of terminating the program or at the very least, cutting it back significantly. Newton was concerned that it was taking on a life of its own, that influential foreign nationals were developing a vested interest in maintaining it, and that they were beginning to consider the program as a virtual entitlement. Following the November 1967 board meeting, Quigg informed a close British colleague that "the Board decided it had no alternative but to substantially reduce the Harkness Fellowships in order to make additional funds available in support of the Fund's [other] activities. ... "[44]

But cutting back the program, much less terminating it, would prove to be far more difficult than Newton could imagine. Although some of his foreign colleagues understood or at least appeared resigned to cutbacks as justified, others rejected explanations of the reasons in almost defiant terms. Gottfried van Benthem van den Bergh, a high-ranking academic in the Institute of Social Studies at The Hague, complained to Malcolm Aldrich, "I must confess that I find it difficult to believe that [redirection of Fund resources to medical education] is the only reason. I believe that it is better to be frank about my doubts. ... I conjecture [that there] might be political reasons behind it." Addressing the feeling among some on the board that certain fellows had developed anti-American feelings, van den Bergh stoutly defended such perspectives: "The Harkness program has brought mainly social

scientists and humanists to America. They could not avoid being critical about many aspects of contemporary America and of American
foreign policy, in the same way as their counterparts in the American
universities. ... Yet they are critical because they *care*, however they *identify* with America (emphasis his).[45] In conclusion, van den Bergh
fervently urged board members to reconsider the Fund's position.

During the remainder of Newton's presidency, he and his colleagues at the Fund grappled unsuccessfully with the issue of the
Harkness Fellowships. In a few words, the leaders of the Fund simply
could not, in the final analysis, say "no." On several occasions, they
announced that they planned to cut back the number of fellowships here
and there, but they repeatedly "reconsidered" their decisions in response
to storms of protest from former fellows, anguished appeals from key
associates in countries affected by the projected cutbacks, and the objections of a few board members determined to uphold this tradition at all
costs. As Newton recalled, one of the realities of managing a prominent
benefactor's foundation was that one had to pay close attention to traditions, even when one believed they had outlived their usefulness.[46] In
1975, the year Newton resigned from the presidency of the Fund, the
Harkness Fellowships consumed $1,086,097, or nearly 15 percent of
the Fund's disbursements.[47] That percentage was virtually unchanged
from the proportion of fellowship allocations when Quigg took over the
Fund twelve years earlier.

Changing Leadership

In some respects, Newton was very comfortable running the
Commonwealth Fund. He was very proud of the organization's initiatives, particularly in medical education and expanding health care
service in many urban areas. In addition, by the time Quigg had been
with the Fund for a decade, the board of directors had developed enormous confidence in his judgment. Although a liberal on most social,
economic, and political issues, Quigg demonstrated a natural human
touch with even the most conservative board members. Testimony to
that fact was that, over the years, the board regularly increased the

amount of money Quigg could dispense at his discretion, without formal approval by the board. When Malcolm Aldrich was running the Fund, he had available a discretionary fund of $10,000, which was seldom used. In 1965, two years into Newton's regime, the amount was raised to $25,000 per year. Two years after that, it was doubled to $50,000, and in 1972, the board virtually gave Quigg carte blanche in earmarking $225,000 annually for his personal commitments.

Yet beneath the surface, certain tensions were developing within the hierarchy at the Fund. Much to Newton's disappointment, his close friend and Fund vice president, Robert J. Glaser, resigned his position in 1972 to return to Palo Alto, California, and become president and chief executive officer of the Kaiser Family Foundation. At that point, because Newton was sixty-one and nearing conventional retirement age, the board of directors wanted to hire a vice president who would eventually succeed him. Although he was just four years younger than Newton, Carlton B. Chapman, M.D., was named executive vice president early in 1973. Chapman had impressive credentials. After graduating from Davidson College, he was a Rhodes Scholar at Oxford, and he then earned his medical degree from Harvard in 1941. Chapman spent nineteen years at the Southwestern Medical School at the University of Texas in Dallas, where he specialized in cardiology. He became dean of the medical school at Dartmouth College in 1966.[48]

For the first few months of their association, Newton and Chapman appeared to get along well. The general focus of the Fund's commitments remained the same. At board meetings and public gatherings, Chapman provided strong verbal support for his boss's programs. Soon, however, Newton developed a sense that Chapman was getting restless and he wanted to push his way into the president's chair sooner rather than later. As Newton recalled almost thirty years later, "He thought the time had come when he should be President. I concurred, thinking that the board would name me Chairman." The decision was reached at the November 1974 board meeting, and Chapman was to take over as president of the Fund in February 1975. Newton anticipated an "easy and friendly" two-year transition period, during which control gradually shifted over to his successor. But the Fund did *not* name him chairman. Further complicating matters was that following Malcolm Aldrich's retirement, his brother, Hulbert "Huck" Aldrich, had assumed the role of chairman, and he decided he wanted to stay on. In a face-saving gesture fooling almost nobody, the board appointed Newton as vice chairman. Newton had always enjoyed a comfortable working relationship with Malcolm Aldrich, but such was not the case with his brother. According to Quigg, "Huck was top dog, and he liked being so. He was very much a chauvinist; the board was all male. The board was pretty rigid, and my boundaries seemed more restricted."[49]

What made Newton's situation increasingly uncomfortable was that, once he was assured the presidency, Chapman pushed for a significant change in the direction of the Fund. In Quigg's view, Chapman wanted to impose his blueprint with unseemly haste. At the very meeting where it was determined that he would take over as president, Chapman unveiled a laundry list of recommendations for a shift in focus that he had been developing for a year. Although Chapman agreed in general that Newton's initiatives had been sound, he made it equally clear that he also believed they were outdated. Newton had devoted considerable attention to health care delivery. But in the late 1960s, the Robert Wood Johnson Foundation, which provided at least six times more funding annually than the Commonwealth Fund, had moved into that field. The Johnson Foundation had actually taken over some programs the Commonwealth Fund had started. Chapman also questioned many of the Fund's "experiments" in health care delivery. In some cases, their results were intangible, extremely long range, and very difficult to quantify. As Chapman saw it, the Fund was spread too thin and needed "an even sharper focus on education for the entire sweep of the health professions."[50]

Regardless of how effectively the officers of the Fund smoothed over the transition in leadership in press releases and internal documents, Newton felt, with good reason, that he was being put out to pasture. He was definitely not ready to retire. At sixty-three, he still had plenty of energy and was in superb health, with nearly three decades of life ahead of him. Quigg was a member of and served on the boards of many prestigious organizations, and some of them provided enormous stimulation and satisfaction. During his years at the Commonwealth Fund, he served the board of the National Arbitration Society, an organization devoted to settling disputes without lengthy and expensive litigation. He also contributed time to the Nutrition Foundation. Thirty years ago, nutrition was seldom on the "menu" of most medical schools' curricula. Newton and many of his associates believed aspiring doctors needed training in that field.

These activities alone would not provide the stimulation he needed. He spent a year as president of the New York Young Men's Christian Association (YMCA), but, as he recalled, "By no means was it a spectacular year." Newton sensed that he was really a figurehead at the YMCA and that he had been named to the position largely in hopes that he could raise funds for the organization. Although he was on salary with the Commonwealth Fund, the YMCA position was unpaid. There was a very small staff, which operated on a shoestring. Previous YMCA presidents had sometimes partially subsidized the organization by bringing along large numbers of staffers from their parent corporations.[51]

During Newton's years as president, the Commonwealth Fund distributed over $60 million in support for various endeavors. The following table identifies the primary beneficiaries, excluding the Harkness Fellowships.

Special Development Awards to Medical Schools 12,013,000

Planning Development of New Medical Schools 4,854,000

Innovations in Medical Education 9,736,000

Improvements in Teaching through Research
        in Medical Education .1,299,000

Interface between Medical Schools and
        Their Communities .10,129,000

Training of Physicians' Assistants and Other
        Health Professionals .3,235,000

Awards to Collateral Organizations to Improve
        Medical Education 5,909,000

Developing International Medical
    Education Programs 4,028,000
Interface between Medicine and Social
    Programs 3,330,000
Development of National Health Policy 1,739,000
Education and Research in Human Sexuality 2,145,000
Population Control 2,064,000
Total $60,481,000

Shortly after he left the Fund, Newton responded at length to a letter from a trusted associate still working there who was evidently feeling very uneasy about his own future. In providing advice to his friend, Quigg conveyed a sense of residual bitterness over his departure, a belief that he had been betrayed. First, he urged his friend to make sure he had a solid job offer from another employer before "evidenc[ing] in your conversation any more than absolutely necessary your hostility toward, and criticism of, Carl [Chapman]." He advised his friend to keep his emotions in check, get key recommendations in writing, and plan his exit carefully. Newton confided, "I have had emotional reactions under similar circumstances twice in my life."[52]

Quigg's wounds healed slowly. In the mid-1980s, the Newtons were in New York and unexpectedly ran into Chapman while waiting for a taxi. The encounter evidently was awkward, and their conversation was undoubtedly strained, but the chance meeting induced Chapman to write an "apology letter" to his former boss: "This is to convey my regret for having handled the whole matter as I did. I knew then, and I know now, that I owe a great deal to the Fund, to you, and to Bob Glaser. My years as President were not especially happy ones but the reasons were more endogenous than otherwise."[53]

One naturally raises the question when it became clear in 1975 that Newton's position at the Commonwealth Fund was increasingly uncomfortable, why didn't he quit immediately? In Quigg's mind, that would be admitting defeat; as he stated later, "I didn't want to go back to Denver with my tail between my legs."[54] Fortunately, he did not have to. Newton was a nationally known and enormously respected figure in many realms of human achievement. Decades of effective networking had earned him admirers and friends in the highest echelons of government, academe, science, business, and the arts. When he applied for a fellowship at the prestigious Center for Advanced Study in the Behavioral Sciences in Palo Alto, California, there was never much suspense over whether or not his application would be successful. In his correspondence with administrators at the Center, the only issues were the level of funding needed and the timing of his fellowship. By the summer of 1976, the final terms of an agreement were hammered out. The four girls were out of the nest and leading their own lives. Quigg and Ginny packed up their belongings and headed for the Golden State.

CHAPTER 12

∾

WINDING DOWN

N ewton could look back on his decade-plus of work at the Commonwealth Fund and take great satisfaction in what he had achieved. However, following an unsatisfying year in which he exercised little real authority as vice chairman of the Fund and basically felt out of place as president of the Young Men's Christian Association of New York, he looked forward to some time removed from the hustle and bustle of day-to-day problems. In the spring of 1976, he applied for a prestigious fellowship at the Center for Advanced Study in the

Ginny and Quigg celebrate his seventy-fifth birthday at daughter Abby's home in Shokan, New York, in 1986.

Behavioral Sciences. The center was essentially an academic "retreat" above the golf course at Stanford University where individuals could read, meditate, write, present seminars on research projects, and interact socially on a regular basis. Fellows selected were senior scholars and other individuals who, for the most part, had made noteworthy contributions in the public arena.

In his application for a fellowship, Newton stated that if selected as a fellow, he wished to evaluate grants made to the Commonwealth Fund during the years of his leadership: "The purpose of this evaluation will be not so much to identify the Fund's successes and failures, but, rather, to see whether we can learn something that will be useful to the Fund, and perhaps to other foundations, about how to evaluate foundation grants, how to improve the grant making process, and how to do a better job of program development."[1]

It took Newton some time to negotiate the financial terms of his departure from the Commonwealth Fund. He had been very well paid at the Fund. Quigg eventually secured a generous two-year payout from the Fund, including annuities, deferred compensation, supplemental retirement and guaranteed consulting fees, and round-trip airfares for him and Ginny from New York. Newton asked the Center for a total of $14,900 for the 1977–1978 academic year, which basically represented the difference between his annual salary at the Fund and his smaller buyout stipend. He also expressed hope that the Center could make room for Ginny, who would "wish to devote our Fellowship year to her own project." Ginny had been working for several years for a nonprofit group, the Economic Development Council of New York City. She was involved in a project labeled "High School Renewal," trying to make the high school experience more meaningful and relevant to students in danger of dropping out. She was working "with a view of publishing the results of her study" and was on a modest salary, which she would lose when the couple moved to California. Eventually Quigg worked out an arrangement by which, in consideration of Ginny's losing her salary, the Center would increase its stipend to the couple from the $14,900 originally requested to a total of $24,000 for the fellowship year.[2]

In the summer of 1977, the couple moved to Palo Alto. They rented a home at 745 De Soto Drive for a short time, and then purchased it. Quigg claimed that after a stressful final year with the Fund, it was "really a year of leisure" and a "healing process" for him. As he remembered, "I was going to work on the effect of foundations on American life, but I didn't get anything written." He also recalled that he "really broadened" his reading, including "a lot of books unrelated to the subject I was planning to work on: foundations."[3] Yet Ginny recalled that he contributed significantly to the intellectual climate. Although the fellows worked independently in their offices, they lunched together every day, and on Wednesday evenings, one person would conduct a seminar on the topic he or she was researching. In Ginny's words, "Quigg contributed enormously by asking the right questions." The couple also entertained other fellows at their home, having two or three couples over for dinner approximately twice a month. Their discussions were invariably interesting and lively.[4]

As one of the most senior fellows in terms of age, Newton may have somewhat resembled a "father figure" to some of the younger fellows. Most important, he was respected and very much liked. At a farewell dinner for fellows at the end of their year, someone penned a truly dreadful limerick, supposedly characterizing Newton:

> There was a fellow named Quigg
> Whose hairline never called for a wig
> His perpetual youth
> Could be traced to Vermouth
> And anything else he could swig
> His record of course is great
> He labored for city and state
> With both Boulder and Denver he could grapple
> Not to mention the Big Apple
> We wish the best for Quigg and his mate

In his final report on his activities during the fellowship year, Newton stated that he had hoped, at the very least, to prepare a major paper containing the conclusions reached during his year of research and reflection "that would provide some guidance to foundations. But I have not yet succeeded in this endeavor. Such a paper, however, has a high place on my agenda." Although he downplayed his own achievement during the fellowship year in terms of serious scholarship, the "time out" marked considerable intellectual growth. Before turning attention to what he had originally planned to study in depth, the present and future of American foundations, he provided an extremely thoughtful year-end assessment of the year's impact on his own personal development. He only wished that the year had come earlier in his career: "Had I had the good fortune of spending a year at the Center in mid-career, I believe I would have dealt with the institutional problems I encountered with a great deal more insight, imagination and understanding." He urged the Center to consider bringing in more midcareer professionals so they could use insights gained at the center to provide "more enlightened leadership to their institutions."[5]

Newton originally intended to come to some conclusions about private foundations, and he did make some important observations. He understood that foundations faced a definite "image" problem in the eyes of the general public: "As institutions they are somewhat anomalous newcomers in our society and seem never to have gained wholehearted acceptance. To too many people they appear to have an elitist aura, to be tax dodges, whereby the very rich perpetuate family control over their fortunes. ... [They] lack public scrutiny and accountability [and appear] unresponsive to urgent public needs." In addition, Quigg argued that they sometimes came across as "arbitrary and whimsical in their dealings with seekers of their funds." Equally worrisome, Newton contended that they were "dominated by big business, that they devote a large pro-portion of their resources to 'safe fields of interest,' that they are instruments for the preservation of the status quo, and that they neglect the urgent problems of the underserved populations. ... " By the latter phrase he meant racial minorities and the poor. According to Newton, in part because of foundations' collective failure to convince the public of their pure intentions, politicians had enacted a rather "punitive Tax

Reform Act" in 1969. Among other goals, this law was an effort to snuff out phony charitable organizations. He concluded that unless foundations made more intelligent, concentrated efforts to define and clarify their missions, "they will continue to be easy prey for demagogues."[5]

Newton had spent much of the early fall of 1977 reading extensively in the professional literature concerning foundations, and he realized that foundation officers with the courage to confront society's toughest issues often received few kudos for their efforts. Groups of Americans facing enormous social and economic problems were often extremely sensitive to perceived criticism from "outsiders." Even initiatives taken with the purest of motives could backfire, particularly if sensitive representatives of minority groups believed "whites" were trying to impose "elitist" cultural values on their communities. Growth and changes within almost any community are difficult and stressful, as they are generally accompanied by at least initial pain. As Newton put it, "The serving of those needs often leads to social change which in its turn arouses hostility from those adversely affected. ... It takes a very sensitive foundation staff to navigate these turbulent waters."[6]

Newton had begun his inquiry with the idea of devising strategies to help foundations actually *measure* the impact of their grants. He believed that many foundations basically frittered away money "in response to local pressures and often to personal whims." After considerable reading and reflection, he came to believe that measurement, or attempts to quantify objectively the impact of grants, was an unrealistic goal. In most cases, too many individuals would inject too many complicated variables. Devising a process that would work for large numbers of foundations would be nearly impossible. "[A]s an alternative, I decided to study in some depth a few of the highest priority problems of our society, especially those that might be susceptible to foundation intervention." He narrowed his inquiries into three general areas: inflation, medical care, and poverty. He admitted frankly that his studies of poverty and inflation were basically for self-education. But he had been directly involved in facilitating the diffusion of medical care for two decades, and his assessment of the current state of medical care rang true:

"The chaotic conditions of medical care in the United States has [*sic*] resulted in escalating costs which jeopardize our economy and in many inequities which threaten to make a sham of the concept that access to decent medical care is a basic human right."[7] Unfortunately, more than a quarter-century later, Quigg's words still resonate with truth.

The happy and stimulating year at the Center passed quickly for the couple, but Newton was not worried about his next step. His close friend and colleague, Bob Glaser, had assumed the presidency of the Kaiser Family Foundation, which was at the time headquartered in Palo Alto. The late American industrialist Henry J. Kaiser had founded one of the nation's first health maintenance organizations (HMOs) in the 1930s, and following World War II, he and his staff were offering prepaid health care to millions of Americans.[8] Although the Kaiser Family Foundation disbursed money to numerous causes deemed worthy by Kaiser's heirs and fund administrators, much of its focus was on medical matters. Therefore, Glaser and Newton worked up an arrangement by which the fund would benefit from the latter's advice. For a stipend of $1,500 per month to

begin in September 1978, Glaser understood that Newton would "devote part of [his] time to foundation matters, giving us the benefit of [his] long experience and judgment in the field of philanthropy, and particularly in the health care area."[9] The Newtons spent two more enjoyable years in Palo Alto, and Quigg provided guidance to the Kaiser Family Foundation on a regular basis. He also read a great deal, and he and Ginny continued to travel.

Quigg, at temporary rest, approaching eighty. At the time, he served "of counsel" for his brother-in-law's Denver law firm, Davis, Graham and Stubbs. (ca. 1991).

By the winter of 1980, the couple had resided in California for three years. Although they owned a home in Palo Alto and enjoyed life in the warm sunshine, they had been away from Colorado for seventeen years. Both of their extended families were centered in Denver. When Quigg's brother-in-law, Dick Davis, urged Quigg to rejoin his law firm, now named Davis, Graham and Stubbs, they decided to return home to Denver. Although construction of their unit was not completed when they first examined it, the couple purchased half of a duplex in a new development just south of Cherry Creek and east of University Boulevard called Polo Club North.

Although Newton was nearing his seventieth birthday when the couple returned to Denver, neither he nor Ginny had any intention of turning exclusively to a life of leisure. Dick Davis's overture to Newton to rejoin his old law firm in 1980 was not his first invitation. In 1966, Davis had tried to lure Quigg back to Denver from the Commonwealth Fund to become managing partner of the firm. Even in 1966, Davis understood that, having not practiced for more than a quarter century, Newton's expertise in law would not be up to date. As Davis related to his partners, however, Quigg was so highly respected and well connected regionally and nationally that his renewed association with the firm would greatly enhance the firm's prestige and help bring in new business.[10]

Although flattered by the proposal, Newton did not seriously consider it. He had just begun his work at the Commonwealth Fund, and Ginny was starting her work in a doctoral program at New York University. The girls had settled into new schools and developed new circles of friends. He didn't want to uproot the family yet again so soon after their move from Boulder.

During the first seven decades of his life, Newton had never made an important move without knowing where he would land, and this pattern continued late in 1980. When the couple decided to return to Denver, Quigg was assured that he would receive a warm welcome at his old firm. His old associates immediately set him up in an office on the twenty-sixth floor of the firm's headquarters in the Colorado National Bank Building, where he served "of counsel." By early 1981, Newton had not practiced law for forty years; he made no pretense of mastering the intricacies of modern law, so he did not take on legal clients. But he worked full-time at the firm until he was about eighty years old, mostly in public relations and representing the firm at civic events.[11] For example, within months of his return to the local scene, Newton was named vice chairman of Denver Civic Ventures, a "public purpose corporation" heavily involved in continued downtown development. He also handled some tasks inside of the firm that many of the younger partners and associates found distracting and time consuming, such as soliciting contributions for the Mile High United Way.[12] Newton also served on the Legal Foundation Board and with the Anti-Defamation League.

In the late 1930s, he had started and become first president of the Denver Committee on Foreign Relations, which was an effort to bring together people interested in international relations. Over the years, the group had attracted a number of influential people, including Joseph Korbel, the father of Madeleine Albright, future secretary of state, who was a professor at the University of Denver. Korbel had helped establish the Graduate School of International Studies (GSIS) in the early 1940s. In the 1980s, Newton returned to Denver University and served as an advisor to the Social Sciences Foundation and GSIS.

The city and region that the couple had left in the early 1960s had been transformed in two decades. Although the city of Denver had maintained a pretty stable population, suburbs such as Aurora and Lakewood had mushroomed; tens of thousands of acres of formerly open fields had been filled in by tract homes. Following the OPEC oil cutoffs and restrictions in the 1970s, the region had experienced a phenomenal energy boom in oil shale and natural gas. Seemingly overnight, downtown Denver's skyline was transformed, now featuring many dazzling new fifty-plus story office buildings. When Newton returned, reporters sought out his views on what had happened since he had left. In typically modest fashion, Quigg discounted the role he had played in helping place the region in a position where his successors could take advantage of opportunities. Newton referred to the Denver he had left as a "cozy little city," and he expressed amazement at an "exploding

metropolis, marked by striking changes and marvelous excitement."
Quigg believed that the changes were for the better, and he fully
approved of the new growth. He also commented that he felt "a little
like Rip Van Winkle must have felt."[13]

Newton was inundated with requests to serve on boards of local
charitable organizations and foundations, plus countless civic committees. The executive director of the Anschutz Family Foundation asked
Newton to provide guidance as an advisor in its efforts to "alleviate the
misery of the poor. ... "[14] The chairman of the Department of Medicine
at the University of Colorado Health Sciences Center (UCHSC) asked
Quigg to become co-chair of a committee to select the recipient of an
endowed chair in adult diabetes research at the institution.[15] Shortly
after his return to Denver, the dean of the UCHSC attempted to enlist
his help in establishing a committee to monitor a planned relationship
between the University of Riyadh College of Medicine in Saudi Arabia
and UCHSC. The dean revealed that if the Saudis signed the agree-
ments, "we will over the space of the next few years be sending faculty
to the University ... receiving faculty from there for training, train some
of their graduates in our residency programs and in general provide academic support for the development of their medical school."[16]

The dean promised that the evaluation meetings would only
occur once quarterly, taking no more than an hour or two. Newton
recalled that he initially accepted the "Saudi" request, but that he
quickly grew disillusioned with the program and did not join the committee: "I became negative. I thought it distracted from focusing on
solving problems at the CU Medical School. Kaiser Permanente had
done the same thing and had tried to set up a Kaiser Permanente program there. Basically, people wanted to take junkets over there."[17]
Although Newton had been removed from the presidency of the
University of Colorado for more than a quarter-century, in early 1990
Regent Richard Bernick asked him to participate in a scheduled assessment of the performance of the current president, E. Gordon Gee.[18]
Since he was a deeply respected former mayor of Denver, current and
aspiring office seekers often sought both his advice and endorsement.

Whether or not Newton's public support was essential, Mayor Federico
Peña received his solid public endorsement and won a second term in a
landslide in 1987.[19]

While continuing to work full-time at Davis, Graham and Stubbs
and engaging in many local and regional civic and charitable projects,
Newton continued serving numerous national organizations. He
remained a "true blue" graduate of Yale; he and Ginny regularly returned
to New Haven for reunions of former Yale Corporation members. As in
the past, he continued to serve Yale. He was chair of the Committee on
Medical Affairs, which annually reviewed fundraising efforts, all facets
of the performances of the medical and nursing schools and their faculties, and the activities of the Yale–New Haven Medical Center, Inc.[20]
Newton regularly attended national gatherings of the Council on
Foreign Relations until the end of his life. He was also a board member
for the New York Life Mutual Fund. Newton enjoyed the work because
it gave him a view of the business world from the inside of a large corporation, including perspectives he would not have gained otherwise.
Quigg had served as trustee of his father's estate, and he continued to
provide financial advice to many family members. Since none of his
daughters was particularly interested in managing money, he devoted
considerable time to helping guide their financial affairs.[21]

Although he had left California, Newton still served on the board
of the Kaiser Foundation Health Plan, Inc. Following a board meeting
in Oakland in summer 1981, he wrote a long letter to Dr. James A.
Vohs, president of the organization, in which he stated that one of the
most fundamental problems HMOs faced was a widespread public perception that they provided "substandard care." Newton argued that as
competition between HMOs and "fee for service" providers stiffened in
the future, "quality of care [was] going to be much more in the forefront
of public discussion." Quigg again played down his contributions,
adding a postscript, "What I said above I realize belabors the subject
unmercifully, which is what comes from having too much spare time."[22]
Vohs apparently didn't think so; he demonstrated his profound respect
for Newton in part by drafting a twenty-eight-page report to Newton

and the board, enumerating all of the steps the program was taking in an effort to assure quality control.[23]

Newton maintained personal connections with former colleagues at the Commonwealth Fund, particularly after Carl Chapman left the presidency. Yet attending Fund functions could touch off long-suppressed feelings and occasionally result in fireworks. In the years since leaving the Fund, Quigg may have forgotten just how conservative certain board members were. He liked Chapman's successor, Margaret Mahoney, who invited him to lunch at Harkness House following the funeral of a longtime board member that Newton had attended. At the luncheon, Quigg evidently expressed strongly negative views toward former President Ronald Reagan, and he later confessed to Mahoney, "I am afraid I was a little too 'wound up' at lunch. I was then at the peak of my resentment toward people in high office who betray their trust, and there have been so many of them in recent years."[24] Knowing of Newton's past long-term connection to the Fund, applicants for support, including some people whom he had never met, asked him to endorse specific proposals. In most cases, Newton demurred, explaining that he did not wish to impose his opinions in the delicate process of determining the most worthy proposals.[25]

Quigg (right) and Ginny with an unidentified classmate at Quigg's seventieth reunion at Andover in the spring of 1999.

Fortunately, in Quigg's later years, most of his long-term institutional associations were totally noncontroversial and provided unending pleasure. As a youth, Newton had turned over profits from operating the school yearbook at Andover to the school. As an adult, he continued making important contributions to the school and underwrote the Phillipian Prize, a scholarship awarded annually to a deserving student. Over the years, recipients of the award wrote Newton thanking him for his generosity and describing their lives, hopes, and ambitions. Newton greatly enjoyed receiving these letters, and he always responded at length.[26]

Quigg was also very generous with Yale. When his brother-in-law and former law partner, Dick Davis, died in the late 1980s, Newton made a gift to establish a student aid fund in Dick's name.[27] Late in his life, Quigg donated assets totaling more than $300,000 to the university, which set up two scholarships in his name, one in the undergraduate college and the other at the Yale Law School. As with the Andover award, the Newton family continued receiving appreciation letters from university administrators and the scholarship recipients from Yale, even after his death.[28] Newton's habit of providing crucial assistance to young people was a source of continuing satisfaction throughout his life, particularly in his last years.

The Newtons were involved in other efforts that benefited Colorado and the region. Back in 1937, as a recently minted Yale Law School graduate, twenty-six-year-old Quigg had been one of three incorporators of the Boettcher Foundation. He served on the board as a trustee and was its secretary for the next eighteen years. In 1952, Newton was very actively involved with the board, and he helped establish the Boettcher Scholarship. Nearly fifty years later, in May 2000, Quigg and Ginny made a generous contribution to the University of Colorado Foundation to help establish a "faculty enhancement fund." Wishing to honor the Newtons, the Boettcher Foundation awarded $500,000 to the university to help set up an endowed chair in their name. It would be called the Quigg and Virginia S. Newton Endowed Chair in Leadership at the University of Colorado. Within weeks after

Quigg's death in April 2003, numerous admirers from Colorado and around the country had contributed another $173,000, and the position was on its way to being fully funded.[29]

Although the couple was involved in myriad activities after their return to Denver in 1980, their world was hardly one of constant work. By then, all four girls had married and were starting their own families. Holidays usually brought visits from one or more of the girls, along with spouses and grandchildren. They played a good deal of tennis at the Denver Country Club, and they occasionally used the swimming pool and enjoyed Thursday night specials in the dining room. In their later years together, their favorite use of leisure time was travel, and they took some fascinating and memorable trips. In 1936, Ginny had taken a cruise around the world, and Quigg shared her interest in seeing as much of the world as they could.

One memorable journey in the spring of 1985 involved a sailing jaunt in Tonga, an island kingdom in the South Pacific. It was a journey reminiscent of scenes from Daniel Defoe's adventure classic, *Robinson Crusoe*. Three couples, the Newtons, Seth Milliken, and an old Yale friend, Mac Parsons, and their wives, made up the party. Both Parsons and Milliken were very experienced sailors. They flew into Tonga, where, thanks to introductions from well-connected friends, they received royal treatment as VIPs from local authorities. They were greeted at the airport by a high-ranking government official and taken to the International Dateline Hotel. He and other officials remained with them for what Quigg remembered as "a very gala beer-drinking evening." The next morning the three couples spent a half-hour with Honorable Baron Tuita, the acting prime minister. Then they were escorted in two limousines on a tour of the main island, including a stop for a swim along a lovely shoreline, followed by a lobster lunch at a fancy restaurant. After lunch they "drove across the entire island to the western shore through many native villages and dense groves of banana trees and stately coconut palms before arriving at the Good Samaritan Inn, where they enjoyed another seafood meal." However, the highlight of the trip was a chartered flight to the remote Vava'u Islands, where they snorkeled and sailed for several days. They cooked on the boat, which was well stocked with steaks, lobsters, and other wonderful foods, largely because there were no restaurants and many of the islands were uninhabited. However, other islands had small populations, and the adventurers enjoyed tropical fruits brought to them by friendly natives who also sold them shells and other native crafts.[30] For people used to the hustle and bustle of late-twentieth-century urban life in America, the trip constituted a remarkable, very welcome change of pace.

The Newtons made their own arrangements for most trips, and they preferred not to travel in large tour groups. During her around-the-world trip as a teenager, Ginny had recorded her impressions in amazing detail: a diary of two thick volumes. As an undergraduate, then later as a graduate student, she had developed the habit of taking extensive lecture notes. A half-century after the world cruise, she was recording all of their experiences in great detail. On a trip to Eastern Europe in 1986, she described staying at all manner of hotels, including some that featured pricey rooms, lukewarm water, and cacophonous outside noise. They often looked up former University of Colorado professors and good friends from other stops in their life's journey scattered around the world. Many of these reunions included wonderful, spontaneous adventures.[31]

Ginny at the Wailing Wall in Jerusalem.

Another promising trip the couple undertook late in 1987 had a less happy result. The couple had invested considerable time in reading up on China and visited the country with Joe and Toni Stepanek, who had lived and worked there. Their trip was semiofficial, in that Colorado governor Roy Romer had since 1982 been taking preliminary steps to investigate possibilities of establishing trade ties with the People's Republic.[32] Newton would be talking informally with both American representatives and several Chinese officials, particularly in the Hunan Province. A day or so before they left for China, Ginny had whacked her head getting into a new car they had purchased, but she didn't think too much more about it at the time. Her vision soon became blurred, but she tried to ignore it.

The couple's journey started well. They flew into Guilin, where they enjoyed a river cruise through the ethereal mist-shrouded sugarloaf-shaped mountains celebrated by the brushes of thousands of artists, from schoolchildren to the masters. They viewed the beginning stages of the excavation of thousands of terra-cotta warriors at Xian, and then they

Ginny and Quigg in Guilin, China, during their memorable trip in 1987.

took a train to Beijing. Unfortunately, Ginny's vision was becoming increasingly blurry. They planned to visit the Great Wall when they got to Beijing. Ginny urged Quigg to go, but she wanted to stay behind and find an ophthalmologist. This effort turned into more of an ordeal than she had imagined. Following a long taxi ride to a remote part of the city, long waits in line, and the necessity of running a gauntlet of entreaties from acupuncturists, Ginny finally found a qualified eye doctor who informed her she had a detached retina requiring immediate treatment.[33]

The Newtons immediately canceled the rest of the trip and caught the first available flight back to the United States. In Denver, she had surgery, but unfortunately, ten days afterward, the retina detached again. Eye doctors could not correct the situation, and she lost complete sight in one eye. A few weeks after the accident, Quigg reassured one concerned friend, "I am glad to say she is taking this misfortune in stride, and looks forward to getting back into her tennis, bicycling, and music in the near future."[34]

Her husband was right. Ginny bounced back and was soon bicycling and playing her usual competitive brand of tennis. She hid her loss of vision so well that acquaintances, even good friends, could not remember which eye was affected. Nor did the China misadventure dim

A pensive Quigg looking out over the Golan Heights in Israel.

the couple's urge to travel. There were many more trips, including a memorable journey to Egypt and Israel in 1995. In Egypt, they cruised the Nile, visited the Aswan Dam, the pyramids, and the Sphinx, and spent days touring ancient ruins and tombs, and then wandering through fabulous museums. The couple enjoyed the outdoor bazaars, where Ginny bargained for a beautiful tablecloth.

Ginny was struck by the incredible gulf between the few who enjoyed enormous wealth and the millions upon millions living in abject poverty. During the trip to the Middle East, the couple was for the first time conscious of the emergence of a new force in international relations: terrorism. There were no incidents, but many people noticed the reduced number of tourists. Nevertheless, they took their chances and proceeded to Israel, where they visited the Dead Sea, the River Jordan, and the Golan Heights. In Tel Aviv, they were moved by the exhibits in the Diaspora Museum. They toured a modern kibbutz and were impressed with the modern schools and medical facilities. Ginny was struck in particular by the inferior status of women in Egypt, where their potential for human development was severely repressed. In contrast, in Israel women were expected to play prominent roles in all realms of life, including the military. The Middle East trip posed many challenges, not the least of which was getting home. A major snowstorm had closed all airports on the East Coast, so they could not return home through New York. Instead, they had to fly to Paris and then continue to Boston, where they were held up for another day before being able to return to Denver.[35]

Some of the couple's trips in later years were far less challenging logistically, yet enormously stimulating. They enjoyed theater and music, and they became regulars in a University of Colorado group that made extended visits to London during the Christmas holiday season. Just after Christmas 1996, they left Denver for a two-week stay in England. Their tour group headquartered for the first week in London at a comfortable hotel at Russell Square, a convenient downtown location. They visited all the famous tourist sights, and they enjoyed services at Westminster Abbey and St. Paul's Cathedral. The London theater menu is one of the most extensive in the world, and every day they could attend at least one performance. For several days they reveled constantly in theatrical and musical productions, some of them unforgettable. On occasion, they enjoyed both a matinee and an evening performance, yet they also took time to wander through bookstores in the shopping districts and enjoy sumptuous lunches and dinners at outstanding restaurants. After more than a week in London, they took a bus to Stratford-on-Avon and spent the remainder of their stay in England attending Shakespearean productions.[36]

The initial music/theater trip was so enjoyable that they decided to repeat it the following year. On the 1997–1998 tour, the group added a side trip to Norwich and extended the trip to include several more days of sightseeing in London. They stayed at the same hotels in both London and Stratford-on-Avon, and once again they enjoyed the fine array of musical and theatrical offerings.

After returning to Denver from the West Coast, Quigg and Ginny spent much of their time together, but they also pursued some separate interests. Quigg joined an all-male organization named the "Cooking Club," a tongue-in-cheek title, since members met once monthly for sumptuous meals that few, if any, of them helped prepare. The group consisted largely of influential Coloradans, and they enjoyed their repasts at a clubhouse near the Broadmoor Hotel in Colorado Springs. After one monthly gathering, Quigg received a flattering letter from his old friend Donald Hoagland: "All the people at the dinner were unanimous about one thing—admiring you. They handled it nicely—not excessively—but that theme carried through the whole evening, and I couldn't have been more supportive of it. If you didn't hear it all, that's probably good for your character. But believe me—your parents would have been pleased."[37]

Despite the conditions under which Quigg departed from the University of Colorado, he regularly acknowledged that those were the happiest years of his professional life. Without question, that is where he met many of his closest lifelong friends, including Bob Glaser, Oz Tippo, Leo Hill, Ken Clark, and others. He and many of his close colleagues often looked back nostalgically at those years. In the summer of 1989, twenty-six years after Newton and most of his top administrators left the university, they arranged a gala three-day reunion of old friends at a lodge at the Garden of the Gods Club, below Cheyenne Mountain in Colorado Springs. It was about as different from an "academic" conference as any gathering could have been.

For three days, old friends regaled each other with long-remembered past events. During one evening dinner in which numerous irreverent tributes were exchanged, Quigg attempted to "run" the meeting but with little apparent success. Despite his feigned efforts to maintain order by tapping a gavel, his friends constantly interrupted him. Outlandish ditties were submitted by Bob Glaser, Oz Tippo, Leo Hill, William E. "Bud" Davis, and former regent Al Smith. It was truly an evening of lovingly recounted nostalgia. Tippo remembered being seated near Ginny Newton at a graduation ceremony and remarking how appropriate it was to be awarding honorary degrees. Ginny reportedly exclaimed, "We at Vassar do not give honorary degrees." Tippo replied, "You at Vassar never had anyone who deserved one." Whereupon, Tippo recalled, she playfully slugged him. Bud Davis served as unofficial scribe of the event, and he concluded eloquently, "Too soon the evening ended. The table was cleared. The trophy heads on the wall were bleary-eyed. We agreed … this was an event we could talk about to our grandchildren. We moved from the warmth of the lodge into the fresh crispness of the mountain air. Flecks of snow speckled the ground to remind us that we were indeed in Colorado, and low clouds reflected the lights of the city far below. We had been to the heights of the mountain, and the meeting was adjourned."[38]

When they were in Denver, both Quigg and Ginny remained active in many local and regional civic and cultural endeavors. Both greatly enjoyed reading, and Quigg corresponded with former associates and old friends such as Oz Tippo about which new books provided the most stimulating ideas. Tippo suggested numerous biographies, including several works by noted historian David McCullough. After urging Newton to read biographies of Woodrow Wilson and University of Chicago president Robert M. Hutchins, Tippo remarked puckishly, "After reading about Wilson at Princeton and Hutchins at Chicago, I'm beginning to think we had a picnic at Colorado."[39] To one friend who had written an article providing advice about living life to the fullest at an advanced age, Quigg expressed total agreement about "the desirability of having an intellectual focus in retirement." He went on to state that he had "done some study of history," but that it was "all without much focus." Newton expressed mild frustration over the fact that he was not a particularly fast reader, adding a classic understatement: "My own reading is eclectic. I am very curious about many topics." He and Ginny regularly visited the Tattered Cover, a wonderful bookstore just blocks from their home. He would bring home five or six books at a time. "I am always buying books that I intend to read. None of it is light reading. Well, maybe the kids will read them."[40]

As he aged, Newton kept physically active. Although Ginny was a more regular participant in tennis, the two still occasionally played together. In his late seventies, Newton also took a membership at a nearby Bally's Health Club, which he visited two or three times a week. At Bally's, he used a treadmill and stair-climbing machine, and he occasionally lifted light weights. Still, age eventually caught up with him. On their second trip to England late in 1997, rather than taking a taxi to a remote attraction, the couple took a subway and then had to walk quite a distance at one end. A few days after their return to the United States, Quigg, then eighty-six, experienced such pain in his knees and back that he was confined to a wheelchair for some time. He fought through that experience and got back on his feet, although he had to use a cane.

He received fine medical care from his personal physician, Dr. Richard Byyny, whom he visited regularly. Byyny prescribed therapy and exercise through swimming, which Newton did regularly for the rest of his life. For a time, Quigg did physical therapy at his home. Staff members at the pool where Newton swam until his very last days remembered him as an enthusiastic participant in his therapy and one who constantly provided encouragement to other swimmers.

On August 3, 2001, Quigg celebrated his ninetieth birthday surrounded by numerous extended family members. Although he was clearly slowing down physically, he was as curious, mentally alert, and articulate as ever. He enjoyed people of all ages, and particularly young people. Young and old alike, most of those privileged to visit with him, later realized that he invariably asked more questions about them than they had about him. Although younger family members had little real sense of what he had done for the city of Denver, the state of Colorado, and his country, they had a sense that he was somebody special and had done remarkable things in the past.

One of his most prized letters came from his granddaughter, Justine Rice, on his ninetieth birthday. She wrote, "I just want you to know how much I love you and how proud I am to have you as my grandfather. I have so much respect for you and all you have accomplished and I can only hope to make you proud. ... I love hearing your stories and appreciate all your advice. You are such a great role model for me and everyone and have accomplished more than I could ever dream."[41]

Newton was extremely modest and self-effacing, but in his last years, he must have had a sense of how widely he was admired, even loved. In his eighties and early nineties, Quigg realized that although he had stepped down from positions of authority and power, he was not forgotten. Newspaper reporters in the region frequently interviewed him and wrote complimentary stories about many of the decisions he had made during the years he had led Denver and the University of Colorado. Political candidates and officeholders welcomed him at forums where participants discussed past, present, and future.

In 1997, Newton's former business manager at the University of Colorado, Leo Hill, hosted and helped mastermind a celebration of the "Newton Years" at the Heritage Center on the Boulder campus. Dozens of former colleagues and countless admirers wrote eloquent tributes to various achievements under his watch at the university. Many of his closest associates from the university years gathered for a two-day celebration in Boulder, where they enjoyed gala receptions, dinners, and fond reminiscences. At the end of the festivities, Hill presented Newton with a beautifully bound volume containing scores of fulsome written tributes to his leadership. After some reflection, Newton wrote Hill a letter that suggested the exhibit and gathering had done a good deal to heal some festering wounds left by the football mess, Regent Bromley's antics, and the Goldwater fiasco: "I believe, in sum, that, due to these controversies and headlines, our administration has suffered from a lack of appreciation of its accomplishments, both in the public mind and among many of our friends, from the day we departed to this day. ... [I]t was so great that you brought us all together again as a team perhaps for the last time. I believe each of us is full of appreciation to you for all you have done. Thank you! Thank you!"[42] Newton was honored when Mayor Wellington Webb announced that following a multimillion-dollar face-lift, the Denver Auditorium would bear his name. In his final years, it seemed, controversy and contention seemingly melted away, and Newton was fully recognized for the remarkable contributions that he had been making to the city, state, and nation for fully seven decades.

CHAPTER 13

TAPS

At about noon on April 2, 2003, a longtime friend, Jerry Harrison, met Newton at his home and drove him to the Denver Country Club, where they enjoyed a leisurely lunch. The two men had met perhaps a decade earlier, when they were both members of the Federal Fiscal Policy Institute, a group interested in helping elected officials address problems connected to the rapidly escalating national debt. The group included ex-Colorado governor Richard D. Lamm, lawyer Donald Hoagland, and other well-connected Colorado politicians, businessmen, lawyers, and other professionals.

Harrison had been meaning to arrange a lunch with Quigg for some time but had put off calling him, largely because he had not yet completed a mutually agreed-upon task of drafting a letter to the Commonwealth Fund regarding future directions the organization might pursue. Harrison had written down some ideas, and he wanted feedback from his friend. As they drove to the club, Newton informed Harrison that his vision had deteriorated to the point where it was difficult to read, so Harrison gave Quigg a draft of his letter, which he could review later at his leisure, with help from Ginny. The two friends weren't really meeting to talk about business; they mainly enjoyed sharing ideas. As Harrison recalled, "Losing the main topic of 'unfinished business' would certainly not be any restraint to our conversation since we normally tried to cover every important topic of interest to either of us at the moment."[1]

When Newton and Harrison arrived at the club, they climbed the stairs to a second-floor dining room, sat down, and ordered lunch.

301

Quigg requested a roast beef sandwich and a cup of soup. Their minds were focused more on ideas than food. Harrison was a board member for J. D. Edwards, a securities company, and the two men talked briefly about the volatility of the firm's stock price. Talk quickly turned to George W. Bush's recently launched war in Iraq and whether the invasion was a wise decision. Believing at the time that Iraq did, in fact, have weapons of mass destruction, they agreed, reluctantly, that it was. Years earlier, Harrison had written a book dealing largely with spiritual issues in which he raised the question of how a moral, ethical person would react if an axe murderer approached him and his family with evil intent. He would have two choices: succumb to the murderer "and hope for your reward after death" or "kill the axe murderer before he killed you." As Harrison recalled, "Neither Quigg nor I could see any better way around this dilemma."[2]

That raised the issue of God. Both men were agnostics. Quigg stated that he did not deny God's existence; he simply did not see sufficient proof of it. Harrison was somewhat more willing to believe in a definable higher power. Quigg asked Harrison if he believed that God was "an old man with a white beard living some place in the universe." He then raised the question of whether God had any personal relations with humans as individuals. "Neither of us thought it likely that He kept track of our particular life or arranged events to help or harm us." This launched the friends into a discussion of six basic philosophical questions: who, what, where, when, why, and how. They thought they had a pretty good handle on five of the six, but could not fully grasp why they were here, why this universe. The men talked about how brief human lives were in the course of the history of the universe. How could they possibly develop the ability to understand in their fleeting moments on Earth?

Talk then turned to Jesus. Quigg was convinced that Jesus had been a flesh-and-blood human being, not a "God figure" or religious construct. Neither man could recall how long it had taken after Christ's crucifixion before the story of Jesus of Nazereth had been "reduced to a writing that survives to today." Newton believed developing the account might have taken about forty years, and Harrison thought it was two to three hundred years. They agreed that it didn't much matter, given the "impressive ability of oral societies to transmit information seemingly accurately over many generations." Talk then turned to what had inspired Harrison to write his book, which probed some of the deepest philosophical questions concerning mankind. Harrison stated that he hoped to "distill the wisdom of the world into useful principles stated in simple words that any reasonably literate eleven-year-old could understand." Harrison reminded Quigg that they had, in fact, had a similar conversation eight years earlier, when the book had been published. At the time, when the two men had talked of universally successful social behaviors, Newton had responded, "How is that any different from the Golden Rule?" Harrison responded that his comment hit the nail on the head, that "it all boiled down to that." Quigg stated that the Golden Rule was "the most useful device he had ever discovered in working with people, especially in difficult circumstances." He had used it all his life, and it seldom failed. The friends talked on. Newton asked Harrison how libraries classified his book, and they agreed that it could be filed under any one of a dozen categories. They spent some time talking about how they organized their libraries.[3]

Finally, as afternoon shadows began to lengthen, the two men paused in their conversation and looked about. The restaurant staff had disappeared, and no other members were at nearby tables. They were alone in the dining room. Three hours had passed. They got up from the table and continued their conversation as they walked down the hall. Quigg was wholly focused on the conversation, not his surroundings. As he started down the steps, he reached out for a handrail but missed it. It all happened in a split second. He fell headfirst to the bottom of the steps, where he lay, unconscious. Quigg never knew what hit him. He was rushed to the emergency room but never regained consciousness. Harrison stayed with Ginny at the hospital as other family members were called. Family members realized that keeping him on life support was useless, and they ordered that it be turned off. Quigg Newton died peacefully on April 3, 2003.

Almost immediately, tributes to Newton began pouring in. Out of respect for the former leader, government officials in city hall and the statehouse lowered flags halfway. In the next few days, local newspapers printed lengthy obituaries, including fulsome praise that concentrated on his achievements as mayor, president of the University of Colorado, and president of the Commonwealth Fund. His passing also drew attention from major eastern papers, including an obituary in *The New York Times*. A few days later, the family held a private ceremony honoring him at the Polo Club North clubhouse in the complex where the couple had lived ever since their return to Denver in 1981. In late May, the University of Colorado hosted a memorial service at Old Main Hall, followed by a reception at Alumni House, formerly the president's house, which the Newtons had occupied during his years as president.

The family received hundreds of condolence letters, most coming directly to Ginny. To many, Quigg had been a hero. One old friend wrote, "I've had very few living and personally known heroes, maybe eight or ten, and Quigg was one of them." Tom Farer, dean of the Graduate School of International Studies at the University of Denver, wrote eloquently, "A great man has fallen. Through the years I have met many men of ability in academic and public life. Not one of them has matched Quigg in combining high intelligence with generosity of spirit, deep compassion and understanding for fellow human beings, commitment to the public good and true sweetness of character."[4]

Some letters arrived from prominent public officials. Congressman Mark E. Udall (Democrat-Colorado) remembered Newton as "a shining example for all of us elected officials." Udall remembered gratefully that Quigg and Ginny had encouraged him to run for Congress from Boulder. Former United States senator Tim Wirth (Democrat-Colorado) recalled, "Quigg was the first politician I ever knew about—my mother worked on his campaign in 1947—and I grew up with an abiding sense that there was real integrity and political joy in the process." Wirth was deeply grateful that when he initially decided to run for his first elected office in 1974, "valuable counsel from men like Dick Davis, Bruce Rockwell and Don Hoagland helped pass on the Newton tradition and commitment." Wirth commented on how much he enjoyed crossing paths with Quigg at public gatherings, and he noted wryly that the Newton influence on him must have been deep, as he had even followed him into the foundation world.[5]

Many fond recollections reflected on the style and grace Newton brought to the table of any organization he led. One Denver neighbor who always showed his regard for the couple by addressing them as Mr. and Mrs. Mayor when encountering them on walks around their complex at Polo Club North recalled with more than a touch of nostalgia, "Your style of governance was appreciated and absent in today's environment." In his mind, however modern and farsighted Newton's ideas may have been, Quigg and Ginny Newton represented a more genteel tradition in terms of personal style.[6] A former employee with the City and County of Denver who graduated from a Denver University program called government management in 1950 and worked four years for the city, recalled the unique leadership Newton provided: "He was demanding, setting high standards but always ready to consider a novel suggestion. Those habits I acquired working for him stayed with me during my working years. Although four years is not a long time, I was proud to say that 'I was in the Newton administration.'"[7] Coloradans knew that meant something. William E. "Bud" Davis, who was "fill-in" football coach at the university in 1962 following the Grandelius firing, later went on to serve as president of several universities. Davis emphasized the striking camaraderie of the leadership group in Boulder, stating that Quigg led a "band of brothers (and wives)—we few, we happy few." Davis called it a "special Camelot" and repeated the refrain:

> Let it never be forgot
> That once there was a spot
> That for one shining moment
> Was known as Camelot[8]

Others commented on Newton's superb people skills. Maggie Coval, director of the Colorado Endowment of the Humanities (CEH) recalled, "I remember how carefully Quigg *listened* to you ... and how he offered his quiet wisdom as we struggled with divisions inside CEH" (emphasis added).[9]

Two longtime friends wrote to Ginny expressing how Quigg had affected their lives. Eleanor Harper, one of Ginny's classmates from her days at Kent Denver School, recalled that she and her husband "were both hoping to see Quigg again to talk history and passionate politics as we had on our other visits and now won't have the chance. He didn't have to talk politics for me. I just liked seeing the mix of warmth and integrity he projected, rare qualities that are getting rarer." From Cape Cod, Ruth Plimpton recalled, "Quigg was so special. Once he stepped foot in Osterville, you never would have guessed he was president of a college or mayor of a great city. He gave his all for whatever he was involved in. He was so *loved* by everyone who had any contact with him."[10]

As is true of almost any conscientious and well-intentioned leader, Newton inspired others even when unaware of it. Donald Hoagland, who joined Newton's law firm and enjoyed a very distinguished career in Colorado, recalled that Newton deeply influenced his decision to come to Colorado in the first place. In the early 1950s, the recent law school graduate lived in New York and saw a picture of Newton, then serving as mayor. "He was in a white shirt with the sleeves rolled up, and he had his elbow on a split-rail fence. He looked more like a partner in a Wall Street law firm than a man who spent a lot of time on split-rail fences, but I liked the looks of him and what he was trying to do." It turned out that Hoagland had a good friend who knew Dick Davis at Yale. Hoagland decided to look for a job in Denver. He came out and interviewed with the firm. Although Quigg offered him a job working for the city attorney's office, it was at a low salary of just $1,850 per year. Hoagland decided he could do better in the private sector, and he went to work in Dick Davis's law firm at a somewhat higher starting salary. Through the years, Hoagland became a close friend to Newton and was a powerful figure in his own right, with seasoned political instincts. His assessment of Quigg's influence in the city, state, and nation was deep and shrewd. After his friend's death, Hoagland wrote, "Quigg's *happy mind* never stopped looking for a positive, constructive resolution to any problem, whether it was tiny or massive, personal or political. His influence was everywhere, and it won't stop now" (emphasis added).[11]

Margaret Mahoney, who came to the Commonwealth Fund when Newton was president and eventually assumed that position herself, recalled the essence of his executive leadership: "He set standards both as mayor and as university president that made him stand tall amongst others who would and did take the easy paths. ... What I saw was his ability to *move institutions forward.* ... It was his Commonwealth role that I knew best. I was not just a witness but a willing subject. He taught me how to pursue a problem, and in his work at Commonwealth I observed how he moved ideas ahead, against and around obstacles that short-sighted people put in his path. What he left was a monumental change in medical care" (emphasis added).[12]

Newton spent a lifetime making thoughtful gestures toward people he did not know well, or even at all. One admirer wrote of visiting Denver with his young wife when Quigg was mayor. A mutual acquaintance suggested that he look up Newton when he got there. He was surprised at the result: "Feeling most brazen, we did. And what a good reception from Quigg. 'Come for dinner.' Amazed and delighted we were graciously received by you both—and served mint juleps and dinner!"[13] Others remembered that both Quigg and Ginny frequently went to great lengths to provide help at critical moments. A former female undergraduate at the University of Colorado who looked after the girls one summer at Osterville, on Cape Cod, recalled needing to travel to Annapolis, Maryland, on very short notice for an important family event. Unfortunately, she had to depart on a Sunday, and she was stranded because there were no trains to take her into Providence, Rhode Island, where she could catch a connecting train: "I was sunk because I didn't want to let [my family] down, but Ginny and Quigg came to the rescue and drove me all the way to Providence. I will never forget this trip because we laughed all the way to Providence, even though I am sure driving there was the last thing they wanted to do that afternoon."[14]

Although he was closely associated with many of the nation's most influential and powerful people, Newton was equally engaged with people in all walks of life. One admirer remembered that "he seemed to enjoy talking with everyone, regardless of their status or personal importance." Another friend who was decades younger wrote, "He *never* let the age in years that separated us hinder our having a wonderful relationship." Gordon Saunders, whose father, Donald, had worked closely with Quigg at the University of Colorado, recalled "the instant bond that formed between our two year old son … and Mr. Newton on the balcony of my parents' apartment." In his last months, Newton had worked out in the swimming pool at the rehabilitation center at the University of Colorado Health Sciences Center. A dozen or so members of the staff at the pool sent a card filled with heartfelt recollections of the joy he brought with him every Monday, Wednesday, and Friday. As one staff member succinctly stated, "We will miss our buddy."[15]

Newton treated everyone with respect; condescension was foreign to his makeup. One friend remembered, "As so many of the newspaper articles said, he was always more interested in learning about the other person than talking about himself." A woman who had worked for Davis, Graham and Stubbs when Newton returned from California recalled, "In the five years I worked for the firm, my most pleasant experiences were with him." She continued, "I found Quigg to be one of the 'old school' types I'd grown up with from the fifties. He knew how to treat people, had social graces that were not taught in law school, and never forgot how to treat a lady." Other younger lawyers would sometimes barge in, demanding that their copying had to be done immediately, that others' work would have to wait. But never Newton: "I'd see him out of the corner of my eye, coming toward my desk with something to copy for him, gingerly approaching for fear I was too busy. … I had trouble convincing him that he could interrupt me with something he needed at any time he wished."[16]

What was Newton's long-term impact on the city, state, and nation? In ninety-one packed years, Quigg lived a rich, productive, and happy life. He was born into privilege, and he could have easily slipped into a sybaritic life of leisure and self-indulgence. That choice held no temptations. From his teenage years forward, he rarely spoke of his own needs but instead focused on the concerns of others. He sincerely believed that in being permitted to serve the people of Colorado and the nation, he was being granted a wonderful privilege. His was truly a life of service. As Margaret Mahoney eloquently stated, "Quigg left the world a better place than when he arrived on earth. I would like the universe to know how he was and what he did, for he was a great man." Another admirer stated simply, "He was a great man who was seemingly unaware of his greatness." Finally, as Nils Wessell, an old friend and associate from his years in the world of foundations, beautifully summarized: "His distinguished career as a lawyer, university president, mayor and foundation president was testimony to his many abilities, no two of these careers calling on the same assets that were his: Renaissance man."[17]

⚭

APPENDIX

The extended Newton clan contained just a few leaders and risk-takers. Quigg Newton's known forebears included neither royalty nor aristocrats, but they go back to this nation's origins. Richard Newton disembarked in Boston in 1638, arriving in Massachusetts toward the end of the so-called Great Migration from England, which occurred between 1630 and 1641.[1] By the time his ship sailed into Boston Harbor following a journey that probably took between eight and ten weeks, several thousand Puritans were already settled in the Bay colony. Like almost all newcomers to the continent, Newton intended to acquire land of his own that he could pass down to his progeny. Boston itself was already heavily settled, earlier arrivals having claimed all desirable property. Newton headed due west approximately fifteen miles to a new settlement named Sudbury, where he planted family roots.

Little is known about Newton's roots in England, but earlier genealogical work, the efforts of previous scholars, and considerable circumstantial evidence permit the modern researcher to make several inferences. Family lore held that Richard Newton was an uncle of Sir Isaac Newton, the famous scientist and mathematician, but genealogical evidence almost certainly disproves such claims.[2] Evidently, Richard was married before he moved to New England to Anne Loker, the daughter of a glover in the county of Essex, in England. Being in his mid-thirties, he was slightly older than the average emigrant to Massachusetts. Although a slight majority of migrating families brought along servants,[3] there is no mention of Newton enjoying such a luxury. In other respects, he and Anne almost certainly blended in with their shipmates. Like fully four-fifths of his shipmates, he was a "husbandman," or farmer, and many men brought their families.

Richard Newton may have made arrangements to settle in Sudbury before leaving England. Town records reveal that he was among the fifty-seven original proprietors to whom lands had been assigned by 1640. In virtually every respect, his life unfolded as that of a typical New England farmer of the seventeenth century. He and Anne raised seven children, including four sons. Like most fellow Puritans, Newton was keenly intent upon acquisition of property, and he gradually expanded his landholdings, first in Sudbury and then in Marlborough, located approximately eight miles farther west. At the time of his death in 1701, Richard Newton owned 130 acres, scattered across several locations. The size and nature of his landholdings were approximately average for first-generation New England settlers.[4]

Richard Newton was involved in a significant sectional dispute between those residing close to the center of Sudbury and those living on "outlying" districts. In the Massachusetts colony, the Puritan church was the dominant force in society. Members of the community were obliged to attend church regularly. Those who refused to attend services or even slacked off in at least outwardly devout participation were threatened with unappealing, sometimes even frightening, consequences. In many communities, "outlying" farms were often several miles from churches, and attending several religious services per week became increasingly time-consuming for settlers in remote areas. Hence, in 1684, by which time he was settled in Marlborough, Richard Newton and eight other landholders petitioned the magistrates of Sudbury for permission to establish their own church.[5] Responsible authorities approved the request in principle, although the expense and difficulty of establishing an adequate facility and hiring and retaining a capable minister precluded a functional separation from the established church in Sudbury for many years.

Richard Newton's eventual success in meeting his and his neighbors' needs independently from those of his more distant and centrally located townsmen was not necessarily the norm. Throughout the late seventeenth and most of the eighteenth century, "most Massachusetts towns contended with varying success against the ambitions of their outlying districts. ... In places like Dedham, years of sectional sparring culminated in voting fraud, resort to muskets at town meetings, and 'complete paralysis of the mechanisms of town government.'"[6]

In one respect, Newton far surpassed his fellow townsmen, as he lived to be "almost a hundrid [*sic*] years old."[7] His choice of Boston as his debarkation point may have been an important contributing factor to his remarkable longevity. Although the New England climate was far harsher than those in other colonies farther south, life expectancy for Puritans was considerably higher than in other colonies. One noted scholar's statistical sampling revealed that the average life expectancy for New England men was seventy-one years, while women could expect to survive until age sixty-seven. In the Chesapeake colonies, dysentery, typhoid, and malaria struck down settlers in droves; life expectancy for men was just forty-three years, and women lived, on average, only into their late thirties.[8]

Since he survived for more then six decades in the emerging New England commonwealth, Richard Newton witnessed firsthand some of the critical shaping events in New England's history: the slackening of rigid Puritan self-denial and the emergence of the "half-way" covenant in 1662; uprisings of Native Americans and the destruction of several Puritan villages during King Philip's War in 1675 and 1676; and the Salem witchcraft trials during the early 1690s. On March 26, 1676, Indians attacked Marlborough, where Richard and several family members were living, and destroyed a considerable amount of property. Evidently, no lives were lost in the raid, but Newton family members were distinctly aware that they lived on the outer fringes of white man's settlement.

Richard died as the eighteenth century opened. His wife, Anne (in some documents named Hannah), had died in 1697, and all of the family's assets were divided among the children. As was the custom of the day, the sons inherited almost everything, daughters very little. Colonial Massachusetts was essentially a man's world. John Winthrop, the colony's governor, proclaimed in 1645 that "A true wife accounts her subjugation [as] her honor and freedom and would not think her condition safe and free but in subjection to her husband's authority."[9] According to at least one respected scholar, "Married women ... had even fewer legal rights than a slave." They could not vote, file suits, enter contracts, testify in court, or file wills of their own. Dowries brought into marriages became the husband's property, and any wages earned by a wife belonged to her husband. Law required her to obey her mate, and men were allowed to beat their wives. Adultery was strictly a female offense; public censure might constrain a philandering male, but the law did not.[10] In seeking economic security, New England's daughters had extremely limited options. If they remained "spinsters," they often lived with parents or married siblings. Unless they were from affluent families, their status in society was generally low and their roles were vaguely defined. They might not even have a room or a portion of the home that they could truly consider a private refuge. Yet, women who married often simply exchanged one master for another.

In his will, dated in 1684, Richard left a double portion of his estate to his oldest son, John, also common practice at the time. Since bad feelings between inheriting siblings erupted occasionally, particularly when wills were carelessly drawn up, Richard Newton's division of lands, household furnishings, and all of his possessions was extremely detailed and explicit. Although not provided with land, the daughters received household furnishings and modest amounts of money. Evidently, there was enough property to go around, as none of the second-generation Newton men felt a need to move far from the Sudbury/Marlborough region. John Newton was born in Sudbury in 1641 and became a proprietor of Marlborough in 1660. In 1666, he married Elizabeth Larkin, who also lived in Marlborough. He lived there his entire life, dying at the age of eighty-two. He largely followed his father's career as a farmer, but he also practiced house carpentry on the side in order to raise additional income.[11]

The oldest son of that union, John Newton Jr., was born in Marlborough in 1667, lived his entire life there, and died in nearby

Southborough at the ripe age of eighty-six in 1754. Like his father, John Jr. was the oldest son, and he inherited a double portion of the family's lands, which amounted to about 125 acres.[12] He was evidently reasonably well off, and he felt little reason to migrate farther west. Like his forebears, John Newton Jr. practiced husbandry, became a pillar of the local Puritan church, and led what by all official accounts appeared to be an exemplary life. During the "Indian troubles" accompanying King Philip's War in 1675–1676, more than half of the ninety Puritan villages in New England were attacked, and thirteen were completely destroyed. Several thousand colonists died fighting. Advancement of frontier settlement was delayed for two generations while the northern colonies recovered.[13] John Jr., then just eight or nine years old, may well have had searing memories of the dangers of war, since his father's home was designated as one of twenty-six local frontier "garrisons."[14]

Except for these events, John Newton Jr. probably led a relatively uneventful, pedestrian life from that point forward. He and his wife, Hannah, were parents to several children, including Phineas, who was born in 1707. Available records do not reveal the order of birth of the children, but Phineas was evidently not the firstborn son, as his land inheritance, if he received any at all, was quite modest. In 1730 or 1731, he married Patience Howe of Marlborough. His wife was appropriately named. Rearing and attempting to provide for at least ten children must have consumed the combined strength of husband and wife, as they became the first generation of Newtons to move frequently, presumably in search of more farmland and improved economic opportunities. It appears that Phineas's search for security was reasonably successful, as he acquired additional property holdings in Windsor, Connecticut, and later in Springfield, Massachusetts. Although reasonably healthy, Phineas did not enjoy quite the longevity of several of his forbears, dying at age seventy-one in 1779.

A quick reading of his will, drafted eight years before his death, might lead one to believe that Phineas's holdings were very modest: a house in Springfield valued at nine pounds, two horses, four oxen, six cows, ten goats and sheep, three swine, ten acres of pasturage and fifteen acres suitable for tilling. In earlier years, however, Phineas had deeded nearly 200 acres in separate parcels to several sons. His listed assets also included three "ratable polls." In the late eighteenth century, such a term is subject to various interpretations. It could mean slaves, free blacks, or servants, but it could even refer to sons over the age of sixteen still living at home.[15] In all likelihood, only two of his sons might have been living under his roof when the will was drawn up in 1771. Circumstantial evidence suggests that several assistants may have helped Phineas in two trades: house carpentry and shipbuilding. Phineas willed numerous tools of these trades to his oldest son, Francis.

For the colonists in Massachusetts during the seventeenth and early eighteenth centuries, warfare was a relatively common experience. Following "Indian troubles" during King Philip's War in 1675–1676, there were significant outbreaks of fighting during King William's War in 1689–1697, Queen Anne's War in 1702–1713, Governor Dummer's War in 1722–1725, and King George's War in 1744–1748. In most of these conflicts, fighting was sporadic and colonists were "inconvenienced" in relatively rare cases. But the French and Indian War (1754–1763) was different. Several thousand Massachusetts men were drafted, willingly or otherwise. Many of those forced to serve under British regular officers were shamefully abused. Some were "pressed" to serve in His Majesty's royal navy; others were forced to march hundreds of miles under difficult conditions to fight the French in Canada. Hundreds of men died in battle or due to disease; others were horribly maimed. Family records do not prove conclusively that Phineas fought in the French and Indian War, but circumstantial evidence suggests his participation, as he was identified in 1763 Springfield town records as a "Lieut." At least Phineas survived the war; his oldest son, Artemas, was not so fortunate.[16]

Thaddeus Newton, the sixth son of Phineas and Patience, evidently had to scramble even harder for survival than his parents. He was born in 1750 and married Sarah Damon in 1776. Thaddeus became a soldier during the American Revolution, evidently serving very short enlistments in several different companies. He answered one call to arms when Bennington, Vermont, was under threat of attack by the British in

August 1777. A month later, he returned to the same company, signing up for duty in the Northern Department as a private, but one week later Thaddeus apparently left camp without permission. Evidently, he was either not charged with desertion or he was reinstated, since he enlisted once again in Berkshire County in the summer of 1779. He returned to Springfield six weeks later.[17]

Was Thaddeus Newton a "low-life" slacker? His response was fairly typical among men of his generation. Historian Robert Gross, an authority on the American Revolution, observed that after the outbreak of hostilities at Concord in April 1775 and for the first year or so of the war, local men swarmed to the cause, and officers usually had little difficulty filling the ranks of willing volunteers for military service. Not surprisingly, as both casualties and the cost of war mounted, and as food, supplies, and even pay for the soldiers became more sporadic—even nonexistent—the initial enthusiasm waned. In Concord, half the men under age fifty received at least one draft notice. Many well-to-do men paid for substitutes, and some adventurers accepted bounties to enlist.[18] Thaddeus Newton's multiple short-term enlistments suggest that he may have been a "bounty jumper." Robert Gross stated flatly, "From 1777 on, the Continental ranks were manned largely by the lower social orders. ... The longer the war went on, the poorer and more degraded in status were the recruits."[19]

Yet if Thaddeus Newton's zest for combat was less than robust, he pursued economic opportunities with admirable persistence. Following the British surrender in 1781 at Yorktown, Virginia, and the official end of the American Revolution in 1783, the former colonists rapidly expanded their areas of settlement. Thaddeus did not become a pioneer settler west of the Alleghenies, as did thousands of his new countrymen, but he began the migration of the extended Newton clan westward, away from Massachusetts.[20] During the 1780s and early 1790s, Thaddeus tried his hand at various enterprises in at least four towns in the vicinity of Springfield, Massachusetts. His primary commercial interest appears to have been buying timber lands in western Massachusetts. Either he achieved only limited success, or wanderlust took over. In 1795, at age forty-five, he moved his family permanently to Buckingham, in Wayne County, Pennsylvania, just across the Delaware River in the northeast corner of the state. When settled, he once again began buying up property containing large stands of timber. Thaddeus thus began an extended Newton family tradition of engaging in the lumber business, which continued in several states without interruption until Colorado family members finally sold off the last lumber business more than a century later, in the early 1900s.

Evidently, Quigg Newton's great-great-grandfather, Ezra Newton, was one of the few Newton men not to demonstrate any particular initiative or drive. Nor was he blessed with a long and full life. Born a child of the American Revolution in Wilbraham, Massachusetts, on April 24, 1777, he was the oldest of Thaddeus and Mary Newton's many children. In about 1800, Ezra married Mary Carr, one of twenty-three children (by three wives) of Caleb Carr, of West Greenwich, Rhode Island. Evidence suggests that he worked in his father's lumber enterprises for his entire life, and he died in summer 1816 at age thirty-nine after becoming ill while at his father's home in Wayne County. Ezra fathered seven children, the last of whom, Ezra Artemus, Quigg's great-grandfather, was born several months after his father's death on March 23, 1817.[21]

As the youngest (and fatherless) son, Ezra Artemus Newton perhaps realized from a very early age that he faced a particularly hard row to find success. The first major economic depression experienced by the newly emerging republic began in 1819, just two years after Ezra's birth. The Bank of the United States failed; in large cities, wage scales—for those lucky enough to keep their jobs—declined by two-thirds. Land sales in almost all sections of the country declined precipitously. Perhaps Mary Carr Newton found shelter for herself and her youngest children in the home of her in-laws or at least in their hometown of Buckingham, Pennsylvania. It was Ezra Artemus Newton who was responsible for the settlement of an important branch of the family in Colorado.

ENDNOTES

Chapter 1: Family Roots

[1] Thomas L. Connelly, *The Marble Man: Robert E. Lee and His Image in American Society* (New York: A. A. Knopf, 1977); Jean Strouse, *Morgan: American Financier* (New York: Random House, 1999); and Jack Shephard, *The Adams Chronicles: Four Generations of Greatness* (Boston: Little Brown, 1976).

[2] David M. Donald, *Lincoln* (New York: Simon and Schuster, 1995); Geoffrey S. Perrett, *Ulysses S. Grant: Soldier and President* (New York: Random House, 1997); Mark S. Foster, Henry J. Kaiser, *Builder in the Modern American West* (Austin: University of Texas Press, 1989); Ron Cherny, *Titan: The Life of John D. Rockefeller, Sr.* (New York: Random House, 1998); and Neil Baldwin, *Edison: Inventing the Century* (New York: Hyperion, 1995).

[3] The study of "success" has generated massive amounts of research. For excellent reviews and summaries of this literature, see Walter A. Friedman and Richard S. Tedlow, "Statistical Portraits of American Business Elites: A Review Essay," *Business History* 45:4 (October 2003): 89–113; see also Alan B. Kreuger, "The Apple Falls Close to the Tree, Even in the Land of Opportunity," *The New York Times*, November 14, 2000. Relevant books include Edward Pessen, (ed.), *Three Centuries of Social Mobility in America* (Lexington, Mass. D. C. Heath, 1974), and Kevin Phillips, *Wealth and Democracy: A Political History of the American Rich* (New York: Broadway Books/Random House, 2002): chapter l. "Peter Temin recently concluded that, while the American political elite has become more representative of the general population over the past century, the business elite has not done so." See Temin, "The American Business Elite in Historical Perspective," in Elise S. Brezis and Peter Temin (eds.), *Elites, Minorities, and Economic Growth* (Amsterdam: Elsevier Science B.V, 1999), 19–39. I am indebted to my colleague, Pamela Walker Laird, for these references.

[4] The definitive work on this subject is by Pamela Walker Laird, *Pull: Networking and Success Since Benjamin Franklin* (Cambridge: Harvard University Press, 2005).

[5] For details on Newton family genealogy, see the Appendix.

[6] W. B. Vickers, *History of the City of Denver, Arapahoe County and Colorado* (Chicago: O. L. Baskin & Co.: 1880), 536–537.

[7] *Rocky Mountain News*, September 24, 1941.

[8] Ibid., 537; Newton family genealogy, 125–126.

[9] Ellen K. Fisher, "Newton Family History," n.p., unpublished, undated manuscript, Newton family papers.

[10] Ibid.

[11] For a useful discussion of the denuding of the Front Range landscape, see Kathleen A. Brosnan, *Uniting Mountain and Plain: Cities and Environmental Change Along the Front Range* (Albuquerque: University of New Mexico Press, 2002): 146–150, 155.

[12] *Rocky Mountain News*, September 24, 1941.

13 Ibid.

14 Centennial 1903 Annual (Pueblo, Colo.; Cadet Corps of Pueblo High School: 1903); passim.

15 Untitled and undated genealogical typescript in possession of Abby Newton, Newton family papers.

16 James Newton to Mrs. Joseph Parker, September 2, 1913, Newton family papers; Interview of Quigg Newton by author, February 26, 2003.

Chapter 2: Youth

1 *Rocky Mountain News*, September 24, 1941.

2 Quigg Newton, interview by author, September 4, 2002.

3 *Rocky Mountain News*, September 24, 1941.

4 John M. Barry, *The Great Influenza: The Epic Story of the Deadliest Plague in History* (New York: Viking, 2004).

5 Quigg Newton, interview by author, September 4, 2002.

6 Quigg Newton to Mother and Dad, July 21, 1925, Newton family papers.

7 Ibid.

8 Jim Newton to Culver Military Academy, June 29, 1923, Newton family papers.

9 Quigg Newton, undated letter to "Daddy," (ca. July, 1923), Newton family papers.

10 Quigg Newton, interview by author, November 20, 2002.

11 Undated newspaper clipping, Newton family papers.

12 Quigg Newton, interview by author, September 24, 2002.

13 Ibid.

14 Quigg Newton imparted this view in numerous personal interviews with the author. Throughout their lives, Quigg provided Ruth considerable financial advice and attempted to shield her from trouble and conflict.

15 Jim Newton to Quigg Newton, May 5, 1926, Newton family papers.

16 Jesse M. Hamilton to Mr. Newton, undated memorandum, Newton family papers.

17 Quigg Newton, interview by author, September 13, 2002.

18 Jim Simmons, "A Few Recollections," *Colorado Classicist* 27:4 (December 1989): 12.

19 Quigg Newton, interview by author, March 26, 2003.

20 Robert P. Newton to Quigg Newton, September 2, 1926, Newton family papers.

21 Irving Eaton to Quigg Newton, November 8, 1926, Newton family papers.

22 Jim Newton to Quigg Newton, undated, (September, 1926). It is important to remember that in 1926 air mail was just barely established; since this service was expensive, it was seldom used except for important business transactions. See A. Scott Berg, *Lindbergh* (New York: G. P. Putnam's Sons, 1998): 84–89.

23 Quigg Newton to Dad and Mother, September 29, 1926, Newton family papers.

24 Ibid.

25 Quigg Newton to Dad and Mother, October 31, 1926, Newton family papers.

26 Quigg Newton to Mother and Dad, October 2, 1926, Newton family papers.

27 Quigg Newton to Dad, October 23, 1926, Newton family papers.

28 Quigg Newton to Dad and Mother, October 31, 1926, Newton family papers.

29 Quigg Newton to Dad and Mother, September 29, 1926, Newton family papers.

30 Quigg Newton to Dad and Mother, October 31, 1926, Newton family papers.

31 Quigg Newton to Dad, November 10, 1926, Newton family papers.

32 Quigg Newton to Mother and Dad, February 3, 1927, Newton family papers.

33 Quigg Newton to Dad and Mother, October 31, 1926, Newton family papers.

34 Quigg Newton to Dad, November 11, 1926, Newton family papers.

35 Quigg Newton to Uncle "Jim," December 8, 1926, Newton family papers.

36 Quigg Newton to Dad, November 10, 1926, Newton family papers.

37 James Newton to A. E. Stearns, November 23, 1926, 1926, Newton family papers.

38 Nelle Newton to Quigg Newton, January 24, 1927, and Nelle Newton to Quigg Newton, February 17, 1927, both in Newton family papers.

39 Quigg Newton to Mother and Dad, February 18, 1927, Newton family papers.

40 Quigg Newton to Mother and Dad, February 3, 1927, Newton family papers.

41 Quigg Newton to Mother and Dad, February 13, 1927, Newton family papers. One needs to remember that Quigg was attending prep school in the late 1920s, by which time Americans in general, and particularly upper middle class adults, had for the most part lost most of any remaining respect for the institution of Prohibition. Millions of adults openly flaunted the law, frequenting "speakeasies" and serving alcohol in their living rooms during ritualistic "cocktail hours." Organized gangsters who supplied the liquor, including Chicago's notorious Al Capone, were in their heyday. The tobacco industry was equally successful in expanding cigarette consumption, directing advertising campaigns not just to adult males, but to women and adolescents. It is hardly surprising that smoking and drinking among pseudo-sophisticates at America's leading prep schools were endemic.

42 Phillips Academy, Andover, Massachusetts, Report for the Term Ending March 24, 1927, Newton family papers.

43 Quigg Newton to Mother and Dad, September 17, 1927, Newton family papers.

44 Quigg Newton to Mother and Dad, November 15, 1927, Newton family papers.

45 R. G. Bulkley to Quigg Newton, November 15, 1927, Newton family papers.

46 Jim Grant to Quigg Newton, December 2, 1927, Newton family papers.

47 Jim Newton to Quigg Newton, November 18, 1927, Quigg Newton papers, box 4, Western History Collection, Denver Public Library.

48 Clarence H. Adams to Jim Newton Jr., February 18, 1927, Quigg Newton papers, box 4, Western History Collection, Denver Public Library.

49 Dad to Quigg Newton, November 1, 1927, Newton family papers. Before widespread availability of penicillin, diseases such as syphilis could lead to death.

50 Quigg Newton to Dad, November 17, 1927, Newton family papers.

51 Quigg Newton to Mother and Dad, March 10, 1928, Newton family papers.

52 Quigg Newton to Mother and Dad, January 19, 1928, Newton family papers.

53 Quigg Newton, interview by author, December 19, 2002.

54 Ibid.

55 Quigg Newton telegram to Mr. and Mrs. Jim Newton, June 26, 1928, Newton family papers.

56 Quigg Newton, interview by author, September 9, 2002.

57 Quigg Newton to Dad, April 9, 1928, Newton family papers. One reader of this manuscript, David Wetzel, raised the insightful question "How do we know this isn't just an excuse that he'd been rejected by the big fellows?"

58 Ibid.

59 Ibid.

60 Quigg Newton to Dad and Mother, April 15, 1928, Newton family papers.

61 For an account of this incident, see "Preface."

62 Quigg Newton to Mrs. Taylor, undated letter, (ca. 1931), Newton family papers. Interestingly, other Andover students shared Newton's perspective on the school. Yardley Beers, who graduated from Andover a year after Newton, visited the institution fifty years later. He found the Andover of 1981 far more interesting and challenging than the school had been in 1930. "The school that I visited in 1981 is more intellectually healthy and one with much more human understanding than the one I knew in 1930. ... The Andover of my day was too much dominated by the "Success Theory," and the activities in which one could be a socially acceptable "success" were rigidly limited by custom, mostly being a letter man in the major sports or being senior editor of the "Phillipian." An interest in the arts or a scientifically related hobby caused a student to be branded as eccentric." See Yardley Beers, "The

State of Phillips Academy," undated manuscript, Newton family papers, p. 1. At least one of his former teachers was sufficiently impressed with Quigg's concerns about the school that in the summer of 1933, just after Quigg had graduated from Yale, he asked his former student's thoughts on the institution. "It's your turn to tell me some things, many things about Andover, the place, the men, the boys, and me in my relations with them." Art Darling to "Jim" Newton, August 31, 1933, Newton family papers.

[63] College Entrance Examination Board, examination number 4680, June 18–23, 1928, Newton family papers.

[64] Quigg Newton, interview by author, September 9, 2002.

Chapter 3: Branching Out

[1] Quigg Newton, interview by author, September 9, 2002.

[2] Perhaps the most readable single volume on the stock market frenzy of the late 1920s is John Kenneth Galbraith, *The Great Crash* (Boston: Houghton Mifflin, 1954). Books presenting other views of the crash include Robert Sobel, *The Great Bull Market: Wall Street in the 1920s* (New York: W. W. Norton, 1968); William K. Klingaman, *The Year of the Great Crash: 1929* (New York: Harper and Row, 1989); and Maury Klein, *Rainbow's End: The Crash of 1929* (New York; Oxford University Press: 2001).

[3] James Newton to June Burns, November 8, 1929, Newton family papers.

[4] Quigg Newton, interview by author, September 9, 2002.

[5] Quigg Newton to Mother and Dad, May 9, 1930, Newton family papers.

[6] Historiography is essentially the history of history itself, usually focusing on theory and the evolution of various historical approaches.

[7] Quigg Newton, interview by author, September 9, 2002.

[8] Quigg Newton, interview by author, October 14, 2002.

[9] James Newton to Quigg Newton, June 17, 1932, Newton family papers.

[10] Ibid.

[11] Quigg Newton telegram to James Newton, February 3, 1932, Quigg Newton papers, box 4, Western History Department, Denver Public Library.

[12] Mary Rose Newton to Quigg Newton, December 19, 1932, Newton family papers.

[13] *History of the Class of 1933* (New Haven: 1933): 630.

[14] Quigg Newton to "Allan and Tom," October 28, 1997, Newton family papers.

[15] Quigg Newton, interview by author, September 9, 2002.

[16] Quigg Newton to Dad, undated letter (ca. September 1933).

[17] Quigg Newton to Mother and Dad, undated letter (ca. May 1934), Quigg Newton papers, box 4, Western History Department, Denver Public Library.

[18] James Newton to Quigg Newton, April 17, 1934, Quigg Newton papers, box 4, Western History Collection, Denver Public Library.

[19] For more insights into the thought of Thurman Arnold, see his autobiography, *Fair Fights and Foul: A Dissenting Lawyer's Life* (New York: Harcourt Brace and World, 1951).

[20] Quigg Newton, interview by author, September 13, 2002.

[21] "Chick" to "Jim," July 12, 1934, Newton family papers.

[22] Wilbur Newton to Quigg Newton, July 3, 1934, Quigg Newton papers, box 4, Western History Collection, Denver Public Library.

[23] Harriett Thompson to Quigg Newton, Quigg Newton papers, box 4, Western History Collection, Denver Public Library.

[24] Quigg Newton to Harriett Thompson, Quigg Newton papers, box 4, Western History Collection, Denver Public Library.

[25] Quigg Newton, undated letter (ca. summer, 1934) to Mother and Dad, Quigg Newton papers, box 4, Western History Collection, Denver Public Library.

[26] Wilbur Newton to Quigg Newton, July 23, 1934, Newton family papers.

27 Quigg Newton to Mom and Dad, undated letter (ca. summer 1934), Quigg Newton papers, box 4, Western History Collection, Denver Public Library.

28 Quigg Newton to Dad, undated letter, (summer 1934), Quigg Newton papers, box 4, Western History Collection, Denver Public Library.

29 Bruce A. Murphy, *Wild Bill: The Legend and Life of William O. Douglas* (New York: Random House, 2003): 81–135, passim. However, a Pulitzer prize-winning scholar of American jurisprudence recently concluded, "Unfortunately … most legal historians now see his judicial track record as having been no better than his domestic one … a huge disappointment." David J. Garrow, review of Murphy, *Wild Bill*, in *The Nation* (April 14, 2003): 25.

30 "William O. Douglas: 1898–1980," *American Bar Association Journal* 66 (March 1980): 321.

31 Douglas's most recent biographer, Bruce Murphy, casts profound suspicion on his subject's tales of youthful poverty. By his account, Douglas at least partly invented an impoverished past to enhance his mystique. He quotes Douglas responding to the fact that such accounts appeared repeatedly in newspapers and national magazines: "If the darn fools want to write that stuff, who am I to contradict them?" See Murphy, *Wild Bill*, 121.

32 Insights into Douglas's life and career were taken from his lengthy obituary in *The New York Times*, January 20, 1980.

33 Yale University School of Law, Official Transcript, issued January 26, 1942, Newton family papers.

34 Quigg Newton to Mother and Dad, undated letter (ca. May1936), Newton family papers.

35 Quigg Newton to Mother and Dad, undated, "Thursday" (ca. late May 1936), Quigg Newton papers, box 4, Western History Collection, Denver Public Library.

36 James Newton to Quigg Newton, August 21, 1936, Quigg Newton papers, box 4, Western History Collection, Denver Public Library.

37 James Quigg Newton Trustee—Stock Inventory, July 20, 1936, Quigg Newton family papers.

38 Quigg Newton to Mother and Dad, undated letter (ca. summer 1936), Quigg Newton papers, box 4, Western History Collection, Denver Public Library.

39 James Newton to Quigg Newton, August 21, 1936, Quigg Newton papers, box 4, Western History Collection, Denver Public Library.

40 James Newton to Quigg Newton, September 19, 1936, Newton family papers.

41 Later, when Douglas was on the Supreme Court, Douglas told Quigg that the job of justice only occupied his mind part-time, and that it left him with plenty of time to write, travel, and attempt to understand the world. Quigg Newton, interview by author, September 23, 2002.

42 The Nye Committee, convened by Congress in 1934, spent many months unveiling profiteering by some of the nation's biggest suppliers of the military during the war. Coming at a time when the nation was suffering the worst of the Depression, from a public relations perspective, the timing could not have been worse for big business.

43 Quigg Newton, interview by author, September 13, 2002.

44 Quigg Newton to Charlie (Noyes), February 16, 1937, Newton family papers.

45 John Knox, *The Forgotten Memoir of John Knox* (Chicago: University of Chicago Press, 2002): 177–178.

46 Quigg Newton to Charlie Noyes, February 16, 1937, Newton family papers.

47 *Rocky Mountain News*, April 10, 1949.

Chapter 4: Searching for Self-Identity

1 Quigg Newton to Harriett Thompson, December 12, 1936, Newton family papers.

2 Ibid.

3 Dick Davis to "Quiggle," undated letter, Newton family papers.

4 Carl Abbott, *Colorado: a History of the Centennial State* (Boulder, Colo.: Associated University Press, 1976): 230.
5 Dick Davis to "Quiggle," November 9, 1936, Newton family papers.
6 James Newton to Quigg Newton, undated letter (ca. summer 1936), Newton family papers.
7 James Newton to Quigg Newton, July 24, 1937, Newton family papers.
8 Quigg Newton to Dick Davis, July 15, 1937, Newton family papers.
9 Quigg Newton to Dad, March 17, 1940, Newton family papers.
10 Bill Sheldon to Quigg Newton, June 4, 1935, Newton family papers.
11 Dick Matthews to Jim [Quigg's name at Andover and Yale] Newton, July 23, 1936, Newton family papers.
12 Dick Matthews to Jim Newton, September 13, 1936, Newton family papers.
13 Quigg Newton to Ben Lieb, August 4, 1936, Newton family papers.
14 Quigg Newton to Ben Lieb, March 12, 1937, Newton family papers. The remark about being pursued by bill collectors is almost certainly jocular.
15 Quigg Newton to Vinton Lindley, March 15, 1937, Newton family papers.
16 Quigg Newton, interview by author, September 23, 2002.
17 Quigg Newton, tribute to Dick Davis, undated, p. 4, Newton family papers.
18 Quigg Newton, interview by author, September 23, 2002.
19 *Rocky Mountain News*, August 21, 1940.
20 "David Graham and Stubbs: History of the Firm, 1915–1975," mimeographed, n.d., 31, Newton family papers.
21 Quigg Newton, interview by author, September 23, 2002.
22 Newton tribute to Dick Davis, 6.
23 Ibid., 8. See also Stanley M. Walker and Martin Van Sickel, "Report on Hydroponic Experiment Under Commercial Conditions," mimeographed August 1938, Quigg Newton papers, box 4, Western History Department, Denver Public Library.
24 *The Denver Post*, April 5, 1944. See also Roscoe Fleming, "The Story of James Quigg Newton," *Rocky Mountain News*, September 24, 1941.
25 Newton's private papers contain voluminous reports on such issues between 1935 and 1938.
26 "Address by Quigg Newton, Jr., Over Radio Station KLZ, June 30, 1938 at 8:30 PM re. Reorganization of Colorado State Government," mimeographed June 1938, pp. 1, 6, Newton family papers.
27 Quigg Newton to Frank G. Arnold, August 9, 1938, Newton family papers.
28 Quigg Newton to Edward D. Foster, August 10, 1938, Newton family papers.
29 Quigg Newton, "Civil Service Reform," speech delivered at the Colorado Legislative Conference, December 9, 1938, Newton family papers.
30 Quigg Newton to E. O. Griffenhagen, July 31, 1939, Newton family papers.
31 E. O. Griffenhagen to Quigg Newton, July 26, 1939, Newton family papers.
32 Quigg Newton, interview by author, October 23, 2002. Newton's involvement with founding the Denver chapter of Council of Foreign Relations eventually helped the University of Denver create the entity that became the Graduate School of International Studies.
33 "Our Present Task is a Unified America," article by Quigg Newton Jr., in *The Denver Post*, March 16, 1941.
34 Quigg Newton to Paul C. Smith, July 2, 1941, Newton family papers.
35 Quigg Newton, interview by author, November 13, 2002.
36 Quigg and Virginia Newton, interview by author, February 26, 2003.
37 Virginia Newton, "For SARA Celebration of the Colorado Women's Forum: Philosophy, Influences, and Pathways," manuscript in possession of author, November 1991, n.p.
38 The result was an extraordinarily detailed and highly insightful two-volume work. The diary reveals remarkable maturity and insight for a sixteen-year-old girl. Many of her

comments on the cultures she observed reveal both knowledge of and sensitivity to foreign cultures. Ginny Newton, "Travel Diaries," 1936, in possession of author.

[39] See Quigg Newton to Brunson MacChesney, January 7, 1942, Newton family papers.

[40] Quigg Newton, interview by author, September 23, 2002.

[41] Katharine Graham, *Personal History* (New York: A. A. Knopf, 1997): 106, 107.

[42] Virginia Newton, interview by author, March 4, 2004.

[43] Oscar Cox to Members of Draft Board # 8, City and County of Denver, January 26, 1942, Quigg Newton papers, box 1, Western History Collection, Denver Public Library.

[44] James Newton to Harold Stark, May 17, 1940, Newton family papers.

[45] James Newton to "Harold" (Stark), September 23, 1940, Newton family papers.

[46] James Newton to "Harold" (Stark), March 10, 1942, Newton family papers.

[47] Quigg Newton to Paul C. Smith, January 24, 1942, Quigg Newton papers, box 1, Western History Collection, Denver Public Library.

[48] Quigg Newton to William Hutchinson, February 19, 1942, Quigg Newton papers, box 1, Western History Collection, Denver Public Library.

[49] Quigg Newton to Lt. Commander L. C. Quiggle, March 23, 1942, Quigg Newton papers, box 1, Western History Collection, Denver Public Library.

[50] The engagement announcement was front-page news in the society section of *The Denver Post*. April 10, 1942.

[51] Virginia Newton, interview by author, March 3, 2004.

[52] R. M. Griffin to the Vice Chief of Naval Operations, May 25, 1942, Quigg Newton papers, box 1, Western History Collection, Denver Public Library. See also Naval Air Transport Service Command, "Statement of Mission, Tasks and Objectives of Legal (Contracts) Officer," mimeographed, undated, Newton family papers.

[53] Virginia Newton, interview by author, October 14, 2002.

[54] Quigg Newton, interview by author, September 23, 2002.

[55] *The Denver Post*, April 5, 1944.

[56] In reviewing an earlier draft of this manuscript, my esteemed colleague, Pamela Walker Laird, wrote, "This might be unfair to him. That issue didn't have the salience it gained after World War II." After some thought, I decided to leave it in. Combat duty had helped vault numerous political candidates, some of them most undistinguished, into higher office. Although presidents George Washington, Andrew Jackson, and Theodore Roosevelt might have earned their elevation to the nation's highest office even without combat duty, it is hard to imagine Zachary Taylor and Ulysses S. Grant advancing any higher in public affairs without it.

[57] Quigg Newton to Captain Don Smith, March 23, 1945, copy in Quigg Newton papers, box 1, Western History Collection, Denver Public Library.

[58] J. P. Whitney to Assistant Chief of Staff (NATS), April 14, 1945, copy in Quigg Newton papers, box 1, Western History Collection, Denver Public Library.

Chapter 5: Entering the Public Arena

[1] One can only speculate on whether Jim Newton's death influenced the couple's decision to settle "permanently" in Denver. Although Quigg missed his father, he may have felt a sense of relief that his father would not be looking over his shoulder and analyzing every move he made.

[2] Quigg Newton to Mr. McGregor, February 16, 1942, Quigg Newton papers, box 1, Western History Collection, Denver Public Library.

[3] Quigg Newton, interview by author, October 7, 2002.

[4] James Newton to Quigg Newton, October 7, 1942, Quigg Newton papers, box 4, Western History Collection, Denver Public Library.

[5] *The Denver Post*, April 10, 1946.

[6] *Rocky Mountain News*, September 5, 1946.

[7] Quigg Newton to Dave Northrup, March 19, 1946, Newton family papers.

[8] *The Denver Post*, January 21, 1947.

[9] Fortas enjoyed a brilliant legal career and a rapid rise through the ranks of the judiciary, but his nomination as chief justice of the Supreme Court was derailed when a U.S. Senate ethics probe in 1968 uncovered questionable ethics conduct. See William Manchester, *The Glory and the Dream: A Narrative History of America, 1932–1972* (Boston: Little Brown, 1973): 1138–1139.

[10] Quigg Newton, interview by author, September 30, 2002.

[11] For a good sketch of Stapleton, see George V. Kelly, *The Old Gray Mayors of Denver* (Boulder, Colo.: Pruett Publishing Company, 1974): 23–54

[12] Kelly, *The Old Gray Mayors*, 1. Historians are divided over the long-term significance of Stapleton. Although crediting him with helping to bring aviation to Denver and expanding the mountain park system, effecting flood control, and securing and developing Lowry Air Force Base, Kelly basically dismisses him as a typical machine politician, awash in graft and tolerating inefficiency and corruption among his associates. Phil Goodstein sees Stapleton as basically an opportunist who enjoyed early support from the Ku Klux Klan then avoided association with the hooded order once it had outlived its usefulness. See Goodstein, *The Seamy Side of Denver: Tall Tales of the Mile High City* (Denver: New Social Publications, 1993): 243–246. A very different assessment of Stapleton had been presented in *The Queen City: A History of Denver* (Boulder, Colo.: Pruett Publishing, 1986) by historians Lyle W. Dorsett and Michael McCarthy. They argue that Stapleton and Robert Speer were the city's two greatest mayors. Although admitting Stapleton's Klan ties—"he did what was politically advantageous" (200)—they argue that he directed the city's government in "a conservative, constructive, and efficient manner. Independent, responsible, and a good administrator, he instinctively served the interests of the power elite, freeing them to attend to business" (199). Furthermore, Dorsett and McCarthy state, "Critics who charge that he allowed the city to stagnate during those years are wrong" (200).

[13] Harland Bartholomew, "Review of Report of the Advisory Committee on Civic Planning for Denver," mimeographed (St. Louis, Mo.: Bartholomew and Associates, September, 1946): 2, Newton family papers.

[14] Undated *Denver Post* newspaper clipping (ca. August 1946).

[15] *The Denver Post*, June 9, 1946; *Rocky Mountain News*, June 17, 1946; *The Denver Post*, June 20, 1946.

[16] See, for example, a *Denver Post* story, "Builders Demand Better Street Signs," July 16, 1946.

[17] *The Denver Post*, June 20, 1946. But *The Post* urged every civic organization to apply pressure to force the administration to move more quickly. In late July, a *Post* editorial chided the chamber of commerce and the board of Realtors for not confronting Stapleton: "This inaction is said to be out of friendship of many members for the city administration. ... Loyalty has its place; so, too, does civic duty." See "Civic Paradox," July 27, 1946.

[18] *The Denver Post*, October 15, 1946.

[19] Ibid., March 21, 1947.

[20] Ibid., June 4, 1946.

[21] *Rocky Mountain News*, February 18, 1947.

[22] *The Denver Post*, February 18, 1947.

[23] Ibid., October 16, 1946.

[24] Ibid., December 16, 1946.

[25] Ibid., December 24, 1946.

[26] Ibid., April 20, 1947.

[27] Ibid., June 20, 1946.
[28] Ibid., September 6, 1946.
[29] Ibid., September 8, 1946.
[30] Ibid., September 9, 1946.
[31] Ibid., October 16, 1946 and February 7, 1947.
[32] *Cervi's Journal*, December 16, 1946.
[33] *The Denver Post*, January 27, 1947.
[34] *Rocky Mountain News*, June 29, 1946.
[35] *The Denver Post*, July 3, 1946.
[36] *Rocky Mountain News*, August 11, 1946. Burke failed to indicate whose skirts they might be hiding behind.
[37] *The Denver Post*, September 8, 1946.
[38] Ibid., October 2, 1946.
[39] *Rocky Mountain News*, March 1, 1947.
[40] *The Denver Post*, December 24, 1946 and January 12, 1947.
[41] Ibid., September 11, 1946.
[42] Quigg Newton, interview by author, October 20, 2002.
[43] Louis E. Gelt to Quigg Newton, September 13, 1946, Newton family papers.
[44] Henry W. Hough to Quigg Newton, September 13, 1946, Newton family papers.
[45] *Rocky Mountain News*, September 14, 1946.
[46] *The Denver Post*, November 23, 1946.
[47] Ibid., December 24, 1946.
[48] Quigg Newton, "Statement to the Press for Release 6:00 PM, Saturday, February 22, 1947," mimeographed, Newton family papers.
[49] "Quigg Newton's Program for Denver," pamphlet, Newton for Mayor Club, 1947.
[50] Childe Herald, "Ideas and Comments," *Rocky Mountain Herald*, March 1, 1947.
[51] Kelly, *The Old Gray Mayors of Denver*, 20.
[52] Quigg Newton, interview by author, September 30, 2002.
[53] By 2004, of course, political campaigns cost many times these dollar amounts. To conduct a serious campaign for an office such as mayor of Denver, a candidate would need at least $1,000,000, and perhaps more.
[54] Harry Combs to Quigg Newton, February 26, 1947, Newton family papers.
[55] "Second Mayoralty Study," Research Enterprises, mimeographed report, released March 12, 1947, Newton family papers.
[56] *The Denver Post*, April 23, 1947.
[57] Ibid., April 13, 1947.
[58] Ibid., April 14, 1947 and April 15, 1947.
[59] Ibid., April 27, 1947 and May 1, 1947.
[60] Ibid., April 16, 1947, April 18, 1947, and April 20, 1947.
[61] "Employee" to Mr. Newton, May 9, 1947, Newton family papers.
[62] See, for example, Quigg Newton to Ina Aulls, May 12, 1947, Newton family papers.
[63] *Rocky Mountain News*, April 23, 1947.
[64] Ibid., May 2, 1947 and May 9, 1947.
[65] *The Denver Post*, May 13, 1947.
[66] Ben Loeblein to Quigg Newton, May 22, 1947, Newton family papers.
[67] Pogue and Neal to Quigg Newton, May 26, 1947, Newton family papers.
[68] Ben Leib to Quigg Newton, May 27, 1947, Newton family papers.
[69] Elwood Brooks to Quigg Newton, May 21, 1947, Newton family papers.
[70] Earl Mann to Quigg Newton, May 21, 1947, Newton family papers.
[71] Wendell T. Liggins to Quigg Newton, June 11, 1947, Newton family papers.

Chapter 6: Grasping the Reins of Power

1 George V. Kelly, *The Old Gray Mayors of Denver* (Boulder, Colo.: Pruett Publishing, 1974): 26; Quigg Newton, interview by author, December 19, 2002.

2 "Speech by Mayor Newton to City Employees," June 17, 1947, pp.1, 3, mimeographed, Newton family papers.

3 Maxine Kurtz, "Knocking Down Bars of the Invisible Cage," unpublished memoir, 2001, p. 4, Newton family papers.

4 For a sketch of Radetsky, see his obituary in the *Rocky Mountain News*, October 15, 1967.

5 Bruce Rockwell, interview by author, February 23, 2004.

6 *The Denver Post*, June 13, 1947.

7 "The Residents ... 1500 and 1600 Blks S. Josephine to Mr. Newton, December 31, 1953, Quigg Newton papers, box 3, Western History Collection, Denver Public Library.

8 *New York Herald-Tribune*, November 12, 1947.

9 Kelly, *The Old Gray Mayors*, 27–28.

10 "From the Mayor's Office For Release after 5 PM," October 18, 1947, mimeographed statement, Quigg Newton papers, box 4, Western History Collection, Denver Public Library.

11 Edgar M. Wahlberg to Quigg Newton, November 17, 1947, Quigg Newton papers, box 3, Western History Collection, Denver Public Library.

12 Quigg Newton, "Address by Mayor Newton, Yale Law Club, April 28, 1949, p. 2, Newton family papers.

13 Quigg Newton, interview by author, December 19, 2002.

14 *Mayor's Mailbag*, April 10, 1949, transcripts in Quigg Newton papers, Western History Collection, Denver Public Library.

15 Ibid., September 5, 1948.

16 Undated newspaper clipping, Newton family papers; Quigg Newton, interview by author, January 23, 2003.

17 Kelly, *The Old Gray Mayors of Denver*, 24.

18 *Des Moines* (IA) *Tribune*, March 13, 1951.

19 "Report on Benefits Received by City Employees," May 5, 1955, Quigg Newton papers, box 3, Western History Department, Denver Public Library. Modern-day readers should bear in mind that the cost of living index has multiplied approximately sevenfold since the late 1940s.

20 Mrs. Selma Wolf to Quigg Newton, July 1, 1947, Newton family papers.

21 "From the Mayor's Office For Immediate Release," July 31, 1947, Quigg Newton papers, box 3, Western History Collection, Denver Public Library.

22 Ibid., November 21, 1948.

23 Bruce Rockwell, interview by author, February 23, 2004.

24 Ibid.

25 *Rocky Mountain News*, April 4, 1950.

26 *Mayor's Mailbag*, March 7, 1948.

27 Ibid., January 30, 1949.

28 Ibid., April 18, 1948.

29 Virginia Newton, interview by author, March 10, 2004.

30 *Mayor's Mailbag*, September 26, 1948.

31 Ibid., June 20, 1948.

32 Virginia Newton, interview by author, March 10, 2004.

33 *Mayor's Mailbag*, May 11, 1949.

34 Quigg Newton, interview by author, December 13, 2002.

35 Nan Newton, interview by author, January 31, 2003.

36 Abby Newton, interview by author, November 30, 2002.

37 Ibid., November 6, 2002; Virginia Newton, interview by author, July 9, 2003.

38 *Denver Business Journal,* June 28–July 4, 2002.
39 Quigg Newton, interview by author, September 30, 2002.

Chapter 7: Regional Visionary

1 *Working Denver: An Economic Analysis by the Denver Planning Office* (Denver: The
   Mayor's Office, 1953): 7.
2 Charles W. Eliot to Quigg Newton, October 11, 1947, Quigg Newton papers, box 3,
   Western History Collection, Denver Public Library.
3 Quigg Newton, interview by author, December 19, 2002.
4 See *Mayor's Mailbag,* December 26, 1948, 5–7.
5 "From the Mayor's Office for Release After 5:00 PM," February 14, 1948, copy in Quigg
   Newton papers, box 3, Western History Collection, Denver Public Library.
6 *Intermountain Jewish News,* April 14, 1995.
7 *Mayor's Mailbag,* October 2, 1949.
8 Quigg Newton, interview by author, March 5, 2003.
9 Apparently, Zeckendorf thought very highly of Newton. When Newton left the city to
   become vice president of the Ford Foundation in the mid-1950s, Zeckendorf offered him
   a job in his own corporate empire. Quigg Newton, interview by author, March 5, 2003.
10 Quigg Newton, interview by author, December 12, 2002.
11 Newton described the trip in detail in his regularly scheduled Sunday afternoon radio talk
   shortly after his return. See *Mayor's Mailbag,* March 13, 1949.
12 In 2003, Denver International Airport hosted 37.5 million arriving and departing passengers. This total was actually a drop from its peak year, 2000, when 38.8 million
   passengers passed through the facility. See the *Atlanta Constitution,* February 9, 2004.
13 Quigg Newton, interview by author, November 13, 2002.
14 *Mayor's Mailbag,* May 1, 1949.
15 Quigg Newton, interview by author, March 5, 2003.
16 *Rocky Mountain News,* December 16, 1953.
17 American Municipal Association, "Problems and Prospects in National Committee of
   Defense Planning" (mimeographed November 1954), Quigg Newton papers, box 3,
   Western History Collection, Denver Public Library.
18 John Buchanan, "City Hall," *The Denver Post,* April 11, 1955.
19 Quigg Newton, interview by author, November 13, 2002.
20 For a more in-depth discussion of these issues at the national level, see Mark S. Foster, *A
   Nation on Wheels: The Automobile in American Culture Since 1945* (Belmont, Calif.:
   Thompson Wadsworth, 2002): chapter 1.
21 Ibid., chapter 2.
22 Quigg Newton, interview by author, November 13, 2002.
23 *Mayor's Mailbag,* June 6, 1948.
24 *Rocky Mountain News,* June 3, 1950.
25 The literature on the decline of mass transit and the emergence of the automobile in the
   postwar years is massive. Much of it is contentious and one-sided. One school of historians and public policy analysts condemns the automobile industry and highway
   lobby as venal and corrupt, fantasizing about a utopian world of efficient mass transit that, in fact, never existed. Another group steadfastly defends the highway lobby
   and automobile industry as simply providing what the public wanted. For a refresh-
   ingly even-handed overview of the emergence of public policy regarding mass transit
   during these years, see George M. Smerk, *The Federal Role in Urban Mass Transportation* (Bloomington and Indianapolis: Indiana University Press, 1991): 43–55.
   For another recent synthesis of the subject, see Foster, *A Nation on Wheels.*
26 Mark H. Rose, *Interstate: Express Highway Politics, 1939–1989,* rev. ed. (Knoxville:
   University of Tennessee Press, 1990).

[27] *Mayor's Mailbag*, October 28, 1951.

[28] Quigg Newton, interview by author, November 13, 2002.

[29] *Rocky Mountain News*, June 15, 1947. According to Denver historian Thomas J. Noel, Campbell donated his services to the city as a $1 per-year man during Newton's years as mayor.

[30] Henry A. Barnes, *The Man with the Red and Green Eyes: The Autobiography of Henry A. Barnes, Traffic Commissioner, New York City* (New York: E. P. Dutton, 1965): 72, 75–84.

[31] Virginia Newton, interview by author, March 10, 2004.

[32] Barnes, *The Man with the Red and Green Eyes*, 87–88.

[33] Ibid., 88–98.

[34] For an excellent analysis of this political issue at the national level, see Robert M. Fogelson, *Downtown: Its Rise and Fall, 1880–1950* (New Haven: Yale University Press, 2001) 282–304.

[35] "Advance Release from the Mayor's Office, after 5 PM," July 19, 1947, Quigg Newton papers, box 3, Western History Department, Denver Public Library.

[36] *Mayor's Mailbag*, October 23, 1949.

[37] Ibid., March 26, 1950 and December 17, 1950.

[38] Quigg Newton, interview by author, November 13, 2003.

[39] "A Summary Report of Major Accomplishments City and County of Denver, 1947–1955, Management Office, June 15, 1955," Quigg Newton papers, box 3, Western History Department, Denver Public Library.

[40] William C. Jones and Kenton Forrest, *Denver: A Pictorial History* (Boulder, Colo.: Pruett Publishing, 1973): 171.

[41] Rose, *Interstate*, 30.

[42] "From the Mayor's Office for Immediate Release," June 26, 1947, Quigg Newton papers, box 3, Western History Collection, Denver Public Library.

[43] "Basic Facts on the Valley Highway," undated mimeographed report, Quigg Newton papers, box 3, Western History Department, Denver Public Library.

[44] Ernest Koutnik to Quigg Newton, May 31, 1947, Quigg Newton papers, box 3, Western History Department, Denver Public Library.

[45] *Rocky Mountain News*, June 12, 1947.

[46] "The Denver-Boulder Turnpike: Chronology and Interesting Facts," undated mimeographed report, Newton family papers.

[47] *Mayor's Mailbag*, May 7, 1950.

[48] Ibid., April 27, 1952.

[49] Ibid., January 30, 1949.

[50] Maxine Kurtz, "Knocking Down Bars of the Invisible Cage," unpublished memoir, 2001, 9–10, Newton family papers.

[51] Quigg Newton, "City Club Speech, April 2, 2002, p. 4, Newton family papers.

[52] Tom Noel, "Health Crusader Florence Sabin Should Be Hero to All Coloradans," undated newspaper clipping, Newton family papers.

[53] Quigg Newton, interview by author, October 7, 2002; for a detailed account of the episode, see Kelly, *The Old Gray Mayors of Denver*, 38–44.

[54] Jerry B. Tillman to Edward O. Greer, March 3, 1954, Quigg Newton papers, box 3, Western History Collection, Denver Public Library.

[55] *Mayor's Mailbag*, January 22, 1950.

[56] McEnroe, *Denver Renewed*, unpublished manuscript, pp. 21–22. Quigg Newton papers, box 3, Western History Collection, Denver Public Library.

[57] Helen Peterson to Quigg Newton, May 6, 1954, Quigg Newton papers, box 3, Western History Collection, Denver Public Library.

[58] *Mayor's Mailbag*, February 13, 1949, Quigg Newton papers, box 3, Western History Collection, Denver Public Library.

[59] Helen Peterson, undated interview (ca. 1994), p. 5, Newton family papers.

[60] *Rocky Mountain News*, May 16, 1951.

[61] *Philadelphia Inquirer* magazine, July 22, 1951.

[62] "For Release on Delivery 6:15 P.M. EST," mimeographed December 28, 1948, Newton family papers.

[63] Quigg Newton, interview by author, January 23, 2003.

[64] "Nichols" to J. Edgar Hoover, office memorandum, April 18, 1950, Newton family papers.

[65] Unidentified agent to "Honorable_____, the assistant to the president, June 23, 1953," Newton family papers. Unfortunately, Newton died before I could ask him if he had ever joined the organization in question.

[66] *Mayor's Mailbag*, February 19, 1950.

[67] For coverage of the campaign for U.S. Senate, see chapter 8.

[68] *The Denver Post*, April 10, 1955.

[69] *Cervi's Rocky Mountain Journal*, September 24, 1953; undated clipping, "Mile High Observations" by Gene Cervi.

[70] See "Past, Present and Future," *Cervi's Journal*, September 20, 1967.

[71] Lyle W. Dorsett, *The Queen City: A History of Denver* (Boulder, Colo.: Pruett Publishing Company, 1977): 253.

[72] *The Denver Post*, April 1, 1995.

Chapter 8: Dead End

[1] Quigg Newton, interview by author, October 30, 2002.

[2] *The Denver Post*, April 2, 1954.

[3] Undated, unidentified newspaper column, Newton family papers.

[4] Mark S. Foster, *The Denver Bears: From Sandlots to Sellouts* (Boulder, Colo.: Pruett Publishing, 1983): 51–53, 57.

[5] *The Denver Post*, April 2, 1954.

[6] Ibid.

[7] Ibid. and *Pueblo Star*, April 2, 1954.

[8] *The Denver Post*, April 4, 1954.

[9] Ibid., April 7, 1954.

[10] Ibid.

[11] Ibid.

[12] Perkin's sketches of Newton and Carroll were taken from undated *Rocky Mountain News* clippings (ca. April 1954) in the Newton family papers.

[13] *Durango Herald*, April 11, 1954.

[14] *The Denver Post*, April 25, 1954.

[15] Ibid., May 7, 1954.

[16] *Rocky Mountain News*, May 9, 1954.

[17] Johnson to Newton, May 17, 1954, Quigg Newton papers, box 3, Western History Collection, Denver Public Library.

[18] "Subscriptions Received During 1953," undated manuscript, Newton family papers.

[19] Mahlon Thatcher to Dick Davis, May 28, 1954, Newton family papers.

[20] Tyson Dines to Richard M. Davis, June 9, 1954, Newton family papers.

[21] Richard M. Davis to Robert F. Newton, September 2, 1954, Newton family papers.

[22] Thomas K. Younge to Richard M. Davis, September 3, 1954, Newton family papers.

[23] Morrison Shafroth to Quigg Newton, June 7, 1954, Newton family papers.

[24] "Suggestions for Speech," undated, mimeographed ca. June 1954, Newton family papers.

[25] *The Denver Post*, May 20, 1954.

[26] *Rocky Mountain News*, June 29, 1954.

[27] Ibid., July 6, 1954.

28 *The Denver Post*, July 12, 1954.
29 Ibid., July 29, 1954.
30 Virginia Newton to author, notes on first draft of this manuscript, in possession of author.
31 *Rocky Mountain News*, August 11, 1954.
32 *The Denver Post*, August 18, 1954.
33 "Speech by Quigg Newton for Release at 8:00 PM, Wednesday, August 18, 1954," mimeographed, Newton family papers.
34 *The Denver Post*, August 25, 1954.
35 Ibid.
36 Ibid., August 26, 1954.
37 Ibid.
38 Ibid., August 28, 1954.
39 *Rocky Mountain News*, August 25, 1954.
40 "Text of Quigg Newton's Address to be Given Before the City Club, Tuesday, August 31," mimeographed, Newton family papers.
41 "Period of Old Age," mimeographed, undated speech, Quigg Newton papers, box 3, Western History Collection, Denver Public Library.
42 After Franklin D. Roosevelt's vice president for two terms, John Nance Garner of Texas, left the administration, Roosevelt selected Wallace to run with him against Wendell Willkie in 1940. Wallace's outspoken liberalism alienated many party regulars, however, and Roosevelt was encouraged to replace Wallace after one term. Ultimately, that led to the choice of Harry Truman to run on the Democratic ticket with Roosevelt in 1944.
43 *Rocky Mountain News*, September 3, 1954.
44 *The Denver Post*, September 8, 1954.
45 *The Denver Post*, September 3, 1954; "Text of Newton's Address at 8 P.M., September 7 on the Gold Nugget TV Network: KOA-TV, Denver; KRDO-TV, Colorado Springs; KLSJ-TV, Pueblo," mimeographed, Quigg Newton papers, box 3, Western History Collection, Denver Public Library.
46 "Text of Address by Quigg Newton, Democratic Candidate for U.S. Senator, on KBTV, Denver and KKTV, Colorado Springs, 8 P.M., Thursday, September 9," mimeographed, Newton family papers.
47 Bruce Rockwell, interview by author, July 28, 2003.
48 *Rocky Mountain News*, September 11, 1954.
49 *The Denver Post*, September 12, 1954.
50 Ibid., September 15, 1954. Shafroth was evidently a close student of history. Lincoln lost a popular vote of the people in 1832 when he ran for the Illinois state legislature. See David H. Donald, *Lincoln* (New York: Simon and Schuster, 1995): 45–46.
51 Quigg Newton, interview by author, January 23, 2003.
52 Ed Johnson to Quigg Newton, September 17, 1954, Quigg Newton papers, box 3, Western History Collection, Denver Public Library.
53 Kenneth C. Penfold to Quigg Newton, September 15, 1954, Quigg Newton papers, box 3, Western History Collection, Denver Public Library.
54 Ben Cherrington to Quigg Newton, September 24, 1954, Quigg Newton papers, box 3, Western History Collection, Denver Public Library.
55 Walter A. Gail to Quigg Newton, September 16, 1954, Quigg Newton papers, box 3, Western History Collection, Denver Public Library.
56 Bruce Rockwell, interview by author, July 28, 2003.
57 Hugh B. Terry to William B. Lewis, August 4, 1955, Newton family papers.
58 *Rocky Mountain News*, February 25, 1956.
59 See, for example, John J. Sullivan to Quigg Newton, June 20, 1955, Newton family papers.
60 Robert H. Hudson to Quigg Newton, September 5, 1955, Newton family papers.
61 Quigg Newton, interview by author, October 14, 2002.

[62] Unidentified and undated newspaper clipping. The interviewer was Max Goldberg, a Denver-area columnist.

[63] Quigg Newton, "Public Relations Problems and Policies," confidential mimeographed internal memo, June 1, 1956, pp. 2, 3, and 4, Newton family papers.

[64] Quigg Newton, interview by author, October 14, 2002.

[65] Unidentified and undated newspaper clipping. The interviewer was Max Goldberg, a Denver area columnist.

[66] *Rocky Mountain News*, February 26, 1956.

[67] John J. McCloy to Rowan Gaither, November 7, 1956, Newton family papers.

Chapter 9: The Halls of Academia

[1] Ward Darley to Quigg Newton, December 8, 1955, president's office papers, series I, box 102, folder 6, Archives, Norlin Library, University of Colorado at Boulder.

[2] *Rocky Mountain News*, October 28, 1956.

[3] Frederick S. Allen, et. al., *The University of Colorado* (New York: Harcourt Brace Javonovich, 1976): 184.

[4] See Dayton D. McKean, *The Boss: the Hague Machine in Action* (Boston: Houghton Mifflin, 1940).

[5] *Rocky Mountain News*, October 28, 1956.

[6] See Allen, et. al., *The University of Colorado*.

[7] Mrs. Blue may have been pressured by Bromley, or perhaps by Republican Party officials, to vote against Newton's appointment. Newton, of course, had declared himself a Democrat before running for the party's nomination to United States Senate in 1954, and many Republicans resented him. Until very recently, Mrs. Blue had apparently held positive personal feelings for Ginny and Quigg. Before Quigg was formally offered the position, one of Ginny's good friends, Susan Marsh, wrote to Darley, "Virginia Blue, an old friend of mine, told me I wouldn't do any harm if an ordinary citizen should write a personal letter on behalf of Quigg Newton." Susan Marsh to Ward Darley, October 15, 1956, president's office papers, series I, box 102, folder 6, Archives, Norlin Library, University of Colorado at Boulder.

[8] Quigg Newton, interview by author, October 7, 2002.

[9] Ibid.

[10] Leonard Kinsell to Quigg Newton, October 29, 1956, Newton family papers. Former university president Robert L. Stearns was also convinced that the regents would make the appointment unanimous, just as he was convinced that the appointment of Newton was a wise move and that Newton would do a splendid job. See Robert L. Stearns to Ward Darley, November 1, 1956, Newton family papers.

[11] Quigg Newton, interview by author, October 7, 2002.

[12] *The Denver Post*, undated newspaper editorial, November 1956; *Rocky Mountain News*, undated newspaper editorial, November 1956, both in Newton family papers.

[13] Ward Darley to Quigg Newton, November 4, 1956, president's office papers, series I, box 103, folder 6, Archives, Norlin Library, University of Colorado at Boulder.

[14] Laurence M. Gould to Quigg Newton, November 5, 1956, Newton family papers.

[15] John C. Banks to Newton, November 6, 1956, and Newton to Banks, November 12, 1956, both in Newton family papers.

[16] Speech at "School and University Conference" (April 1959), mimeographed, Newton family papers.

[17] Quigg Newton to William O. Douglas, November 12, 1956, Newton family papers.

[18] Quigg Newton to Arthur B. Darling, November 30, 1956, Newton family papers.

[19] Quigg Newton to Louis T. Benezet, November 30, 1956, Newton family papers.

[20] Quigg Newton, interview by author, November 20, 2002.

[21] *The Denver Post*, December 6, 1956.

[22] Quigg Newton, interview by author, November 30, 2002.

[23] "Persons Entertained in President's House," mimeographed 1961, Newton family papers.

[24] Quigg Newton, interview by author, December 13, 2002.

[25] Quigg Newton, interview by author, February 26, 2003.

[26] *Boulder Daily Camera*, May 24, 1957.

[27] Virginia Newton, telephone interview by author, March 23, 2004; *Colorado Daily*, January 17, 1958.

[28] Untitled Speech to the Colorado Legislature, (ca. December 1956), pp. 5, 6.

[29] This translates into about $46,000 in 2000 dollars.

[30] *Rocky Mountain News*, December 11, 1956.

[31] Untitled Speech, 7.

[32] *Rocky Mountain News*, December 11, 1956.

[33] *The Denver Post*, April 6, 1986.

[34] Ibid.

[35] Quigg Newton, interview by author, November 30, 2002.

[36] *Boulder Daily Camera*, April 9, 1959.

[37] Quigg Newton, interview by author, October 7, 2002

[38] Quigg Newton, interview by author, November 20, 2002.

[39] Calvin Grieder, untitled talk at AAUP Meeting with the Board of Regents, January 1, 1961, mimeographed, pp. 5–6, Newton family papers.

[40] *Boulder Daily Camera*, December 11, 1958.

[41] See Glenn Terrell to Quigg Newton, December 16, 1960, Newton family papers.

[42] Quigg Newton, interview by author, October 21, 2002.

[43] William Manchester, *The Glory and the Dream: a Narrative History of America, 1932–1972* (Boston: Little Brown, 1973): 792, 819.

[44] William Shakespeare, *Julius Caesar*, Act IV, scene 2, line 96.

[45] "The National Center for Atmospheric Research (NCAR) Background—for the Display Designer of the Newton Exhibit," undated paper, Newton family papers.

[46] *Rocky Mountain News*, August 25, 1960.

[47] Copies of three undated and unsigned letters, Newton family papers.

[48] Lewis M. Branscomb, "The Joint Institute for Laboratory Astrophysics: A Fully Integrated Partnership Between Government Laboratory and University," *Education and Federal Laboratory-University Relationships, Proceedings of a Symposium, October 29–31, 1968*, sponsored by the Federal Council for Science and Technology and the American Council on Education (Washington, D.C.: Smithsonian Institution, 1969): 42–44, 46.

[49] David A. Lind to Quigg Newton, February 28, 1997, Newton family papers.

[50] Undated clipping in *The Denver Post* (ca. November, 1961), Newton family papers.

[51] Dr. Robert J. Glaser, interview by author, April 18, 2003.

[52] Allen, et. al., *The University of Colorado*, 188.

[53] Quigg Newton speech, "National Fund for Medical Education," mimeographed April 1959, Newton family papers.

[54] Dr. Robert Glaser, interview by author, April 18, 2003.

[55] Dr. Robert Glaser, "University of Colorado: The Quigg Newton Years and the Medical Center," manuscript written on September 2, 1997, Newton family papers.

[56] Dr. Richard Krugman, interview by author, March 14, 2003. For more information, see also Mary E. Helfer, Ruth S. Kempe, and Richard D. Krugman (eds.), *The Battered Child Syndrome*, 5th ed. (Chicago and London: University of Chicago Press, 1997).

[57] Quigg Newton, interview by author, February 12, 2003.

[58] Dr. Robert Glaser, interview by author, April 18, 2003.

[59] Quigg Newton to Morrison Shafroth, July 21, 1958, Newton family papers.

[60] Ibid.

Chapter 10: Storm Clouds over Boulder

1. For background information on the history of football at the university, see James Whiteside, *Colorado: A Sports History* (Niwot: University Press of Colorado, 2000): chapter 6.
2. *Rocky Mountain News*, January 24, 1959.
3. Ibid. Likely at the behest of his boss, Jack Foster, who by the early 1960s had become an arch foe of the Newton administration and virtually everything it stood for, Nelson became a staunch defender of Bromley during the investigation of coach Sonny Grandelius. See his column, *Rocky Mountain News*, March 16, 1962.
4. Quotes from football players are all from the *Rocky Mountain News*, January 24, 1959.
5. William E. Davis, *Glory Colorado: A History of the University of Colorado, 1858–1963* (Boulder, Colo.: Pruett Press, 1963): 721.
6. *The Denver Post*, February 9, 1959.
7. Whiteside, *Colorado: A Sports History*, 217–218.
8. Ibid., 218.
9. Quigg Newton, interview by author, October 21, 2002.
10. Minutes, regents of the University of Colorado, special meeting, March 17, 1962, p. 8.
11. Herrick Roth to Sonny Grandelius, September 15, 1959, president's office papers, series I, box 30, folder 1, Archives, Norlin Library, University of Colorado at Boulder.
12. Whiteside, *Colorado: A Sports History*, 219.
13. *Colorado Daily*, March 20, 1962.
14. *Rocky Mountain News,* March 16, 1962.
15. Whiteside, *Colorado: A Sports History*, 219. For extended analysis of the football scandal at the University of Colorado, see Bill Furlong, "Anatomy of a College Recruiting Scandal," *Sport* 34 (November 1962): 14–17, 88–92.
16. William E. Davis, "Colorado Football's Galloping Disaster: Memoirs of a Big-time Coach," *Harper's Magazine* (October 1965): 52.
17. Minutes, regents of the University of Colorado, special meeting, March 17, 1962, p. 21.
18. Quigg Newton, interview by author, October 20, 2002.
19. Don Saunders to Quigg Newton, August 22, 1975, Newton family papers.
20. Copies of unsolicited remarks, undated, Newton family papers.
21. Best to Richard J. Bernick, July 25, 1961, Newton family papers.
22. Undated statement, Newton family papers.
23. Calvin Grieder, "Talk at AAUP Meeting with Board of Regents and Administration," University Club, January 1, 1961, pp. 4, 5, Newton family papers.
24. Edward Rozek to President Newton, April 23, 1959, regents' papers, University of Colorado.
25. Blaine Mercer to Edward Rozek, April 23, 1959, and Gordon Barker to President Newton, copies in regents' papers, University of Colorado. Rigorous external review of scholarly work by candidates for promotion and tenure is now routine at virtually every respected university in the nation.
26. President Newton Remarks to Faculty Senate, May 16, 1961, memorandum on Edward Rozek, associate professor of political science, undated mimeographed manuscript, pp. 7–8, Newton family papers.
27. Earl A. Wolvington to Quigg Newton, November 7, 1961, president's office papers, series I, box 92, folder 2, Archives, Norlin Library, University of Colorado at Boulder.
28. Earl A. Wolvington to Quigg Newton, November 10, 1961, Newton family papers.
29. *The Denver Post*, January 26, 1962.
30. *Colorado Daily*, February 12, 1962.
31. Buena Vista *Republican*, February 2, 1962.
32. *Rocky Mountain News*, January 27, 1962.
33. Mimeographed memo from Woody Hewitt to Earl [Wolvington], undated, Newton family papers.

34 Ibid. At the bottom of the Hewitt memo is a comment from an unidentified writer, "Any ideas or suggestions as to authenticity, validity, etc."

35 Mimeographed memo, January 30, 1962, Newton family papers.

36 *Colorado Gadfly*, December 1, 1961.

37 *Colorado Daily*, December 1, 1961.

38 *The Boulder Daily Camera* stated that the Young Socialists "were given" the front-row seats. The *Rocky Mountain News* stated that they "swarmed in" and grabbed them.

39 "Memorandum on Barry Goldwater, Republican Senator, Arizona," October 19, 1963, pp. 1–3, Newton family papers.

40 Aurora *Star*, March 8, 1962; *Rocky Mountain News,* March 10, 1962.

41 "Memorandum on Barry Goldwater," pp. 5, 8.

42 *Rocky Mountain News*, March 10, 1962; "Memorandum on Barry Goldwater," p. 8.

43 Quigg Newton to Barry Goldwater, May 2, 1962; Quigg Newton to Gordon Allott, May 2, 1962, both in Newton family papers.

44 Jeff Hofman, "Origins and Motives of the Political Assault on James Quigg Newton, President of the University of Colorado, 1956–1963," senior thesis, Department of History, 1992, p. 31–33. Hofman observed that the newspaper suspended publication a year later, after Newton left office. It had, by then, achieved its primary purpose. See Ibid., 54–55.

45 Mitcham quoted in Lawrence G. Weiss, "Goldwater and Colorado U," *The Nation* (December 8, 1962): 403.

46 Ibid. On September 28, the Board of Publications wrote a lengthy letter to Newton, which basically exonerated Althen. Although acknowledging that the editor was skirting close to the edge of journalistic license, the board, which consisted of six faculty members, assumed considerable responsibility for the situation. The chair noted that five of its six members were new to their responsibilities, and for this reason they might not have recognized their obligation to at the very least weigh in guidance for the editorial staff. See William J. Hanna to Quigg Newton, September 28, 1962, Newton family papers.

47 "Memorandum on Barry Goldwater," 10.

48 *Boulder Daily Camera*, October 2, 1962.

49 "Memorandum on Barry Goldwater," 11–12.

50 Weiss, "Goldwater and Colorado U," 404; *Rocky Mountain News*, October 9, 1962.

51 Weiss, "Goldwater and Colorado U," 404.

52 Ibid.

53 Robert W. Oliver to Quigg Newton, November 11, 1962; support letters from friends were numerous. See also Philip Wylie to Quigg Newton, November 2, 1962. Both are in Newton family papers.

54 John F. Kennedy telegram to Quigg Newton, April 23, 1961, Newton family papers.

55 Quigg Newton, interview by author, February 26, 2003.

56 Hofman, "Origins and Motives," 16.

57 "Charles D. Bromley," mimeographed memo, December 1962, p. 8, Newton family papers.

58 *The Denver Post*, August 29, 1962.

59 Ibid., August 30, 1962.

60 Ibid., October 13, 1962.

61 Ibid., October 23, 1962.

62 *Rocky Mountain News*, November 8, 1962.

63 *The Denver Post*, January 20, 1963.

64 *Rocky Mountain News*, April 14, 1964; *The Denver Post*, April 15, 1964.

65 Quigg Newton to Don Saunders, April 22, 1964, Newton family papers.

66 Quigg Newton, interview by author, October 21, 2002.

67 Lloyd Worner to Quigg Newton, October 12, 1962, Newton family papers.

68 Rufus Putney to Quigg Newton, November 6, 1962, Newton family papers.

69 *Arapahoe Herald,* December 11, 1962.

70 Robert L. Stearns to Quigg Newton, December 28, 1962, Newton family papers.

71 "Special Report on the CU Controversy," *The Denver Post,* December 6, 1962.

72 *The Denver Post,* March 2, 1963.

73 Ibid., March 3, 1963.

74 Ibid., March 24, 1963.

75 Irving Seidman, *Oswald Tippo and the Early Promise of the University of Massachusetts: A Profile in His Own Words* (Amherst, Mass.: Friends of the University Library, 2002): 36–37.

76 Ibid., January 20, 1963. See also "Transcript of proceedings relative to personnel matters, as recorded by Mr. Irving Seidman," minutes, meeting of the regents of the University of Colorado, January 19, 1963.

77 Lowell Brooks, "The University and Political Mud," *Colorado Engineer* (March 1963): 8.

78 *The Denver Post,* May 5, 1968.

79 Quigg Newton to Henry W. Sherman, April 2, 1963, Newton family papers.

80 Quigg Newton to Wilmarth S. Lewis, December 18, 1963, Newton family papers.

81 Quigg Newton to Milton H. Elefant, May 24, 1963, Newton family papers, May 24, 1963.

82 Mrs. Edward Kingery to Quigg Newton, June 22, 1963, Newton family papers.

83 Quigg Newton to Mrs. Edward Kingery, September 4, 1963, Newton family papers.

84 *The Denver Post,* March 5, 1963.

85 *The New York Times,* April 14, 1963; John Ogilvy to Quigg Newton, February 26, 1963, Newton family papers.

86 "Memorandum on Progress University of Colorado, 1956–1962," mimeographed report, December 1962, pp. 1, 7, 18, 21, 26, 27, Newton family papers.

87 William E. Davis, "A Personal Remembrance: The Quigg Newton Years, 1956–1963," June 20, 1997, Newton family papers.

88 For coverage of the Smiley years at the university, see Frederick S. Allen, et. al, *The University of Colorado, 1876–1976* (New York and London: Harcourt Brace Jovanovich, 1976); 209–236.

Chapter 11: Medical Visionary

1 Quigg Newton to James Webb, October 2, 1963, Commonwealth Fund papers, board of directors, series 7, box 6, folder 49, Commonwealth Fund Archives, Rockefeller Research Center.

2 Quigg Newton, introductory remarks for Dr. David Hamburg at a cocktail reception, October 28, 1974, p. 1, Newton family papers.

3 Commonwealth Fund, Financial Statements and Supplemental Schedules for the Year Ended June 30, 1963 and Accountants' Report, p. 2; and Commonwealth Fund Financial Statements, Supplemental Schedules, and Summaries for the Years Ended June 30, 1975, and Auditor's Opinion, p. 3.; both in Commonwealth Fund Archives, Rockefeller Research Center.

4 Virginia Newton, telephone interview by author, May 27, 2004.

5 Abby Newton to author, undated (ca. March, 2004).

6 Quigg Newton, interview by author, December 13, 2002.

7 Carl E. Taylor to Quigg Newton, November 1, 1966, Newton family papers.

8 Quigg Newton to Samuel B. Kirkwood, October 24, 1966, Newton family papers.

9 "Itinerary Mr. and Mrs. J. Quigg Newton, Jr., January 19, 1968—February 4, 1968, Newton family papers; Virginia Newton, telephone interview by author, February 4, 2004.

10 A. McGehee Harvey and Susan L. Abrams, "For the Welfare of Mankind; The Commonwealth Fund and American Medicine" (Baltimore: Johns Hopkins University Press, 1986): 405–406; direct quote from 407.

11 Ibid., 365.

12 Paul Starr, *The Social Transformation of American Medicine* (New York: Basic Books, 1983): 347.

13 Ibid., 355, 358–359.

14 Robert J. Glaser, "The Medical Deanship," *Journal of Medical Education* 44 (December, 1969): 1119.

15 Quigg Newton, "Recommendations Concerning the Fund's Future Programs in the Health Field," presented to the board, November 22, 1964, box 22, Folder 183, Commonwealth Fund Archives, Rockefeller Research Center.

16 Starr, *The Social Transformation of American Medicine*, 335.

17 Ibid., 360.

18 For more on the Kaiser health care initiatives, see Mark S. Foster, *Henry J. Kaiser: Builder in the Modern American West* (Austin: University of Texas Press, 1989): chapter 13 and Rickey L. Hendricks, *A Model for National Health Care: The History of Kaiser Permanente* (New Brunswick, NJ: Rutgers University Press, 1991).

19 Harvey and Abrams, "For the Welfare of Mankind," 349.

20 Ibid., 350–351.

21 Ibid., 354–355.

22 A. A. Bliss, *The Physicians Assistant—Today and Tomorrow*, 2nd ed. (Cambridge: Ballinger Publishing Co., 1975): 1–2; W. G. Reiss, et. al., "The Current Status of Physicians Assistants," *Maryland State Medical Journal* 33 (1984): 288.

23 Harvey and Abrams, "For the Welfare of Mankind," 367–368.

24 Ibid., 359.

25 Ibid., 360.

26 "Summary of the Achievements of the Center for the Study of Sex Education in Medicine, 1968–1974," pp. 1–9, Commonwealth Fund Archives, Rockefeller Center; Harvey and Abrams, "For the Welfare of Mankind," 360–362.

27 Harvey and Abrams, "For the Welfare of Mankind," 377.

28 "NAACP Interview with Mr. Roy Wilkins, Secretary, and Dr. Marcel, May 12, 1965," by Quigg Newton, series 7, box 6, folder 49, Commonwealth Fund Archives, Rockefeller Research Center.

29 Harvey and Abrams, "For the Welfare of Mankind," 458.

30 Ibid., 452.

31 Quigg Newton to Hulbert "Huck" Aldrich, Chairman of the Board of the Commonwealth Fund, February 3, 1976, Commonwealth Fund Archives, Rockefeller Research Center.

32 C. Henry Kempe, *The Battered Child*.

33 Harvey and Abrams, "For the Welfare of Mankind," 413.

34 Ibid., 416–417.

35 See Kingman Brewster to Quigg Newton, June 27, 1966 and "Draft, Statement of Goals and Objectives of the Yale—New Haven Medical Center," March 14, 1969, both in Commonwealth Fund Archives, Rockefeller Research Center.

36 Harvey and Abrams, "For the Welfare of Mankind," 430.

37 Florence S. Wald to A. McGehee Harvey, March 8, 1983, quoted in Harvey and Abrams, "For the Welfare of Mankind," 430–431.

38 Leon E. Rosenberg interview with A. McGehee Harvey, December 3, 1982, quoted in Harvey and Abrams, "For the Welfare of Mankind," 420.

39 Harvey and Abrams, "For the Welfare of Mankind," 431.

40 Ibid., 432.

41 Quigg Newton to Jane Goodall and David Hamburg, November 15, 1974, Commonwealth Fund Archives, Rockefeller Research Center.

42 Quigg Newton to Carleton B. Chapman, May 6, 1975, series 2, sub-series 3, box 21, file 173, Commonwealth Fund Archives, Rockefeller Research Center.

[43] Quigg Newton, "The Harkness Fellowship Program," mimeographed January 23, 1974, pp. 5, 9, Quigg Newton Files, series 2, sub-series 3, box 18, folder 141, Commonwealth Fund Archives, Rockefeller Research Center.

[44] Quigg Newton to Sir Eric Ashby, November 10, 1967, Quigg Newton Files, series 2, sub-series 3, box 18, folder 142, Commonwealth Fund Papers, Rockefeller Research Center.

[45] Gottfried van Benthem van den Bergh to Malcolm Aldrich, April 19, 1968, Commonwealth Fund Archives, Rockefeller Research Center.

[46] Quigg Newton, interview by author, February 6, 2003.

[47] "Harkness Fellowship Program Administrative Cost," mimeographed memo, undated (ca. 1976), Commonwealth Fund Archives, Rockefeller Research Center.

[48] Harvey and Abrams, "For the Welfare of Mankind," 440–441.

[49] Quigg Newton, interview by author, January 29, 2003.

[50] Harvey and Abrams, "For the Welfare of Mankind," 462–463.

[51] Quigg Newton, interview by author, January 29, 2003.

[52] Quigg Newton to Dr. Robert L. Johnston, July 31, undated letter (ca. 1977), Newton family papers.

[53] Carl Chapman to Quigg Newton, November 16, 1984, Newton family papers.

[54] Quigg Newton, interview by author, January 29, 2003.

Chapter 12: Winding Down

[1] Quigg Newton to Preston S. Cutler, July 6, 1976, Newton family papers.

[2] Preston S. Cutler to Quigg Newton, July 13, 1976 and Preston S. Cutler to Quigg Newton, August 2, 1976, both in Newton family papers.

[3] Quigg Newton, interview by author, February 12, 2003.

[4] Virginia Newton, interview by author, February 12, 2003.

[5] Quigg Newton to Gardner Lindsey, May 15, 1978, Newton family papers

[6] Ibid.

[7] Ibid.

[8] For more information, see Mark S. Foster, *Henry J. Kaiser: Builder in the Modern American West* (Austin: University of Texas Press, 1989), chapter 13; and Rickey L. Hendricks, *A Model for National Health Care: the History of Kaiser Permanente* (New Brunswick, NJ: Rutgers University Press, 1991).

[9] Robert J. Glaser to Quigg Newton, August 16, 1978, Newton family papers.

[10] Richard M. Davis, "Confidential Memorandum," May 4, 1966 and Richard M. Davis to Quigg Newton, May 23, 1966, both in Newton family papers.

[11] Quigg Newton, interview by author, February 12, 2003.

[12] Quigg Newton memo to "All Personnel," undated (ca. 1986), Newton family papers.

[13] *The Denver Post*, September 13, 1981. Newton described himself as "pro-growth" in the 1980s, but in several conversations with the author in 2002 and 2003, he stated his belief that growth in the 1990s and early twenty-first century had gotten out of control, with far too little consideration for future sources of water or energy, too little planning for traffic congestion, and too little concern for the deteriorating quality of life along the Front Range.

[14] Robert F. Leduc to Quigg Newton, February 14, 1983, Newton family papers.

[15] Robert W. Schrier to Quigg Newton, July 1, 1983, Newton family papers.

[16] M. Roy Schwartz to Quigg Newton, May 4, 1981, Newton family papers.

[17] Quigg Newton, interview by author, February 12, 2003.

[18] Richard J. Bernick to Quigg Newton, March 2, 1990, Newton family papers.

[19] Untitled, mimeographed draft endorsement (ca. 1989), Newton family papers.

[20] "The University Council: Report of the Committee on Medical Affairs," May 2, 1980, mimeographed, Newton family papers.

[21] Quigg Newton, interview by author, November 13, 2002.

[22] Quigg Newton to James A. Vohs, July 14, 1981, Newton family papers.

[23] James A. Vohs to Quigg Newton, September 27, 1981, Newton family papers.

[24] Quigg Newton to "Maggie" (Mahoney), December 12, 1989, Newton family papers.

[25] Quigg Newton to Margaret Mahoney, June 6, 1989, Newton family papers.

[26] Douglas E. Lorenz to Quigg Newton, July 7, 1956; Quigg Newton to Douglas E. Lorenz, July 30, 1956; David Chase to Quigg Newton, August 9, 2002; all in Newton family papers.

[27] Quigg Newton to C. Davis Weyerhaeuser, June 17, 1988, Newton family papers.

[28] Josh Boehm to Mrs. Quigg Newton, November 6, 2003; William B. Bidwell to Quigg Newton, January 27, 2003; William B. Bidwell to Mrs. Quigg Newton, September 24, 2003; and William B. Bidwell to Mrs. Newton, December 22, 2003; all in Newton family papers.

[29] "Amended and Restated Fund Agreement, Quigg and Virginia S. Newton Endowed Chair in Leadership," March 3, 2003, Newton family papers.

[30] Quigg Newton to Samuel Gary, March 14, 1985; Quigg Newton to Sione Kite, March 22, 1985; and Quigg Newton to Hon. Baron Tuita, March 25, 1985, all in Newton family papers; Quigg Newton, interview by author, December 3, 2002.

[31] Virginia Newton diary, 1986 trip to Czechoslovakia, Newton family papers.

[32] Roy Romer to Honorable Xiong Qing-quan, January 29, 1988; Anonymous, "A Note on Colorado/China Relations," first draft, undated (ca. January 1988), both in Newton family papers.

[33] Virginia Newton, interview by author, February 11, 2004.

[34] Quigg Newton to Bill Dodge, January 15, 1988, Newton family papers.

[35] "Round Table Report," 1995, Newton family papers.

[36] "London Theater/Music 1996–1997 Itinerary," Newton family papers.

[37] Donald Hoagland to Quigg Newton, September 1, 2002, Newton family papers.

[38] William E. Davis, "Minutes of the Last Meeting of the J. Quigg Newton Younger Than Springtime Club, Cheyenne Mountain—The Cooking Club Lodge, Colorado Springs, Colorado, June 3, 1989," mimeographed, June 2, 1989, Newton family papers.

[39] Oswald Tippo to Quigg Newton, July 27, 1993, Newton family papers.

[40] Quigg Newton to "Went," undated letter, Newton family papers; Quigg Newton, interview by author, November 20, 2002.

[41] Justine Rice to Quigg Newton, undated, August 2001, Newton family papers.

[42] Quigg Newton to Leo Hill, October 5, 1997, Newton family papers.

Chapter 13: Taps

[1] Gerald Harrison, "Lunch With Quigg, April 2, 2003," dated April 5, 2003, p. 2, Newton family papers.

[2] Ibid., 1.

[3] Ibid., 3, 4.

[4] Donald E. Barnes to Ginny Newton, undated (ca. April, 2003); Tom Farer to Ginny Newton, undated, both in Newton family papers.

[5] Mark E. Udall to Ginny Newton, April 30, 2003; and Tim and Wren Wirth to Ginny Newton, April 5, 2003, both in Newton family papers.

[6] Richard C. Tucker to Ginny Newton, April 2003, Newton family papers.

[7] James D. Keyes to Ginny Newton, April 10, 2003, Newton family papers.

[8] William E. Davis to Ginny Newton, April 9, 2003, Newton family papers.

[9] Maggie Coval to Ginny Newton, undated letter (ca. April, 2003) Newton family papers.

[10] Eleanor E. Harper to Ginny Newton, August 1, 2003 and Ruth Plimpton to Ginny Newton, September 2003, both in Newton family papers.

[11] Donald Hoagland to Ginny Newton, April 6, 2003, Newton family papers.

[12] Margaret E. Mahoney to Ginny Newton, May 19, 2003; Donald Hoagland to Ginny Newton, April 6, 2003, both in Newton family papers.

[13] Art and Nan Delaney to Ginny Newton, undated letter (ca. April 2003), Newton family papers.

[14] Wendy Wilson Greer to Ginny, Nan, Abby, Nelle, and Ginna Newton, May 26, 2003, Newton family papers.

[15] Ruth and Peter Philpott to Ginny Newton, undated letter (ca. April, 2003); H. Benjamin Duke to Ginny Newton, April 6, 2003; Gordon Saunders to Ginny Newton, April 8, 2003; and Pool Rehab to Ginny Newton, undated letter (ca. April 2003), all in Newton family papers.

[16] Sydney S. Macy to Ginny, Nan, Nelle, Abby, and Ginna, April 9, 2003 and Sandi G. Gastin to Ginny Newton, April 7, 2003, both in Newton family papers.

[17] Margaret Mahoney to Ginny Newton, May 19, 2003 and Nils Wessell to Ginny Newton, April 14, 2003, both in Newton family papers.

Appendix

[1] In terms of numbers, the outflow of settlers to New England was small compared to those in the southern colonies. Between 1630 and 1641, between 17,000 and 21,000 settlers arrived in New England. The numbers arriving in the Chesapeake region during the same period were several times that large. See Stephen Innes, *Creating the Commonwealth: The Economic Culture of Puritan New England* (New York: W. W. Norton, 1995): 23.

[2] Richard Newton was born in approximately 1601. Sir Isaac Newton's father, Isaac, was born and baptized in 1606, and he was the eldest of four brothers, of whom Richard was the *youngest*. Thus, the Richard Newton who migrated to Boston was almost certainly not Sir Isaac Newton's uncle. *Newton Genealogy: A Record of the Descendents of Richard Newton of Sudbury and Marlborough, Massachusetts, 1638,* compiled by Ermina Newton Leonard (De Pere, Wis.: Bernard Ammidown Leonard, 1915): 2, 14.

[3] Virginia D. Anderson, *New England's Generation: the Great Migration and the Formation of Society and Culture in the Seventeenth Century* (New York: Cambridge University Press, 1991): 222, table 1.

[4] Numerous books have been written depicting everyday life in the early Massachusetts settlements. See John Demos, *A Little Commonwealth: Family Life in Plymouth Colony* (London and New York: Oxford University Press, 1970); Kenneth A. Lockridge, *A New England Town: The First Hundred Years Dedham, Massachusetts, 1636–1736* (New York: W. W. Norton, 1970); and Philip J. Greven Jr., *Four Generations: Population, Land, and Family in Colonial Andover, Massachusetts* (Ithaca and London: Cornell University Press, 1970).

[5] Newton family genealogy, 7.

[6] Robert A. Gross, *The Minutemen and Their World* (New York: Hill and Wang, 1976): 18. For descriptions of such conflict in Dedham, see Lockridge, *A New England Town: The First Hundred Years, Dedham, Massachusetts, 1636–1736,* 93–118.

[7] Newton family genealogy, 2.

[8] Innes, *Creating the Commonwealth*, 23; Anderson, *New England's Generation*, 180–181, 225, table 8.

[9] Nancy Woloch, *Women and the American Experience: A Concise History*, 2nd ed. (New York: McGraw-Hill, 2002): 5.

[10] Gross, *The Minutemen and Their World*, 102. Yet other sources disagree over interpretations of Massachusetts law and practice. According to Nancy Woloch, "Marriage was recognized as a civil contract based on the mutual consent of both parties. Husbands were compelled to support and cohabit with their wives; deserters could be hounded

or errant husbands hauled into court for adultery or failing to provide. In New England, where authorities kept an especially 'watchfulle eye' over the home, 'disorderly carriage' within it was likely to evoke reprimands. Statutes outlawed of limited physical abuse of wives. The Massachusetts Body of Liberties in 1641 prohibited wife-beating, 'unless it be in his own defense upon her assault.'" Woloch, *Women and the American Experience*, 5–6. For more analysis of gender relations in Colonial New England, see Edmund Morgan, *The Puritan Family: Religion and Domestic Relations in Seventeenth-Century New England* (New York: Harper and Row, 1966); Laurel T. Ulrich, *Good Wives: Image and Reality in the Lives of Women in Northern New England, 1650–1750* (New York: A. A. Knopf, 1982); Carol Berkin, *First Generations: Women in Colonial America* (New York: Hill and Wang, 1997); and Mary Beth Norton, *Founding Mothers and Fathers: Gendered Power and the Forming of American Society* (New York: A. A. Knopf, 1996).

[11] Newton family genealogy, 22.

[12] Ibid., 60.

[13] Gary B. Nash, et. al., *The American People: Creating a Nation and a Society, volume I to 1877* (New York: Harper and Row, 1986): 76.

[14] Newton family genealogy, 60.

[15] Telephone interview with Virginia Anderson by author, March 7, 2003. A source including an authoritative historical account of slavery in the northern colonies, including Massachusetts, is Ira Berlin, *Many Thousands Gone: The First Two Centuries of Slavery in North America* (Cambridge and London: Harvard University Press, 1998). See also Edgar J. McManus, *Black Bondage in the North* (Syracuse, NY: Syracuse University Press, 2001) and Lorenzo J. Greene, *The Negro in Colonial New England* (New York: Columbia University Press, 1942). An excellent source on indentured servitude is Abbott Smith, *Colonists in Bondage: White Servitude and Convict Labor in Colonial America, 1607–1776*, 2nd ed. (New York: W. W. Norton, 1971).

[16] Newton family genealogy, 69, 70, 71. For an authoritative account of the experiences of colonial soldiers during the French and Indian War, see Fred Anderson, *A People's Army: Massachusetts Soldiers and Society in the Seven Years' War* (Chapel Hill: University of North Carolina Press, 1984).

[17] For excellent accounts of the everyday lives of American troops during the Revolution, see Robert Gross, *The Minutemen and Their World* and Fred Anderson, *A People's Army*. For additional details of Thaddeus Newton's service in the Continental Army, see Newton family genealogy, 82–83.

[18] Gross, *The Minutemen and Their World*, 147–150.

[19] Ibid., 150, 152.

[20] Gross observed that after the Revolutionary War, the economy in towns near Boston were depressed, that Concord, for example, was "more of a place to be from." Ibid., 169. By the mid-1790s, more than half of the young men had left the town they had fought so hard to defend. Ibid., 177.

[21] Newton family genealogy, 102–103.

INDEX